# International Handbook
# on Alcohol and
# Culture

# International Handbook on Alcohol and Culture

EDITED BY
## DWIGHT B. HEATH

GREENWOOD PRESS
Westport, Connecticut • London

**Library of Congress Cataloging-in-Publication Data**

International handbook on alcohol and culture / edited by Dwight B.
  Heath.
     p.    cm.
  Includes bibliographical references and index.
  ISBN 0–313–25234–3 (alk. paper)
  1. Drinking of alcoholic beverages—Cross-cultural studies.
2. Drinking customs—Cross-cultural studies.  3. Alcoholism—Cross-
cultural studies.  I. Heath, Dwight B.
HV5035.I57  1995
394.1'3—dc20      95–7184

British Library Cataloguing in Publication Data is available.

Library of Congress Catalog Card Number: 95–7184
ISBN: 0–313–25234–3

First published in 1995

Greenwood Press, 88 Post Road West, Westport, CT 06881
An imprint of Greenwood Publishing Group, Inc.

Printed in the United States of America

The paper used in this book complies with the
Permanent Paper Standard issued by the National
Information Standards Organization (Z39.48–1984).

10 9 8 7 6 5 4 3 2 1

**Copyright Acknowledgments**

The editor and the publisher gratefully acknowledge permission to use the following:

Excerpts from *Preventing Alcohol Abuse: Alcohol, Culture, and Control* by David J.
Hanson. 1995. Praeger Publishers: Westport, CT. Used with permission of Praeger
Publishers, an imprint of Greenwood Publishing Group, Inc., Westport, CT.

To

A New Beginning

# Contents

# Tables

# Preface and Acknowledgments

Over the years it has been one of my preoccupations to try to keep abreast of the rapidly expanding literature that deals with alcohol in cultural context, cross-culturally throughout the world, and throughout human history. As an anthropologist, I revel in unusual tidbits of information and instances where general propositions are contradicted by local realities. Also as an anthropologist, I am intrigued by the recurrence of some phenomena across widely divergent ways of life and the universality of a few features in the human experience. Furthermore, it is striking to see the many different ways in which people use, think about, and react to what at first appears to be a simple chemical compound.

Recently it has become evident that a number of colleagues in fields other than anthropology are interested in how various peoples deal with alcohol, and for a great variety of reasons. Often their data and insights are phrased in terms of nation-states rather than of local populations. The idea behind this book is to merge these levels of awareness and concern, trying to understand what various peoples in the complex world around us believe and how they behave with respect to alcohol.

Like almost every book, this one grew slowly as an idea for some time before the actual compilation and writing began. It was Clyde Kluckhohn at Harvard who stimulated my original interest in culture, and my academic interest in alcohol sprang from a chance meeting with E. M. Jellinek and Mark Keller at Yale. They all encouraged me to write, from the earliest stages of my professional career, and David J. Pittman and Charles R. Snyder served as friendly mentors and good examples.

Although much of my early scholarly effort was devoted to understanding land reform and social revolution in Latin America, and other historical, economic, and political phenomena there and elsewhere, the idea of alcohol as a window on other aspects of culture stirred my imagination. As I grew more involved with alcohol studies, it became clear that some colleagues would be glad to contribute to comparative studies; a few lacked confidence about their skills to do so in a strictly ethnographic sense; and others felt that their strengths lay elsewhere and that national-level data had another, sometimes stronger, kind of significance.

The existence of a distinguished series of International Handbooks on various subjects at Greenwood Press made a compilation such as this seem feasible. Maureen Melino and other editors there have been supportive and helpful, especially in understanding the many delays that are inherent in such a complex venture. Shirley Gordon lent her expertise by converting innumerable component drafts into a final unified manuscript. As usual, my friend and colleague A. M. Cooper was a steadfast enabler, in the best sense of that word.

This volume is clearly a collaborative effort, and I am immensely grateful to the many friends and colleagues who have helped me bring the idea to a reality. The contributing authors have invested considerable time, thought, and effort in making a complex subject understandable, within severe constraints of both time and space. They have threaded their various ways through a virtual minefield of controversies and politically sensitive issues without diluting their descriptions or analyses.

In recognition of the fact that a book such as this is a joint venture, royalties have been assigned to support further social and cultural research on alcohol.

Dwight B. Heath

# 1

# An Introduction to Alcohol and Culture in International Perspective

## Dwight B. Heath

Alcohol has long been one of the most popular chemicals used by human beings to enhance their moods, and it has been one of the most widespread throughout history. Ironically, it is a tranquilizer, appetizer, disinfectant, anesthetic, food, solvent, and economic commodity, as well as a potent symbol—all in various ways in different cultures. A relatively simple chemical compound, alcohol occurs in nature without any human input and is often appreciated by animals other than humans (Siegel 1989). Like salt, it is toxic if taken in excessive quantities but, also like salt, it is often refined or diluted and consumed with other substances to make them taste good and to make people feel better.

## WHY ALCOHOL MATTERS

A chemist can rightly insist that there are several "alcohols," but the one that most interests most people is ethyl alcohol (also known as ethanol, ETOH, or $C_2H_5OH$). It is the only alcohol that people customarily drink—although too often they get methyl alcohol by mistake, and suffer severe gastric disturbances, if not blindness and death. Ethyl alcohol is soluble in water, has no distinctive taste, does no physical harm (in moderate quantities), and is metabolized at the rate of about 7 grams (or 0.3 oz.) per hour in a normal human body, leaving only carbon dioxide (which is what we breathe out anyway) and water. That is a little less than the amount in an average "drink" in the United States in the 1990s—for example, a 12-ounce bottle of beer (at 4%), a 3.5-ounce glass of wine (at 12%), or a 1-ounce shot of spirits (at 86 proof, which is 43%). Drinking larger quantities or drinking faster leads to an accumulation of alcohol for the liver to process, and can result in many kinds of complications. The rapid diffusion of alcohol throughout the system (absorbed in the blood) can affect all our senses and abilities, in varying ways and to varying degrees, depending in part on the amount ingested (Gomberg et al., 1982).

The drinking of alcohol in beverages is so unremarkable that, in English as in many other languages, beverages containing very little are often called "alcoholic beverages" (or even "alcohol") not only in common parlance but also in some legal contexts, and even in the burgeoning multidisciplinary field of "alcohol studies." (To qualify as "nonalcoholic," a beer sold in the United States must contain no more than 0.5% by weight or by volume, a level similar to that found in many fruit juices.) Another indication of the pervasiveness of drinking alcohol as part of the human experience is the fact that, again in many languages, the verb "to drink" often implies alcohol rather than just any liquid. For example, "She drinks, you know" or "He's a drinking man" or "I'll drink to that" (Heath 1986a).

## WHY CULTURE MATTERS

As common as the drinking of beverages containing alcohol is, it is often treated as if it were a special kind of behavior (Marshall 1979). For example, in some cultures, young people are supposed to abstain. In others, women should be very discreet about where, when, with whom, and how much they drink. Men are subject to other, generally less restrictive, norms about drinking. Governments often fix on alcoholic beverages as special targets for taxation, and both laws and regulations spell out, often in great detail, where they may be sold, when, to whom, in what relation to solid foods, and many other conditions that are considered irrelevant with relation to other drinks.

Since the mid-1940s, there has been a growing scientific interest in various aspects of "alcohol studies"—some have even called for the recognition of a new field, "alcohology." It is intellectually exciting, just as it is scientifically relevant and practically useful, to consider this single substance that is used by people throughout the world in very different ways, for very different purposes, and with very different consequences (Pittman and White 1991). It is an ideal realm for trying to sort out the distinctions between what is cultural and what is biological, what comes from nature and what from nurture. No matter how thorough a chemical analysis is made of trace elements in alcohol, they have little bearing on the attitudes and values of people who drink it. No matter how complete a psychological assessment can be made of an individual, his or her behavior will change in approximately dose-related ways that tend to be predictable in terms of social norms of the local population. No matter how thorough our understanding of historical and sociological aspects of alcohol use in a given society, it matters whether people are drinking beer (at about 4–12%) or wine (at about 8–20%) or spirits (over 30% alcohol), and how fast they drink it. In short, alcohol is a biopsychosocial phenomenon, and ignoring that complexity can only result in partial understandings, or even misunderstandings.

## THE PURPOSE OF THIS BOOK

This book has been compiled with the aim of providing easier access to information about alcohol in relation to cultures throughout the world. Human populations have always tended to distinguish themselves on the basis of shared understandings about the nature of things, proper relationships among people, right and wrong behaviors in various contexts, links with the supernatural, how to communicate, and many other aspects of life. Such a design for living can be called a culture, and we find many such that differ markedly in some aspects although they may be similar in others. Only during the last few centuries have boundaries and the political apparatus of the nation-state been imposed as an overlay upon the patchwork of human cultures, many of which long preceded nations and most of which still survive and influence the ways people think and act, far more than do state institutions.

In the workaday routine of most individuals, it is aspects of the culture that shape most of what they do, even if they are not particularly aware of it at any given time—for example, in language, gender relations, dress, child rearing, age roles, cuisine, or subsistence activities. At another level, citizenship in the nation can become crucially important in certain contexts—such as obeying the law, serving in the military, getting a passport, or dealing with money.

We often talk as if nation and culture are identical, or at least congruent (Heath 1986b). There is so little cultural variation in Denmark and Iceland, for example, that such a view seems justified. By contrast, cultural variation is so striking in Australia that the authors of that chapter speak of ''Aboriginal territory'' as quite apart from the European-dominated urban fringe of the country. And the difference is not just a matter of size: Sri Lanka's various distinctive cultures are given far more political, economic, and social importance than the single traditional minority in Sweden.

## SCOPE OF THE BOOK

An encyclopedic treatment of the subject would be enormous and difficult for anyone to comprehend. But a sampling, designed to provide information on a basic core of subjects, from a limited number of very different countries around the world, can both reveal the rich diversity of roles that alcohol has played in human cultures and allow for meaningful comparisons and contrasts.

This book should serve as a basic reference source for students and laypersons, as well as for the international and multidisciplinary scholarly community. Jargon has generally been avoided, and a glossary provides quick identification of those few specialized terms that could not easily be rendered in colloquial English. The straightforward expository style should not, however, be interpreted as implying oversimplification.

The bulk of this volume is a series of chapters, each written by a recognized authority (or two), describing the place of alcohol in the culture or cultures of a country. Countries were chosen to represent each continent, various government and economic systems, a size range including the largest and some of the smallest, some homogeneous in population and some very diverse. They include not only major urban and industrial nations but also young and developing nations, and a remarkable variety of popular practices and of public policies with respect to beverages containing alcohol. Some countries of obvious interest were left out because they are well described elsewhere; others, because colleagues were reluctant or unable to undertake the burdensome task of writing such a chapter. The culture or cultures within each country that are described were chosen by each author independently. As an anthropologist, I might have devoted more attention to various tribal or peasant groups, but it is interesting to see how the concept of culture was viewed as congenial and appropriate by colleagues in other fields.

The chapters are not identical in outline, but they usually include some historical context, dominant patterns of alcohol use and some variant usages among different populations, how social and demographic factors (such as age, sex, socioeconomic class, schooling, income) affect drinking and its outcomes, and legal, regulatory, and policy issues. Some of the authors offer recommendations for action.

It was no surprise that each country presents a unique and distinctive combination of factors that relate to the importance of alcohol there. It was a surprise, however, that many of the contributing authors chose to ignore a standard outline that might have facilitated comparisons and contrasts because they felt that it would hamper their presentations. As an editor, I have conscientiously let each of the authors speak with his or her own voice rather than homogenizing them to an unnatural uniformity. Minor stylistic revisions have been made in the interest of clarity and comprehension, but the organization and content of each chapter, and the tone of each author, remain intact. This explains why some chapters may seem so favorable toward drinking and some so critical, some quite liberal in their evaluations and recommendations, and some authoritarian. On a very few occasions, I have inserted brief editorial comments, located at the end of a chapter, to inject an editorial note where it seems crucial to understanding, or where the author's view appears to differ from that of mainstream Western science.

## FORMAT AND USE OF THE BOOK

A reader who wants to learn about drinking in a given country will find that the chapter in this book is the most recent and authoritative source that is easily accessible. Almost every chapter includes a list of selected references that will be helpful to anyone who chooses to pursue the subject in greater detail. In quantitative terms, the chapters differ considerably. This is partly a reflection of the fact that nations and cultures differ in terms of how people treat alcohol, and what it does to them. It also reflects the significant differences among nations in terms of numerical data that are available. This is partly a function of the wealth that a government (or police system, or hospital, or other agency) chooses to devote to enumeration. It is partly a function of how important research is thought to be (in competition with other demands on limited resources). One might even argue that it reflects a people's view of how important—or unimportant—numbers may be in relation to other ways of knowing. Any reader who is unfamiliar with the meaning and significance of the numerical index known as per capita consumption, which so many authors cite, should read the Appendix for a simple explanation, together with large-scale international comparison.

In qualitative terms, there is also some variation. It is evident that the authors are practicing scientists and other professionals in many different fields. Readers should also keep in mind that English is, at best, a second language for most of them.

Following the twenty-seven national chapters are two chapters by the editor. One provides an anthropological overview of alcohol use, emphasizing linkages with other aspects of culture. The other points out some of the more striking regularities that occur among the countries that have been described by local authorities, and offers some tentative generalizations. In the hope that journalists, legislators, and others who play active roles in shaping and communicating policies will pay attention to the value of these accounts as "natural experiments," I also mention some of the policy implications that derive from so much experience.

A brief appendix both illustrates the wide range of per capita consumption figures for various countries and explains the strengths and some of the shortcomings of such figures. A glossary provides definitions of words that are used in distinctive ways in various parts of this book; some are specific to an individual country, and some are terms that have special meanings in relation to alcohol studies.

The bibliographic essay is intended to help anyone who wishes to pursue the subject in greater depth. With no pretense at being complete or encyclopedic, it aims at guiding the reader to a few key sources, most of which are available at any major research library, for original writings, both descriptive and analytic, by authoritative specialists.

"About the Editor and Contributors" gives brief information about each of the authors and the editor, emphasizing present affiliation so that they can be contacted by interested readers, rather than simply chronicling their many and varied achievements.

The index is intended to help the interested user, even one with little prior knowledge of the subject, to find relevant information on concepts, types of beverages, social groups, cultures, religions, and other topics. Abundant use of cross-referencing avoids the problem that might arise from too much use of a specialized vocabulary or jargon.

In a sense, an international handbook should be viewed as a tool, with the measure of its worth being the success of those who use it. The contributors join me in hoping that these essays will be helpful, no matter what your reason for seeking them out.

## REFERENCES

Gomberg, Edith L., Helene R. White, and John A. Carpenter (Eds.). 1982. *Alcohol, Science and Society Revisited.* Ann Arbor: University of Michigan Press.

Heath, Dwight B. 1986a. Cultural definitions of drinking: Notes toward a semantic approach. *The Drinking and Drug Practices Surveyor* 21:17–22.

———. 1986b. Concluding remarks. Pp. 234–237 in Thomas F. Babor (Ed.). *Alcohol and Culture: Comparative Perspectives from Europe and America. Annals of the New York Academy of Science* 472. New York: NYAS.

Marshall, Mac (Ed.). 1979. *Beliefs, Behaviors, and Alcoholic Beverages: A Cross-Cultural Survey.* Ann Arbor: University of Michigan Press.

Pittman, David J., and Helene R. White (Eds.). 1991. *Society, Culture, and Drinking Patterns Reexamined.* New Brunswick, N.J.: Rutgers Center of Alcohol Studies.

Siegel, Ronald K. 1989. *Intoxication: Life in Pursuit of Artificial Paradise.* New York: E. P. Dutton.

# 2

# Australia

## Wayne Hall and Ernest Hunter

Australia today is an anglophone, predominantly European nation-state that occupies an island continent the size of the continental United States. Its population of 17 million is one of the most suburbanized on earth, with 40% living in the cities of Sydney and Melbourne, and two-thirds clustered in the suburbs of the eight capital cities that hug the coastal areas of the largely barren continent (Australian Bureau of Statistics 1992a). It is a federation of six states (New South Wales, Queensland, South Australia, Tasmania, Victoria, and Western Australia) and two territories (Australian Capital Territory and the Northern Territory) that were separate British colonies before federating in 1901. It has a parliamentary system of government in each state and the commonwealth. The head of state is the constitutional monarch, Queen Elizabeth II, who is also queen of England.

Australia originated in 1788 as a British penal colony on the shores of Sydney Harbor. In the subsequent two centuries its indigenous population has been submerged in an English-speaking society of predominantly Anglo-Celtic origin, supplemented by a large influx of European immigrants after World War II and a smaller, more recent intake of Asian immigrants after the relaxation of the "White Australia" immigration policy in the early 1970s. Australia's indigenous people—Aborigines and Torres Strait Islanders—comprise about 1.5% of the population.

## HISTORY OF DRINKING IN AUSTRALIA

Heavy alcohol use has long been a part of the cultural identity of Australians, forming a central part of "mateship"—egalitarian, convivial relations among workingmen, as celebrated by Henry Lawson, Banjo Patterson, and other writers at the start of the twentieth century. Heavy drinking was a feature of the early penal settlement, among both jailers and prisoners. It remained so after free settlers began to arrive, and during the frontier period after the gold rush of 1850, when many young single men were employed as itinerant workers in mining and agriculture. The dominant pattern was binge drinking, when wages would be consumed in a drinking bout; a special feature was the tradition of "shouting," in which a group of male drinkers would take turns buying drinks for all members of the group.

Aggregate per capita consumption was high during the period of early settlement and remained so during the first half of the 1800s. During the early years of settlement, rum was used as a form of currency, and attempts to control the rum trade contributed to a military revolt against Governor William Bligh in 1808. Nevertheless, the stereotype of exceptionally heavy, if not heroic, drinking during this time is misleading because it ignores the fact that for much of this period, the European population of Australia was dominated by young working-class males (either convicts or soldiers), with a ratio of three men to every woman, and relatively few children. When per capita consumption is adjusted for gender and age (Powell 1988; Room 1985), Australian alcohol consumption during the first half-century of settlement was at most only marginally greater than in contemporary Britain, and probably lower than in both Britain and the United States.

Over the two centuries of European occupation there have been long waves in Australian alcohol consumption similar to those observed in other anglophone and European societies. Consumption remained high until after the gold rush in the 1850s, thereafter steadily declining (with small perturbations during economic booms and depressions) until, by the end of the century, it had approximately halved. It continued to decrease throughout the early 1900s, reaching a historical low in the depths of the depression in the early 1930s. Then it began a steady increase during the postwar period, reaching its highest point in the late 1970s, when per capita consumption was comparable with that of the mid-1800s. Since then consumption has declined by about 12%.

### Reasons for the Long Waves in Alcohol Consumption

Recent analyses of the causes of the long waves of alcohol consumption in Australia (e.g., Lewis 1992; Powell 1988; Room 1985, 1988) have suggested a number of explanations for the long decline in consumption between 1860 and 1930. A major factor was a shift from the male-dominated society of the penal era (ending in 1840 in New South Wales) and the frontier period (approximately 1850 to 1900) to a more equal sex distribution. With this demographic change Australia became an increasingly settled, urbanized, and family-oriented society. Its population became better educated because of free secular education, and there were greater opportunities for forms of recreation other than drinking, especially sport.

A shift in the type of preferred alcoholic beverages during this period also played a role. Spirits-drinking dominated the colonial period in the absence of a native brewing or distilling industry and because of technical difficulties in importing any alcohol other than spirits. The emergence of a local brewing industry and improvements in the transportation of beer in the late 1800s encouraged a transition from a spirits-drinking to a beer-drinking culture.

The development of an active temperance movement in the latter part of the 1800s also contributed to the moderation of alcohol consumption, and perhaps encouraged the shift toward beer. A temperance movement that began in the mid-1830s preached moderation rather than abstinence, and advocated the drinking of beer and other lighter alcoholic beverages. A later, more politically successful, abstention-oriented temperance movement emerged in the 1880s under the influence of the U.S. temperance movement. Although powerful, the abstentionist form of temperance was unsuccessful in achieving legislative prohibition, despite a long campaign for local option and for a referendum to prohibit alcohol sales.

The major legislative success of the temperance movement was a restriction on the trading hours of hotels (the major alcohol outlets in Australia). Hotel closing at 6 P.M. was introduced in most Australian states during World War I (which Australia entered in 1914 along with Britain), when temperance sentiment coincided with a patriotic preparedness to make sacrifices for the war effort.

Six o'clock closing endured until the middle of the century, despite attempts to liberalize trading hours. It had consequences for the alcohol trade, drinking practices, and the drinking environment. One consequence was the development of a black market in alcohol known as "sly grogging," especially during World War II. The elimination of sly grogging proved to be one of the major reasons for the repeal of early closing in New South Wales. Early closing also encouraged a drinking practice called the "six o'clock swill," in which hotels were packed with workers who had an hour, between finishing work and closing time, in which to consume as much alcohol as they could. This practice produced spartan "public bars" from which women were excluded and in which the walls and floors were tiled to expedite hosing out of spillage and effluvia of the "swill."

The long period of increasing consumption that began in the late 1930s has been attributed to a number of factors (Lewis 1992; Room 1988). One was growing affluence as the economy continued to expand until the mid-1970s, which was reinforced by the commodification of leisure and the decline in "wowserism"—the Australian name for puritanism. During this period alcohol was incorporated into everyday life as controls on its availability were liberalized in the late 1960s and early 1970s. It again became respectable for women to drink alcohol in public. Alcohol was heavily promoted and advertised, largely through the sponsorship of major sports, such as cricket, rugby league football, and horse racing.

The reemergence of wine-drinking in the late 1960s also contributed to increased per capita consumption by making the use of alcohol with meals a common event. The resurgence of wine consumption was encouraged by postwar migration from European wine cultures like Italy and Greece, and increased travel by Australians to European wine-drinking countries. Increasing access to postsecondary education in the late 1960s helped to destigmatize wine, which had hitherto been the beverage of skid-row drinkers. The increasing popularity of wine was aided by the introduction of a sales tax differential in the early 1970s that favored wine over other forms of alcohol.

## CONTEMPORARY CONSUMPTION PATTERNS

By international standards, Australia's 1989 per capita alcohol consumption (8.5 liters) is within the top twenty countries, but well behind the wine-drinking societies of France (13.4), Spain (12.0), and Italy (9.5). It has the highest per capita alcohol consumption in the English-speaking world, ahead of New Zealand (7.8), Great Britain (7.6), and the United States (7.5). About 4.3% of household expenditure is estimated to be on alcohol.

The distribution of alcohol consumption in the European population of Australia was not systematically studied until very recently. Population studies of alcohol consumption have been few, and have used such a variety of methods of assessment that it is difficult to compare their findings either over time or across different surveys conducted at the same time. There have been very few special-purpose alcohol surveys, most having been undertaken as part of surveys of health status (e.g., Australian Bureau of Statistics 1992b; Risk Factor Prevalence Study Management Committee 1990). Consequently, few studies have inquired about drinking patterns beyond typical frequency and quantity of alcohol consumed, or the consumption in the past week. Questions about alcohol-related problems in the population have been rare, as have sociological studies of drinking patterns (e.g., Hamilton 1986; Sargent 1979), except in Aboriginal populations in remote areas that have been comparatively well studied.

Gender and age are the major differentials in alcohol use. The proportion of abstainers is around 18%, and higher among women (21%) than men (15%), and among persons older than fifty-five (32%) than those under fifty-five (13%) (Commonwealth 1992). Among those who drink, approximately equal proportions drink less than weekly, one to two days a week, and three or more days a week. Women are much more likely to drink less than weekly, and men more likely to drink three days or more a week (Risk Factor Prevalence Study Management Committee 1990). The frequency of drinking increases with age among both men and women.

In terms of the typical quantity consumed, over half of drinkers report that they usually consume one to two standard drinks (10 g. ethanol) per drinking occasion. This pattern is true for three out of four women who drink, and for half of the men who drink. A fifth of drinkers typically consume three to four drinks (one in four men and one in six women). About one in six drinkers consume five or more drinks on a drinking occasion (about one in four of men and one in ten of women who drink).

Beer was the most popular beverage in the 1989–90 National Health Survey, (Australian Bureau 1992b), with 37% of drinkers consuming it in the previous week, compared with 26% who drank wine and 23% who drank spirits or fortified wine. There is a strong gender difference in beverage preference. Males are much more likely to consume light and full-strength beer than women, who are much more likely than men to consume wine.

These overall patterns suggest that the majority of the population are relatively restrained and infrequent drinkers: two out of three either do not drink or drink fewer than three days per week, and two-thirds drink two or fewer standard drinks per drinking occasion. There is, nonetheless, a substantial minority of drinkers who drink most days of the week and who drink five or more standard drinks on an occasion. They are disproportionately found among young men, one in four of whom typically drink five or more standard drinks. The Northern Territory—a "frontier" area with a large population of young blue-collar males—has the lowest proportion of nondrinkers and the highest per capita consumption of alcohol in the country, a state of affairs that has prompted policy changes to reduce consumption.

Despite recent decreases in per capita consumption, the typical quantity consumed and the frequency of drinking among young women has increased (Corti and Ibrahim 1990). Although there remain major differences between men and women, the pattern of young women has grown closer to that of men, with higher frequency of drinking and larger amounts consumed per drinking occasion, probably a reflection of the greater participation of women in paid work, increasing incomes, and a weakening of taboos against women drinking.

With the conspicuous exception of Aboriginal alcohol use, ethnic differences in alcohol use have not been investigated. According to the National Health Survey (Australian Bureau 1992b), average consumption was higher among Australians of an English-speaking background (15.8 ml.) than among drinkers from southern Europe (10.4 ml.). Beyond this aggregate consumption data, the opportunities for studies of the impact of Australian drinking patterns on those of migrants, and of migrants' drinking on that of Australians, have largely been ignored.

The ways in which drinkers learn to drink have not been well studied, although surveys of alcohol and other drug use among high school youth suggest that the majority of juvenile drinkers have tried alcohol well before the age of eighteen, when they can legally purchase it in hotels and bars. Substantial minorities of those age twelve to sixteen (one in four boys and one in five girls) drink alcohol on a weekly basis, although this has declined in recent years (from one in three boys and one in four girls in 1983), perhaps in response to alcohol education campaigns directed toward adolescents.

## Alcohol-Related Problems

According to estimates (Holman et al. 1988), the major cause of alcohol-related deaths in Australia is cancer of the oral cavity, colon, esophagus, pharynx, and pancreas among men, and of the breast, colon, esophagus, and pancreas among women. The remaining major alcohol-related causes of death among men are accidents (especially motor vehicle accidents), liver cirrhosis, and suicide, and among women they are diseases of the circulatory system, accidents, cirrhosis, and suicide. When account is taken of the life lost, accidents and suicides are the major causes of alcohol-related deaths in both men and women. Motor vehicle accidents are a major cause of morbidity when assessed by bed-days, as are alcohol dependence and the treatment of its medical complications.

There are limited data on changes in alcohol-related mortality and morbidity over time. Liver cirrhosis shows the predicted variation with per capita consumption, and the contribution of alcohol to motor vehicle accidents has declined since the mid-1980s, in part because of measures such as random breath-testing for alcohol. The interpretation of trends in data on drunkenness and alcohol-related offenses is more difficult because of variations in policing and changes in state legislation governing such offenses. The application of the methods of Holman et al. (1988) to time-series data indicates that alcohol-related mortality has declined along with alcohol consumption. On the limited evidence available, then, alcohol-related health problems seem to have increased while consumption increased and to have decreased more recently as it has declined.

## ALCOHOL CONTROL MEASURES

The rise in alcohol consumption and alcohol-related problems during the 1970s prompted various efforts at amelioration. State governments radically liberalized controls on the availability of alcohol while increasing treatment provision for the alcohol-dependent and introducing measures to reduce public drunkenness and alcohol-related motor vehicle accidents. Treatment provision for alcohol dependence greatly expanded in the late 1970s and early 1980s when federal and state governments increased funding to services previously provided by voluntary and charitable agencies, most of which were based upon the disease model of alcoholism that legitimized liberal alcohol control policies. Drunkenness was gradually decriminalized to reduce the number of problem drinkers coming before the courts and being compulsorily treated in mental hospitals.

State governments enacted tough legislation to reduce alcohol-related motor vehicle accidents. Australia was one of the first countries to introduce compulsory blood tests for persons involved in accidents, and has since progressively reduced the blood alcohol level regarded as per se evidence of intoxication (from 0.08% to 0.05% in most states). Random breath testing (RBT), in which police stop drivers at random and submit them to breath tests for alcohol, was introduced in the late 1970s in Victoria and in 1982 in New South Wales. The majority support RBT had when it was introduced has grown because of its apparent success in reducing road fatalities (Homel 1988).

More recently, professionals in the alcohol field, many of whom have come from a treatment background, have begun to advocate policies that aim to reduce aggregate alcohol consumption by reducing availability, increasing the price, and banning alcohol advertising and promotion. These ideas were first propounded in the early 1970s and most forcefully stated in the influential 1977 report of the Senate Standing Committee on Social Welfare, *Australia: An Intoxicated Society?* These proposals were popularized when alcohol was included as part of the National Campaign Against Drug Abuse that was launched in 1985 as a campaign against illicit drugs. A National Health Policy on Alcohol was developed in 1986, the first draft of which incorporated many alcohol control measures (including taxation on alcohol content). It was substantially modified before final acceptance in 1989 in the face of opposition from South Australia, the state most dependent on income from the wine industry (which would be economically disadvantaged by the abolition of the taxation advantages enjoyed by wine).

## ABORIGINAL DRINKING

Alcohol use among the indigenous peoples of Australia (Aborigines and Torres Strait Islanders, hereafter referred to as ''Aborigines'') has been a central and recurring theme in the development of enduring stereotypes of Aborigines, which have been reinforced by the high visibility of Aboriginal drinking in remote areas of Australia. Aboriginal disadvantage is a critical reason for this. Among Aborigines 40 percent of the population is under fifteen years of age (compared with 25% in the non-Aboriginal population). Aboriginal youth have lower educational achievement, three to four times higher rates of unemployment into and throughout adulthood, and greater likelihood of relying on social security (welfare) for their income. At the end of the 1980s, rates of police detention were twenty times, and rates of imprisonment were fifteen times, higher than for non-Aborigines. Aboriginal life expectancy is sixteen to twenty years less than in the wider population, with very high rates of infant mortality and excess mortality in middle adulthood from ''lifestyle'' diseases and non-natural causes. Alcohol has been implicated as a cause of 10% of Aboriginal deaths (three to four times the percentage for non-Aboriginal Australians).

### History

Although various Aboriginal groups used psychoactive substances prior to 1788, European settlement brought unprecedented exposure to alcohol. As the pastoral and mining frontiers relentlessly expanded from the penal settlements of the east coast, so did Aboriginal experiences of alcohol. Alcohol was introduced to Aboriginal populations of the south and east as they were being decimated by disease and violence, leaving them dispossessed and dislocated.

Aborigines seeking shelter on the fringes of European settlements were, within a few generations, incorporated into a new (European) landscape in which they were the outsiders. Drinking was one of the behaviors that prompted legislation to prohibit Aborigines access to alcohol as early as 1838. The states progressively restricted and controlled Aborigines, entwining prohibition in a framework of discriminatory laws that intruded into every domain of Aboriginal life. Escape from the draconian restrictions was available only to a small group of Aborigines who had extinguished any vestiges of their Aboriginality. Conditional "citizenship" brought them rights to education, ownership of land, free movement, hospital treatment, the retaining of income earned, the vote, and consumption of alcohol. For the majority, who were unable or unwilling to make this transformation, prohibition came to symbolize their status as noncitizens.

Prohibition did not prevent consumption; it reinforced patterns of furtive and rapid drinking in town and fringe-camp settings, consolidating the value of alcohol as a reward and a way of obtaining sexual access to Aboriginal women. As a secretive activity, "grogging" developed its own codes and norms that reflected both traditional patterns of reciprocity and obligation, and the exigencies of prohibition. Drinking was hidden but drunken behavior was not, intoxication providing a rare avenue for confronting Europeans' expectations of right and proper behavior. Aboriginal drunken comportment was, and remains, a rejection of the norms of the dominant culture.

The association of prohibition with citizenship was reinforced when prohibition was lifted at the same time the Aborigines were given the right to vote. Although a 1967 referendum included Aborigines in the national census for the first time, and gave the federal government authority to legislate for them, it was not until 1972 that prohibition was finally lifted in the last regions of remote Australia.

Since the abolition of prohibition, Aborigines have experienced extraordinary rates of incarceration, with more than half of the detentions in the late 1980s being for drunkenness. The Royal Commission of Enquiry into Aboriginal Deaths in Custody, implicated alcohol use as a major cause of incarceration and a contributory cause of some deaths in custody. Since then, public drunkenness has been decriminalized in most states, and some states and territories have legislated to allow Aboriginal communities to control access to alcohol and its public consumption. The effects of these initiatives have been mixed; the most successful have been initiated by individual Aboriginal communities and supported by statutory enforcement.

## Contemporary Alcohol Use

The alcohol consumption of Aborigines and other Australians is similar in a number of respects: men are more likely to be drinkers and to consume more than women; the amount consumed declines with age; living in a town and having a job are associated with more moderate use of alcohol; and remote or rural residence is associated with heavier but less frequent drinking.

Such similarities are ignored in the stereotypes of Aboriginal alcohol use in the wider society, according to which heavy drinking is thought to be universal among Aborigines. The limited quantitative studies of Aboriginal consumption that have been done contradict this stereotype. The proportion of Aborigines who are nondrinkers is consistently twice that for Australia as a whole, and at all ages men are more likely to be drinkers than women. Among young adults, nearly all men and about two-thirds of women are drinkers, but these proportions fall with age for both sexes, leveling off at about half of the male population for those in their fifth decade and older. Among women the proportion of current drinkers falls steadily from around two-thirds of young adults to one in ten elderly women. Nondrinking men are far more likely to be ex-drinkers, whereas nondrinking women are more likely to have been lifetime abstainers.

Among young men there is substantial peer pressure to drink and strong discouragement of attempts to stop. For some young men their identity as drinkers becomes conflated with their Aboriginality, supporting the stereotypes of the wider society that they symbolically reject through their extreme drinking. Attempts to "traditionalize" aspects of alcohol use (such as sharing and reciprocity) and its associated violence have been rejected as a rationalization by some within the Aboriginal community.

The clearest refutation of the stereotype of Aborigines as "hopeless drunks" is the fact that about a third of Aboriginal male drinkers over the age of forty have given up alcohol. The vast majority have done so without any formal intervention, demonstrating a capacity for self-motivated sobriety after many years of heavy drinking. The effects of alcohol on family life and health are the main reasons given for stopping. Christian fundamentalist groups have provided a structure supportive of abstinence, and as a consequence have polarized some communities into "drinkers" and "church men." More recently, Aboriginal communities have adapted treatment programs that have proven successful in treating alcohol dependence among native North American peoples.

Alcohol use has increased tensions within communities in other ways. Many older Aborigines who have successfully given up alcohol lament youths' lack of interest in their traditions, and younger Aborigines, often rebelling against their elders, point out that it was older Aborigines who "taught" them about alcohol. Open conflict has emerged in some areas between men, who are more likely to be drinkers, and women, who are more likely to be abstinent, yet bear the social, economic, and traumatic consequences of men's drinking.

Although Aborigines are less likely to drink than the Australian population as a whole, the majority of those who drink consume at harmful levels (more than 60 g. of alcohol per drinking day). Among young men in the remote Kimberley region of Western Australia, for example, the median consumption of alcohol on drinking days is between fifteen and seventeen standard drinks (each of 10 g. of alcohol).

The way in which alcohol is consumed largely reflects availability, which is limited by location, legal restrictions, and resources. Where alcohol is not readily available, those who drink do so episodically. In urban, town, and fringe-camp settings, the major determinant of the pattern and quantity of alcohol consumed is the availability of money. Because most Aborigines are poor and rely on social security, alcohol consumption diverts sustenance from others in the community.

In the autonomous Aboriginal communities of remote Australia, a range of measures have been adopted to control the supply of alcohol. At the one extreme are communities that have obtained liquor licenses as a collective economic enterprise, often taking over from hoteliers who had profited from the community. At the other extreme are communities that have declared themselves "dry," and in between are communities that have canteens (or bars) but place restrictions on the beverages that are available (e.g., only beer), the days and hours of operation, and where the alcohol can be consumed (e.g., away from the canteen).

These measures have not stopped those who choose to drink. Aboriginal drinkers living in communities that have gone "dry" move to town to live and to drink. Communities where alcohol is available and problems have been substantial, have had some of the people move to towns where larger populations and greater social resources provide a greater measure of security. The elderly often choose to live in alcohol-free "outstations" remote from their communities. For heavy drinkers who travel regularly between these settings, the remote communities and outstations provide "time out" between binges.

Aboriginal drinking in urban centers occurs more often in hotels and clubs, whereas in remote settings, drinking usually takes place away from the point of sale. The site of consumption may be a customary or improvised gathering point that draws together family, countrymen, and groups who may not have associated in the past. Drinking circles contain women and men; children are often present but do not participate in the drinking. An atmosphere of amiability and communion that typifies the early stages of "grogging" may give way unpredictably to disputes and violence as old enmities and jealousies are rekindled and new ones ignited.

Aboriginal drinking has functions in addition to pleasurable effects. It structures communities along drinker/nondrinker lines and is a significant factor in consolidating social relationships between drinkers. As a sought-after and easily distributed commodity, alcohol is nicely adapted to rituals of obligatory sharing and reciprocity that were characteristic of traditional resource use. Having and giving alcohol constitutes a marker of prestige and an affirmation of relatedness, providing a convenient mechanism for the negotiation of emotional, social, and material credit. In certain circumstances alcohol may be interchangeable with money.

The beverage of choice among Aboriginal drinkers is full-strength beer. Sweet white wine (Moselle) emerged in 1980s as the main challenger to beer, reflecting the aggressive marketing of two- and four-liter wine casks that are portable, easily shared, contain relatively robust wine, and are cheap. Fortified wines (port and sherry) also remain popular; spirits are less so because of the cost and concerns about the toxicity of such "hot stuff."

The behaviors associated with drinking and the comportment of intoxication have protean manifestations. The most obvious is in the propensity for personal violence, which, although reflecting fundamental intercultural forces, is largely confined to violence between Aborigines. In 1990–91 the homicide rate for Aborigines was nine times that for the general population; Aboriginal victims were more likely to be female and to be affected by alcohol than other victims. Offenders, who were usually male, also were more frequently affected by alcohol than offenders in the general population, and twice as likely to have had previous convictions for assault.

The conjunction of alcohol and violence has become so frequent in some settings as to be virtually expected among young men. Poverty, the paucity of services in remote settings, the divisions between young adults and older Aborigines, and the undermining of the latter's authority and of mechanisms for traditional conflict resolution have reduced the means to contain such violence. This is compounded by cultural constraints on the right to challenge freedom to do as one wishes. Arrest for violence is a normative experience for young adult males in some remote communities and has become almost an adolescent rite of passage. Alcohol is still commonly invoked as a means of explaining violence and absolving the perpetrator of responsibility—"It's the grog" is often an acceptable excuse.

Alcohol has by and large had a negative effect on family, community, and traditional life in remote Aboriginal communities. Its consequences have prompted initiatives by governments and Aboriginal organizations to support sobriety or moderation. The overall patterns of consumption in Aboriginal Australia may moderate as a result of these interventions and as the social and economic disadvantages of Aborigines are redressed.

The situation is in flux. The first generation of Aborigines who could legally drink as young adults are now in late middle age. Given the penetration of alcohol among men, the lifespan distribution has probably stabilized among men; this is not the case for women, however, among whom the prevalence of alcohol consumption is slowly increasing. As a consequence, family integrity and functioning may be further compromised as the widespread reliance on older, nondrinking women as the primary caretakers is threatened.

Family instability is normative for Aboriginal children in heavy-drinking environments. Learning about drinking often begins in childhood, and the first direct experience is usually during the early teens or midteens. Such experimentation, which may be facilitated by older teenagers and young adults, is generally not sanctioned by parents or older adults. However, although there may be sharp words of censure, punishment is uncommon, and at times adolescent drinking may be overlooked or rationalized.

## SUMMARY

Alcohol use has played an important but understudied cultural role in Australia. Heavy consumption, especially of spirits, was the norm during the early years of the male-dominated population of the penal colony and the frontier period. Consumption declined from the mid-1800s until the end of the 1930s with the achievement of equality in numbers between men and women, increasing urbanization, the education of the population, a rise in temperance sentiment, and a shift from spirits to beer. Consumption rose steadily from 1930 to 1980 with decreasing restrictions upon the availability of alcohol and its incorporation into many aspects of everyday life, then began to decline in the early 1980s. Drinking in the 1990s shows a higher frequency and quantity of alcohol use among men, although the gender differential has decreased.

Aboriginal alcohol use is a special variant pattern that has attracted more research attention than that of non-Aboriginal Australians, largely because the latter have long regarded Aboriginal alcohol use as "problematic." Contrary to stereotype, Aborigines are less likely to consume alcohol than non-Aboriginal Australians, but those who drink, consume much larger quantities. The gender and age differentials in drinking mirror those of the wider community: men are more likely than women to drink, and to drink to excess, and consumption is highest among young men. Social disadvantage is a potent contributory cause of Aboriginal drinking, as indicated by the fact that moderate drinking is found among the minority of Aboriginal people who live in towns and are in paid employment.

## REFERENCES

Alexander, K. (Ed.). 1990. *Aboriginal Alcohol Use and Related Problems.* Canberra: Alcohol and Drug Foundation.

Australian Bureau of Statistics. 1992a. *Social Indicators No. 5, 1992.* Catalog no. 4101.0. Canberra: Australian Government Publishing Service.

———. 1992b. *1989–90 National Health Survey: Alcohol Consumption, Australia.* Catalog no. 4381.0. Canberra: Australian Government Publishing Service.

Brady, M. 1992. Ethnography and understandings of Aboriginal drinking. *Journal of Drug Issues* 22 (3):699–712.

Commonwealth Department of Health, Housing and Community Services. 1992. *Alcohol the Facts.* Canberra: Australian Government Publishing Service.

Corti, B., and J. Ibrahim. 1990. Women and alcohol-trends in Australia. *Medical Journal of Australia* 152:625–632.

Hamilton, M. 1986. Understanding the alcoholic in the context of community consumption patterns. *Australian Drug and Alcohol Review* 5:215–224.

Holman, C. D., et al. 1988. *The Quantification of Drug-Caused Morbidity and Mortality in Australia.* Canberra: Commonwealth Department of Community Services and Health.

Homel, R. 1988. *Policing and Punishing the Drinking Driver.* New York: Springer-Verlag.

Hunter, E. 1993. *Aboriginal Health and History: Power and Prejudice in Remote Australia.* Cambridge: Cambridge University Press.

Langton, M. 1993. Rum, seduction and death: "Aboriginality" and alcohol. *Oceania* 63 (3):195–206.

Lewis, M. 1992. *A Rum State: Alcohol and State Policy in Australia.* Canberra: Australian Government Publishing Service.

Lyon, P. 1990. *What Everybody Knows about Alice: A Report on the Impact of Alcohol Abuse on the Town of Alice Springs.* Alice Springs: Tangentyere Council.

Ministerial Council on Drug Strategy. 1989. *National Health Policy on Alcohol in Australia.* Canberra: The Council.

Powell, K. C. 1988. *Drinking and Alcohol in Colonial Australia 1788–1901 in the Eastern Colonies.* National Campaign Against Drug Abuse Monograph no. 3. Canberra: Australian Government Publishing Service.

Risk Factor Prevalence Study Management Committee. 1990. *Risk Factor Prevalence Study Survey No. 3, 1989.* Canberra: National Heart Foundation and Australian Institute of Health.

Room, R. 1985. "An intoxicated society?": Issues then and now in Australia. In J. Cavanagh, F. Clairmonte, and R. Room (Eds.). *The World Alcohol Industry with special reference to Australia, New Zealand and the Pacific Islands.* Sydney: Transnational Corporations Research Project, University of Sydney.

———. 1988. The dialectic of drinking in Australian life: From the Rum Corps to the wine column. *Australian Drug and Alcohol Review* 7:413–437.

Sackett, L. 1988. Resisting arrests: Drinking, development and discipline in a desert context. *Social Analysis* 24:66–84.

Sansom, B. 1980. *The Camp at Wallaby Crossing: Aboriginal Fringe Dwellers in Darwin.* Canberra: Australian Institute of Aboriginal Studies.

Sargent, M. 1979. *Drinking and Alcoholism in Australia: A Power Relations Theory.* Melbourne: Longman Cheshire.

# 3

## Canada

### Yuet W. Cheung and Patricia G. Erickson

To many Canadians, enjoying a hockey or baseball game on TV with friends, drinking beer, shouting and cheering for the favorite team, is a familiar social gathering scenario. Indeed, drinking is a popular activity among Canadians, especially on social recreational occasions. In 1989, an estimated 78% of Canadians fifteen years or older had taken at least one drink in the previous year (Health and Welfare Canada 1990). In that same year, the mean consumption was approximately 9.5 liters of pure alcohol for every drinker aged fifteen or older, and the value of sales of alcoholic beverages was $9,896 million, about U.S. $8.4 billion (ARF 1992). The level of alcohol consumption in Canada is higher than in most South American, Asian, and African countries, although compared with other Western countries, it is probably in the medium range.

Before we further describe the current drinking pattern in Canada, a brief introduction to the history of alcohol use in Canada is in order. It was believed that before the arrival of the Europeans, native inhabitants in the land now called Canada were totally abstinent (Smart and Ogborne 1986). When trade was established between Indians and Europeans, brandy and rum became major commodities sought by the former. Native peoples became the first heavy drinkers in Canada. Heavy drinking also was an aspect of the lives of early European settlers, especially lumbermen, miners, boatmen, and railwaymen. In the mid-1700s, liquor became a source of government revenue. The church also held a permissive attitude toward drinking. Taverns and wayside inns, abundant throughout Canada, were places where excessive drinking often took place. Per capita alcohol consumption was probably 25–30% higher than it is today.

Alcohol use in Canada did not become a social issue until the early decades of the 1800s, when the temperance movement began. Alcohol was identified by the movement as the root cause of moral degradation and all kinds of social problems. Supporters of the movement were mainly middle-class, Anglo-Saxon, Protestant fundamentalist, and rural; they believed that prohibition of alcohol would eradicate the major social evils in society. Temperance societies proliferated throughout the country except in Quebec, where the Catholic Church was more in favor of moderate drinking than of complete prohibition.

In spite of opposition from drinkers and those involved in the sale and distribution of alcohol, the temperance movement culmulated in the prohibition of drinking in all ten provinces early in the twentieth century. Except for Prince Edward Island, which passed prohibition laws in 1907, all other provinces started prohibition in the late 1910s. But the success of the prohibitionists was short-lived. As people continued to drink, an active illegal market for alcohol distribution was engendered. Prohibition laws were difficult to enforce. More important, poverty, crime, disease, and other social miseries did not disappear with prohibition. Changes in the demographic structure of the Canadian population during the postwar years, due to increasing numbers of immigrants and city dwellers, also undermined public support for prohibition, which had greater appeal to rural, middle-class, Protestant fundamentalists. Except for Prince Edward Island, which was the strongest holdout for prohibition (1907–1948), other provinces repealed prohibition in a relatively short time, ranging from only one year for Quebec (1918–1919) to thirteen years for Nova Scotia (1916–1929). The failure of prohibition marked the end of the biggest and longest social movement in Canadian history.

## CONTEMPORARY DRINKING PATTERNS

Although prohibition of drinking was a ''great experiment that failed,'' it did bring about a reduction in the rates of drunkenness and deaths from alcoholism in the several decades that followed. From the 1930s to the 1960s, surveys of alcohol use were scanty and scattered. One source of data on drinking habits has been the Gallup Poll, which found in its surveys that the percentage of drinkers (ever used alcoholic beverages) twenty-one years and over increased from 59% in 1943 to 65% in 1958, and the percentage of drinkers eighteen years and over increased from 67% in 1969 to 78% in 1978, then dropped to 73% in 1983 (Smart and Ogborne 1986). Since the 1970s, large-scale national and provincial surveys have collected a large amount of information on the drinking patterns of Canadians.

### General Prevalence Trends

Three national surveys on health and related issues have been conducted since 1978 by Health and Welfare Canada. These are the 1978/79 *The Health of Canadians* (Health and Welfare Canada 1981), the 1985 *Canada's Health Promotion Survey* (Health and Welfare Canada 1988), and the 1989 *National Al-*

*cohol and Other Drugs Survey* (Health and Welfare Canada 1990). The last was the first national survey to focus exclusively on alcohol and other drug issues.

All three national surveys asked the respondent whether he or she was a current drinker, defined as one who had taken at least a drink in the year preceding the survey. Results showed a trend of slight decline in the estimated percentage of current drinkers age fifteen or over, from 82% in 1978/79 to 81% in 1985, to 78% in 1989. There were fewer abstainers in 1989 than before (7%, compared with 8% in 1985 and 13% in 1978/79), but more Canadians had stopped drinking for at least a year (15%, compared with 10% in 1985 and 4% in 1978/79).

Among current drinkers, there was a decline in the proportion of "frequent drinkers" (those who drink alcohol at least once per month), from 67% in 1978/79 to 61% in 1985 and 52% in 1989, and an increase of "occasional drinkers" (drink alcohol less than once per month) from 15% in 1978/79 to 20% in 1985 and 26% in 1989.

## Current Drinking Habits and Attitudes

The richest collection of information on current drinking habits, attitudes toward drinking, and alcohol-related problems in Canada was gathered by the above mentioned 1989 *National Alcohol and Other Drugs* (NAD) Survey, which interviewed by telephone 11,634 respondents fifteen or older in randomly selected households in ten provinces (Yukon and the Northwest Territories were excluded). Data for this chapter on the current drinking situation in Canada were mainly extracted from that survey (see Health and Welfare Canada 1990; ARF 1992).

How frequently and how much do Canadians drink? About a quarter of current drinkers (those who had taken at least a drink in the twelve months preceding the survey) drink less than once per week, another quarter drink less than once per month, 38% drink one to three times per week, and 11% consume four or more drinks per week. On the average, a current drinker consumes 3.7 drinks per week. Half of the current drinkers had not consumed five or more drinks on one occasion in the last twelve months.

The most popular alcoholic beverage consumed by Canadians is beer, followed by spirits and wine. In 1989–90, the sale of beer accounted for $4,981 million (about U.S. $4.2 billion, 50% of total sale of alcoholic beverages); that of spirits and wine accounted for $3,174 million (U.S. $2.7 billion, 32%) and $1,741 million (U.S. $1.5 billion, 18%), respectively.

The most popular drinking setting for Canadians is a bar or tavern; almost three-quarters of current drinkers always drink whenever they visit such places. Canadians are also likely to drink at parties, weddings, and other social gatherings (half of current drinkers do), and in a restaurant while having dinner (almost one-quarter of current drinkers do). Drinking is much less likely to take place at home, during lunch at a restaurant, or at concerts or sporting events.

Canadians do not like to drink alone. The most common drinking companions are friends, followed by spouse/partner and family members (other than spouse)/ relatives. About half of the current drinkers drink with their friends a few times per month or more, three-tenths of them drink with their spouses that frequently, one-quarter drink with their family members/relatives, and slightly more than one-tenth drink with coworkers. Less than one-tenth of current drinkers drink by themselves once per week or more, and they are more likely to be older or heavy drinkers.

Because much drinking takes place in bars/taverns and at parties/social gatherings, and many Canadians drink with friends or spouse/relatives, it is not surprising that they hold a permissive attitude toward drinking in bars/taverns and on social occasions. Almost 60% of all respondents of the 1989 NAD Survey feel that it is acceptable for a man to take one to two drinks in a bar with his friends, and 22% think it is permissible for a man to drink enough to feel the effects of alcohol in that context. A woman drinking at a bar with friends is also acceptable, although a smaller percentage (16%) permit woman to drink enough to feel the effects in that context. Drinking enough to feel effects at parties or social gatherings is as acceptable as drinking at a bar with friends.

However, when it comes to work-related contexts, Canadians are much more restrictive about drinking. For example, almost 60% of respondents believe that coworkers should not drink when they are out to lunch.

Generally speaking, the norms of male drinking and female drinking are *not* the same. In almost all drinking contexts, Canadians hold a more permissive attitude toward drinking by males than drinking by females.

In sum, drinking is prevalent among Canadians; an estimated 78% of Canadians fifteen years or older are "current drinkers," consuming an average of 3.7 drinks per week. Drinking is very much a social recreational activity, the most common contexts for drinking being the bar/tavern and social gatherings, and alcohol being always consumed with friends or spouse/family members/ relatives. Canadians generally hold a permissive attitude toward drinking on social occasions, although male drinking is more acceptable than female drinking. Drinking in work-related settings is not acceptable. These findings suggest that alcohol use is very much part of the socialization in the family, among peers, and in the workplace.

## Sociodemographic and Regional Variations in Drinking

Underneath the general patterns of alcohol use in the Canadian population are quite a few sociodemographic and geographic variations.

### Region

In general, alcohol use is more prevalent in western provinces than in eastern provinces. For example, British Columbia in the west has the highest proportion of current drinkers (83%), and Prince Edward Island in the east has the lowest proportion (64%). The proportions of current drinkers in Manitoba and Sas-katchewan, two provinces in central Canada, are 79% and 78%, respectively.

However, the average number of drinks consumed by a current drinker per week is highest in Ontario and Quebec (both 3.9), although the percentage of current drinkers in these two provinces is close to the Canadian average (78% for Ontario and 76% for Quebec). The average number of drinks per week consumed by a current drinker in British Columbia is 3.8, and that in Prince Edward Island is 3.1.

### Gender

In Canada, as in many other countries, men are more likely to consume more alcohol than women. In the 1989 NAD Survey, 84% of men were current drink-ers, compared with 72% of women. Men also consume alcohol more frequently and in larger quantities than do women; 15% of male current drinkers drink four times or more per week, whereas only 6% of female current drinkers do. The average number of drinks per week consumed by male current drinkers is 5.3, compared with 2.0 for female current drinkers.

### Age

In general, age is inversely related to prevalence of alcohol use. The per-centage of current drinkers is highest in the youngest subgroup of 15–34 (84%), decreases to 80% for 35–54, and drops sharply (63%) for fifty-five or more. The greatest average number of drinks per week (4.3) is found in the 20–24 and the 45–54 subgroups. The 15–19 subgroup consumes the smallest average number of drinks per week (2.4).

### Marital Status

Married, separated, and divorced Canadians have similar percentages of cur-rent drinkers (79%, 76%, and 78%, respectively). The highest percentage of current drinkers (82%) is among those who have never been married, probably because this subgroup of people is the youngest. Widowed Canadians have a much lower percentage of current drinkers (49%) than other subgroups, probably because this subgroup has the largest proportion of older people. Among all the subgroups, those who are separated consume the highest average number of drinks per week (5.2), followed by those who are divorced (4.4) and never married (4.3).

### Education

There is a substantial difference in the percentage of current drinkers between Canadians whose education level is secondary school or less and those with postsecondary schooling. Those with secondary schooling or less have a smaller proportion of current drinkers (73%), whereas the proportion for those with some postsecondary schooling is 87% and that for those with a postsecondary degree is 86%. Although level of education seems to be positively associated with prevalence of alcohol use, those with the highest level of education (post-secondary degree) consume fewer drinks per week (3.6) than those at other education levels (3.8 for secondary or less and 4.2 for some postsecondary).

*Occupation*

Alcohol use is more prevalent among Canadians who are in the work force or are looking for jobs than among those who are not. Among employed Canadians, managers/professionals have the highest percentage of current drinkers (88%), followed by blue-collar workers (86%). However, blue-collar workers consume more drinks per week (5.8) than managers/professionals (3.8).

Among those not in the work force (students, retirees, and homemakers), students have the highest percentage of current drinkers (77%), compared with 59% of retirees and 63% of homemakers. However, retirees consume more drinks per week (3.8) than the other two subgroups (2.6 for students and 1.5 for homemakers).

*Income*

Household gross annual income is positively related to alcohol consumption. The proportion of current drinkers is 60% in the lowest income subgroup (less than $10,000 [U.S. $8,500]), rising to 66% in the $10,000–$19,999 [U.S. $8,500–16,999] subgroup, 80% in the $20,000–$39,999 [U.S. $17,000–33,999] subgroup, and 89% in the highest income subgroup ($40,000 or more [over U.S. $34,000]). The average number of drinks per week consumed also increases with income, from 2.7 in the lowest subgroup to 4.2 in the highest subgroup.

*Ethnicity*

Canada is a multiethnic society, with people of British and of French descent being the two earliest and dominant nonnative ethnic groups. Immigrants from other parts of Europe came in large numbers in the last two centuries. Since the 1960s, growing numbers of immigrants from Central and South America, Asia, the Middle East, and Africa have arrived, significantly changing the ethnic composition of the country. The country is also divided along linguistic lines, with French being the dominant language in the province of Quebec and English being spoken in most other parts of the country. Apart from these two official languages, ethnic languages are widely used among different groups, especially by immigrants who have little knowledge of either of the two offical languages.

In spite of the enormous ethnic variations in the Canadian population, very few research efforts have been made to document the prevalence of alcohol consumption and alcohol-related issues in different ethnic groups. Some insights can be gained by examining the data of the 1989 NAD Survey, although meaningful comparisons of alcohol use among ethnic groups await more sophisticated research. The survey asked respondents what language they most often spoke at home, and what ethnic or cultural group they belonged to. The former question assesses whether the respondent is English-speaking (an anglophone), French-speaking (a francophone), or neither (i.e., a user of ethnic language only). The latter information is a respondent's subjective identification with an ethnic group or heritage. If a respondent could not name a group that he or she identified with, he or she was assumed to be significantly acculturated to mainstream Canadian culture and to retain little ethnic culture. Those who mentioned a group without making reference to the Canadian identity (i.e., not a "hyphenated Canadian") are likely to be recent immigrants and to retain and practice a large amount of the ethnic culture.

Findings show that anglophones and francophones do not differ significantly in the proportion of current drinkers (79% for anglophones and 77% for francophones). Ethnic language users have the smallest percentage of current drinkers (66%). Anglophones and francophones consume an equal number of drinks per week (3.8); ethnic language users consume fewer drinks per week (3.2).

Regarding ethnic group identification and alcohol use (figures obtained from the analysis in Cheung and Eliany 1992), those not identifying with any particular ethnic group have 79% current drinkers. Among those who identified with an ethnic group, without making reference to the Canadian identity, the Ukranian/Polish subgroup has the largest percentage of current drinkers (82%), followed by the German/Dutch subgroup (80%). Contrary to popular stereotypes, the Irish, the Scottish, and the Italian/Portuguese subgroups all have lower, rather than higher, percentages of current drinkers (73% for Irish and 76% for Scottish and Italian/Portuguese) than the Canadian average. The English and French subgroups have similar percentages of current drinkers (79% and 78%, respectively). Those who gave "other" group identities (Jewish, Chinese, and others) have the smallest percentage of current drinkers (72%).

Native peoples in Canada have been known to consume more alcohol and have more alcohol-related problems than other Canadians. Although there have been many studies of alcohol use among Indians and other native peoples in Canada, no large-scale alcohol and drug epidemiological survey has been conducted. Alcohol sales data for Yukon and the Northwest Territories, inhabited mainly by native peoples, suggest that the levels of alcohol use of the native peoples are high (ARF 1992). For example, the number of drinks per week per person aged fifteen and over, computed from sales data, for Canada as a whole was 12.5 in 1980–81, 11.7 in 1984–85, and 11.2 in 1988–89. The consumption rate was twice as much in Yukon: 26.9 in 1980–81, 20.9 in 1984–85, and 20.1 in 1988–89. The rate in N.W.T. was lower than in Yukon but still substantially higher than the Canadian average: 15.4 in 1980–81, 15.7 in 1984–85, and 14.6 in 1988–89.

## ALCOHOL-RELATED PROBLEMS

Canadian drinkers experience a variety of personal and social problems as a result of their drinking. Among the current drinkers in the 1989 NAD Survey,

12% reported that they had at some time in their life felt that their alcohol use had a harmful effect on their physical health. Difficulties with friendships or social life was the next most common consequence of drinking (experienced by 11% of current drinkers at some time in their life). Other problems resulting from alcohol use reported by 2–6% of drinkers included negative outlook on life, financial difficulties, problems with marriage or home life, and problems with employment or studies.

Further analyses of the 1989 NADS data (Single and Wortley n.d.; Cheung and Eliany 1992) show that, although some sociodemographic variables (e.g., gender, age, education, income) correlate significantly with alcohol-related problems, a drinker's total alcohol consumption and extent of heavy drinking are most predictive of his or her lifetime alcohol-related problems and alcohol-related problems in the last twelve months.

In Canada, alcohol is a cause of a variety of physical problems (ARF 1992). In 1988, the number of alcoholics (based on the Jellinek estimation calculated from cirrhosis deaths) was estimated at 476,800, or 2,600 alcoholics per 100,000 population age twenty and over (excluding Yukon and N.W.T.). This alcoholism rate has been dropping since the mid-1970s, from 4,200 alcoholics per 100,000 population age twenty and over in 1975 to 3,700 in 1980, and to 2,800 in 1985.

During 1987–88, the total number of discharges from Canadian general hospitals of patients with an alcohol-related diagnosis was 36,872, 67% of which were for mental disorders and 30% for diseases of the digestive system. The rate per 100,000 population age twenty and over was 200.6. This represents a drop of 7.2% from the previous year.

The rates of alcohol-related mental disorder cases and alcohol-related diseases of the digestive system cases have been declining. For example, the rate for alcohol dependence syndrome cases per 100,000 population aged twenty and over was 105.5 in 1984–85 and 88.0 in 1987–88. The rate for alcohol-related chronic liver disease and cirrhosis cases per 100,000 population age twenty and over was 30.1 in 1984–85 and 29.2 in 1987–88.

Data on alcohol-related problems in the native population are scattered and incomplete, although many studies have found high rates of alcohol-related diseases and disabilities among native peoples. One compilation of data (ARF 1992) indicates that the alcohol-related mortality in Yukon and N.W.T. is higher than the Canadian average. The percentage of deaths from direct alcohol-related problems relative to total deaths for all diagnostic categories for Canada as a whole was 1.7 in 1986 and 1.6 in 1989. That for Yukon was 4.4 in 1986 and 4.2 in 1989; that for N.W.T. was 3.0 in 1986 and 2.0 in 1989.

Alcohol intoxication is one of the major contributory factors in traffic accidents. The rate of drinking-and-driving offenses per 100,000 population age sixteen and over was 677.1 in 1990. Like alcohol-related physical problems, the rate of drinking-and-driving offenses dropped during the 1980s: 878.6 in 1983, 770.1 in 1986, and 708.7 in 1989. Yukon and N.W.T. had much higher rates than the rest of Canada: 4,102.4 and 1,798.7, respectively in 1983, and 3,473.7 and 2,941.3, respectively, in 1990.

In sum, there has generally been a decline in the rates of alcoholism, alcohol-related physical problems, and drinking-and-driving offenses in Canada since the 1970s. The decline is concomitant with the decrease in alcohol consumption in the same period.

## ALCOHOL POLICIES

### Control Policies

Although the federal government is in charge of the manufacture, import, and export of alcoholic beverages, each province regulates the marketing and distribution of alcohol within its boundaries. This has meant considerable variation in control policies across Canada.

Each of the ten provinces has a monopoly on the off-premises sale of spirits, imported wine, and beer. Domestic wine and beer are sold through both monopoly and private outlets. Quebec permits the sale of beer and wine in grocery stores; a similar recent initiative in Ontario was defeated. The number and types of on-premises outlets, as well as hours of sale, have generally been increasing since the 1950s. Self-service has replaced ordering from clerks. The price of alcoholic beverages in real dollars (unaffected by inflation) has been growing cheaper in Canada since the 1960s. These various components of the liberalizing trend in alcohol availability likely contributed to the increase in alcohol consumption from 1950 to the mid-1970s (Single et al. 1981).

During the period between 1970 and 1975, the drinking age was lowered from twenty years in Quebec and from twenty-one years in all the other provinces. The legal drinking age is now eighteen years in about half the provinces and nineteen in the rest. Although parents are permitted to serve alcohol to underage children in their own homes, legal penalties exist for underage drinkers and those who supply them in other settings.

Advertising of alcoholic beverages has been a controversial issue in Canada. By federal law, beer and wine commercials, but not those promoting spirits, are permitted on radio and television. This resulted in the distillers' launching a charter challenge [Ed. note: a lawsuit charging unconstitutionality] that such a ban was an infringement of their industry's right to equal treatment. As of 1995, the final ruling had not been given. The sponsorship of sports and other cultural events by the alcoholic beverage industry is widespread in Canada. Advertising regulations vary by province, and numerous guidelines restrict the types, content, and location of ads. Generally, Canada permits far less alcohol advertising than is commonplace in most parts of Europe and the United States (Smart and Ogborne 1986).

Public attitudes toward alcohol control policies were assessed in the NAD Survey (Health and Welfare Canada 1990). A majority of 74% favor both the continued ban of alcohol sales in grocery stores and the introduction of warning labels on alcoholic beverages. About half (51%) support a complete ban of alcohol advertising on radio and television. Respondents are more likely to favor an increase both in alcohol taxes (27% vs. 18% for a decrease) and the drinking age (50% vs. 3% approving a decrease). More respondents agree with a proposal to decrease permitted hours of operation of government monopoly stores than would expand business hours (17% vs. 7%). Thus a majority of Canadians appear to oppose the "liberalizing" trends of past decades.

## Prevention and Treatment Policies

There is a trend in Canada toward more comprehensive prevention programs that include a variety of psychoactive substances. Such programs are usually seen as part of provincial jurisdiction over health. The majority of programs are school-based, but some advertising campaigns have been developed that center on health promotion. Public attitudes support educational methods for the prevention of alcohol problems: 61% favor an increase in anti-drinking advertisements; 82% support more server training (to stop serving alcohol to intoxicated persons); 81% want more government prevention programs (Health and Welfare Canada 1990).

In Canada, treatment directions have shifted away from more expensive, specialized inpatient care to a mix of in- and outpatient services. These include detoxification facilities, long- and short-term residential facilities, and a variety of outpatient programs. Alcohol dependency and related problems are dealt with in a broader system of universal health care accessibility. Treatment for alcohol problems is widely available, but the vast area of the country means that access is more limited in sparsely populated areas than in urban centers. Self-help groups are also numerous, and Canada has a high proportion of Alcoholics Anonymous groups compared with most other countries.

In conclusion, Canada has been a leader in the recognition that many alcohol problems are self-inflicted "lifestyle" diseases. The most effective approaches, in the long run, are likely to be basic prevention, early intervention, and health promotion strategies.

## REFERENCES

Addiction Research Foundation. 1992. *Canadian Profile: Alcohol & Other Drugs.* Toronto: Addiction Research Foundation.

Cheung, Yuet W., and Marc Eliany. 1992. Predicting alcohol use and alcohol-related problems in Canada: How useful are socio-demographic variables? Toronto: Addiction Research Foundation.

Health and Welfare Canada. 1981. *The Health of Canadians: Report of the Canada Health Survey.* Ottawa: Ministry of Supply and Services of Canada.

―――. 1988. *Canada's Health Promotion Survey: Technical Report.* Ottawa: Ministry of Supply and Services of Canada.

―――. 1990. *National Alcohol and Other Drugs Survey: Highlights Report.* Ottawa: Ministry of Supply and Services of Canada.

Single, Eric, Norman Giesbrecht, and Barry Eakins. 1981. The alcohol policy debate in Ontario in the post–war era, Pp. 127–157 in Eric Single, Patricia Morgan, and Jan de Lint (Eds.). *Alcohol, Society and the State,* vol. 2, *The Social History of Control Policy in Seven Countries.* Toronto: Addiction Research Foundation.

Single, Eric, and Scot Wortley. 1993. Drinking in various settings as it relates to demographic variables and level of consumption: Findings from a national survey in Canada. *Journal of Studies on Alcohol* 54: 590–599.

Smart, Reginald G., and Alan C. Ogborne. 1986. *Northern Spirits: Drinking in Canada Then and Now.* Toronto: Addiction Research Foundation.

# 4

---

# Chile

## *Eduardo Medina Cárdenas*

## SOME GENERALITIES ABOUT ALCOHOL

The use of alcoholic beverages is as old as mankind's existence in the world. In ancient times some people must have realized that natural juices from a number of fruits or the broth of any grain boiled in water and then left for some days into the open air, gained a very special "spirit" or "power," inasmuch as they produced some very interesting mental modifications in any person who drank them. Because the search for substances, procedures, and techniques for a voluntary change of perceptions, moods, or behaviors of their members appears to be a constant in all human groups as early as primitive hunting-and-gathering bands, beverages that had such properties acquired an important role in ceremonies and rites associated with private family life or public collective feasts. Concentration of these fermented beverages by distillation seems to be an invention of Arab civilization, during the 1200s; the word "alcohol" (meaning "subtle spirit"), reflecting this new power of beverages, is derived from Arabic. In reality, the natural fermentation of a variety of plant products to produce alcohol, and their subsequent distillation and transformation into liquors, were technical procedures developed long before the beginning of modern chemistry. Not until the 1700s did chemists isolate the ethyl alcohol (or ethanol) that is responsible for those mental changes, and discover oxygen and its role in the production of wines, ciders, and beers.

Very early in this process, and parallel with the use of alcoholic beverages, there emerged concern for the consequences of their consumption. By trial and error, the favorable and unfavorable effects, both for the individual and for society, were discovered and rules were developed to assure safer utilization. Examples include reserving beer for special feasts in Sumer, specific limits on consumption that were included in the Code of Hammurabi, the religious cults of Dionysus and Bacchus in Greek and Roman civilizations, warnings about the perils of alcoholic excess spelled out in the Bible and the punishment by death for unauthorized drunkenness among the Aztecs.

## ALCOHOLIC BEVERAGES IN CHILE

Various alcoholic beverages were known to the majority of aboriginal American peoples before the Hispanic conquest. During pre-Columbian times some *chichas* (home brews) were made by fermenting different fruits, grains, and other plant raw material; the grapevine was not known then, and there were no techniques to keep those beverages from going sour; neither was distillation known. Spaniards introduced the grapevine into America, partially motivated by the necessity of providing wine for Christian religious services; the grapevine was introduced from Spain to Cuba during the second voyage of Christopher Columbus, and from Spain to Mexico shortly after the conquest of that territory by Hernando Cortés (around 1531). Vines were brought from the Canary Islands to Peru sometime later, and vineyards were established there by 1551. Other Spanish conquerors contributed techniques for preserving fermented beverages and for distilling rums and brandy.

The grapevine was introduced to Chile from Cuzco, Peru, and wine was produced as early as 1555. The central part of colonial Chilean territory, between the northern city of La Serena and the southern city of La Concepción (latitudes 30°S to 38°S) proved to have extremely favorable conditions for this activity. At the end of the 1700s, exportation of wine to other colonies of Spanish America began. Its course followed the economic conditions of Chile and the varying commercial dispositions of the Spanish Crown, sometimes tolerant and sometimes restrictive, depending on the requirements of European interests.

Throughout the colonial period and up to the mid-1800s, Chilean grapevine cultivation was characterized by the fewness of varieties of grapes and the simple manufacture of wines. In 1851, a new and favorable period began with the importation of French grapevines and modern techniques of wine production, both of which prompted an important increase in both the area devoted to vineyards and the volume of wine production. This industry became the most successful agricultural activity in 1870, exporting wines to both Europe and America. From then until the 1980s, there was a sustained increase in vineyard area and in the manufacture of wines and *chichas*.

According to Chilean wine producers, demand has steadily diminished since 1950: the per capita annual average consumption was 65 liters during the 1950s, 60 liters during the 1960s, 50 liters in the 1970s, and 45 liters in the 1980s. However, the annual average per capita consumption of all kinds of alcohol experienced fluctuations (between 8 and 12.5 liters of pure ethanol annually) during those decades. There was not a lesser consumption of alcoholic beverages but a reorientation of preferences, especially among young people, from wine toward beers and distilled liquors (which are often combined with soft drinks). This is demonstrated by the impressive increase in domestic production of both newly favored types of alcoholic beverages and extensive importation in recent years.

Annual export of alcoholic beverages has never exceeded 2–5% of each year's production. A number of negative individual and collective consequences result from chronic excessive consumption among the adult population, mainly males. The concern of public authorities is reflected in the enactment of specific legislation, since the beginning of the twentieth century, to control quality; to apply taxes; to control sale hours and licensing; to set punishment for public inebriety; to provide compulsory medical treatment for alcoholics; and to promote preventive education programs in public schools.

## URBAN CONSUMPTION

The individual and collective effects of heavy alcohol consumption among the adult population have been realized by public health authorities for a long time. The Chilean Ministry of Public Health distinguishes four different but complementary criteria for the classification of alcohol consumption:

A. Quantity of ethanol consumption. This is calculated not in terms of the volume drunk but according to the proportion of the calories in the individual's daily diet that are derived from alcohol. For example, if a male adult weighing 80 kilograms requires a daily total intake of some 2,800 calories (35 cal. per kg. of body weight), he could safely receive up to 560 calories from alcohol daily (approximately 80 g. of absolute ethanol), an amount roughly equivalent to 0.75 liter of wine, 2 liters of beer, or 0.25 liter of distilled liquor. Deriving more than 20% of one's total caloric intake from alcohol is considered excessive drinking.

B. Mode of consumption. Any drinker can take ethanol in three different patterns:
    1. Remittent. The consumption is on isolated occasions, during a brief period of time, with intervals of a month or more between drinking occasions.
    2. Discontinuous. The consumption is on isolated occasions or during a period of some days, with an interval of a few days or weeks between intakes.
    3. Continuous. The consumption is daily, with only a few hours between successive intakes.

C. Bodily effects of ethanol intake. This refers to the presence or absence of episodes of drunkenness, the appearance of manifestations of lack of motor coordination ranging from "superficial drunkenness" to a stupor ("profound drunkenness") due to the effects of alcohol. One such episode in a month or twelve in a year is acceptable—if there is no significant damage to the drinker, his or her family, or his or her work; more than that is considered "excessive."

D. Inductive factors for consumption, that is, reasons or motivations that lead a person to drink:
    1. Sociocultural factors. The motivation for drinking springs from an adaptation to the norms or mores of the social group the person belongs to.

2. Psychopathological factors. The motivation for drinking derives from the search for relief of some intrapsychic stress (a mood upset, an anxiety reaction, etc.).

3. Physiopathological factors. The motivation derives from relief of the alcohol withdrawal syndrome, the ensemble of disturbing bodily signs and symptoms that the drinker experiences as the result of previous alcohol intake, minutes or hours before. This pathological drive to consume alcoholic beverages is called "physical dependence on ethanol" (a factor found only in an alcoholic).

These criteria allow us to classify the adult population as normal or abnormal drinkers, as follows:

A. Normal drinkers.

1. Abstemious (or abstainer). A person who never drinks alcoholic beverages or drinks them no more than five times a year, in small quantities, and without drunkenness. They comprise 20% of the adult population.

2. Moderate. A person who drinks in a discontinuous or continuous manner, up to 0.75 liter of wine during a day (or its equivalent in other alcoholic beverages) and/ or gets drunk no more than once a month or twelve times a year. Such a person is assumed to drink due to sociocultural factors alone. They comprise 65% of the adult population.

B. Excessive/abnormal drinkers.

The first subtype drinks in a discontinuous or continuous manner, over 0.75 liter of wine during a day (or its equivalent in some other alcoholic beverage), and/or gets drunk more than once a month or twelve times a year. Such persons are assumed to drink due to sociocultural and/or psychopathological factors. They represent 10% of the adult population.

The other subtype is called an alcoholic, a person who drinks because of his or her physical dependence on ethanol. Such persons may also have sociocultural and/ or psychopathological reasons for alcohol consumption. The amount of alcohol intake is similar to that of excessive drinkers, and he or she need not be habitually drunk. They represent 5% of the adult population.

Epidemiological surveys published between 1950 and 1990 are consistent on these approximate prevalence rates. These publications also demonstrate that abnormal drinking is associated directly with male gender and inversely with socioeconomic level.

## USE OF ALCOHOLIC BEVERAGES AMONG MAPUCHE INDIANS

Beers and *chichas* were consumed long before the arrival of the Hispanic conquerors. When the Spaniards arrived in the territory that is now Chile, they used the term "Araucanos" for all the people who lived in an extensive region (parallels 33°S to 42°S) because of their common language and similar habits. The natives called themselves, according to their respective zone of origin, Picunches (in the north), Huilliches (on the south coast), Pehuenches (in the forested southern Andes), and Mapuches (in the central valley). The Mapuche resisted more than any other ethnic group. Despite military and civil efforts to integrate them during the colonial period, they surrendered to the Chilean army and came under the national jurisdiction only in 1880. Now they constitute the main ethnic minority of the country.

Due to such an extended period of cultural contact and acculturation between the Hispanic conquerors and the Mapuche, there is much information regarding alcohol consumption in a number of documents written by chroniclers, travelers, missionary-priests, public officials, and other witnesses. As soon as the Europeans arrived during the 1500s, they remarked on the variety of native *chichas* made from local fruits or grains. The occasions of consumption—as part of collective celebrations associated with war plans or victories, marriages, economic transactions, or the meting out of justice—usually included deliberate and socially accepted drunkenness. During such festivities, the behavior of the participants changed from glad and cheerful songs and dancing to licentiousness and verbal or physical violence.

Documents of the 1600s are more descriptive. Feasts, sometimes with artistic performances, are detailed. Important occasions for ceremonial alcohol consumption by adult men included worship of the earth, collective agricultural work, and house-building. Procedures for making alcoholic beverages introduced by the Spaniards changed some native habits. In the past, when they produced their fermented beverages, it was usually necessary to drink them in a few days, before they became too acid; now, people who lived near new urban settlements could acquire better fermented and distilled beverages in commercial establishments or from rural peddlers.

Drinking habits are described in more detail during the 1700s. The common habit of heavy drinking ended on the eve of a war venture, and natives devoted themselves to physical fitness. Colonial authorities were worried about the negative consequences of alcohol consumption among the indigenous population who lived near the cities. There were attempts at moderating that consumption by controlling sale hours and instituting police patrols to avoid disorders. Indian people placed on royal land grants were partially paid with wine, even when that was illegal.

During the 1800s, Spanish domination ended and the Republic of Chile was established. Then came the military surrender of the Mapuches, their final pacification, usurpation of the majority of Indian ancestral lands, and a settled life inside small, rural communal properties known as *reducciones* (reductions, or reservations). Alcoholic beverages sold in rural areas usually were diluted with water. Indians who lived in cities as part of the lower class continued to attract the concern of the authorities because of their propensity for drinking and getting drunk.

Authors of the early 1900s refined our understanding of those patterns. During the pre-Hispanic epoch, about seventeen different kinds of *chicha* were made. Maize was introduced during the Inca domination; grapes, apples, wheat, and technology for the production of wine and spirits arrived with the Spaniards. Some years later, the Mapuche produced only apple and maize *chichas,* and bought other types of alcoholic beverages.

The ancestral feasts—mainly the *nguillatun* (a traditional propitiatory rite for the fertility of land and crops that invoked supernatural protection and was celebrated at the winter solstice)—in ancient times were marked by moderate alcohol consumption; as traditions and customs became secularized, those feasts became occasions of diversion, with much more male drunkenness and growing participation of women in them. The increasing impoverishment of the Mapuche restricted celebrations and, consequently, diminished the frequency and intensity of their occasions for excessive drinking.

Natives who frequently went to local markets on the periphery of cities and villages, as well as mestizos, showed individual and group effects of heavy drinking such as health problems, quarrels and other violent behavioral out-bursts, absenteeism from work, and economic hardship. In public drinking places, they often were exploited by unscrupulous merchants and spent the majority of what money they received for the sale of their domestic production; sometimes, when they did not have enough cash, they were induced to sell personal belongings to pay for their drinks.

By the end of 1800s, a difficult cultural contact had been established between the Mapuche and the Chilean dominant society. The socioeconomic and cultural instability of the Indians was associated by foreign observers with their inmoderate drinking, and many Chileans believed that this aggravated their life situation and influenced their cultural degradation. A very negative stereotype of the "lazy and drunken Indian" developed, with official acquiescence. From this grew measures for forcibly acquiring Indian lands, based on a negative stereotype that indiscriminately considered them corrupt, degenerate, and inferior.

Some modern descriptions of Mapuches who live on reservations or in cities appear in ethnographies based on anthropological fieldwork. Reservation Mapuche maintain the social role of alcohol intake, more associated with males but with higher frequency of consumption due to easy access to alcoholic beverages by means of purchase or barter. Nevertheless, normal consumption involves fewer days of drunkenness than in the past: like the dominant Chilean pattern, less quantity but more frequency. The opportunities for drinking are parties, Catholic celebrations, journeys to the village or city, and various informal occasions. Drinking alone is criticized, and so is abstention; such behavior is interpreted as a lack of trust.

The Mapuches who live in cities look for social relations with other Mapuches, mainly when they first arrive, which generates social support groups. They also interact with friends in their neighborhood or workplace. Group drinking reinforces group cohesion. At the beginning of this new life in the city, some heavy drinking episodes typically occur, but drinking later stabilizes toward the norms of the dominant population. Now that cash is needed for everything, it can no longer be spent so freely as it was in rural areas, where food could be obtained without it.

Affiliation with some religious groups can modify these consumption patterns. This is the case when a Mapuche joins a Protestant church, many of which demand abstinence and in turn offer a real confraternity of aid and support.

## SOCIAL LEARNING OF ALCOHOL CONSUMPTION

As in other countries, the intake of alcoholic beverages is a very common social custom in Chile. Most people drink in a wide variety of formal or informal social and personal interactions. There is general acceptance of consumption, mainly with respect to the adult male; in both urban and rural settings, male drunkenness is accepted, a cultural trait that has led some authors to propose the existence of a national subculture of excessive intake. (That subculture includes a group of adult lower-class men who consume alcohol in bars and cantinas, mainly on weekends; drunkenness is an outcome.) There is evidence that an important proportion of abnormal male drinkers in that lower-class stratum acquired the habit when they were children, imitating the behavior of their adult reference figure, mainly their father. Drunkenness is criticized among men in upper socioeconomic levels and among women in all levels.

Social interactions that occur during drinking, and their effects on drinkers, particularly those of the urban lower-class subculture, have resulted in the creation of slang and proverbs related to beverages, bottles or other containers, modalities of drinking, ways of inviting one to drink, drunkenness, alcoholism, and so on. The ethnolinguistics of alcohol has been an interesting development among national folkloric studies.

Drinking begins during childhood or adolescence, within the family itself or under the influence of peers. Adolescents, like adults, drink alcohol at social events; when the consumption is out of the family context, it is more frequently inmoderate, mainly among men. The reasons why young people drink include curiosity, relaxation, imitation of adults, customs, easy access, and advertisements. A minority highlight the role of more individual reasons, such as changes of mood, anxiety, feelings of incomprehension, or difficulties in interpersonal relations. In spite of legal prohibition of the sale of alcohol to youngsters in restaurants and bars, unrestricted sale of bottles to children and adolescents in grocery stores and supermarkets facilitates its consumption in public places.

The adolescent population shows a 30% rate of abstainers, 60% moderate drinkers, and 10% excessive drinkers. Gender and socioeconomic associations are similar to those among adults. Among wealthy young people, there is no correlation between knowledge about the negative effects of immoderate consumption and the modalities of intake: the same high school group who earned grades of 98% in alcohol education had 12.6% excessive drinkers.

## PROS AND CONS OF ALCOHOLIC BEVERAGE CONSUMPTION

The Chilean vineyard cultivation comprises some 90,000 hectares (about 225,000 acres), which represents 1% of the total cultivated agricultural land. Fully 85% of each annual harvest is devoted to alcohol production, and the remainder to fresh grapes for domestic consumption and export. Fiscal control of production is under the Ministry of Agriculture. Beer barley cultivation occupies about 15,000 hectares (37,500 acres).

About 5% of the active labor force of the country is engaged in production and commercialization of alcohol. The wine industry employs 10% of the agriculturally active population, and some 100,000 families are involved. Total taxes paid by alcohol-related industries in the country represent 30% of all taxes related to agricultural activities. The consumption of alcoholic beverages is fostered by advertising that associates their use with cultural values, youth, wealth, social refinement, sports, and so forth.

This favorable relation to the national economy is the image held by the majority of the population. The problems associated with abnormal drinking most directly affect the drinker and his or her family, and impact only on police, health, and judicial services, which have a little contact with most people. But social problems are greater than those generated by abnormal drinkers alone, because the whole society may be involved in different ways with various drinking problems. In fact, we pay attention to at least six problem areas in this connection:

1. Alcoholics have a physical dependence on ethanol and, as a consequence of their pathological consumption, may have many individual and social problems.

2. Excessive drinkers, even though they do not have physical dependence on ethanol, can experience negative consequences similar to those of alcoholics.

3. Moderate drinkers may, on a very rare drinking occasion, be involved in a traffic accident, violence, and/or other harmful situations.

4. Increased immoderate consumption among adolescent and young adult males and among adult women is facilitated by the ease of purchasing alcoholic beverages.

5. The association of abnormal drinking with the consumption of another psychotropic substance is very typical in young adults. It has been determined that abstainers rarely use drugs, and drug addicts are frequently excessive drinkers. Among those arrested for using and/or trafficking in drugs, 51% of their fathers and 9% of their mothers were abnormal drinkers.

6. The consequences of abnormal drinking are spread over the entire population. Any person, even an abstainer, may be involved in an accident or violence with people who are under the influence of alcohol; any citizen can suffer the costs of abnormal drinking, such as the negative economic effects of public health costs and the destruction of property and wealth.

The negative consequences of problem drinking are multiple and important. Some of them will be briefly described here.

1. During 1981–89, drinking was directly or indirectly associated with one-third of ambulatory medical consultations, 38% of hospital discharges, and 43% of hospital mortality.

2. As in other countries, the annual per capita average consumption is directly associated with mortality from liver cirrhosis and traffic accidents: the more the individual intake, the higher these figures become, and vice versa.

3. It is estimated that each problem drinker has twenty days of work absenteeism a year, and his or her productivity and that of his or her direct coworkers decline 25% and 10%, respectively.

4. During 1991–92, alcoholism and its direct and indirect impacts on the health of workers resulted in 5–8% of the disability retirements under social security.

5. The economic cost of abnormal drinking is generated indirectly by premature mortality of the worker, his or her lower productivity and work absenteeism, and directly by reallocation of resources of the social welfare system and the destruction of physical property. A study made in 1981 estimated the global cost at U.S. $1.82 billion; health expenses were only U.S. $116.5 million (in this same year, the budget for education, health, justice, and welfare was U.S. $1.57 billion).

6. During 1980–89 police arrests for public drunkenness and DWI were 28.6% and 0.6%, respectively, of total arrests.

7. Violent deaths associated with alcohol consumption in the metropolitan region of Santiago during 1981–88 were high; 33–50% of fatal traffic accidents, homicides, and suicides were alcohol-related. This association was probably similar in deaths due to drowning and burns.

The analysis of some official strategies to prevent excessive drinking and alcoholism offers different perspectives on supply and demand of alcoholic beverages. At various times there have been absolutely and relative dry zones, high taxes and prices, control of vineyard areas, and so forth. There have been educational campaigns, some oriented to stimulate normal consumption among adults; a program of primary prevention of alcoholism incorporated into the public school curriculum; and mutual-help groups among alcoholics. Their value is uncertain, and many experts are skeptical about their effectiveness. To many, it seems that a sustained shift to moderate consumption among excessive drinkers, and to abstinence for alcoholics, can be reached only when effective interpersonal support and religious or ideological reorientations have come into play.

## CONCLUSIONS

Alcoholic beverages are an integral part of Chilean culture. Their types and uses vary according to sociocultural traits and technological development of the human groups who have lived in the national territory.

Chile has a tradition of frequent consumption of wine. Nevertheless, due to a sustained change in the preference of drinkers to beer and liquor during recent years, wine consumption probably represents only half of the total alcohol intake in the 1990s.

Individual and collective negative effects of abnormal consumption have interested those concerned with Chilean public health for many years. This awareness is expressed by means of clinical, epidemiological, and sociocultural investigations, and in the development of detailed classificatory parameters of the different types of drinkers.

The Mapuche and other aboriginal groups in the national territory have been changing their ancestral patterns of drinking (traditionally corresponding to ceremonial intake) to patterns similar to those of lower-class urban and rural groups. This change is the manifestation of historical and acculturative dynamics between these native groups and the dominant society.

Even though the processes related to alcoholic beverages constitute one of the most important agricultural activities of the country, the enormous dimensions of the economic cost of the undesirable results of immoderate consumption surpass the benefits of their production, distribution, and commercialization.

Even though preventive strategies for excessive drinking and alcoholism exist, mainly in public health and education, experts are skeptical about their efficacy.

## REFERENCES

Dobert-Versin, M. T., B. Gómez-Maldonado, and E. Medina-Cárdenas. (1983). *Alcohol y alcoholismo.* Santiago: Edit. GALDOC.
Encina, F. A. 1983. *Historia de Chile.* Santiago: Ercilla.
Gay, C. 1973. *Historia física y política de Chile.* vol. 2, *Agricultura.* Santiago: Instituto de Capacitación e Investigación en Reforma Agraria.
Heath, D. B. 1982. Historical and cultural factors affecting alcohol availability and consumption in Latin America. Pp. 128–188 in Institute of Medicine. *Legislative Approaches to the Prevention of Alcohol-Related Problems.* Washington, D.C.: National Academy Press.
Hernández, A. 1985. Análisis de la situación vitivinícola actual. *El campesino* 116 (10): 51–58.
Hernández, A., P. Prczcolkowski, and P. Morandé. 1986. *La viña y el vino en Chile.* Santiago: Facultad de Agronomía, Universidad Católica de Chile.
Lomnitz, L. 1976. Alcohol and culture: The historical evolution of drinking patterns among the Mapuche. Pp. 177–198 in M. W. Everett, J. O. Waddell, and D. B. Heath (Eds.). *Cross-Cultural Approaches to the Study of Alcohol: An Interdisciplinary Perspective.* The Hague: Mouton.
López, A. 1987. Mortalidad por cirrosis hepática, producción y precio del vino en Chile: 1950–1982. *Boletín de la Oficina Sanitaria Panamericana* 102:346–358.
Medina-Cárdenas, E. 1989a. Consumo de sustancias psicoáctivas en Chile. *Boletín epidemiológico de Chile* 16(4–6):53–74.

————. 1989b. Uso de alcohol y otras drogas por los indígenas de Chile. In *V Congreso iberoamericano sobre drogodependencias y alcoholismo.* Madrid: CIDA.

————. 1991a. Alcoholismo, tabaquismo y drogadicción. Pp. 1550–1558 in J. Meneghello, E. Fanta, E. Paris, and J. Rosselot (Eds.). *Pediatría,* vol. 2. 4th ed. Santiago: Publicaciónes Técnicas Mediterráneo.

————. 1991b. Epidemiología del alcoholismo y de otras drogadicciones. *Revista AIE-PAD* 7:26–84.

Medina-Cárdenas, E., and H. Boccardo-Zapata (Eds.). 1980. Alcoholismo y salud pública. Special issue of *Cuadernos médico-sociales* 21(1).

Ministerio de Salud de Chile. 1989. *Plan nacional de salud mental y psiquiatría: 1989–1990.* Santiago: MSC.

Vial-Correa, G. 1986. *Historia de Chile.* Santiago: Editorial Santillana del Pacífico.

# 5

---

# China

## *Xiao Jiacheng*

The origins of alcohol and culture in the world are ambiguous, but China is almost certainly the birthplace of spirits distilled from a yeast-fermented base. In respect to the variety of such liquors, China is still important and distinctive. Throughout history, and even today, the Chinese people have stressed the role of alcohol in sociocultural life, affecting overall patterns of belief, behavior, values, and attitudes. Religion often involved alcohol, especially in connection with sacrificial activities. Some ancient Chinese considered alcohol itself to be sacred, and drank it only in sacrificial ceremonies; eventually, they would sacrifice whenever they wanted to drink. They also used alcohol before drinking, as an offering dedicated to the sky, to the earth, to ghosts and deities, or to their ancestors. As early as the sixteenth century B.C., there are inscriptions on bones and tortoise shells describing offerings of millet wine and tulip-flower wine to the dead "big chief" and "the soldier." These earliest documents signal alcohol's religious importance, a bond that continues undiminished, and show that since before the Shang dynasty (1711–1066 B.C.), there has been a close link between religious beliefs and alcohol, especially as a means of worshipping the sky, the earth, ancestors, and other spirits.

Because of its supposed power, alcohol was an important part of various secular rituals as well. Some rites stemmed from a religious background, but many evolved into wholly new forms. For example, some focused on the political system; others celebrated the harvest; and still others stressed ethics and morality, especially respect for the aged. In the spring, there was a huge ritual at court when the emperor received visiting nobles; parades and military reviews came in the autumn. There were six separate rites of initiation at various life stages of a growing boy; rites in connection with weddings and funerals; and rites to celebrate the first shooting by troops while in training. In rural areas, any meeting of friends was celebrated with drinking. Although such rites were varied and diverse, they all had alcohol as an important component.

In relation to marriage, alcohol still plays a role at almost every step. Among the Hans (the major ethnic group in China), the suitor's family offers alcohol to the prospective bride's family, a practice well documented as long ago as the Song Dynasty (A.D. 960–1279). Similar customs prevail among the Dai, Jingpo, and Lahu ethnic minorities. Among the Ewenkis, once the gift is drunk, it is understood that the parents have approved the marriage. Among Mongolians, engagement is a two-step procedure: a preliminary (or minor) approach is made by the suitor and matchmaker, taking liquor and two plates of pancakes to the girl's parents; the major, confirming ritual involves the man's relative offering gifts of liquor, roast mutton, cake, and a *khatag* (a silk scarf). At the time of the wedding, a Mongolian bridegroom gives quantities of alcohol, and toasts each member of the bride's household separately. When the couple return to his house, they are welcomed at the gate by horsemen displaying butter, milky tea, roast mutton, and other gifts, always including kumiss (fermented mare's milk), which is considered especially auspicious. The Manchus also treat alcohol as an integral part of the engagement process and a key wedding gift. Among the Han, the bridegroom toasts all his new relatives, and drinking by the couple is taken as a confirmation of their pledge to each other. Many of the ethnic groups consider alcohol so important that a special batch is prepared soon after a girl's birth, to be saved for use in rituals that will occur when she leaves home to marry. It is noteworthy that this practice contradicts the popular stereotype that Chinese parents often have nothing to do with a daughter.

Alcohol is also an important adjunct to hospitality. A host and guest often serve each other as a combined expression of welcome and thanks. Meetings of old friends are enhanced by drinking together. A popular story from the Jin Dynasty (A.D. 265–420) tells of a host's being so concerned to serve drinks to his friends that, having no other resources, he sold his hair to a wigmaker in order to buy liquor. Even today, there is a saying: "Alcohol without tea is no slight; but food without alcohol is." Drinking is an important part of hospitality and sociability, thought to lend an air of festivity and relaxation to any meeting, and to signal respect for the guest. Mongolians serve three cups at a time; a guest should drink two of them quickly or risk being exhorted to do so by toasting songs. Among Tibetans, two cups of barley ale may be declined, but a guest is expected to accept and toast his host with the third. Among the Ewenkis, a host offers cowberry wine after pouring a little on the fire as a sacrifice and tasting it himself, as an indication that it is not poisoned. Clearly, alcohol is an integral part of the various cultures throughout China, in spite of the misguided notion many Westerners have to the effect that it is unimportant.

## HISTORY

Alcohol has a long history in China, including what many Chinese sources call "natural alcohol," which is not deliberately manufactured but an unintentional outcome of the process of fermentation. Stories from the Tang Dynasty refer to apes and monkeys making alcohol. In the Song Dynasty, it was recognized that pears stored too long change into wine. During the Ming Dynasty (1368–1644) people are said to have placed wild flowers and fruits, to make wine, in shallow, stone-lined depressions, and there are several accounts of woodsmen finding it in the remote mountains of Canton. The details of these stories may sometimes be apocryphal or mythological, but the theme is so consistent and pervasive as to suggest that there may be some grounding in fact for "natural alcohol," which can occur anywhere that microorganisms survive on sugars, and has been described as causing insects, birds, and even mammals to become drunk on naturally fermented fruits or berries.

Concerning the invention of "manufactured alcohol," there are three ancient theories, each identified with an individual. One of the earliest accounts is a legend recorded in the Warring States Period (475–221 B.C.) that refers to the time of Emperor Yu (around 2140 B.C.). Yi Di, a female servant of the emperor's daughter, found that a gruel of grain that had been left for a while both tasted good and felt good. The emperor found out about it, predicted that it would cause great troubles, and exiled Yi Di.

A more widespread story attributes the origin to Du Kang (sometimes called Shao Kang), a posthumous son of the fifth prime minister of the Xia Dynasty (2140–1711 B.C.). He grew up in his mother's family, herding sheep with her father-in-law. One day he was caught in a shower on the mountaintop. In the rush to drive the sheep home, he forgot his lunch of cooked and husked sorghum that was hanging in a bamboo bucket on a tree. When he returned a few days later, it smelled good and tasted sweet. His father-in-law was a well-known cook, and they experimented together until they produced a fine rum called *li xun.* Another version of this story is that Du Kang's father was killed by the traitor Han Zhuo, but that Du Kang escaped to a village in the mountains of Henan. There he found a cave where apes and monkeys fermented flowers and fruit. Enchanted with the smell, Du Kang imitated them and produced alcoholic beverages that everyone enjoyed. Drinks were such a great gift to humankind that after Du Kang's death, the deity Jade Emperor supposedly invited him to join the celestial court and named him god of alcohol. His name is now synonymous with alcohol, as in the refrain "What can relieve sorrow? Nothing but Du Kang," which is still popular throughout China.

A third theory attributes winemaking and "mellow sap alcohol" to the great doctor Qibo, who used fermented rice as medicine for the Yellow Emperor (around 2500 B.C.). His medical book is still a basic reference, containing many mentions of the benefits of rice wine.

Each of these theories carries the name of the maker of alcohol, and marks the introduction of alcohol as an important historic event. They are not simply oral myths, but each is documented in ancient literature. Undoubtedly the evolution from primitive origins to the many and elaborate drinks we know today involved gradual contributions from innumerable ordinary people.

## MAJOR DRINKING PATTERNS

A number of drinking patterns can be identified, given the pervasive importance of alcohol in the various cultures that comprise the immense and diverse People's Republic of China.

### Ritual Drinking

Apparently from the beginning, alcohol has been important in many rituals, both sacred and secular. Toasting is an integral part of any large meal, and it is important when friends get together or separate, even in the lowliest of families. The welcoming of guests and their departure are occasions for elaborately stylized drinking, and sometimes for eating.

Kumiss (sometimes called milk wine) is a home brew based on the milk (of horse or rarely of cow). It has long been favored among the Mongol and Khazak ethnic minorities in the north. Mongolians have the richest variety: *qige* from fresh horse milk; *salinarihe* distilled from sour buttermilk; *ariji,* double-distilled *salinarihe;* and *jieriji* further distilled from *ariji.* Marco Polo told of his travel about Kublai Khan's serving *qige* at a grand royal banquet. Mongolians and Khazaks still drink much kumiss at their annual fair and reunion, and it is an integral part of every wedding ceremony.

### Festive Drinking

Even when drinking is not specifically integrated into a ritual, it is often important as a normal part of a festive day or holiday, such as the annual festival to welcome springtime, the lantern festival, the dragon-boat festival, the midautumn festival, and the double-ninth festival. On all such occasions, drinking itself is an important activity, and special drinks are prepared as part of the festive observances.

Ever since the Han Dynasty, liqueurs made from peppers and cypress leaves, and a medicinal liquor called *tusu,* have been important in celebrating the new year, one of the major holidays in the Chinese tradition. Everyone toasts for a happy new year, for good health, and for long life for their elders. The lantern festival, which celebrates the first full moon of the new year, is marked with the eating of special sweet dumplings, the floating of lighted lanterns, and the drinking of special cordials. The dragon-boat festival falls on May 5 (in the Chinese lunar calendar). Because that month was thought in ancient times to be unhealthful, customs surviving from the Tang Dynasty emphasize the medicinal properties of alcohol. One favorite is distilled from calamus (the dried rhizome of the sweet flag), and another is flavored with realgar (disulfide of arsenic, yielding red alcohol); both are thought to protect one from poisons and a variety of diseases, as well as to help purify the blood. The midautumn festival falls on August 15 (lunar) and features drinking while watching the moon, still a favorite custom in both urban and rural areas.

In some southern areas, home brew is placed in a large pot containing several hollow reeds or bamboo tubes as straws. People sit in a circle around the pot, and each sips through a straw. Good-natured talking and laughing are a normal accompaniment of such drinking. In a large group, longer straws may be used so that the circle can be enlarged. Singing, dancing, and the recitation of traditional epic poetry are common in this context. This custom is at least as old as the Wei Dynasty (sixth century A.D.) because it is described in detail in the first Chinese book on agriculture, which was published then. It is still frequent among the Quiang and Han peoples of Sichuan, and the Miao of Guizhou. There is no better way to entertain a guest than such "happy drinking."

## Recreational Drinking

From the perspective of Chinese culture, alcoholic beverages can stimulate one's mind and stir one's sentiments. Therefore, drinking goes hand in hand with music, dance, poetry, song, novels, and other literary and art forms. The ideal form of leisure and recreation, for many people, is to combine drinking (to heighten one's senses) with musical or artistic appreciation.

As early as the Zhou Dynasty (1066–256 B.C.), books tell of the delights of combining drinking with listening to songs and watching dances. Among the ethnic minorities in Liao, in the north, plays and acrobatics were entertainments that could best be appreciated while drinking. A Tibetan host today will sing, often improvising poetically, while offering alcohol to a guest. Antiphonal singing, with the men responding to the women and vice versa, occurs during banquets in Tibet, especially in the Dong society, where it is highly esteemed as "an ocean of songs." In many parts of the country it is customary for a guest to offer a singing toast to the oldest person in his host's household, and there are songs that everyone sings, while drinking heartily, as an important part of almost any meal that includes more than the immediate family. The host may sing a toast to the guest, who must drink quickly and respond with another toast. Such exchanges can go on for a long time, involving much humor and imagination in improvising, as well as considerable drinking. Classical Chinese poetry contains abundant references to such recreational drinking, and to the drunkenness that usually ensued, which was highly esteemed as signaling unbridled joy and camaraderie.

There are a number of drinking games described in ancient literary sources that survive today as a form of recreational drinking. In the poem game, for example, players are called on in turn to compose a poem with a specific pattern of rhyme and meter within a very brief time. Failure to comply means that one must take a large drink quickly—and doing well is the cue for a toast of recognition. Clearly, both the poetic improvisation and the drinking are appreciated as forms of recreation. Similarly, the riddle game is popular at all social levels, with players taking turns at making up and solving riddles, always punctuated by drinking a long draft. There are several other drinking games, some of which require a sophisticated knowledge of history and literature (the ivory dominoes game, the *Analects* game, the *Four Books* game) and some of which are simple (the dice game, the cheerful game). Some involve the Chinese predilection for playing with language (the cycling-overlapping-word game, the tongue-twister game, the altering Chinese characters game), and others deal with knowledge of people or symbols (the who's who game, the bouquet game). All combine sociability, enjoyable play, and heavy drinking.

## Medicinal Drinking

Throughout history, alcohol has played an important role in Chinese medicine. In fact, the Chinese characters for "alcohol" and "medicine" share the same root, and there is an old proverb that "Alcohol is the best of all medicines." Fully 2,000 years ago, a classic text, *The Yellow Emperor's Canon of Medicine,* included a chapter titled "The Decoction of Liquor" that contains many references to its use for treating a variety of ills. In succeeding centuries, Chinese curers have consistently stressed the curative and preventive roles of alcohol. The famous *Compendium of Materia Medica,* by Li Shizhen of the Ming Dynasty, lists seventy-nine different alcoholic beverages, some recommended for general nourishment and others for healing specific illnesses. Some drinks are cited to stimulate the appetite, to aid digestion, as a general tonic, or to "warm the waist." Others are said to assuage kidney disorders, resist the cold, or even improve one's overall appearance. Yellow rice wines, grape wines, millet spirits, and many other beverages, both fermented and distilled, occur in the Chinese pharmacopoeia, each with specific values attributed to it.

This obvious link with medicine and curing makes the Chinese toasting one's health more than a pro forma salutation; there is a genuine and profound belief that drinking is good for you. It is commonly thought that alcoholic beverages can heal many illnesses and can prevent others, help to maintain one's health, lend strength, and eventually stave off the degeneration of old age. Medicinal drinking is not an oxymoron in China today, any more than it was in many Western countries until recent years. One might expect that the increasing scientific evidence that is accumulating about the greater longevity of moderate drinkers would prompt others to recognize what has been known in China all along—that moderate drinking is healthful, whereas excessive drinking can be harmful.

### Moral Drinking

According to traditional Chinese philosophy, alcohol is not only a need in the physical and material sense but also such a strong stimulant to people's sentiments that it can shape one's destiny toward good luck or bad. Mankind embodies both good and evil, and moral drinking can emphasize the former, promoting social as well as individual welfare and well-being.

Ancient Chinese literature abounds with references to "drinking virtue." King Zhou of the Yin Dynasty (1324–1066 B.C.) was sad at heart and a poor administrator, but he excelled at the "virtue" of drunkenness. The reaction of his successor, Zhou Gong, was to ban drinking, but custom intervened and the prohibition quickly evolved into an elaborate set of rules for correct drinking. Emphasis was put on achieving drunkenness without investing too much money or effort, and favored group drinking—but only if there was "good reason for it." Confucius did not oppose drinking but warned against too much, on grounds that it might result in fighting. Drinking was a good and pleasant thing in moderation, but not something to be overdone. There was even a moral value to drinking because it could "harmonize the blood" and improve one's health, cheer the spirits of a person or a group, dispel melancholy, and add happiness to life.

These are not ideas that disappeared long ago; they remain vital today. Moderate drinking is not just acceptable; it is a moral imperative. Excessive drinking, by contrast, is unequivocally viewed as bad.

### THE NATIONAL SCENE

Statistical data are always difficult to evaluate in a country so large and diverse as China, but authors from other countries also apologize for their lack of precision, so I do not hesitate to provide some numbers for comparison. The majority of men are moderate drinkers (64.2%), whereas a majority of women abstain (51.3%). A remarkably low percentage of the population are heavy drinkers (10.4%, all male); more are moderate drinkers (15.8%); many are light drinkers (32.6%). Infrequent drinkers are 11.7%, and abstainers, 29.5% (Chi et al. 1989). Beyond such general categories, a number of drinking styles should be identified.

We have seen that alcohol is an important part of many social activities and of daily life for most contemporary Chinese. Nevertheless, attitudes about alcohol vary markedly. In praising alcohol, people often refer to it as "jade" or "sweet dew," terms conveying value and affection. To be sure, there are some who fear alcohol, saying that it leads to failure, sexual promiscuity, illness, or even death. According to them, every king who lost his country, or every son who hurt his family, did so because of drinking. But they are in a usually silent minority; most see alcohol as the ideal gift or prize, as the perfect accompaniment to eating, celebrating, or even mourning.

There is also a sense in which alcohol permeates Chinese legends. There is no great god of wine, like Dionysus in ancient Greece, but the legend of Du Kang is analogous. There is an astronomic constellation called "the alcohol stars flag" that is associated with good fortune and happiness. Since alcohol is not a human invention, the Chinese think it must have some sacred component, so that drinking while eating is not only healthful but positively religious. People delight in tracing the origins of particular drinks that are especially sacred, and an elaborate mythology has grown up around beverages.

In this chapter, I have deliberately neglected to chronicle the many brief periods of prohibition in Chinese history. All were short-lived, and reflected nothing of the opinions of the majority of the people. It also appears that they rarely had much impact beyond the narrow circle of the royal or imperial court. Similarly, I have not discussed "the flushing response." Much has been written in recent years about the tendency of many Chinese, Japanese, Korean, Eskimo, and Native American individuals to turn red in the face, have irregular heartbeat, and suffer subjective discomfort after a few drinks. This combination of reactions has been traced to a hereditary factor, an unusual form of alcohol dehydrogenase that results in slower metabolism of alcohol. This has often been described in Western literature on alcohol as a genetic "defense mechanism" or "immunization" against alcoholism, or even as preventing excessive drinking among those who inherit it. A few authors view it in just the opposite way— favoring heavy drinking (in order to "get through" the initial discomfiture). Ironically, Chinese people are generally unaware of, or have little to say about, flushing, and it plays no apparent role in shaping either attitudes or behaviors in relation to alcohol. For that reason, there is no reference to it in connection with the varied drinking customs discussed earlier, although I am well aware that some researchers are interested in and curious about it.

The major points that should probably be kept in mind by anyone who is beginning to study Chinese drinking, or to compare it with drinking elsewhere, are the close integration of alcohol with many and diverse aspects of Chinese culture; the long-esteemed and colorful roles that various forms of beverage alcohol have played in Chinese history; and the significant variation that can still be found among ethnic groups (or nationalities) within the huge and diverse landmass that is the People's Republic of China.

## EDITOR'S NOTES

In the interest of simplicity, we have used "China" to refer to the People's Republic of China (sometimes colloquially called Mainland China or Communist China). There were traditionally similar (but in recent decades a range of very different) influences on alcohol and culture in Taiwan (sometimes called Republic of China, Nationalist China, or Formosa).

In keeping with standard Chinese practice, Dr. Xiao's surname is given first. In referring to this chapter, a citation should read, and be alphabetized as, Xiao, Jiacheng.

Centuries-old Chinese manuscripts are not customarily identified in so much detail as are those in Western libraries. For this reason, some of the References may appear to be incomplete; however, they are as complete as the conventions of Chinese historical scholarship allow.

## REFERENCES

Chi, Iris, J. E. Lubbin, and H. H. L. Kitano. 1989. Differences in drinking behavior among three Asian-American groups. *Journal of Studies on Alcohol* 50:15–18.

Confucius. Ca. 500 B.C. The mandate of alcohol. In *The Book of Esteem, or Book of the Zhou Dynasty.*

Dou Ping. Ca. 1000. *The Genealogy of Alcohol.*

Fang Xinfang. 1989. Re-expounding the origin and development of fermenting alcohol with yeast in China. Pp. 3–31 in *Chinese Culture of Alcohol and Famous Liquors in China.* Beijing: Foodstuff Press of China.

Gao Yun. Ca. 400. Instruction on alcohol. In *History of the Northern Dynasty.*

Ge Hong. Ca. 350. Admonition on alcohol. In *Bao Pu Zi.*

Gu Yanwu. Ca. 1650. A ban on alcohol. In *Records on Knowledge Day by Day.*

Guo Panxi. 1989. *Chinese Customs of Alcohol.* Xi'an: People's Press of Shanxi Province.

Heath, Dwight B. 1986. Drinking and drunkenness in transcultural perspective: An overview. *Transcultural Psychiatric Research Review* 21 (1):7–42; 21 (2):103–126.

Huang Pusong. Ca. 850. *Life in an Intoxicating Home.*

Li Ying. 1989. Rich, fantastic, wonderful, profound and touching: Legends and mythologies about Chinese alcohol. Pp. 129–151 in *Chinese Culture of Alcohol and Famous Liquors in China.* Beijing: Foodstuff Press of China.

Liu Ling. Ca. 300. *Ode to the Virtue of Drinking.*

Luo Zhiteng. 1980. Contributions of the ancient Chinese people to the chemistry of brewery. *Journal of Zhongsan University (Natural Science Edition)* 1:81–89.

Su Shi. Ca. 1075. *Dongpo's Canon on Alcohol.*

Wan Guoguang. 1987. *Talking about Alcohol.* Beijing: Press of Popular Science.

Xiao Jiacheng. 1992. On the ethnicity of alcohol. *Nationality Studies* 4 (5):38–47.

Zhu Gong. Ca. 1125. *A Canon of Alcohol in the Northern Mountains.*

# 6

# Denmark

## *Peter Schiøler*

In Denmark alcohol has been enjoyed throughout history. No period has been known for a high prevalence of abstaining. The Vikings, their kings, and their chieftains drank the beverages of their time. Of these mead (a honey-based beer) and various kinds of grain-based beer are the best known.

## HISTORY OF ALCOHOL

The anecdotes that have survived from the Viking period (around 800–1250) relate enjoyment of alcohol to the specific male stereotypes: the Vikings were, according to most of the literature that has survived, physically strong, muscular, bearded, courageous, adventurous, and ruthless to their enemies and domineering to their thralls (a term including serfs, servants, and slaves). Drinking enhanced these male characteristics. The Vikings killed, raped, robbed, and burned in the foreign lands they visited. Slaves and women were brought back to Denmark and other Nordic countries. The Vikings had strong women at their side, but they did not drink alcoholic beverages to the same extent as the men.

One disturbing aspect about this stereotype of the Vikings is that we lack information about the moderate use of alcohol, which must have been typical for a large part of the alcohol consumption of the people at the time.

Why did the Vikings drink in this dramatic way? The reason for the strong expansion of the Nordic people in the early Middle Ages was that the communities developed into successful villages, families, and groupings. Sailing developed because the geography called for sea transport: Denmark consisted of a peninsula and several hundred inhabited islands close to each other; the Norwegians lived along the coasts, between which there were mountains that hindered traffic for much of the year; and even the Swedish Vikings could trade and transport more easily on the Baltic Sea than overland.

The Vikings developed administration of their municipalities, which they brought with them to eastern and northern Great Britain, Ireland, Normandy, and eventually even to Galicia in northwestern Spain, Sicily, and southern Italy. Even though danegeld (Danish taxation) in East Anglia and Yorrick's land (now Yorkshire) was unpopular at the time, the administrative structure introduced (the taxation system with fiscal norms and values) was successful and functioning long after the Vikings.

It can hardly be believed that the Vikings' expansion and modernization were led by an upper class who were brutes and drunkards. We must assume that they could not have conquered strong countries and kept them dominated for centuries exclusively by the force of drunken, violent behavior.

The exaggerated tales about the Vikings' consumption of alcoholic beverages are often made even more shocking because they are also said to have taken ergot, a hallucinogenic fungus that would have brought them into a state of blind rage, but there is little scientific basis for such stories. Unfortunately, we lack information about how alcohol was integrated into the everyday life of the Viking societies. From the ubiquitous findings of drinking jars, which often were extensively ornamented or decorated, it appears that alcohol was widespread and frequently used in those societies.

However, all this does not give a full description of the alcohol culture of Viking times. We hear about warriors, kings, and princes, but little about those who stayed at home: the women, the children, the servants, and the thralls. We know little about norms and rules, and how they were passed from one generation to the next. We know little about any differences or variation in consumption patterns and behaviors. But, from the material remains alone, we presume that they were not intoxicated all of the time.

While Vikings expanded their frontiers outward, their commercial relationships with Europe and the Near East opened doors inward. Danish culture especially shows a combination of Nordic influences with cultural impacts from the south. Traders from France and Germany, and the Roman Catholic Church, brought wine and fresh fruits and vegetables to Denmark. Importation was troublesome, and hence rather expensive. It was the well-to-do and educated groups who could afford to drink wine, imported from France, Spain, and Italy. The use of wine in no way lessened the consumption of beer and similar products among the masses.

In the 1500s, the Chinese (and presumably Arabic) art of distilling alcoholic liquors became known in Denmark, and soon the north European version of spirits came into general use. This technique was introduced by European monks and alchemists (hoping to use their art to produce gold from lesser metals). The Danes called distilled alcohol *snaps* (a word of German origin). This beverage was strong, usually close to 50% alcohol by volume. Many drinks were made from potatoes, barley, and other grains. Nothing was new in this. Grain is at least as old as grapes, both plants having been cultivated for nutritional purposes in the Old World for 4,000 years.

The quality of early distillates was often very poor, but all grades gave their users a sense of well-being, especially welcome for peasants, artisans, soldiers, and others who were exposed to the harsh climate. The tradition of drinking "firewater" became so integrated that peasants and workers began to receive the landowner's homemade spirit as a part of their wages. In this way they became even poorer.

In the latter half of the 1700s, life at the court in Copenhagen became influenced by the coarse hospitality of the king. Drinking, often of fine wines in great amounts, became considered a bad influence on the noble youth and on the sons of rich and influential commoners, merchants, and seafarers, and a few others. Monasteries were converted to boarding schools. The first classes contained equal numbers of young noblemen and commoners, setting the pattern for social equality that has distinguished Denmark ever since.

The interest in alcohol as an unhealthful commodity has increased in recent centuries. In the 1500s, schools for adolescents were placed far from the court in Copenhagen. In the latter half of the 1600s, drinking was considered a nuisance, both in Copenhagen and in the other towns. In this period coffee-drinking was forbidden or frowned upon, and smoking was widespread. Denmark then decided to legalize the coffeehouses and to introduce the English system of using them for collecting mail, especially for transport by ship. Alcohol was not allowed in such establishments. Pietism (a strong religious revival) came to Denmark in this period, giving support to a more open dislike of drunken behavior. Here it was the behavior, and not the alcohol, itself, that was the concern.

The major dramatic writer in the 1700s, Ludvig Holberg, described human frailty in several of his plays. While applying an often acid humor in the production and direction of his plays, he always sought some sort of explanation for what he described. In one play he let a poor and subdued peasant (Jeppe), who was afraid of the authorities and His Lordship, but who really feared his wife even more (because she beat him with a whip) exclaim: "They say that Jeppe drinks. But nothing about why Jeppe drinks" (my translation). It is typical of Ludvig Holberg that the interest is what we today would call the social-psychological problem, and only secondarily the untoward behavior at which he makes us both laugh and weep. He does not believe in general explanations. It is Jeppe's problem. It is common for all those using substances or other means to soothe their tragic and deprived lives, but they each have their own history, and it is there we should seek the cause of Jeppe's frailty. I believe that this scene contains one of the first modern indicators of the Danish opinion on alcohol-related problems and how they can be approached.

In the 1800s industrialism was introduced, and with it, a new approach to alcohol-related problems as an element of the alcohol culture. Denmark joined the Napoleonic side of the great international conflict after the French Revolution. Napoleon was eventually defeated and exiled, and Denmark suffered. In

1813, the state declared bankruptcy. In 1814 Norway was separated from Denmark, and the Danish economy suddenly served a smaller market. Exportation became important; industrialism swept through the country; and shipping began to expand.

In the 1864 war with Prussia and Austria, Denmark lost a very important area, Schleswig-Holstein. This meant that about 40% of the best farmland and some of the richest and most industrialized cities were lost to the country. It also meant that the large harbor in Hamburg was far from the Danish-German border. The Danish market was again reduced. All these events had an impact on the place of alcohol in the culture.

Earlier in the 1800s the concept of the "little man" (or "common man") and his family was conceived. After the war of 1864 this concept was developed strongly in a number of ways. One was the formal establishment of workers' unions and their political front. The same people who organized these also founded the temperance movement, which quickly gained strength. An even more influential source of temperance movements was various religious groups.

Until the 1870s *snaps* was offered, and accepted, as part of wages, but then its low quality was considered a cause of ill health even in moderate amounts. The practice was attacked by both the unions and the temperance people, and disappeared before the end of the century.

This is but one of the major changes in the Danish alcohol culture from earlier times to what it is today. The process of change occurred in a period during which Denmark evolved into a country where social welfare was given high priority by a larger and larger part of the population, thus helping the "little man" to become part of the middle class.

From 1870 to 1910 the consumption of spirits decreased, and the use of beer increased. Then World War I started in 1914; although Denmark was neutral, it left a strong impact on the alcohol culture in the country. As a result of the war and Denmark's position close to Germany, supplies of many commodities were cut off. Exports to Great Britain, which had been the largest Danish market, shifted toward Germany. Germany soon had a severe shortage of food; so much was exported from Denmark to Germany that malnutrition was observed. The strongest symptoms were an increase in the incidence of pulmonary tuberculosis and a new but high incidence of night blindness (nyctalopia). This, together with the good income from increasing exports to the German market, led the government to act. It was decided to increase the retail price of spirits from about 0.90 krone (U.S. $0.26) to about 11 kroner (U.S. $3.17) per liter. This increase was effective. The rich had never used low-quality spirits, and did not begin then. The poor changed to beer. Thus, potatoes and grains became available for eating instead of fermentation. Barley was, of course, still used for beer production.

Denmark had imported rum from the Danish West Indies, notably St. Thomas, St. Croix, and St. John. It was used widely in Denmark: in tea, in toddies, and in desserts. The place of rum is a clear example of the fact that alcohol is to a great extent very closely associated with eating. A central function of alcohol is to accentuate the taste of foods and to stimulate the appetite. In April 1917, the United States bought the Danish West Indies and used them as a link in the fight against German submarines. The price was U.S. $25 million. The islands were renamed the U.S. Virgin Islands. The price of rum increased sharply. Being now a foreign product, customs duties were charged.

The overall result of these events was that Denmark left the Nordic group of spirit-drinking countries (Finland, Norway, and Sweden) and became a beer-drinking one with a relatively low total consumption of alcohol. Within five years this change was complete, and Denmark is still a beer-drinking country like Germany, Belgium, and the United Kingdom.

## CONTEMPORARY DRINKING PATTERNS

In spirit-drinking countries a considerable part of the population seems to get drunk, as if this were the purpose of their drinking, even when drinking with meals. This feature of alcohol-related behavior is seen in the Nordic countries and in many of the eastern European cultures. This behavior is not observed in most of the western or southern European cultures. Denmark's geographical position, intermediate between these parts of Europe, could lead us to expect several patterns of alcohol consumption. There are great variations in any culture, but the studies available show that intoxication is *not* the aim of drinking alcohol in the very large majority of cases, or for the very large majority of alcohol consumers, throughout most of the world, nor is it in Denmark.

The prevailing style of drinking in all Danish social strata is, and has been since the 1890s, to use alcohol in moderate amounts. Alcohol is considered an integral part of meals; it is used between meals to facilitate social contacts and stimulate a collective feeling of well-being. From a Danish perspective, it is strange that there seems to be no Anglo-Saxon word for the first, and lasting, pleasurable effect of drinking alcohol. All of the descriptive terms in English and German seem to be reserved for negative effects, which are not usually apparent until larger quantities have been drunk. There are many Danish words that describe various aspects of intoxication, for example, to specify subtle degrees of change in behavior, progressive lowering of inhibitions, and so forth. "Intoxication" is too strong a term to be used for the primary exhilarating effect of drinking alcohol, a sensation that is the most usual for the great majority of Danish drinkers.

The Danes know these exceptional effects of alcohol, and some debate revolves around such questions as: Are these extremes of usual consumption, or are they marginal and related to an abnormal behavior clearly distinct from generally accepted human behavior? Is intoxication a state of poisoning, or is there a group of human beings with intrinsic biological variations that cause them to be different from the majority, who both physiologically and psychologically can tolerate and control the effects on body and mind, and thus avoid any untoward effects and real harm? Another possibility must be taken into account: that some individuals, because of a deprivation or failure in upbringing, have grown up without sufficient learning about alcohol. All these and other elements of the ongoing debate about the place and function of alcohol in the social and cultural life are clearly derived from the traditions and their development, and mirror the high respect with which the Danish people regard their social welfare system.

Ongoing research has permitted a further study of the patterns of alcohol consumption. But before referring to the cultural indicators, it will be useful to mention some considerations regarding norms and values associated with alcohol-related behavior. For this purpose I will introduce a few concepts typical of Danish thinking about everyday consumption of alcohol.

The first is called "wrong consumption of alcohol." All historical and cultural evidence leads to the conclusion that most consumers have learned to take responsibility for their consumption of alcohol in relation to their own health and well-being. It is risky to consume alcohol in the "wrong" way. The wrong way is where the amount consumed and/or the behavior resulting from consumption substantially deviates from the accepted norms for the occasion. Consumption can be "wrong" if it strongly increases the risk of short-term effects of alcohol, leading to a release of aggression or violence, or driving a motor vehicle when the blood alcohol concentration is too high, or forgetting family obligations, causing martial problems, and so on. Or it can be "wrong" over the long term, as in drinking at work, persistently neglecting family commitments, ignoring the warning symptoms of the body, continuing to drink after the diagnosis of an illness—for example, liver cirrhosis—or simply by being drunk over extended periods of time. All these "wrong" types of consumption increase the risk that an individual will be unable to remain a functioning member of the local culture or subculture.

This is one reason for maintaining a sustained educational and informative preventive effort, particularly in a society that is always changing. Culture also develops very quickly. What was learned in childhood and youth sometimes does not retain its validity. However, the learned responsibility about decisions and behavior relating to alcohol seems to survive.

Social problems may be caused by untoward alcohol-related behavior, or alcohol may be one factor among several that provoke or aggravate social difficulties. These difficulties will depend on tolerance of variant behavior in the community and, consequently, on the prevailing culture. This means that the nature of social difficulties cannot always be explained or understood without knowledge of the sociocultural determinants against which an individual's social behavior is perceived by others in the family, the peer group, the workplace, or the community.

This was recognized at the World Health Organization Conference at Alma Ata in 1976 (WHO 1978). WHO's major program, Health for All in the Year 2000, included this aspect of alcohol-related problems when targets for achieving healthy or health-promoting lifestyles were formulated (WHO 1985). The lifestyle concept is holistic in that it integrates the entire everyday life in all its somatic, psychological, social, and judicial norms and values.

In different cultures, different norms operate, as do time lags between these norms in different sociocultural settings. There are many examples of differences in behavior that, although related to the different psychological makeup of men and women, are not attributable to any biological difference in the effect of alcohol on the two sexes. However, this demonstrates how the "wrong" use of alcohol in some situations can upset the norms and values that are built into cultures to a different extent for men and women. This also holds for the difference in pace of change in the common culture.

Some male behavior associated with alcohol consumption is tolerated even if it is grotesque or ugly. It is as "male" as the stereotypes of the Vikings. It is not the amount, the frequency, or the way in which alcohol is consumed that may be considered "normal" in such circumstances. It is the related behavior that allows a latitude to men very different from that tolerated in women. This double standard has some serious consequences for individuals, particularly when spontaneous or unthinking reactions come to be accepted in formulating norms and values, and become the basis of possible sanctions or even policies.

Yet, it is through the detailed study of the broad field of variation of the elements of a culture that a basis of knowledge is established on which to raise hopes for the prevention of the many alcohol-related problems that are experienced by a relatively few drinkers.

Another key term is "normal drinking." It is in relation to this that we perceive terms such as "misuse," "overuse," and "abuse." These terms are most often applied without reference to the conditions or quantity of consumption. In this connection it becomes important to establish a concept of "normal consumption." Since cultural differences will be even more marked in the contrasting category of "abnormal" (or "not normal") consumption, the concept must include a considerable degree of flexibility. It must be applicable to the description of an individual's relationship with alcohol as this is integrated into his or her culture and community. Normalcy will, in this way, constitute a cultural concept and reflect a bio-organic or judicial aspect only slightly.

It is perhaps easier to use biological criteria for defining normalcy. This can be done by extrapolating from dose-related morbidities or from known social deviations. The point reached in this way would be a consumption defined as not causing alcohol-related problems under normal (usual) conditions. Flexibility is needed in this type of definition. For women, it is obvious that physiological differences lead to higher blood alcohol concentrations after the intake of a specific quantity of alcohol per kilogram of body weight, compared with the same intake for a man of the same weight. In traffic offenses the blood alcohol concentration is the legal requirement that counts, not the clinical manifestation of an alcohol-induced behavior. For both men and women there will be numerous situations where drinking alcohol is counterproductive and socially undesirable.

It follows that the "normalcy" concept relating to alcohol consumption is made up of at least two quite different parts: one that refers mainly to biomedical and physiological indicators, and one that refers mainly to behavioral, social, and culture-related indicators. The first part may be derived from mean values used in different circumstances—for example, by insurance companies, and increasingly by public health authorities and by WHO. This has precipitated a wide discussion about a "safety" concept, the crux of which is the safety limits of alcohol consumption. These may well be of general use if they are capable of being specified. However, safety limits should be defined only if the conditions that apply to them are also defined. The use of such terms therefore will be variable. The establishment of the culture-related concept "normal drinking" presupposes that research and administrative experience combine to form the database and monitoring capabilities necessary to follow the development of the many indicators available for extending knowledge about a culture and the place of alcohol in it.

This more esoteric discussion has influenced the Danish choice of policy. It slowly developed over the postwar decades, at the same time that consumption rose in tandem with the economic affluence of the general population. From about 1955 to 1973, when the energy crisis began to persuade people that they were consuming too much, the average annual consuption of alcohol had more than doubled. The increase was caused by several phenomena; most important was that affluence enabled people to buy more of all types of commodities than before. Another important factor was the equalization of men and women: female consumption increased both in amount and in frequency. At the same time, the use of alcohol was distributed over the entire week, although the largest quantity was used on weekends. Weekends became longer after the change from a six-day to a five-day workweek. Alcohol also was used on many more occasions. The old pattern comprised ritual drinkings: the presence of guests, family gatherings, Sunday lunch, Saturday evening, festivities during the week, birthdays, weddings, and other events were all noteworthy for how one was expected to dress, topics of conversation, preparation of the introductory drink, when to taste the wine or spirit for each course, which people should be placed close to each other and which people should avoid close contact.

In the upper middle class such items have become a very formal behavior even though one of the major reasons for hospitality is the mutual wish "to relax together." Danish hospitality was, and is, different from that of most other peoples, in that dinner is rather early and guests remain for hours after the table is cleared. After the coffee with liqueurs and brandy that follow a meal, conversation takes place. Much talking makes for thirst, to be quenched by soft drinks, whiskey and soda, or beer. In this way a Danish dinner with a few guests can develop into quite a wet affair.

Here again, the alcohol culture directs or sets the framework for the choice of wines, most often based on the composition of the menu. It also dictates the behavior of both hosts and guests. You are expected to take part in the conversation, but not too loudly and only when it is your turn. You are allowed to show a natural interest in your companion at the dinner table, and there will often be some dance music available. However, the limits of propriety are not relaxed, using alcohol as an excuse. You are likely to be remembered and frowned upon for stupid remarks or untoward behavior of the amorous, or especially the violent, kind. So, although alcohol is used to facilitate social contact and the feeling of warm well-being, the Danish alcohol culture draws limits.

By the beginning of the 1930s, the use of intoxication as an excuse for some crimes was strongly hindered in the Penal Code. This was also the time when harsh intervention and sanctions were introduced against driving under the influence of alcohol. Both of these limits on freedom of behavior were popular, and they continue to be so. However, there are still too many motor vehicles driven by people under the influence. Thus, there are many and wide variations in the alcohol culture and in the decision-making skills in Denmark.

In 1967 Denmark abandoned the clinical tests as decisive in the diagnosis of a driver's degree of intoxication. Since then the police can rely only on blood alcohol concentration as a measure of the extent of intoxication.

## ATTITUDES TOWARD DRINKING

Regarding the Danish attitude to alcohol, we can refer to the work of K.-E. Sabroe at Aarhus University (Sabroe 1993). After a discussion of a lecture (Schiøler 1987) on the concept of "cultural immunity" in regard to alcohol-related problems covering the protective effect arising from the intrinsic experience with alcohol consumption in a drinking population, or in an alcohol culture prevailing in a community, Sabroe developed the concept of "consumer consciousness" regarding alcohol. He studied a wide range of variables with respect to their impact on alcohol-related behavior: sex, age, social group, income, occupation, and political party (often meaningful in a democracy with as many as eight parties in the Parliament). The Amsterdam Group, which issued the volume to which Sabroe contributed, also studied reasons for drinking alcohol and for not drinking it, opinions about alcohol and health, whether alcohol is a "good" in life, the distribution of consumption over the week and during the day, companions when last intoxicated, rituals and traditions, and more. Sabroe's study shows the following:

- Total consumption of alcohol has decreased slowly from the maxima in 1976 and 1983.
- Women drink less than men, but the difference is diminishing.
- Youths drink less than they did in the 1980s.
- The higher the personal income, the higher the consumption of alcohol.
- The higher the education, the higher the consumption. The distribution of beer, wine,

fortified wine, and of spirits is not the same in the different social groups (because they are based upon education and income).

• There is no simple correlation between consumption and political party.

The most frequent reasons why one drinks alcohol are its taste, conviviality, relaxation, and "coziness." The most frequent reasons why one abstains are its health effect and the constant need to be fit to drive a car.

The picture of alcohol, drawn through the responses to a long questionnaire from 2,000 randomly selected persons, is seemingly in accordance with a basic Danish understanding that has been prevalent since World War II: alcohol is a consumer good. It is a view apparently established early in the process of socialization.

Some schoolchildren aged six to eight were asked to draw "a person drinking alcohol," a "person not drinking alcohol," and "children with adults drinking alcohol." No drawing had people from socially marginal situations or displaying improper behavior. Most were "positively imagined" and included happy people or people with mild characteristics of intoxication. Only one of the drinking persons in the drawings was a woman. This study was made in a school in downtown Aarhus, the second largest city in Denmark.

## ALCOHOL POLICIES

A number of studies show the same picture. The lawmakers and most of their advisers have, since the 1940s, understood this relaxed (some say "liberal" or even "lenient") attitude to drinking, which Danes consider normal and not hazardous. Therefore, there has been no trend in the direction of the control-of-availability policies that have long been in operation in Finland, Norway, and Sweden. The Danes do see fellow countrymen with drunken and ugly behavior. They know that about 50,000 to 100,000 individuals have alcohol-related problems, and a few have serious organic dysfunctions. But the Danes consider that these unfortunates were made that way not by alcohol but by its untoward use. Their situations were potentially weak before drinking began. Since alcohol is so deeply integrated in their culture, they presumably used it to alleviate feelings of being deviant, fears, anxieties, and frustrations. Some of them became dependent because of the positive experiences they enjoyed with smaller quantities of alcohol they used as medicine, experiences that they wanted to repeat again and again. In their situations, an alcoholic drink could be a great comfort. In other words, this syndrome is of psychosocial origin; their exaggerated drinking and marginal behavior are learned, and symptomatic of their condition. This symptom is then a cofactor in the person's destruction.

It is, therefore, considered to be the duty of Danish society to use the health system and the social welfare system to make effective help and assistance available to the person and his/her family, if there is one. The Danes apply this principle to any handicap or weakness. Such people are rarely considered to be morally or intellectually deviant from the majority. The system is not perfect, and economic constraints have caused serious cuts in the official support for treatment centers. But the general attitude, as well as the popular will to act accordingly, cannot be disputed.

The Parliament has periodic discussions of alcohol-related problems. The most unbreakable principle observed in these discussions is that unharmed people should be responsible for their health. Help should be given to those who are in need—and in full measure. This means that general restraints and sanctions are given low priority. Only driving while intoxicated is handled with a hard hand. Great weight is placed on health promotion, taught in school and presented in public information for the adults; these instruments are considered to be almost the only rational preventive efforts to reduce the development of alcohol-related problems. The vast majority of the Danes (about 90 to 95% of the total population over fourteen years of age) who use alcohol seem to be able to carry such responsibilities. Only about 2% develop ailments that need treatment, care, or social help. This view is substantiated by a general feeling that Danes generally dislike regulation. They prefer as little interference as possible in their daily lives at home and at work, coupled with a well-equipped apparatus to counter psychosocial ailments and bad luck. This is what the Danish population are willing to support through very high taxes.

The price of alcoholic beverages is the highest within the European Union. But it is not high enough to stop those who drink too much unwisely. About 15% of drinkers account for about 50% of the total consumption. The majority of even these people represent few problems.

It is obvious that membership in the European Community has influenced the pattern of consumption since 1973. Since the 1960s consumption of wine has increased, of spirits has decreased, and of beer has remained rather constant on a high level. Women drink more often than previously, and so do men, but it seems that they drink less at one time because total consumption is decreasing. The amount of homemade beverages consumed is very low compared with Norway and Sweden.

The immigration of workers from Islamic and Mediterranean Roman Catholic cultures in the 1960s and 1970s did not have any impact on the alcohol culture. Neither have the many refugees from Latin America and eastern Europe in the recent years.

## REFERENCES

There are very few general descriptions of the Danish alcohol culture in any language other than Danish. The following may be obtained from libraries or the organizations that produced them.

Sabroe, Knud-Erik. 1993. Alcohol in society. The case of Denmark. In The Amsterdam Group. *Alcoholic Beverages and European Society: A Report of the Amsterdam*

*Group.* Annex 1: *The Historical, Cultural and Social Roles of Alcoholic Beverages.* London: The Amsterdam Group.

Schiøler, Peter. 1987. Cultural immunity toward alcohol-related problems. Paper read at Erasmus University, Rotterdam.

———. 1993. The social and cultural roles of alcohol. In The Amsterdam Group. *Alcoholic Beverages and European Society: A Report of the Amsterdam Group.* Annex 1: *The Historical, Cultural and Social Roles of Alcoholic Beverages.* London: The Amsterdam Group.

WHO. 1978. *Primary Health Care: Report of the International Conference on Primary Health Care.* Geneva: WHO.

———. 1985. *Targets for Health for All.* Copenhagen: WHO, Regional Office for Europe.

# 7

# Egypt

## *Abdel Monheim Ashour*

## WHY ALCOHOL IS NOTEWORTHY IN EGYPT

Egyptian drinking is unique. The drinking pattern and the overall consumption of alcohol have remained stable for over 4,000 years. It is hypothesized that culture and religion were the major determinants of this behavior. Egyptian religion and culture, including drinking, changed little over all these years.

The hallmark of Egyptian drinking is very low consumption. Alcohol was available most of the time, but demand was modest most of the time. Egyptians were essentially drinkers of grain-based beer. They treated the different alcoholic beverages differently. Beer was the everyday food and beverage for everyman. Wine was the drink of episodic festivities. Spirits were (and are) thought to be evil and better avoided.

## ALCOHOL IN EGYPTIAN HISTORY

Egyptian history is unique in the fact that it is highly reliable, being overwhelmingly documented over the last 7,000 years. Carvings or paintings on walls, papyri, and other relics reveal many details of earlier Egyptian life.

### Predynastic and Early Dynastic Drinking

As early as the Predynastic period in Egyptian history (before 3200 B.C.), Egyptians (in both the north and south) had developed a specific belief in the continuation of life after death. This afterlife was envisaged as similar to existence before death. The deceased were provided with the requirements for continued existence, including food and drink.

There were many deities. Priests performed acts of worship before the gods, with offerings of food, drink, and clothing thrice a day. During the First through Fourth Dynasties, burial customs became more elaborate, including special rooms to store food and drink. Funerary temples were built to hold ever-increasing amounts of such offerings. There were many attempts (not limited to the famous) to preserve the body with a lifelike appearance, to help the spirit partake of the food and drink.

### The Old Kingdom (3150 B.C.–2350 B.C.)

Egypt developed into a highly organized and centralized theocracy. The divine king was viewed as the son of the sun and mediator between gods and human-kind. The people were under his strict control. No cult rivaled that of Re (the Sun Cult) in power and importance, and solar temples were constructed. Religion was organized for the benefit of the king and the state. An ethical code had already been developed by Egyptians, supposedly with a divine authorization, and codified in the literature. Only the king could hope to achieve an eternal existence. Vicarious eternity was the religious incentive for people who partic-ipated by contributing labor or offerings in support of the vast mortuary com-plexes that surrounded the pyramids.

The drinking patterns of Egyptians in the Old Kingdom fit well into this culture and religion. In simplest terms, Egyptians in the Old Kingdom saw bread and beer as basic to their sustenance; wine and spirits were still thought to be dangerous.

Beer and bread were inseparable, to the degree that beer was perceived more as a food than as an alcoholic beverage. This notion still survives. Bread and beer, both as food and as offerings, were the focus of many social and cultural activities. They were offered twice daily in the funerary temples to the dead god-king, and were consumed by the staffs of such temples, who could number as many as 300 persons. The Egyptian workman's packed lunch usually con-sisted of bread, beer, and onions. Children and nursing mothers drank beer for health and nutritional reasons. When guests arrived at the door of a host holding a party, the host would greet them with the phrase "Bread and beer" (the equivalent of "hello!"). Most beer-drinking was moderate and social. Yet there were also times and places for getting drunk through excessive drinking. A notorious example of this is the excessive drinking by mourners on the last day of mourning (forty or seventy days after the death). Mourners consumed on that single day what they normally consumed in a whole month. Excessive beer-drinking took place at rich men's parties. It was even hailed in poetry.

Meanwhile, there were warnings against and stigmatization for frequenting beer houses and abusing beer and wine. Beer was home-brewed and also made in special breweries for offerings. Wheat and barley were local products, and so was the storage pottery. Bread was often included in the process of brewing; the beer was thick, nutritious, and had to be consumed fresh. The pottery containers were of porous clay suitable for short-term storage only. This type of beer still exists in Nubia and Sudan, and is called *bouza*. Wine and liqueurs were made from figs, palm dates, and grapes. Because of the considerable loss through evaporation and seepage, most Egyptian wines were probably drunk young.

In the Old Kingdom, religious and cultural rituals were not gestures of piety toward the gods (a sentiment that became common in the New Kingdom) but a self-imposed duty, a gratification, and a familiar and recognized pattern of behavior. In the Old Kingdom, people were confident, hardworking, and optimistic. When they died and were buried with the necessary provisions for the hereafter, it was expected that they would go to the "godly West" and live again, exactly as on earth. This morality and religion were behind the rather liberal use of beer in that period.

## The First Intermediate Period and the Middle Kingdom (2350 B.C.–1600 B.C.)

The First Intermediate Period consisted of the Ninth and Tenth Dynasties. It was a society collapsing from within. The very people who had so wished to prolong the joys of life beyond death now questioned the values of their lives and their society.

The Middle Kingdom (Eleventh and Twelfth) Dynasties, restored stability to Egypt. The omnipotence of Re was replaced by the cult of Osiris (god of land and of grain) and other deities. The ordinary person came to expect an afterlife that was no longer dependent upon the king's favor but could be achieved through the performance of the correct ritual and burial procedures and through devoted worship of Osiris. Every Egyptian believed that upon death he or she was required to face trial before a tribunal of judges. There was an increasing emphasis placed on moral fitness as a hope for individual immortality. The Middle Kingdom was essentially the period when Eyptians of all classes first sought individual eternity and aspired to it through moral righteousness in life.

## The New Kingdom (1600 B.C.–330 B.C.)

The Middle Kingdom came to an end with the Hyksos invasion at the end of the Thirteenth Dynasty. The Hyksos were finally driven out, and the New Kingdom was established with the Eighteenth Dynasty. Its princes (from around Thebes) attributed their ascendancy to support of the local god Amun (air god). They then associated this local god with the old solar god, Re, creating the omnipotent Amun-Re (king of the gods).

There were two types of temples: for the gods and for the dead. There also were two groups of temple rituals. The daily ritual in both cult and mortuary temples provided a dramatization of commonplace events in everyday existence. A second group of rituals were the festivals at regular (often yearly) intervals, the main event being the god's procession. Such festivals attracted huge numbers of pilgrims.

Large quantities of beer were consumed in the daily temple ritual, and much beer and wine was consumed in the temple festivals. Improved technology was available to keep wine for longer periods (e.g., filtering, boiling, and use of storage vessels made of stone).

A festival could last as long as a month, as did Amun's festival at Opet. The increased religious activity in the New Kingdom was associated with material abundance and prosperity. The new cult of Aten (god of the entire kingdom) does not seem to have provided much of a moral philosophy. Once more we can see why much alcohol was consumed. It was in the New Kingdom that two wise men, Ani and Amenehotep, wrote works discouraging students from excessive drinking either at home or at inns. They described symptoms we would now call alcoholism, alcohol-related personality deterioration, and death.

### Greco-Roman Egypt (330 B.C.–A.D. 150)

The Egyptian and Greek cults of the Ptolemies were distinct, but they were both directed to the same monarchs, and as gods the Ptolemies shared the temples of Egyptian deities. Thus the ruler cult was a cement binding together the heterogeneous elements that made up the population of Egypt.

It appears that even the Jews as refugees in Egypt, stranded in a world of Hellenistic paganism, were apt to stray from the narrow path of strict observance, and to become in some degree hellenized. There is no evidence that the religion of the Roman conquerers produced any appreciable effect on the religious life in Egypt. There was no decay in Egyptian religion but a new orientation of religious consciousness. There was a movement away from the old communal cults and toward a more personal relationship to the deity. There was also a reemergence of Osiris and Horus, associated with a general revival of Egyptian sentiment.

The religion of Roman Egypt was a composite of many strands. At its best, it was a noble monotheism, but it also embraced magic and theurgy. Its points of resemblance to Christianity are obvious. The Romans had the policy of letting the Egyptians continue their way of life and their own language, which was Coptic. We can safely say that drinking habits of the Egyptians outside of Greek-dominated cities in the Greco-Roman period differed little from those of the previous 3,000 years.

### The Christian Triumph (150–640)

There is no satisfactory direct evidence for the existence of Christian communities in Egypt during the first century. By the end of the second century, Christianity must have been fairly widespread even in Upper Egypt. The atmosphere of the time was favorable to its spread. For the more educated, the way had been prepared by its monotheism, its high moral standards, its redemptive and sacramental mysteries, and its hope of immortality. Simpler folk found a bridge in the popular worship of Osiris as the god of resurrection. Egyptian Christians took much of their pagan outlook with them into their new creed (e.g., food and wine in tombs, preservation of bodies after death, and other gnostic elements). Egypt's other great contribution was monasticism.

From around 350, we are justified in regarding Egypt as broadly a Christian country. The Christian triumph was no accident. Christianity was a more sophisticated religion for which paganism had paved the way. The Egyptian Christians, the Copts, still appoint their own patriarch of Alexandria and follow their own interpretation of the Scriptures. They regard theirs as the Orthodox Church that held firm to the Nicene Creed.

The stand of Coptic Christianity on alcoholic beverages and drinking is multifaceted. The word "wine" appears in different concrete and symbolic contexts in the Bible. The Old Testament describes wine as a gift of God to believers, short of getting drunk. Wine is part of the offerings in certain festivals. There is much condemnation of drunkenness. The conversion of water into wine by Jesus is meant to be a symbolic miracle rather than an exhortation to consume wine. Jesus is never explicitly reported as having drunk wine (although we presume, on the basis of context, that he did). Jesus uses wine as a symbol for his blood, according to Coptic Christians, because both are extracted by squeezing. St. Paul advocates wine as medicine only for a case of edema in a person who was hurt by drinking too much water. Yet Paul repeatedly speaks against drinking, demonstrating physical and social ailments caused by it. The concluding compromise in face of these controversial biblical stands on wine, as summarized by the Orthodox Coptic Church, is the following: drinking small amounts of fresh wine is allowed, but excessive wine-drinking and drinking any amount of spirits are banned. Although we have no access to documents, we can safely say that Coptic Christianity must have discouraged much drinking, especially of spirits.

## Arab Dominance (641–1805)

Egypt was conquered by the Arabs in 641. The conversion of the bulk of the Egyptian population to the Muslim faith was slow. Arabization and Islamization took several centuries. Historians of this period tell us little about the common people, but it is frequently reiterated that invaders like the Shiite Fatimids did not try to impose their beliefs on the population. The Coptic Church flourished during the Fatimid period (969–1171).

One can safely assume that the Egyptians' culture and habits, including their mild drinking behavior, were rather stable over centuries. To be sure, the enigmatic if not eccentric Caliph Al-Hakim did impose a form of prohibition, and poured beer and wine into the Nile, along with honey. His prohibition was short-lived; he disappeared and his body was never found. Another example to show that the unique Egyptian culture survived regardless of who sat on the throne is the case of the Mamluk Empire (1382–1517). Mamluks, who were nominally Muslims, frequently behaved like pagans. During the Ottoman age (1516–1805), Egypt was relegated to the status of a province within a larger empire that was uniform in religion but varied in language and ethnicity. The alienation between rulers and ruled continued.

Searching in Maccarese's (1436) book on Cairo, I found some anecdotal mention of alcohol in Egyptian life in those days. Because the weather was warm and humid, wines did not keep, so Egyptians learned to add molasses or honey as a preservative. Less beer was consumed. Wine was made only in the early autumn.

Many Christians believe that their religion forbids them to get drunk. They do not drink at all during fast days. Although the Coptic Christian minority was more affluent, their drinking was never excessive. Muslims, who occasionally participated in riots against the churches during the Mamluk regime, looted the sacramental wines together with other items from the churches. Looters are often described as having consumed the wine and fallen drunk in the streets.

## Modern Egypt (1805–present)

Mohamed Ali's modernization campaign expanded agriculture for export, introduced industrialization, and suffered military expansion. A cash-crop economy and changes in land tenure altered agricultural production from grain and fruit to cotton and sugarcane. The *fallah* (peasant, or small-scale farmer) worked 250 days a year on irrigated land and also was expected to provide labor in lieu of paying taxes. The army was feared and the factories were disliked. Aliens manned the army, and Egyptians could not call their land their own. Some Egyptianization of government was started, but it took a century to make a difference. Unfortunately for Egypt, none of Mohamed Ali's successors had his energy, imagination, or political skills. The Suez Canal shares were lost to foreigners, who were granted increasing power as a result of concessions. The British protectorate meant that the English were the real rulers in Egypt from 1881 to 1954. Governor Cromer dissolved what industry there was and transformed diversified farming into monoculture, abandoning food for cotton to feed the mills of Lancashire. Banditry appeared in rural areas. Throughout World War I, Egyptians suffered from inflation. All social problems in Egypt had been shelved by successive governments with the excuse that they had more important matters to worry about, notably negotiating a treaty with England. Egypt was granted independence in 1923 but under a royal family, whom many Egyptians viewed as alien interlopers imposed from without. A fundamentalist religious revival occurred in the early 1900s, which brought an alternative to the constant bickering of political parties over power.

The modern Egyptian problems are disease, ignorance, poverty, and overpopulation. Since 1936 many Egyptians had been worried about the increasing Jewish presence in Palestine. War broke out in May 1948 between Israel and all Arab countries, including Egypt. The course of the war was little short of disastrous, and laid bare the bankrupt nature of internal policies in Egypt. In July 1952 a coup d'état ousted the monarchy, and for the first time in over 2,000 years, Egypt was ruled by Egyptians.

After initial economic progress, by the mid-1960s a period of economic hardship set in. From 1967, Egypt's economic situation deteriorated rapidly, and there was a visible resurgence of religious groups. The regime did not allow the population a real share in government but did give them the semblance of participation. Because of overpopulation and the decline of agriculture, there has been progressive depopulation of the countryside and increasing urbanization.

This review of the history of modern Egypt demonstrates the central paradox of Egyptian identity—the alienation of Egyptians from their rulers. That is why Egyptians hold so strongly to their religion. Alcohol consumption is restricted in Egyptian religion and always has been. Recent Egyptian culture is also reactionary to Western culture, which has a morality that generally permits alcohol consumption.

## MAJOR CONTEMPORARY DRINKING PATTERNS

There is a scarcity of literature on alcohol in Egypt. Scientists concentrate on marijuana and opium consumption, both of which are illegal but nevertheless more prevalent than alcohol in modern Egypt.

In a series of epidemiological explorations of the use of psychoactive substances among young people, Soueif and colleagues (1986, 1987, 1988, 1990) documented current trends in alcohol. Eight percent of twelve-year-old male secondary school pupils had experimented with alcohol, and more had done so in urban areas. This was related to their exposure to the drug culture. Those who continued drinking (at least four times a month) were less socially stigmatized than marijuana or opium users, and they claimed to have an air of modernism about them. The main reason given by those who stopped drinking was the expectation that alcohol would be harmful (41.9%). A religious reason was mentioned by only 8.81%. The majority, in both rural and urban areas, drank beer only. Wine and hard liquor were more prevalent and more experimented with early in urban areas. More rural than urban people took alcohol for self-medication. Urbanites used more narcotics. Some 12.5% eagerly sought their first alcohol drinking experience, and 87% said they first drank in response to pressure from others. Significant persons who pushed for this first drink were schoolmates (34%), friends (31%), and fathers (11%). Fathers often introduced their children to alcohol on a happy social occasion, emphasizing it as a status symbol. Alcohol was used with schoolmates and friends for having a good time.

At a modal age of between eighteen and twenty, Egyptian male university students who ever took beer were 38.5%; wine, 14.6%; and whiskey, 6.7%. Of those who had tried alcohol, 31% said they were still drinking at the time of the interview. The total number of students who took alcohol totaled 42% of the sample. This is a much larger subgroup than any other who admitted using any psychoactive substance, including cigarettes. Similar findings were obtained for secondary school and technical school boys. Like marijuana use, alcohol-drinking appears to be primarily recreational. Contrary to some appearances, the young people (mostly Muslims) had less of an easy conscience toward alcohol than toward prescription drugs.

Soueif and his colleagues reported on a third group (Egyptian males, thirty-five to forty-four years old, working in manufacturing) that showed other interesting aspects of current Egyptian drinking. Only 20.1% admitted ever drinking alcohol; this percentage is much lower than among the students. Alcohol did not seem to be rated highly as a recreational agent in blue-collar, working-class circles. Most of the alcohol drinkers (78.7%) preferred beer; very few drank wine (1.3%) or whiskey (0.9%). These percentages are very different from those of the students, who are assumed to belong to a higher socioeconomic class and to a different generation.

Additional differences exist between the male university students and workers. Young workers tended to begin drinking later than university students. More workers (16%) used alcohol for self-medication; the figure was only 2.5% for students. Of all workers who experimented with alcohol, 27% admitted continuing use. Smoking and being a bachelor stood out as predictors to continuing (vs. stopping) to take drugs. Those who stopped drinking gave the following reasons: anticipating physical and psychological harm (17.2%), financial difficulties (16.2%), and religious rules (13.2%).

There is a two-step association between exposure to psychoactive materials and their abuse. Alcohol users progressed toward their drug of choice, alcohol. Most of the workers shared with students the fact that their use of alcohol started passively: they were introduced to it by someone else rather than having sought out the experience.

Again, what gives meaningful weight to these results is that in all groups of interviewees the information was obtained through highly reliable queries. From the attitude studies of workers who did not drink, we estimate that 20% of them might be vulnerable to alcohol use. The majority (93%) of the workers, both drinkers and nondrinkers, believed that alcohol is harmful.

A fourth report by the Soueif group describes drinking by female Egyptian university students compared with their male colleagues. Although female students had parents higher in the social hierarchy, they had access to less spending money. Very few females smoked cigarettes or used natural narcotics, in contrast to the males. Their age at starting experimentation with narcotics was sixteen, compared with the males' twelve years. Females tried alcohol much more than any other psychoactive substance; 19% admitted ever drinking alcohol, and 38% of those had continued drinking until the time of the interview. A sizable proportion of the females had their first experience before the age of twelve. Their living in an alcohol culture, with a high level of education, permissiveness, and modernism, probably explains their higher and earlier drinking (compared with older workmen). The beverages involved were beer (9.5%), wine (1.5%), and whiskey (0.2%). Obviously, Egypt is still a beer culture.

The mass media were the main channel through which the females learned about alcohol. For the males, friends were more important. Like the male students and like workers, female students said they were prompted in their first drinking experience. Young people in Egypt today are less daring in experimenting with alcohol and narcotics than with prescription drugs. They seem to be drinking in the face of rather powerful (and sometimes even threatening) psychosocial sources of conflict.

## VARIANT DRINKING PATTERNS

Differences by sex have already been summarized. Effects of age and social class are revealed by comparing blue-collar workers and white-collar students. As regards religion, there are no data from systematic research, but we can safely say from observation that there is little difference between the drinking of Muslims (who form 94% of the population) and Coptic Christians (who are most of the remaining 6%). The lives, beliefs, and practices are quite similar among both Muslims and Christians in modern Egypt, and this has been so for a long time. Modern Egyptians are an amalgam of many ethnic groups, but no ethnic minority except the black Nubians is particularly visible. The impression is that the Nubians especially drink the traditional beer, *bouzah,* but this may be a stereotype. Many modern Nubians are highly Islamized and have lived away from their native region in the south for so long that they are like other Egyptians.

There are indicators from Soueif's surveys and other data that an alcohol culture is growing among highly educated and Westernized middle- and upper-class Egyptians. All Egyptians are Arabic-speaking, so the question of linguistic differences in drinking is irrelevant. Tribal groups are evident only on the frontier fringe, as, in Sinai, Matrouh, Sewa Oasis, and Nubia. Although there is little scientific information about their behavior, we can safely state impressions. All of these tribal minorities are Muslim groups of Semitic or Hamitic origins, who share much of the same history and culture of most Egyptians. Their drinking behavior is in no way notorious or characterized by specific features.

Fathers, friends, and mass media are the main sources of information that introduce Egyptians to drinking; the modernized father and mother deserve special mention. Mass media contribute through soap operas and serials, whether made in the West or in Egypt. There is a movement in the country to ban such material on national television, but there is no defense against satellite broadcasts. The advertising of alcoholic beverages is already banned.

Narcotics are illegal in Egypt, but alcohol is not. Still, there are many measures to limit its availability, especially to young people. The aim is to reduce incidence (the numbers of those who start drinking) rather than prevalence (those who already drink). The production of alcoholic beverages is a state monopoly, and all imported alcoholic beverages are highly taxed. There is also much regulatory control of sale of alcohol in regard to time, place, and age.

The trends in alcohol use in Egypt show that per capita consumption of absolute alcohol diminished from 0.061 liter in 1962 to 0.033 liter in 1985. The share of beer is higher: from 0.022 liter to 0.027. Wine dropped from 0.008 liter to 0.004 liter in the same period, and the consumption of distilled alcoholic beverages dropped from 0.031 liter to 0.002. All of these are extremely low figures by all international standards. There is some illicit beer-brewing in the rural areas and some moonshining. Some smuggling presumably occurs. There is no sound way to quantify this illicit alcohol production, but it is certainly not enough seriously to affect consumption figures. Reporting of alcohol-related health and behavior problems is minimal. Such figures are absent from police and employment records, and from health and welfare statistics.

One can safely assume that there is a trend toward more drinking, especially in some sectors of the population, but it is not of any appreciable magnitude. There is a need for focused research with appropriate methodology in order to learn more about alcohol use and its outcomes. The attitudes of most people toward drinking are negative, and alcohol is generally associated with harm, ill health, and religious bans.

## PROS AND CONS OF DRINKING

Egypt's population is predominantly Islamic and Coptic Christian, both religions that ban getting drunk. Islam, the religion of the majority for centuries, bans the mere touch of wine. But Egyptians still hold to some of the concepts of their traditional paganism, which permits beer but not wine and spirits.

According to current law in Egypt, it is not illegal to drink or trade in alcoholic beverages, but there are several clauses that discourage drinking. Penalties are more severe for many crimes if they are committed while drunk. An employer may fire (without compensation) an employee who shows signs of intoxication in the workplace (Law 91/1959). One's license to drive can be suspended for ninety days if one is discovered driving under the influence of alcohol (Law 66/1973). Punishment is even stronger in case of recidivism.

The Shareya (Islamic law) is imbedded in the conscience of all devout Muslims, forming a deterrent to drinking. It is not formally enforced in Egypt, as it is in some other Arab and Islamic countries. According to Shareya, drinking wine in any amount is banned. Any beverage that has similar effects on the mind also is banned. There are penalties, of various degrees of severity, for drinking; there are many conditions necessary to prove any such case, and penalties are not dispensed lightly. The strategy of Shareya to drive the Islamic community into absolute abstention is humanistic, rational, and fair, for those who believe the premises. Non-Muslims in an Islamic society may drink freely behind closed doors. I assume that if Shareya were strictly adopted in modern

Egypt, drinking would change only a little. Consumption is already very low. Problem drinking is also low and is treated as a personal illness rather than a social problem.

Even in the Koran, the source of Shareya, it is mentioned that there are benefits in wine. No detailed clarification is given about the nature of these benefits. Linked with this statement is an assertion that wine causes more ills than benefits. These statements started a four-stage process of banning wine, which extended over thirteen years. Early portions of the Koran mention that it is impossible to meditate or pray while intoxicated. Later verses state that there is a link between wine and a variety of social evils. At last the Muslims were ready for a total ban on wine, including bans on dealing in it and having any association with it. Muslims are still exhorted to keep a wide margin of safety between themselves and wine. Islam, through the word of the Prophet, denies any medicinal value to wine.

Consumption of alcoholic beverages is no longer a rite in Egyptian religious practices or festivities. Some Egyptians drink on the eve of the New Year and at a spring harvest festival called Sham el-Nessim (the smell of the breeze).

The interactional relationship between drinking and hashish smoking is an issue in Egypt. Hashish is the most widely used drug in Egypt. Although it is legally banned, it is not much scorned by either the Egyptians' conscience or their religion. Although the death penalty applies to dealers, consumption has increased in recent years. It was introduced into Egypt in the 1100s, and hashish users still believe that it is beneficial. Some authors claim that hashish provides an outlet that can rival alcohol. But research shows that smoking hashish, like smoking tobacco, is associated with higher risks than drinking.

## CONCLUSION

Egyptian drinking, both old and new, is distinctive. For centuries, the Egyptians consistently drank beer only, and in very modest amounts. Most are spared the many problems that are described elsewhere as being associated with drinking. This stability of Egyptian alcohol behavior is part of an overall generally conservative culture rooted in an old "grain civilization." The restraints on alcohol use come mainly from deep religious sentiments. Egyptian religion matured over thousands of years and protected the Egyptians from drowning themselves in wine. Modernization may yet threaten this stable situation in Egypt, but a revival of religious observance seems to be restoring the stability of the law, including that concerning alcohol consumption.

## REFERENCES

Abdel-Sayed, I. 1988. *Wine from a Christian Point of View.* Cairo: Orthodox Coptic Patriarchy.

Ashour, A. 1989. Egypt's profile. Pp. 461–476 in T. Kortteinen (Ed.). *State Monopolies and Alcohol Prevention.* Helsinki: Social Research Institute on Alcohol Research.

Bell, H. I. 1957. *Cults and Creeds in Graeco-Roman Egypt.* Chicago: ARES Publishers.

David, A. R. 1982. *The Ancient Egyptians.* London: Routledge.

Hassanain, E. 1986. *Alcohol and Drugs between Shareya and Law* [in Arabic]. Cairo: N.p.

Hussain, N. 1990. *The Subculture of Hashish Users in Egypt.* Cairo: American University Press.

Kamil, J. 1987. *Coptic Egypt.* Cairo: American University Press.

Maccarese. 1436. *Al-Mawaez Wa Al-Itebar.* Cairo: N.p.

Marsot, A. L. A. 1985. *A Short History of Modern Egypt.* Cambridge: Cambridge University Press.

Montet, P. 1985. *La Vie quotidienne en Egypt au temps de Ramses.* Cairo: N.p.

Soueif, M. I., and Z. A. Darweesh. 1986. The extent of drug use among Egyptian male university students. *Drug and Alcohol Dependence* 18:389–403.

Soueif, M. I., and M. A. Hannourah. 1987. The use of psychoactive substances by female Egyptian university students. *Drug and Alcohol Dependence* 19:233–247.

Soueif, M. I., and G. S. Youssuf. 1990. Use of psychoactive substances among male secondary school pupils in Egypt: A study on a nationwide representative sample. *Drug and Alcohol Dependence* 26:63–79.

Soueif, M. I., and F. A. Yunis. 1988. The use of psychoactive substances among Egyptian workers. *Drug and Alcohol Dependence* 21:217–229.

Valbelle, D. 1988. *La Vie dans l'Egypt ancienne.* Paris: Presse Universitaire de France.

# 8

# France

## *Véronique Nahoum-Grappe*

France is set apart from most countries by both a high rate of alcohol consumption per person per year, and a steady decrease in drinking during the second half of the twentieth century. An adult over age twenty drank an average of 25 liters of pure alcohol in 1970, 19.6 liters in 1985, and 17.8 liters in 1991. The figures per person per year, provided by the Institut National de la Statistique et des Études Économiques (INSEE[1]), decreased from 13.3 liters in 1985 to 11.9 in 1991. These figures correspond closely to those of Dutch distillers, who compile such data regularly (Dutch Produktschap voor Gestillerde Dranken 1993).

## TRENDS IN FRENCH DRINKING

Since the beginning of the twentieth century, France has been one of the leaders, among those countries for which statistics are available, in annual per capita alcohol consumption. However, this situation, which is due mainly to the great quantity of wine consumed, is changing thanks to a steady decrease in drinking throughout the 1900s, especially since World War II. Even though this decrease primarily concerns wine-drinking, wine has remained the principal alcoholic beverage consumed in France.

We can hypothesize that there will be an eventual homogenization of the statistics concerning alcohol consumption within the European Community, and that the distribution of beer, wine, and spirits will become more nearly equivalent throughout Europe (with the exception of the wine-growing regions surrounding the Mediterranean). This tendency would corroborate a trend toward the drinking patterns in the different European countries becoming less diverse, which began even before economic integration.

The figures concerning wine-drinking allow us to see more precisely the tendency toward a decrease in France: in 1965, average per capita consumption of wine was 90.63 liters; in 1977, it was 64.70 liters; and in 1989, 31.74 (INSEE 1987–1993). In France, beer and cider have never had as great an importance as wine. In the 1990s, wine still makes up two-thirds of the total consumption of pure alcohol in spite of the progressive decline of cheap table wine, which is being replaced more and more by highly regulated wines with the label *appellation contrôlée* (quality-controlled within named regions). More expensive and of higher quality, these wines are consumed mainly on special occasions. The consumption of cider, a popular beverage in northern France, has tended to decrease. In contrast, beers with a high alcohol content (13–17° [equivalent to about 15–16%]), "de luxe" beers, have had increasing sales in France. Although the consumption of distilled liquor has not changed, according to the overall figures, since the 1970s younger people have more often chosen to serve it at their parties. When these same youths become adults, however, they seem to follow the pattern of drinking wine with meals on special occasions. The importance of habitual wine drinking, therefore, remains the overwhelming characteristic of alcohol consumption in France.

Another characteristic of drinking in France concerns the difference between men and women. In 1987, 63% of men over eighteen years old and 30% of women over eighteen claimed to drink at least one glass of wine a day. One out of five men admitted to drinking more than four glasses per day; the same was true of only one woman out of fifty (INSEE 1987). Thus, the heavier the drinking, the more it is a male phenomenon. The majority of habitual or excessive drinkers in France are men and belong primarily, though not exclusively, to the working classes: employees and unskilled workers, artisans, shopkeepers, small business owners, farmers. One example of the gender difference in drinking patterns is that women do not participate in drinking contests, a means of encouraging excessive drinking typical of male sociability in France (Nahoum-Grappe 1989, 1991). The participants in such activities drink over and over again, compelled by an implicit obligation to accept and to pay for rounds in their turn, in order not to lose face. The tacit winner is the man who drinks the most and holds his liquor the best, maintaining control of his speech and actions. By contrast, the water drinker, like those who do not pay for their round, is labeled unmanly, cowardly, and stingy. This practice is found in various forms in different social groups and contexts; it is related to the importance of drinking a toast and to the virtual impossibility for a man to refuse to drink alcohol in certain circumstances. In France, this sort of compulsory drinking has been an integral part of the history of social communication.[2] In this type of excessive, compulsory drinking, in which one tries to outdrink the other—"too much" is never enough—the obligation applies only to men. Women can refuse to drink without losing face; drunkenness on the part of women is looked down upon more than drunkenness on the part of men.

Although the social stigma may be less important for women who drink than for male alcoholics, the moral stigma is greater. For women, though drinking is perceived as a greater human failure than it is for men, it is less related to their social class. For workingwomen, the socioeconomic status does not seem to be statistically significant (INSEE 1987).

In France, consumer patterns differ greatly between men and women; women take more medications, and eat less meat, more sugar, and more vegetables than men. Wine and meat seem to be linked both to a masculine gender identity and to a working-class social identity. A "good meal" in France must include both wine and meat, especially if a man is present. Furthermore, although the intensity of the obligation depends partly on the social class (Bourdieu 1979), it depends more on the type of the meal. "Real men" of the working classes must drink and eat large quantities. The language of this type of virility is incompatible with a bourgeois refinement; the usual representation of the "typical Frenchman" is not someone known for good manners. Furthermore, there is a certain resemblance in the slovenly appearance of the drunkard and the casual style of the typical working-class Frenchman (beret, mustache, baguette [long loaf of bread] under his arm, a bottle of red wine in his hand). Wine-drinking by men is therefore also a symbol of a national lifestyle; in a traditional working-class environment, wine must be served with the meal when a man is present.

For men, wine—a more human beverage because it is the product of careful preparation—replaces water. Women prefer to drink water (as more natural) mixed with a little wine. A French woman will accept a glass of good wine but will refuse a second. At the end of a meal, women and children may dip a sugar cube into the liquor that is served to the men; this traditional act, typically feminine and childlike, reveals a relative cultural proscription concerning spirits, which are thus transformed into a harmless aroma enhancing the real delicacy, the sugar cube.

In France, women drink less than men in quantity as well as in "quality." All gender-specific representations of femininity in France seem to emphasize greater moderation and a preference for "lighter," sweeter, more fruity beverages, like champagne and sweet, aromatic liqueurs.

Many Frenchwomen drink wine in moderation with a meal, but they are rarely among those who systematically drink to excess. The figures on the rate of mortality due to alcoholic cirrhosis of the liver indicate a gender difference in excessive drinking. In 1982, the alcohol-related death rate was 37.2 (gross figure: 37.3) for men and only 13.6 (gross figure: 14.4) for women (INSEE 1987). This is especially striking because women often have higher rates of cirrhosis overall then do men.

A final distinctive aspect of drinking practices in France is a result of the geography of the country; the southern wine-producing regions contrast with the regions located north of the Loire River, where the damage caused by alcohol is more serious. For example, in the north, there is a higher rate of alcohol-related cirrhosis of the liver for both men and women, and, for men, a higher death rate due to cancer of the upper respiratory and digestive tracts, a classic indication of excessive drinking. But regional data on drinking in France do not reveal a significant difference between the north and the south in terms of quantity of absolute alcohol. On the other hand, localized studies show that in the south of France people traditionally drink wine, and in the north they drink more distilled alcohol, cider, and beer, with an increase in wine-drinking after World War I (Nourrisson 1990; Dion 1959). An ethnosociological study (Castelain 1989) focusing on drinking practices among the dock workers in Le Havre,[3] where the rate of alcohol consumption is particularly high, shows that the institutional diagnosis of alcoholism as a pathology does not necessarily correlate with the rate of alcohol consumption. In other words, a high level of alcohol consumption does not necessarily correspond to a high rate of alcohol-related sickness or death. Indeed, drinkers in the wine-producing regions of France consume greater quantities of wine (and not of hard alcohol), but their drinking does not seem to be correlated with a high rate of alcohol-related sickness and death. In fact, the opposite is true, which accords with recent scientific findings that show moderate drinking to be healthful for most people.

It is not clear exactly what sociological or physiological processes may be crucial in producing the different protecting effect that alcohol has in different regions where drinkers consume equivalent amounts. One of the hypotheses that is currently being tested is that wine contains some trace ingredients (probably largely flavonoids) that spirits do not. Or the difference could result from social and convivial drinking in one region, in contrast with solitary and unorganized drinking in the other. Differences in diet, specific cultural practices, regional health care, and other environmental factors are also being examined. For example, in the case of dock workers, the limitation of alcohol-related pathologies may result from an informal system of regulation of drinking that is enforced by the members of a drinking group. Furthermore, though it is evident that wine-producing areas are not subject to a higher rate of alcohol-related sickness and death, the inverse has not been proven. Further detailed, interdisciplinary studies of the drinking patterns in different regions in France are needed in order better to challenge the belief that drinking red wine at a meal does no harm. It is difficult to predict the different rates of morbidity and mortality from the differing levels of consumption, and it has been shown that given an equivalent rate of consumption, we cannot automatically infer an equal risk of alcoholism.

The contrast between the more "alcoholic" north of France and the wine-producing south, which seems better "protected" against the damaging effects of alcoholism, is characteristic of the debate on the subject of alcohol in France in general, and specifically the role that wine plays. Indeed, more than any other beverage, wine acts as a symbol of identity. Not only virile and associated with the working classes, wine is also "French," and even *gaulois* (Gallic), with all the connotations of this term, suggesting a straightforward drinker who laughs and complains, and is always willing to criticize or to tell a bawdy joke, a drink in his hand. In fact, one of the keys to this debate lies in the fact that France has produced wine since the beginning of the Christian era and that this production has played an important role in the history of its national identity. As a result, the specific characteristics briefly described above—the high rate of alcohol consumption and its steady decrease, the importance of wine, the gender difference, and the contrast between drinking patterns in the north and in the south (related to what American researchers call the "French paradox"[4])— cannot be understood without referring to the history of wine and of drinking in France.

## HISTORY OF WINE IN FRANCE

It is essential to take into account the economic, sociological, and cultural roles of wine in France. The southern half of the country (like Greece, Italy, and Spain) belongs to a Latin cultural zone, inseparably identified with vineyards and wine production. The grapevine and the olive tree are two plants emblematic of the region surrounding the Mediterranean. Wine has been mentioned in historical texts ever since the establishment of sedentary settlements following the development of agriculture. Throughout their history, the people around the Mediterranean (Braudel 1979) have known the techniques of wine production and have been familiar with intoxication. Very early, wine trade became a major economic activity in the area (Dion 1959; Lachiver 1988). Laubenheimer (1990) points out, on the basis of archaeological research, wine has been produced in France since the century after the Roman conquest. Wine is present in religious and secular ceremonies, sacrifices and offerings, daily life and special occasions. Catholicism has played a major role in transmitting the technical and semantic culture related to wine.

The social function of wine has always been characterized by great ambivalence: wine has been seen both as a sacred liquid used in liturgical ceremonies, and as a beverage subjected to strict legal, moral, and religious regulations (Austin 1985). The history of medicine also reveals an ambivalent attitude toward wine, which is seen as both a medication and a toxic substance. Galen's ancient axiom, "Wine forms the blood as bread forms the flesh," was transformed into a popular proverb in French oral culture in the 1800s (Loux and Richard 1978). Ancient medicine consistently advised drinking in moderation and proscribed drunkenness. The history of festivities shows the importance of wine as the principal legal psychoactive substance, consumed in excessive quantities on festive occasions (Bakhtine 1970). Throughout its history, wine has been represented as the human beverage par excellence—good for the body, which it revives and heats, as well as for the heart, which it delights—and as a serious risk for the excessive drinker, who may lose his mind, lose control, and behave like an animal (alcohol is sometimes seen as "liberating the beast within the man"). Although excessive drinking is unanimously condemned by religious, moral, and medical authorities, French culture provides a host of literary texts, poems, and songs that praise the drinker and *l'ivresse,* a typically French concept linking the effects of alcohol with ecstasy, rapture, and exhilaration (much like the neglected diverse meanings of the word "intoxication" in English).

The perception of a psychoactive risk related to wine consumption is present throughout Western history, and drunkenness has become both a major model of misconduct (i.e., a good way of behaving badly) and a nearly required experience for every adult male on certain occasions when he must prove both his virility and the social bond that unites him with the group.

Four drinking patterns have appeared consistently throughout French history in religious, medical, moral, legal, and literary texts:

1. Drinking wine with a meal, as part of a diet required to maintain good health.

2. Drinking wine on social occasions, as a contractual sign of sharing, a nonverbal signature of an economic contract, or a marital union. This type of drinking behavior also comprises a "drinking detour" (Nahoum-Grappe 1991)—going out of one's way to have a drink, alone or in a group, for no special reason. Such patterns have developed as a result of the increasing demographic movement in France between the city and the country and within large cities. Inns, taverns, cafés, and bistros are typical sites for this type of social behavior.

3. Drinking wine or other alcoholic beverage on festive occasions in order to become drunk, as a consciousness-altering experience for oneself or others. Temperance movements that have developed since the nineteenth century belong to a more general cultural context, the convention of self-control. Taming one's appetite and passions is required by religious models of behavior and, within the broader context of education since at least the 1600s, by the effects of the Counter-Reformation on schooling in France. The sin of gluttony, which associates excessive drinking with excessive eating, is a concept that is not only religious but also moral and intellectual. The progressive secularization of French society during the 1700s and 1800s did not weaken the pedagogical importance of control, of the social norm of moderation, and of the positive value ascribed to individual discipline.

   Sometimes, however, a controlled excess (planned once a month, for example) is perceived as beneficial. In medical lore from the 1500s to the 1700s, getting drunk was treated as a means of purging the body (Legrand d'Aussy 1782); the repercussions of this medical advice can be seen in the drinking songs and proverbs of the following centuries.

4. Drinking wine as an aesthetic experience linked to wine production. Drinking for oenological purposes, an ancient practice in France, blossomed strongly in the 1800s and persists. Oenological knowledge has become an integral part of the cultural heritage of the French elite since at least the end of the nineteenth century.

Although all four drinking patterns have continued until the present, the first, drinking as part of the diet, seems to have been both the most common and the most traditional form in France. The steady decrease in alcohol consumption in the second half of the 1900s can be linked to the disappearance of the drinking of wine with daily meals by the typical French working-class family.

The variety of criticisms of excess drinking, which are always in danger of being subverted by the drinker's laughter, is proof of both the seriousness of the problem in France and the cultural ambivalence regarding *l'ivresse*. Parallel to the tradition of condemning excessive drinking is a strong tradition of glorifying *l'ivresse:* laughter and humor are on the side of excess drinking. Toasting is another example; the act of raising one's wine glass in the direction of the person one wishes to honor has been a form of nonverbal communication integral to French culture since its historical beginnings. It is probably a secular vestige of ancient sacrificial libations in which a sacred liquid was offered to the gods: blood or wine in exchange for a wish, a prayer summarized in the words "long life!" or "to your health!" In France, a strong belief still persists that one should not make a toast with water, so as not to bring bad luck. Toasting necessarily involves wine. Paradoxically, this act is both an imitation of liturgical rituals and a reference to secular, if not materialistic, values. A reminder of ancient nonverbal sacrifices, toasting has become the lay expression of a specific aspect of French culture that sings the praises of *l'ivresse,* of "one more for the road," thus defying death.

Throughout history, there has been opposition to raising one's glass in this manner. The spontaneous present of *l'ivresse* is expressed in *carpe diem* (seize the day), versus the cold calculations of plotting strategies for tomorrow; the pleasures of the body versus the cool adequacy of reason; and the importance of individual follies as a form of truth more profound than collective norms. In the twentieth century, the act of toasting has become universal in spite of the ambivalence toward the beverage involved and thanks to a philosophy implicit in this act: a profane, typically French philosophy, evoked by Baudelaire as giving preference to "the eternity of sensual pleasure over the infinity of damnation."

In France, wine is the culturally preferred beverage to express this philosophy, as a marker of important moments of social interaction. Wine cannot be replaced at a meal by another beverage, alcoholic or not. If, at the end of the twentieth century, beer can be drunk with a sandwich in town, it is only because a sandwich is not a "real" French meal.

The prestige of wine in France has increased due to its economic and technological history, which, especially since the end of the Middle Ages, has been linked to the progressive elaboration of French gastronomy, greatly appreciated among the elite since the second half of the 1700s, and particularly in the 1800s. Oenological drinking is an aesthetic mode of drinking.

The south of France—the area delimited by an arc running from Alsace down toward Burgundy, dipping down to near the Mediterranean before rising through the Bordeaux region to Nantes—is associated with the production of high-quality wine. Yet, as historians Dion and Lachiver point out, every region in France has been involved in wine production at one time or another. Although the techniques of wine production, storage, and aging (notably of red wine) have changed over time—for example, the use of glass bottles did not become generalized until the 1700s—drinking patterns have changed little. Wine is still

widely drunk in France during a meal (in spite of the decrease mentioned earlier), as a sign of a social bond or transaction, as a means of becoming inebriated,
and as an aesthetic practice.

The history of wine in France—its prestige and its symbolic and aesthetic
value—and that of distilled alcohols has led to a typically French belief that
"wine is not alcohol." Notably since the 1850s, fermented beverages like wine
and cider, deemed beneficial and "hygienic" by Pasteur (Sournia 1986), have
been distinguished from the "harmful" products of distillation like brandy (eau-
de-vie). Popular among the urban working class as early as the 1700s, *eau de
vie* thereafter became perceived as a promise of death. In the 1800s, the term
"alcohol" referred only to beverages produced by distillation; in 1807, for example, the third edition of the *Dictionnaire de poche de la langue française*
defined alcohol in chemical terms: *poudre extrêmement divisée* (extremely refined powder). The term "alcohol" had not yet acquired its current meaning,
relating instead to the Arab word *kohl* (on which it is etymologically based), a
dark, antimonial powder used in makeup.

In France, the vocabulary associated with alcohol-related problems was not
integrated into medical and everyday language until the 1850s. The chemical
definition of alcohol and its appellation, determined by Lavoisier, and the recognition of an alcohol-related pathology, introduced in 1853 with the studies of
Huss, helped to identify a new object of social reflection and condemnation:
alcoholism. The appearance of a new proletariat produced by the industrial revolution and the mass production of distilled alcohol were sociological and economic factors leading to the emergence of alcoholism as a social reality that
took into account the new, harmful drinking patterns of the working class, violent drunkards dragging women and children into their degeneration.

The beneficial effects of wine had been the subject of medical publications
from the 1500s to the 1800s and beyond. These works fought against the use
of alcohol and for a state-regulated anti-alcohol campaign like that in effect in
France today. Indeed, the same "hygienist" doctor who condemns the use of
alcohol may be the owner of a quality wine cellar, thus taking advantage of the
double meaning of the word "alcohol" in French. *L'alcool* refers to a chemical
substance contained in liquids obtained by fermentation, including good wine,
that may cause intoxication. *Les alcools* refers exclusively to the product of
distillation, perceived as more chemical, more "industrial," and less "natural."
The ambiguity caused by this polysemy, and by the fact that the second meaning
often eclipses the first, explains how, in France, one can say that "good wine
is not alcohol" even though it contains ethanol.

This nearly paradigmatic opposition between wine and alcohol has affected
the drinking patterns in France; in the 1800s and 1900s, good wine—assumed
to be natural, blood of the earth, and fruit of human labor—is supposed to be
good for the health, comforting the human body, and "delighting the human
heart" (Nahoum-Grappe 1989). *Les alcools,* on the contrary, are considered
toxic and can be the cause of catastrophic dependency. Traditional French cul-

ture, which condemns both the teetotaler *(le buveur d'eau)* and the drunkard *(le soûlard)* while singing the praises of the wine drinker, is not affected by anti-alcohol propaganda. Both working-class and bourgeois cultures, according to the often mythical distinction established during the 1800s, share the same paradigm: the wine drinker is an aesthete for the second and a model of generous virility for the first.

## ALCOHOLIC BEVERAGES AS A DISTINCT CATEGORY

In order to understand the difficulty the French have encountered in placing wine and alcohol together in the category of alcoholic beverages, we must take into account the asymmetry between the technical, economic, and social histories of wine and of distilled alcohols. The latter first appeared as part of a medical pharmacopoeia; apothecaries held a monopoly over the production and sale of such products until the 1500s. Later, distilled alcohols became popular, especially in urban settings. The violence and burning sensation caused by these "fiery" beverages were interpreted as good for the body and the soul. Thus, distilled alcohol, originating in medical pharmacopoeia, flooded the urban and working-class market from the 1500s to the 1780s before the social alarm was sounded about the danger they presented. The habit of drinking hard alcohol to warm up, to feel good, and as an invigorating lift, rather than to become drunk, had developed before it became possible to evaluate the psychoactive effect of alcoholic beverages. The degree of alcohol contained in a given beverage could not be measured until the 1800s (the alcoholometer was not used until the first half of the century). The strength of an alcoholic beverage could be evaluated only qualitatively or subjectively. The violent effect of intoxicating beverages had therefore made an impact on drinking habits before it was sociologically defined. In France, the fallacious idea that the burning sensation of alcohol was good for the health (Nahoum-Grappe 1991) extended into the 1800s, when chemistry finally joined with medicine to isolate and identify the damage caused by the excessive intake of ethanol.

## *L'IVRESSE:* INTOXICATION IS MORE THAN DRUNKENNESS

There are two different approaches to alcohol-related problems in France. One is a positive approach associated with wine, with *l'ivresse,* with festive drinking, and founded in the long history of French culture. The other is a more negative approach that focuses on dependency and addiction, socially stigmatized as pertaining to the lower classes and caused by *les alcools,* not by "hygienic" fermented beverages. This explains how, well into the 1900s, doctors could continue to advise patients to drink wine in order to fight alcoholism.

In modern French culture, the polysemy regarding alcoholic beverages, including wine, has persisted. Throughout the twentieth century alcohol has been depicted as a source of warmth and a sign of life in children's cartoons like *Les Pieds nickelés* with its anarchist troublemakers, who are heavy drinkers with red noses, or Hergé's *Tintin,* extensively read in France and abroad since the 1930s. The act of drinking when the cold or death threatens to chill your bones arose from the medical value of the warmth, if not a burning sensation, that tempted people to drink (even though the medical practices on which this idea is founded have become obsolete). Representations of *l'ivresse* induce laughter and an attitude of tolerance. Drunks resemble clowns or tottering, rowdy children who transform the urban environment into a burlesque circus in which seeing someone fall becomes entertainment. Such representations of *l'ivresse* have survived in France while more traditional drinking patterns have lost their importance. The consumption of alcohol at meals has been steadily decreasing, and table wine is being replaced at noon by mineral water, a beverage that is considered to be more hygienic, feminine, and distinguished, and is drunk more by white-collar or service workers than by blue-collar workers. This change may be attributed in part to the success of anti-alcohol propaganda as well as to the decline of industrial workers, the social class most associated with drinking wine with a meal. Their drinking patterns have disappeared, and more "elegant" ones have spread with the increase of white-collar workers.

Drinking for the psychoactive effects, for *l'ivresse,* still quite common, has changed in form. We may be witnessing a separation between eating and drinking in France, especially among the younger generations. In fact, moderate, controlled drinking is being replaced by a more irregular form of drinking for psychoactive purposes. Drunken behavior has become more frequent, less socialized, and more anomic than in the festive context.

Drinking as an aesthetic experience, for oenological purposes, may have an institutional future because some authors in France have maintained that training people in wine tasting could prevent excessive drinking by countering the attitude expressed in the saying, "It doesn't matter what we drink as long as we get drunk" *(qu'importe le flacon pourvu que l'on ait l'ivresse).* Focusing on the aesthetic pleasures of alcohol may also reduce the gender gap, in that young women today are also interested in oenology. Yet, drunkenness of an adult or elderly woman still draws greater disapproval than does that of a man.

The introduction of coffee as a common beverage in the 1600s led to a sort of unorganized prevention of the excessive use of alcohol by offering an inexpensive alternative for the occasional drinker. In the 1700s, wine and brandy were the principal beverages in France; black coffee has become the most common drink in the 1900s.

## RECENT CHANGES IN DRINKING PATTERNS

Changes in drinking patterns in France are also the result of more general sociological changes. For example, why do the forms of entertainment chosen by adolescents seem more anomic and less ritualized than traditional forms of celebration? Emptiness and solitude characterize the nightclubs and big parties where these young people choose to have a good time. During the time spent partying, trying to get drunk becomes the principal experience or adventure. Why have elaborate balls and other traditional festivities become obsolete while parties that scarcely provide a break from day-to-day life have increased in number? In a French song of the 1970s, "Dans les Bals populaires" (At village dances), the boys at the bar boast: "We don't dance; we're just here to have a drink, and to have another drink without paying!" These festivities where the men don't dance are no longer worthy of the name *bals populaires*. Singing and dancing, which were learned outside the school environment and limited the alcohol consumption (one didn't drink while dancing), have become obsolete. Festive drinking is therefore related to the way people celebrate and pass the time in a given society. In general, the evolution of drinking patterns needs to be studied within the broader context of an increasingly prevalent type of behavior defined as "democratic individualism," in which the social actor may (or must) take more and more control over his or her actions (Erhenberg 1991). In France the tolerance, or even affection, felt toward the intoxicated drinker is not contradicted by the image of the violent, downfallen drunk, the symbol of failure. In a society where the ultimate goal is self-construction, in terms of both the body and the career, the ultimate risk is the voluntary destruction of this construction. Alcoholism thus appears as an important threat in a culture that has promoted individualism as one of its essential values.

Drinking as a sign of a social bond is the pattern that seems to have undergone the least change. As a general rule, the degree of alcohol consumed is relative to the social investment in the occasion. Certain events—a great fright, a particularly emotional reunion, or important social occasions (contracts, alliances, changes in marital or professional status)—justify alcohol consumption almost as if there were a sociological necessity to drink. Alcohol acts as an indicator of social change; neither coffee nor water can replace it. But alcohol also intervenes when a social void inhibits thinking about change. In the big cities, drinking for no special reason is as common as ritualized drinking; having a drink, which may be simply a minute detour from the routine of workaday life, reveals the possibility of drinking alcohol for no other reason than this very possibility.

Even though young women drink more than before, alcohol consumption remains an expression of a masculine identity. For example, a man whose wife has left him is likely to get drunk (the quantity of alcohol commensurate to the intensity of his love) before crying, whereas a woman will probably break down and cry before having a drink. The feminine identity, less socially determined than men's (according to French estimation), remains incompatible with the image of drunkenness. In moments of success in sports, finance, or politics, for example, men are still expected to offer and to drink alcohol.

The worldwide success of French champagne, developed at the end of the 1600s, reveals the psychological importance of the relationship between a beverage and an occasion, the first being a nearly requisite sign of the other. Even women drink this golden, bubbly wine as a quintessential symbol of festivity. It is probably not by chance that champagne developed in France, not only because this country also produced high-quality wines but also because it is a country where the sociological necessity of alcohol consumption is engraved on the heart of social interactions.

## ACKNOWLEDGMENT

I am grateful to Cecilia Beach, who translated this from the original French. I have approved the translation.

## NOTES

1. INSEE is the source of data concerning alcohol drinking in France. I will be using the figures published by INSEE, Ministère de l'Économie des Finances et du Budget, Direction Générale, 18, boulevard Adolphe Pinard, 75675 Paris Cedex 14, France. INSEE has published *Données sociales* every three years since 1987. Various research institutions like the Conseil National de Recherche Scientifique (CNRS) and Institut National de la Épidémiologie des Drogues (INED) participate in these publications. To these global figures, we can add more specific studies on drinking carried out by public or semipublic institutions: economic studies (financed by the producers), medical studies (carried out within hospitals and/or clinics), and broader sociological studies (carried out by university research teams or in research institutions like CNRS or École des Hauts Études des Sciences Sociales [EHESS]). In France, these studies are supplemented by the work of Marie Choquet and her team Institut National de la Santé et de la Recherche Medicale (INSERM), as well as by studies carried out by the Société Française d'Alcoologie (SFA) and the Association Nationale de Protection contre l'Alcoolisme (ANPA), and those financed by the Institut de Recherche sur les Boissons alcoolisées (IREB).

2. Drinking a toast or drinking to one's health can be traced in the rituals of the French court and other social groups. Not drinking at such moments is considered an insult to the person being toasted and to the group in general. Such shared drinking rituals have been part of European history since Greek and Latin antiquity.

3. Among the social groups in France in which wine is not the primary alcoholic beverage, dock workers are the most affected by alcohol-related problems. But although the probability of alcoholic behavior is almost taken for granted, there were few hospitalized cases during the 1950s. This apparent contradiction is the starting point of J.-P. Castelain's study, *Manière de vivre, manière de boire: Alcool et sociabilité sur le port* (1989). In fact, these dock workers have developed a spontaneous system for controlling drinking patterns.

4. The diet of Frenchwomen in the Toulouse region (southwest), who are moderate wine drinkers, would seem to be a rare case in which regional customs take into account the theory that wine protects against cardiovascular diseases: drinking a moderate amount of wine is considered a "good habit," and epidemiological evidence supports the folk belief.

# REFERENCES

Ansersson-Hassam, E., and E. Astier-Dumas. 1992. Le Paradoxe français: Á la recherche d'une explication. *Médecine et Nutrition* 4, no. 28:231–233.

Austin, G. A. 1985. *Alcohol in Western Society from Antiquity to 1800.* Santa Barbara, Calif.: Southern California Research Institute.

Bakhtine, M. 1970. *L'Oeuvre de François Rabelais et la culture populaire au Moyen-Âge.* Paris: Gallimard.

Bourdieu, P. 1979. *La Distinction.* Paris: Minuit.

Braudel, F. 1979. *Civilisation matérielle, économie et capitalisme.* Paris: Colin.

Castelain, J.-P. 1989. *Manière de vivre, manière de boire: Alcool et sociabilité sur le port.* Paris: Imago.

Dion, R. 1959. *Histoire de la vigne et du vin en France dès origines à la fin du XIXe siècle.* Paris: Flammarion.

Dutch Produktschap voor Gestillerde Dranken. 1993. *World Drinking Trends.* Henley-on-Thames, UK: NTC Publications.

Erhenberg, A. 1991. *Le Culte de la performance.* Paris: Calmann Lévy.

Furet, F., and J. Ozouf. 1975. *Lire et écrire, l'alphabétisation en France de Calvin à Jules Ferry.* Paris: Minuit.

Huss, M. 1853. Analyse de l'alcoolisme chronique. *Annales médico-psychologiques* 5: 60–88.

Institut National de la Statistique et des Études Économiques. 1987- . *Données sociales.* (triennial). Paris: INSEE.

Labrousse, E. 1985. *Esquisse du mouvement des prix et des revenus en France (Ancien Régime).* Paris: Dalloz.

Lachiver, M. 1988. *Vin, vignes, vignerons: Histoire du vignoble français.* Paris: Fayard.

Laubenheimer, F. 1990. *Le Temps des amphores en Gaule: Vins, huiles et sauces.* Paris: Errance.

Legrand d'Aussy. 1782. *Histoire de la vie privée des français depuis l'origine de la nation jusqu'à nos jours* (3 vols.). Paris: P. D. Pierres.

Loux, F., and P. Richard. 1978. *Sagesse du corps: La Santé et al maladie dans les proverbes français.* Paris: Maisonneuve et Larose.

Nahoum-Grappe, V. 1989. Histoire et anthropologie du boire en France. Pp. 83–168 in *De l'ivresse à l'alcoolisme.* Paris: Dunod.

———. 1991. *La Culture de l'ivresse.* Paris: Quai Voltaire-Histoire.

Nahoum-Grappe, V., and J.-J. Yvorel. 1992a. Histoire et anthropologie historique: Etat des lieux. Pp. 191–210 in A. Ehrenberg (Ed.). *Penser la drogue, penser les drogues.* Vol. 1. Paris: Descartes, Ministère de la Recherche et de l'Industrie.

———. 1992b. Histoire et anthropologie historique: Bibliographie. Pp. 133–187 in A. Ehrenberg (Ed.). *Penser la drogue, penser les drogues.* Vol. 3. Paris: Descartes, Ministère de la Recherche et de l'Industrie.

Nourrisson, D. 1990. *Le Buveur du XIXe siècle.* Paris: Albin Michel.

Sournia, J.-C. 1986. *Histoire de l'alcoolisme.* Paris: Flammarion.

# 9

# Germany

## Irmgard Vogt

### CONSUMPTION OF ALCOHOLIC BEVERAGES

Within Europe, Germany has long been notorious for its drinking habits and more so for its permissiveness toward drunken comportment in public. Singing in a pub or on the streets while drunk, gathering in a crowd, quarreling, and eventually fighting just for fun (which quickly may turn into serious situations with people injured or dead) have been described as typically German since the time of Caesar.

Permissive attitudes toward drinking and drunkenness have prevailed throughout German history and persist today. Many famous men have talked against the evils of wine, beer, or spirits: Martin Luther, who in the 1500s loathed wine drinkers, calling them names (such as *Weinschlauch,* wineskin); Böttcher, who in the 1850s stormed against spirit drinkers; Kautsky, who in the 1880s recommended that workers control their consumption of beer. Nevertheless, people developed their own drinking habits, which varied in different regions. Since the 1800s, when the drinking habits we now know were shaped (Völger and von Welck 1981; Vogt 1981, 1985, 1989), clear-cut patterns have been distinguished between the wine-producing regions (such as the Rhine Valley, parts of Swabia, and the Palatinate), those producing spirits (east of the Elbe), and the strongholds of beer production (Bavaria, Berlin, and other highly industrialized areas of the west). Although there are tendencies to hold to customary drinking habits, industrialization has leveled differences between regions and between social classes. Still, there are preferences for wine in the wine-growing regions, for spirits in the east, and for beer in Bavaria.

Some statistics on alcohol consumption in Germany set the stage. As Table 9.1 shows, levels of per capita alcohol consumption have changed since 1900,

**Table 9.1**

**Annual Per Capita Consumption of Alcoholic Drinks (in Liters) in the German Reich and in the Federal Republic of Germany, Including West Berlin: 1900–1990**

| Type of drink | Year | | | | | |
|---|---|---|---|---|---|---|
| | 1900 | 1950 | 1960 | 1970 | 1980 | 1990 |
| Beer | 125.1 | 38.1 | 95.6 | 141.1 | 145.7 | 143.1 |
| Wine, cider, and champagne | 6.7 | 5.1 | 16.0 | 19.5 | 26.6 | 26.1 |
| Spirits | 11.3 | 3.0 | 5.1 | 7.9 | 8.8 | 6.2 |
| Equivalent in liters of absolute alcohol | 10.1 | 3.3 | 7.8 | 11.4 | 12.7 | 11.8 |
| Per capita income (in DM; for US$, divide by about 1.5) | -- | -- | 4,332 | 8,745 | 18,510 | 29,569 |

*Note*: It is assumed that a liter of beer contains 4.4% of alcohol by volume; a liter of wine, cider, or champagne, 12%; and a liter of hard liquor, 38% (Deutsche Hauptstelle gegen die Suchtgefahren 1970–1994).

*Source*: Recalculated from Deutsche Hauptstelle gegen die Suchtgefahren (1970–1994); Hoffmann (1965). The data refer only to West Germany; data on the former German Democratic Republic (East Germany) are not included. For more details, see Statistisches Bundesamt, 1991.

especially since 1950. Measured in liters of absolute alcohol, per capita consumption was around 10 liters in 1900. It decreased drastically during World War I, then rose in the period between the wars. Even so, consumption remained relatively low during the latter period because of economic problems in the 1920s and social problems in the 1930s. It fell to zero during World War II. In 1950, annual per capita consumption of pure alcohol was only 3.3 liters. It rose to a peak of 12.7 liters in 1980, and has leveled off since.

In the two decades after World War II, large numbers of people experienced a steep increase not only in income but also in the consumption of alcoholic beverages. Many women joined their husbands and friends in drinking sessions, first at home and later in restaurants, pubs, and bars. Although there was an association between income and per capita alcohol consumption in the 1950s and 1960s, it more or less disappeared in the 1970s and 1980s. The average income rose until 1990; the level of alcohol consumption has fluctuated around 12 liters of pure alcohol per person per year since the mid-1970s. The data suggest a strong link between income and alcohol consumption after periods of forced abstinence (as during war) and when there is an economic boom. However, there seems to be an upper level for alcohol consumption in highly industrialized countries such as Germany. Thus, increases in per capita income above a certain level have little effect on alcohol consumption, which tends to remain at the same level.

Preferences for specific types of alcoholic drinks have changed since about 1840. In the first half of the 1800s, the consumption of spirits was preeminent in the lower class; the bourgeoisie and the nobles enjoyed white wine from Germany and imported red wine and cognac from France. Around the beginning of the twentieth century, beer, partly due to low price, became the most popular drink among workingmen in the industrial centers and in Bavaria (Vogt 1984a).

Today, beer is the most widely consumed drink among men of all socioeconomic groups, even when one takes regional differences in drinking habits into account. However, there is still a preference for wine in the wine-growing areas and for spirits in the east. But beer is the first choice of frequent and regular drinkers, as can be seen in Table 9.2.

Wine is the second most popular drink, although only a minority of drinkers take it daily. It is more expensive than beer, so its consumption reflects the drinker's income. Wine is frequently linked with special occasions such as Sunday meals, festivities, and celebrations, a tradition less pronounced in wine-producing regions but fairly strong elsewhere. Wine is the most popular alcoholic drink among women (Vogt 1989).

Spirits—including brandy, whiskey, and liqueurs—are least popular. It is as rare for spirits to be drunk daily as it is for wine; however, men of all socioeconomic groups like to drink spirits from time to time, occasionally in combination with beer. Upper- and middle-class men show a preference for imported spirits, whereas blue-collar workers favor German brands. Women, when they drink hard liquor, prefer sweet varieties.

Subtle changes in drinking patterns continue. Although beer is the favorite, wine has attracted new consumer groups, especially affluent families and women. Spirits have lost much of their attraction, due to changing lifestyles as well as to tax increases.

Although the quantity and frequency of alcohol consumption by men is independent of socioeconomic factors, the type of drink preferred is linked to socioeconomic class. More expensive and imported drinks go with high income. They are symbols of affluence and are valued as such. The relationship between income and drinking is most pronounced among women. Those in the higher socioeconomic groups—high income as well as high education—drink more and more regularly than those in low socioeconomic groups. Their favorite drink is wine. The distribution by sex of abstainers and occasional drinkers, moderate drinkers, heavy drinkers, and very heavy drinkers is shown in Table 9.3.

As the data show, the overall differences between the drinking habits of men and women are very pronounced. Whereas 32% of women are abstainers and

**Table 9.2**

**Percentages of the Population of the Federal Republic of Germany and West Berlin Consuming Different Types of Alcoholic Drink, by Frequency of Consumption: 1976–1990**

| Frequency of Consumption | | Year | | | | | |
|---|---|---|---|---|---|---|---|
| | | 1976 | 1978 | 1980 | 1984 | 1987 | 1990 |
| Beer | | | | | | | |
| | Regularly every day | 16 | 11 | 13 | 14 | 13 | 11 |
| | Several times per week | 12 | 11 | 11 | 17 | 15 | 15 |
| | Once per week | 34 | 27 | 20 | 28 | 26 | 30 |
| | Occasionally/seldom | 17 | 16 | 21 | 11 | 11 | 10 |
| | Never | 21 | 34 | 34 | 30 | 33 | 33 |
| Wine and champagne | | | | | | | |
| | Regularly every day | 3 | 3 | 3 | 3 | 2 | 2 |
| | Several times per week | 6 | 4 | 6 | 6 | 5 | 3 |
| | Once per week | 46 | 35 | 30 | 29 | 27 | 29 |
| | Occasionally/seldom | 32 | 31 | 28 | 37 | 34 | 35 |
| | Never | 13 | 26 | 31 | 26 | 31 | 29 |
| Spirits | | | | | | | |
| | Regularly every day | 3 | 3 | 3 | 2 | 2 | 1 |
| | Several times per week | 4 | 2 | 5 | 4 | 3 | 3 |
| | Once per week | 30 | 20 | 17 | 16 | 19 | 19 |
| | Occasionally/seldom | 28 | 22 | 22 | 25 | 22 | 26 |
| | Never | 34 | 52 | 52 | 53 | 52 | 49 |

*Note*: Data reflect a change in frequency categories in 1984; tables do not add up to 100 because of rounding.

*Source*: Recalculated from Bundeszentrale für Gesundheitliche Aufklärung (1984, 1990).

occasional drinkers (defined as drinking small amounts of alcohol once or twice a year), only 13% of men are in this group. Women also outnumber men as moderate drinkers. By contrast, 44% of men can be classified as heavy and very heavy drinkers (alcohol consumption levels of more than 140g/week of pure alcohol). Fully 25% of the respondents in a representative sample report very heavy alcohol use. If one takes into account that people tend to underestimate their alcohol consumption, the real numbers of heavy and very heavy drinkers may be even higher. Men in Germany do drink large quantities and, as can be seen in Table 9.4, beer is their favorite drink.

Women drink moderately at all ages, whatever the type of drink, as is shown in

**Table 9.3**
**Percentages of Abstainers and Occasional Drinkers, Moderate Drinkers, Heavy Drinkers, and Very Heavy Drinkers, by Sex, in Germany: 1990**

| Categories of Drinkers | Females | Males |
|---|---|---|
| Abstainers and occasional drinkers | 32 | 13 |
| Moderate drinkers (up to 140g/week) | 55 | 43 |
| Heavy drinkers (up to 280g/week) | 9 | 20 |
| Very heavy drinkers (more than 280g/week) | 4 | 24 |

*Note*: "Occasional" means no more than once or twice a year.

*Source*: Recalculated from Bundeszentrale für Gesundheitliche Aufklärung (1990). See also Arbeitkreis Alkohol 1979.

Table 9.5. They drink much less beer and spirits than men, and even in the case of wine, they consume smaller quantities. Men are much more willing to indulge in heavy drinking with all types of alcohol; they often consume large quantities during short periods, without paying much attention. Memory lapses and blackouts are fairly common in men who drink: about one-third report experiencing them, compared with 6% of women. Most men find it quite acceptable to get drunk periodically, whereas drunkenness in women is considered inappropriate.

Men and women have different values associated with drinking and drunkenness. From their teenage years, boys are encouraged to drink in peer groups as well as in the company of adult men. There is a saying that "a real man has to be drunk at least once in his lifetime." Thus, excessive alcohol consumption in the teenage years is a rite of passage into adulthood. Such a custom clearly shapes habituation toward drinking and drunkenness. When young men enter military service, most of them are accustomed to drinking regularly. Drinking is "just fun," and during service it helps to fight boredom. Furthermore, to "hold one's drink" is a highly valued virtue of manhood within the military, as in many other all-male institutions. To show off one's skills in drunken comportment, young men compete in drinking games, often with excessive alcohol consumption, not only in the military but also in student clubs and fraternities. Many run the risk of misusing alcohol, and some become addicted.

In contrast, teenage girls are not encouraged to drink much, although today

**Table 9.4**
**Alcohol Consumption among Males in the Federal Republic of Germany and West Berlin: 1990**

| Type and Quantity of Drink | Age Group (%) | | | | | |
|---|---|---|---|---|---|---|
| | - 19 years | 20-29 years | 30-39 years | 40-49 years | 50-59 years | 60 and older |
| **Beer** | | | | | | |
| Do not drink beer | 28 | 18 | 17 | 15 | 8 | 21 |
| Amount consumed per occasion or day | | | | | | |
| 0.2-0.5 liters | 23 | 20 | 18 | 22 | 27 | 37 |
| 0.6-1.0 | 35 | 39 | 40 | 39 | 39 | 30 |
| 1.1-1.5 | 14 | 11 | 14 | 10 | 10 | 6 |
| 1.6-2.0 | -- | 6 | 7 | 8 | 11 | 3 |
| 2.1 or more | -- | 5 | 3 | 6 | 4 | 2 |
| **Wine and champagne** | | | | | | |
| Do not drink wine/champagne | 50 | 29 | 25 | 29 | 36 | 39 |
| Amount consumed per occasion or day | | | | | | |
| 0.1-0.3 liters | 27 | 28 | 22 | 18 | 20 | 24 |
| 0.4-0.5 | 12 | 26 | 29 | 26 | 20 | 20 |
| 0.6-0.8 | 10 | 11 | 14 | 17 | 15 | 12 |
| 0.9 or more | 1 | 4 | 9 | 6 | 8 | 5 |
| **Spirits** | | | | | | |
| Do not drink spirits | 50 | 36 | 33 | 33 | 38 | 40 |
| Amount consumed per occasion or day | | | | | | |
| 2 - 4 centiliters | 30 | 42 | 46 | 47 | 32 | 40 |
| 6 -10 | 18 | 18 | 18 | 14 | 24 | 20 |
| 12-16 | 1 | 3 | 1 | 3 | 3 | -- |
| 18 or more | -- | -- | 2 | 2 | 2 | -- |

*Note*: Tables do not add up to 100 because of rounding.

*Source*: Recalculated from Bundeszentrale für Gesundheitliche Aufklärung (1990).

many of them do so for a short time. The lesson for them is to learn to drink moderately, to avoid getting drunk, and especially to avoid drunken comportment. Most of them adjust to the norms that are set for them.

The following examples of the culture of drinking and drunkenness in Ger-

**Table 9.5**
**Alcohol Consumption among Females in the Federal Republic of Germany and West Berlin: 1990**

| Type and Quantity of Drink | Age Group (%) | | | | | |
|---|---|---|---|---|---|---|
| | - 19 years | 20-29 years | 30-39 years | 40-49 years | 50-59 years | 60 and older |
| **Beer** | | | | | | |
| Do not drink beer | 70 | 39 | 33 | 40 | 51 | 65 |
| Amount consumed per occasion or day | | | | | | |
| 0.2-0.5 liters | 14 | 29 | 41 | 42 | 32 | 26 |
| 0.6-1.0 | 16 | 24 | 22 | 16 | 14 | 5 |
| 1.1-1.5 | -- | 3 | 3 | 2 | 2 | 1 |
| 1.6-2.0 | -- | 3 | 1 | -- | -- | 1 |
| 2.1 and more | -- | -- | -- | -- | -- | -- |
| **Wine and champagne** | | | | | | |
| Do not drink wine/champagne | 48 | 16 | 13 | 19 | 26 | 33 |
| Amount consumed per occasion or day | | | | | | |
| 0.1-0.3 liters | 33 | 32 | 31 | 36 | 30 | 39 |
| 0.4-0.5 | 16 | 28 | 40 | 28 | 29 | 24 |
| 0.6-0.8 | 1 | 17 | 12 | 12 | 9 | 2 |
| 0.9 or more | -- | 6 | 3 | 3 | 6 | 1 |
| **Spirits** | | | | | | |
| Do not drink spirits | 79 | 51 | 50 | 56 | 54 | 67 |
| Amount consumed per occasion or day | | | | | | |
| 2 - 4 centiliters | 17 | 36 | 32 | 33 | 38 | 29 |
| 6 -10 | 2 | 10 | 16 | 9 | 5 | 4 |
| 12-16 | -- | 1 | 2 | 1 | 1 | -- |
| 18 or more | -- | -- | -- | -- | -- | -- |

*Note*: Tables do not add up to 100 because of rounding.

*Source*: Recalculated from Bundeszentrale für Gesundheitliche Aufklärung (1990).

many therefore address male behavior. It is men who come together in pubs and in Bavarian beer gardens to drink, to talk, to play cards, or just to socialize with friends. Women may come with them, but it is often their job to take the drunkards home and help them sober up.

## DRINKING CULTURE IN GERMAN PUBS

Cultural differences within Germany have been stressed, and they are linked to production areas of different alcoholic beverages. Accordingly, drinking patterns, as well as the habits of drinking, differ. Underneath all the differences in drinking patterns, drinking habits, and drinking styles there are similarities that typify German drinking culture all over the country. The German pub (*Kneipe, Wirtshaus, Weinstube*) is the place where men gather to have a beer, a glass of wine, a bit of spirits, or a mixture of these. This section, then, addresses drinking in German pubs (including beer gardens).

The history of public drinking places in Germany goes back to the Middle Ages (Voigt 1973), which need not be dealt with here. However, the number of pubs or bars, saloons, ballrooms, beer halls, and beer gardens increased markedly during the 1800s, and the importance of public drinking places for lower-class men became prominent. First of all, the living conditions of the working class in the early years of the industrial revolution were terrible (cf. Engels 1845; Treiber and Steinert 1980), causing men to look for places other than home to spend free time. Many employers took advantage of that fact by setting up pubs close to their factories, where they served workers alcoholic beverages at prices higher than on the free market. Thus, pubs have been meeting places for workers since the start of industrialization (Reulecke and Weber 1978; Vogt 1984b). Thus, to characterize the pub as "the poor men's social club" holds not only for England but also for Germany.

After the rise of the Social Democratic Party as a strong political force (between 1869 and 1900), pubs were used as meeting places for its members. This was even more the case from 1878 to 1890, when the party was banned. Men came together in pubs "just for a beer," which could not be forbidden, and at the same time discussed party affairs. Police tried to raid some of the pubs that were most notorious as meeting places of the Social Democratic Party, but it was difficult to prove who was there just for a beer and who was there for a party meeting. Thus, pubs acquired a new meaning for working-class men as hideouts in public. Since then, pubs have been the places for party meetings in general, and the Social Democratic Party proudly associates them with its beginnings. Still, the impact of pubs as places where politics are discussed or made is low; people go to pubs not primarily for political reasons but to drink.

To fully understand pubs and the drinking culture, one has to keep in mind their historical roots. The typical pub is close to the living quarters of working-men; it is "the pub around the corner" (*die Eckkneipe;* see Dröge and Krämer-Badoni 1987). It is a modest place without fancy furniture and fixtures. It is divided into two parts: the entrance, with a bar, and one or more rooms in the back, containing tables, chairs, and benches. The light is usually dim, just enough to see the level of beer in one's glass. Beer is the most common drink served in pubs, followed by spirits. Only in the wine-growing regions are there pubs that serve wine as well (Alber 1987). In all others, when customers ask for wine, they can choose between "red" and "white" wine without any further denomination. People who want to drink wine go to restaurants—except in parts of Swabia, the Palatinate, and the Rhine Valley. The drinks offered in pubs indicate that they are not places for women. This does not mean that women may not go to a pub, but most go there only in the company of men.

A pub has its regulars (Runge 1987) who come to the place at least once or twice a week, most of them daily. There are workingmen who come for a beer or two right from the job. They stand around the bar, chat with the bartender and other customers, or just drink in silence. Between 5 and 6 P.M., the noise level is low. Women are explicitly not welcome then. The area around the bar belongs to men, and women who dare to enter it encounter either hostility or (minor forms of) sexual harrassment. In sociological terms, they have crossed the gender border and entered a territory where they are barely tolerated. There are many unwritten rules to be respected in pubs, and a great number of them concern women only.

Normally, the early customers leave after half an hour or so. Some of them may return later in the evening, alone or in the company of friends or their wives. Since pubs do not serve much to eat, people go there after dinner. The place begins to fill around 8 or 9 P.M.; the level of noise rises quickly; the air becomes heavy because of the number of people gathered in a relatively small place; and it is very smoky. There is much laughter at first. With increasing levels of intoxication, tempers rise and people talk to each other loudly, sometimes shouting. In some pubs, quarrels take place quite frequently; in others they are rather rare, depending to a larger part on the bartender. Those who prefer friendly and peaceful customers set up fairly strict informal rules that they are willing to enforce at the cost of losing some of their customers. By doing so, they attract guests who tend to respect the rules of the place, come often, and stay longer. The more aggressive people tend to gravitate to specific pubs, sometimes within the same neighborhood.

However, even in pubs where people often shout at each other, violent fights are rare. Compared with the drinking styles of workingmen in the early 1800s, major changes have taken place. In older descriptions of public drinking places (cf. Medick 1982), fights seemed to have been normal, and workingmen often attacked each other when drunk.

Today, fighting between groups of drunken men is rare except around the famous Octoberfest in Munich, a gigantic public drinking occasion that evolved out of the celebration of the German Thanksgiving Day. The Octoberfest is an amusement park for families during the day, and a place for uninhibited drinking and drunkenness in the evening, attracting people from all over the world. For many, a visit to the Octoberfest is synonymous with getting drunk and displaying drunken comportment at its worst. There appear to be no rules, and it is up to the police to keep public order. People take advantage of the occasion and behave as they like. The results are fighting, injuries, serious (and sometimes fatal) alcohol intoxication, and many people who behave quite extraordinarily.

Whereas going to a pub is embedded in a complex web of informal rules, going to the Octoberfest and to some beer gardens comes close to a visit to the wilderness. Uncontrolled drunken behavior is typically associated with German drinking. Fortunately, it represents just a small part of the multitude of behaviors that go with drinking in Germany.

## REFERENCES

Alber, W. 1987. Trollinger-Poeten, Lemberger-Literaten: Ein einig Volk von Vierte-lesschlotzern. *Hessische Blätter für Volks- und Kulturforschung: Alkohol im Volks-sleben.*

Arbeitskreis Alkohol (Ed.). 1979. *Materialien zum Alkoholmibrauch in der Bundesre-publik Deutschland einschlielich West-Berlin.* Bonn: AA.

Bauer, M. 1903. *Der deutsche Durst.* Leipzig: Seemann.

Böttcher, H.-H. 1839. *Der Branntwein, ein sicherer Zerstörer des Wohlstandes, der Ge-sundheit, des häuslichen Glücks und der Zufriedenheit.* Hildesheim: Gerstenberg.

Bundeszentrale für Gesundheitliche Aufklärung (BzgA) (Ed.). 1984. *Aktionsgrundlagen 1984: Ergebnisse einer Repräsentativerhebung der Bevölkerung ab 14 Jahren der Bundesrepublik Deutschland einschlielich Berlin (West). Teilband Alkohol.* Co-logne: BzgA.

———. 1990. *Aktionsgrundlagen 1990: Ergebnisse einer Repräsentativbefragung der Bevölkerung ab 14 Jahren in der Bundesrepublik Deutschland einschlielich Berlin (West). Teilband Alkohol.* Cologne: BzgA.

Deutsche Hauptstelle gegen die Suchtgefahren (DHS) (Ed.). 1970–1994. *Jahrbuch der Suchtgefahren.* Hamburg: Neuland.

Dröge, F., and T. Krämer-Badoni. 1987. *Die Kneipe.* Frankfurt: Suhrkamp.

Engels, F. 1845. *Die Lage der arbeitenden Klasse in England.* Berlin: Dietz.

Hoffmann, W. G. 1965. *Das Wachstum der deutschen Wirtschaft seit der Mitte des 19 Jahrhunderts.* Berlin: Springer.

Kautsky, K. 1891. Der Alkoholkonsum und seine Bekämpfung. *Die neue Zeit* 9:106–107.

Medick, H. 1982. Plebejische Kultur, plebejische Öffentlichkeit, plebejische Ökonomie. In R. Berdahl et al. (Eds.). *Klassen und Kultur.* Frankfurt: Campus.

Reulecke, J., and W. Weber (Eds.). 1978. *Fabrik, Familie, Feierabend.* Wuppertal: Ham-mer.

Runge, I. 1987. ''Kneipenabende'': Zur Feldforschung im Kiez. In *Hessische Blätter für Volks- und Kulturforschung: Alkohol im Volksleben.*

Statistisches Bundesamt (Ed.). 1984. *Statistisches Jahrbuch.* Stuttgart: Kohlhammer.

———. 1991. *Statistisches Jahrbuch.* Stuttgart: Kohlhammer.

Treiber, H., and H. Steinert. 1980. *Die Fabrikation des zuverlässigen Menschen.* Munich: Moos.

Vogt, I. 1981. Alkoholkonsum, Industrialisierung und Klassenkonflikte. In G. Völger and K. von Welck (Eds.). *Rausch und Realität: Drogen im Kulturvergleich.* Cologne: Rautenstrauch-Joest-Museum.

———. 1984a. Einige Fragen zum Alkoholkonsum der Arbeiter. *Geschichte und Gesellschaft* 8:134–140.

———. 1984b. Defining alcohol problems as a repressive mechanism: Its formative phase in imperial Germany and its strength today. *International Journal of the Addictions* 19:551–569.

————. 1985. Macht Alkohol gewalttätig? *Drogalkohol* 9:119–136.

————. 1989. Federal Republic of Germany. In M. Plant (Ed.). *Alcohol-related Problems in High-risk Groups.* WHO-WGO EURO Reports and Studies 109. Copenhagen: WHO Regional Office.

Voigt, K. 1973. *Italienische Berichte aus dem spätmittelalterlichen Deutschland.* Stuttgart: Klett.

Völger, G., and K. von Welck (Eds.). 1981. *Rausch und Realität: Drogen im Kulturvergleich.* Cologne: Rautenstrauch-Joest-Museum.

# 10

# Guatemala

## Walter Randolph Adams

Alcohol use in Guatemala has been the subject of much comment since the 1940s but has been the subject of little systematic study. Most discussions appear in passing or cover only a few pages. The works by Bunzel (1940), Reiche (1970), and Schwartz (1978) are notable exceptions. There are no official published statistics.

There are five categories of alcoholic beverages in Guatemala: distilled beverages with a sugarcane base; an indigenous, fermented (and illegal) product made from sugarcane; a lightly distilled (and illegal) beverage known by various names; *aguardiente,* a stronger, distilled, and legal version of the latter; and beer.

The Maya produced an alcoholic beverage called *balché* before the Spanish conquest, using honey, water, and the bark of a tree. After the Spanish conquest the sucrose source changed from honey to sugarcane, which has been grown in Guatemala since the early 1600s. In addition to converting this crop into sugar, the country produces rum in several distilleries. Recently, distilleries have begun to put flavorings in the liquor to produce local versions of vodka, gin, and scotch-type whiskey. Some individuals will purchase these instead of the imported brands either for economy or as a sign of nationalism. Because of their high cost, the imported distilled beverages are consumed primarily by the elite. Some nonelite ladinos emulate this behavior, hoping to be perceived as members of that class.

There are a few references to *chicha,* which Tedlock (1985) describes as a corn-based beer. Although *chicha* is a corn-based beer in many other countries, in Guatemala the term more commonly refers to the cane-based, indigenous fermented beverage mentioned earlier. This beverage is used in traditional Indian rituals and is called *boj* by the inhabitants of Alta Verapaz in the northern part of the country. The Pokomam, who live in the central highlands, and the Ixil, who live in the southwestern highlands, have a lightly distilled beverage called *guaro* and *kuxa,* respectively. These beverages are consumed in the same contexts as *boj.* Consequently, when I refer to *boj* in the following pages, one can infer that *guaro* and *kuxa* are used in similar functions.

As many as twenty-three distinct Indian languages were spoken in Guatemala, all of them as different from one another as Spanish is from French. Today, this diversity has diminished for a variety of reasons, and the citizens are grouped into two major ethnic classifications, Indians and ladinos. The term "ladino" refers to anyone who is not an "Indian." Although it is often phrased in terms of "race" and "blood," the distinction is actually based upon lifestyle and cultural features rather than physical features. Consequently, the dividing line between the two ethnic groups is often blurred, and a person can "pass" from Indian to ladino. Precisely because the line is blurred, one's behavior is subject to close scrutiny. For example, Reiche (1970, 103) states that the common perception of Indians is that they are "lazy, stupid, and drunkards." By this definition, people who engage in activities perceived as lazy or stupid, or who drink to excess, can be considered Indians, regardless of whether their lifestyle is Indian or ladino.

The department (state) of Alta Verapaz distinguishes four beverages made from sugarcane, differentiated by the length of time each is allowed to ferment. They range from a fresh sugar-water (with no fermenting) to the alcoholically potent *boj* (home brew). The first serves as a base for other beverages, such as coffee, and is consumed during the day. Reiche (1970) details how *boj* is made in Verapaz and observes that it is frequently produced under unhygienic conditions. One might say this explains why the government has prohibited its manufacture and sale; however, the government's need for revenue from the heavily taxed sale of *aguardiente,* and the need to assimilate the Indians into the national economy, are more likely explanations.

*Aguardiente* is frequently used in public ceremonies, in rituals performed by religious brotherhoods (*cofradías*), and during shamanic rituals where the likelihood that the treasury police will be present is a concern. The participants in these ceremonies risk being arrested if they are caught drinking untaxed *boj.*

Guatemala has two major brands of beer, Cabro and Gallo. Both breweries are owned by members of an upper-class ladino family. In the 1970s, three other breweries opened, creating competition with the traditional companies. None of these competitors is in operation in the 1990s, but, one can occasionally see advertisements for them. In addition to the two domestic labels, beer imported from Mexico is available in supermarkets. This has prompted the two domestic breweries to market a so-called export variety.

Ladinos, especially those in the middle class, drink beer casually with friends and in private settings or at family parties. The elite usually consume a bottle of Mexican or "export" quality beer before lunch or on other informal social occasions. Moore (1973) mentions that Indians use a bottle of beer as a gift to a man when asking permission to marry his daughter. In this sense, the beverage is used as *boj* and is used in more traditional communities. Some researchers have observed Indians drinking beer on market days; however, this may be an attempt to emulate ladino behavior.

## WHY IS ALCOHOL NOTEWORTHY?

There are three reasons why alcohol is noteworthy in Guatemala. First, alcohol is integral to religious activities among the Indians and thus is a marker of ethnic identity. Second, it links the ladino culture with the Indian culture. The government has exploited the Indian drinking pattern by forcing them to consume *aguardiente*. Historically, during religious ceremonies ladinos lent money to the Indians so they could purchase alcohol; the loan was repaid in labor. As Stoll (1993, 33) has poignantly written, alcohol is "only an instrument for the destructive effects of monetizing a subsistence economy."

Third, the sale of heavily taxed *aguardiente* represents a source of income for the government. And, it must be noted, the production of *boj* represents a source of income for many of the rural poor. Reiche (1970) estimated that an Indian household could earn between U.S. $6.00 and U.S. $11.20 in profit from producing 15 to 20 liters of *boj* in a few days. Although this is not much by Western standards, many families found it profitable enough to risk arrest and confiscation of the processing equipment. In a 4-month period, 282 persons were arrested in 3 rural *municipalidades* (counties). Reiche (1970) notes that a little over 52% of those arrested were women. In Guatemala, the production of alcohol is largely a woman's task.

## ALCOHOL IN HISTORY

The Spaniards entered Guatemala in 1524. Little information is available on the Maya consumption of alcohol on the eve of their arrival. Priests, who were the historians and ethnographers during the Spanish conquest, did not arrive in Guatemala to minister to the Indians until the mid-1500s. Even then, they focused on the Indians who were already living in *reducciones,* new towns where Indians were aggregated so they would be under closer Spanish control than in traditional villages. Thus, there is little information about the role of alcohol in traditional Maya society. Our only clues are in the ubiquity and consistency of alcohol consumption patterns in contemporary Maya rituals.

The consumption of alcoholic beverages is mentioned twice in the *Popol Vuh,* the sacred book of the Quiche Maya, an indication that alcohol was consumed before the Spaniards arrived. It states that *quii,* or *chicha,* took three days to ferment and that the consumers "did not feel anything" after drinking it (Tedlock 1985). In both passages in the text, death occurred after the beverage was consumed. One case was a suicide, and the other was a homicide. Due to the absence of other information, it is difficult to determine the significance of this observation.

Thomas Gage, writing during the 1620s and 1630s, provided one of the few statements of early colonial use of alcohol that may accurately reflect indigenous patterns. In his edited diary (Thompson 1958, 225), he states that the Indians made a beverage they called *chicha.* It was made with a little water; molasses, sugarcane juice, or honey "to sweeten it"; some "roots and leaves of tobacco"; and other roots. *Boj* is still made in Alta Verapaz in a similar way (Reiche 1970). Interestingly, these descriptions are almost identical to Roys's (1976) description of *balche,* a beverage consumed by the Maya of the Yucatán as a remedy for loss of speech, as an accompaniment to prayer, and for other purposes (Roys 1965). This document (Roys 1965) may date from the Classic Period (300–900). If that is so, the beverage links the contemporary Maya with their ancestors who lived when Tikal and other archaeological sites were vigorous cities.

Contemporary use of alcohol is consistent throughout Guatemala in spite of the number of distinct Indian groups, and in general follows two distinct patterns. The first pattern probably had its origins in the prehistoric past and is associated with religious ritual. The second pattern had its origin with the coming of the Spaniards in the 1500s and is a product of secular phenomena. The two forms converged in the 1800s, if not earlier.

Many of the rituals during which alcohol is consumed are associated with the *cofradías.* Participation in such a civil-religious hierarchy was and is considered both an honor and an obligation to one's community. Many ethnographies depict this hierarchy as integral to an Indian community's social, political, and religious organization. Holding office in the *cofradía* is very expensive, requiring a large investment of time and money throughout the year. Individuals holding the upper-level positions shoulder the bulk of the cost for elaborate ceremonies, the purpose of which is to maintain community solidarity and world harmony.

Other religious occasions during which alcohol is consumed pay homage to the patron saint of a town. These occasions often coincide with pilgrimages and regional markets. These ceremonies are larger, fully public affairs. Such events were mechanisms by which the Maya ruling class obtained tribute (Adams 1991) and times when people could obtain agricultural and craft products from the larger region.

In the context of such large, public functions, the secular drinking pattern became important. Spaniards had entered Central America in 1524 in search of gold and silver. Their quest for these commodities was in vain. However, they did find cacao (the source of chocolate) and a large labor force. Because the Spanish Crown was in financial straits, conquistadores were given land and were paid in Indian labor instead of money for their services to the Crown.

The Maya planted cacao trees, from which they obtained cacao beans. These beans were used as a currency throughout the area known as Mesoamerica, extending roughly from central Mexico to northern El Salvador and northern

Honduras (Millon 1955). Using established mechanisms for the collection of tribute (such as pilgrimages), the Spanish conquerors displaced the traditional Indian nobility and collected tribute for themselves. The Spaniards, lay and clergy alike, pressured the Indians for ever-larger tribute payments and enticed them to trade cacao (MacLeod 1973) or land (Cambranes 1991) for wine. Thomas Gage (Thompson 1958, 226) stated that Spaniards would make Indians drunk, then "pick their pockets" while they slept.

The Spanish colonizers used many informal and extralegal arrangements, including debt peonage, to induce Indians to work on plantations by the end of the 1700s. Bunzel (1940, 362) states that Indians would "contract debts and sell themselves and their children into slavery" for alcohol. Once they were on the plantations, Indians were paid extremely low wages and charged exorbitant prices for their daily needs, thus keeping them indebted to the landlords.

During the mid-1800s, Guatemala and other Central American republics began planting coffee as a major export crop. Few laborers lived in the primary coffee-growing areas, so laws were passed to secure Indian labor. Agents working for coffee plantations went into Indian towns during the yearly festivals honoring the patron saint. They enticed Indians to sign labor contracts by offering a cash advance that was usually spent on alcohol. In exchange for the loan, the men were obliged to work on distant plantations. Bunzel (1940) indicates that this practice continued well into the twentieth century.

This strategy worked because Indian men liked to drink with friends, to the point of inebriation, but they often ran out of money before they reached that point. Thus, an Indian man would welcome a plantation agent's offer of cash if he had not yet become inebriated, and rarely took the labor commitment seriously. Citing a letter written in 1868, Cambranes (1991, 110) states that some Indians would commit themselves to more than one employer at a time, "without having any intention whatsoever of performing the required work, because most of the time they are either drunk or truant."

## MAJOR DRINKING PATTERNS

The pattern described for the departments of Coban and Verapaz can be regarded as the pattern for Guatemala in general: "The Indian pattern of drinking is more clearly associated with religious ceremony than is that of the Ladino. The Indian also takes the purely social occasion to drink, but the Ladino drinks almost exclusively in the social situations" (King 1974, 194). Schwartz noted in his study that "drinking alone is rare and considered peculiar rather than asocial" (1978, 41). Other researchers state that this holds true in other communities.

Indians consume *boj* and *aguardiente* in large quantities not only in ceremonies associated with the *cofradías* but also in rites of transition. Ritual drinking is required during these important life events because it is thought that one cannot attain the proper religious spirit without it. Inebriation is common on these occasions, but it rarely results in the loss of consciousness. Alcohol consumption to such a state is considered disrespectful to the deities and ancestors. There are some situations in which abstinence or moderate consumption is preferred. For example, Schwartz (1978) observes that alcohol is not consumed on All Souls Day in San Martin; Bunzel (1940) and Stoll (1993) say alcohol is used only moderately during Holy Week in Chichicastenango and Nebaj, respectively.

The one time when drinking to the point of losing consciousness in *cofradía* rituals is tolerated—and even considered proper—is in a "farewell ceremony" when one celebrates the conclusion of the year-long obligatory service in office. One anthropologist observed: "it is common to see the *capitana* [the wife of the highest-ranking male] retiring to her home accompanied by the *vasallas* [her helpers] in a state of alcoholic saturation. This is the only time when a woman is not criticized for being drunk in public" (Reina 1966, 141). This ethnography is one of the few that deals with the participation of women in these ceremonies and implies that drinking by them as well as by men is considered acceptable behavior.

Drinking also takes place on public occasions such as market days, especially those on payday weekends. Drinking to the point of losing consciousness is accepted on such occasions. Both King (1974) and Bunzel (1940) observe that husbands and wives drink together on such occasions in some parts of the country, with men generally drinking more than their wives. Women are less likely to drink than are men, although an inebriated woman is seen occasionally at these events. More often, men will drink with their male friends and invite other friends to join them as they pass by. King (1974, 195) states that Indians drink with friends "to the stage of insensibility" on public occasions such as market days. However, they may have to stop drinking before they reach this point due to lack of funds.

These occasions are more social than religious and involve reciprocity. Alcohol is usually given in exchange for some service or favor to others—whether community service or an exchange of drinks. For example, Sexton (1992) states that when an individual is asked to take part in the Dance of the Conquest, the organizer plies him with *aguardiente* and cigars. Acceptance of these gifts virtually obligates the recipient to grant the request. Many ethnographers observe that requests for an individual to become a godparent or permit the marriage of a daughter are accompanied by ritual gifts of alcohol.

The consumption of alcohol by ladinos approximates the patterns of cosmopolitan Europeans and North Americans. Expensive imported wines and distilled beverages are consumed by the elite, and middle-class ladinos attempt to emulate this pattern. Drinking to the point of losing consciousness is considered improper, and an individual who consumes alcohol "improperly" is looked upon contemptuously, as an Indian. Financial constraints, however, force many to buy the cheaper sugarcane-based counterfeit local gin, scotch, and *aguardiente.*

Lower-class ladinos often appear to drink like Indians. That is, they drink *aguardiente,* some beer, and some *boj.*

Indian men and women will engage in binge drinking on social occasions. This has been attributed to their attempt to seek "release from the extreme pressures of surrounding cultures" (Bunzel 1940, 1976). Lower-class ladinos engage in similar behavior. Their poverty, however, limits their ability to emulate the upper classes. Thus, they engage in behaviors that are considered "Indian," the very label they are trying to avoid.

## VARIANT DRINKING PATTERNS

There is little discussion in the literature of variant drinking patterns, and those that are mentioned are inconsistent. Thus, the discussion here will be a series of anecdotal observations.

King (1974) states that young men and adolescents of all ranks beg drinks or steal bottles from those who can afford good liquor on important social occasions. I have observed this pattern in parts of Guatemala besides Coban and the Verapaz. However, it seems to be practiced primarily by ladinos rather than Indians.

Reiche (1970) states that Indians in Alta Verapaz will drink *boj* in the summer due to the scarcity of water. Children drink *boj* while attending school, resulting in scholastic problems. This is the only area of the country in which this pattern is described.

A few years ago, while participating in a shamanic ritual, I noticed that the shaman—a highly respected curer in the area—used soft drinks instead of the traditional rum in his ceremony. When asked why, he stated that the many years of drinking while performing these ceremonies had damaged his liver, so he changed that part of the ritual.

Guatemala has been the scene of a protracted war of insurgency in recent decades. The Ixil Triangle, located in an isolated region of the western highlands, has been one of the areas most severely affected. Stoll (1993) states that drinking among the Ixil declined during the 1980s due to the war. Warfare has destroyed much economic activity, resulting in widespread poverty. However, the war has also kept outsiders away and fostered increased moonshining.

In the Petén, the northernmost department of Guatemala, Schwartz (1978, 47) describes two distinct groups of "true drunks." The first consists of unmarried or divorced male collectors of chicle (the sap from which chewing gum is made); most are thirty-five to fifty years of age and have no permanent residence. They work in the forest, return to town when they have been paid, drink "until their funds are spent, and then return to work." This pattern is somewhat similar to the drinking behavior observed on market days, except that in this case the men are unmarried. Although community members consider this behavior aberrant, they do not interfere because the drinkers have no families to support and are considered good workers. The same author describes a second group who "barely manage to support their families and who are never really sober" (Schwartz 1978, 47). Although most of them are men, there are two women in this group of heavy drinkers.

For a variety of political, social, and economic reasons, many individuals converted to Protestantism as part of an attempt to shed their "Indianness" and become ladinos. The Guatemalan government encouraged Protestant missions in the mid-1900s in order to "transform the traditional isolated 'folk communities' of the hinterlands into an assimilated proletarianized work force" (Burnett 1989, 139). To do so, the power of the *cofradías* had to be reduced. While Protestantism was taking hold, the Catholic Church, fearing it would lose its following, developed service-oriented groups called Catholic Action. This organization, too, sought to reduce the power of the *cofradías,* and forbade participation in the traditional rituals and alcohol consumption. More recently, however, as Stoll (1993) observes, drinkers and nondrinkers can be found among both Catholics and Protestants.

Changes in the economic climate of Guatemala since the 1950s have reduced the viability of traditional agriculture for Indians in the rural areas of the country. Consequently, Goldin and Metz (1991) observe, more individuals are turning to economic strategies that require them to be absent from the community for longer periods. These strategies emphasize individualism over devotion to the community and require longer work hours than was the case with agriculture. These individuals can justify not participating in the *cofradías* or drinking alcohol because they do not have the time and have less commitment to the community.

## LEARNING ABOUT DRINKING

There is very little information about how individuals learn their alcohol consumption patterns. That which is available suggests they learn from observing their parents and other significant persons. For example, King (1974, 195) notes that Indian husbands and wives will drink together, and take care of each other and children "who usually accompany them."

A parent's drinking behavior can also be a negative model, serving to deter children from drinking. Some authors observe that male heads of household often attribute their religious conversion to their fathers' having drunk too much. Similarly, the conversion of a woman to Protestantism is often a reaction to her husband's, father's, or brother's drinking. Drinking to excess is frequently observed to result in assault and battery of a spouse or other family member. Thus, a woman may become Protestant to find a spouse who is less likely to abuse her.

Conversion to Protestantism suggests something else. Goldin and Metz (1991) observe that conversion is not merely a means of coping or obtaining support for not drinking. Protestantism links sobriety to fundamental ideological and behavioral changes. In short, it is part of the ladinization process.

## PROS AND CONS OF DRINKING

Observers cite the negative effects of alcohol—economic expense, sexual transgressions, and quarrels (Bunzel 1940)—as largely attributable to the consumption of *aguardiente,* not *boj.* There are at least three reasons for this. First, Reiche (1970) notes that *aguardiente* is much more potent (45 proof) than *boj* (10 proof). Second, *aguardiente* is more expensive, causing greater economic hardships for poor families. Third, the money from the sale of *boj* remains in the community, whereas the money from the sale of *aguardiente* leaves the community.

Alcohol consumption to the point of intoxication can result in spousal abuse, especially among Indians and poor ladinos. Ladinos are said to be especially vindictive and severe wife beaters (King 1974).

It may be relevant that Indians can devote more time and resources to other activities, such as sports, games, and travel, if they do not spend their scarce resources on alcohol or religious festivals (Reiche 1970).

Schwartz (1978, 41) and others have stated that when men are asked why they drink, the response is often "There is no other diversion." The traditional pattern of alcohol consumption among the Maya Indians has long been a means of demonstrating community solidarity. Absence of these rituals and other mechanisms would seriously undermine community solidarity unless they were replaced by other institutions.

More important, social relations are extremely fragile because some individuals are forced to be absent from the community for long periods. Others are unwilling to participate in the traditional rituals that promote community solidarity. Drinking in public with friends and neighbors is a symbol of community solidarity. This solidarity was traditionally important because it was a means by which an individual received help, without paying for it, for activities requiring many hands. Such occasions included sowing or harvesting a field, or house-raising, as is the case in many other cultures where helping neighbors has not been commoditized.

A lamentable consequence of much culture change is the destruction of traditional social networks. This is especially true where communities have undergone social upheaval due to the rapid penetration and intrusion of Western culture and economy. These traditional institutions have been, at best, only partially replaced. The government spends very little on public health, education, welfare, and other social programs that would benefit the Indians. As a result, many Indians remain marginal to the country's economy, forced to work and pay taxes but having to find other networks for social support.

Although Protestants refer to one another as *hermano* (brother), the sense of fraternity is not so strong as in the *cofradía.* The economic downturn of the 1980s, which continues in the 1990s, has resulted in decreased employment on plantations and elsewhere. This increases poverty and social unrest, and can lead to migration to other communities or other countries. The emigration of individuals from the communities exacerbates the destruction of traditional social networks. The sense of brotherhood, then, is only temporary in comparison with the traditional system. This would account for the recent development of drinking among Protestants and members of Catholic Action.

## ACKNOWLEDGMENTS

I want to express my gratitude to Dr. John Hawkins, Dr. Dwight B. Heath, Dr. Robert M. Hill, and Dr. Norman B. Schwartz for their help in tracking down elusive references and comments. I also express deep appreciation to Marilyn Baade Adams and Dr. Dwight B. Heath, who read, edited, and made critical comments on an earlier draft.

## REFERENCES

Adams, Walter Randolph. 1991. Social structure in pilgrimage and prayer: Tzeltales as lords and servants. Pp. 109–122 in N. Ross Crumrine and Alan Morinis (Eds.). *Pilgrimage in Latin America.* New York: Greenwood Press.

Bunzel, Ruth. 1940. The role of alcoholism in two Central American cultures. *Psychiatry* 3:361–387.

———. 1976. Chamula and Chichicastenango: A re-examination. Pp. 21–22 in Michael W. Everett, Jack O. Waddell, and Dwight B. Heath (Eds.). *Cross-Cultural Approaches to the Study of Alcohol: An Interdisciplinary Perspective.* The Hague: Mouton.

Burnett, Virginia Garrard. 1989. Protestantism in rural Guatemala, 1872–1954. *Latin American Research Review* 24:127–142.

Cambranes, J. C. 1991. *Coffee and Peasants: The Origins of the Modern Plantation Economy in Guatemala, 1853–1897.* South Woodstock, Vt.: CIRMA/Plumsock Mesoamerican Studies.

Goldin, Liliana R., and Brent Metz. 1991. An expression of cultural change: Invisible converts to Protestantism among highland Guatemala Mayas. *Ethnology* 30(4): 325–333.

King, Arden R. 1974. *Coban and the Verapaz: History and Cultural Process in Northern Guatemala.* Middle American Research Institute Publication 37. New Orleans: Tulane University.

MacLeod, Murdo J. 1973. *Spanish Central America: A Socioeconomic History, 1520–1720.* Berkeley: University of California Press.

Millon, R. F. 1955. When Money Grew on Trees: A Study of Cacao in Ancient Mesoamerica. Ph.D. diss., Columbia University.

Moore, Alexander. 1973. *Life Cycles in Atchalan: The Diverse Careers of Certain Guatemalans.* New York: Teachers College Press.

Reiche, C., Carlos Enrique. 1970. Estudio sobre el patrón de embriaguez en la región rural Altaverapacense. *Guatemala indígena* 5:103–127.

Reina, Ruben E. 1966. *The Law of the Saints: A Pokomam Pueblo and Its Community Culture.* Indianapolis: Bobbs-Merrill.

Roys, Ralph L. 1976. *The Ethno-botany of the Maya.* Philadelphia: ISHI.

————. (Trans. and Ed.). 1965. *Ritual of the Bacabs: A Book of Maya Incantations.* Norman: University of Oklahoma Press.

Schwartz, Norman B. 1978. Drinking patterns, drunks, and maturity in a Peten town (Guatemala). *Sociologus* n.s. 28(1):35–53.

Sexton, J. D. (Trans. and Ed.). 1992. *Mayan Folklore: Folklore from Lake Atitlan, Guatemala.* New York: Anchor-Doubleday.

Stoll, David. 1993. *Between Two Armies: In the Ixil Towns of Guatemala.* New York: Columbia University Press.

Tedlock, Dennis (Trans.). 1985. *Popol Vuh.* New York: Simon and Schuster.

Thompson, J.E.S. (Ed.). 1958. *Thomas Gage's Travels in the New World.* Norman: University of Oklahoma Press.

# 11

# Honduras

## Kenneth W. Vittetoe Bustillo

The general attitude in Honduras toward alcohol use is one of acceptance with some limitations on the time and occasion of drinking. Adolescence is the culturally accepted period to begin drinking, as a predominantly male way of social interaction. A certain degree of permissiveness exists toward the consequences and behavior that result from excessive use and abuse. In the adult population there is no set definition to differentiate the "normal" from the excessive and "habitual" drinker. The term "alcoholic" is reserved for the individual who suffers extreme damage from the disease.

Health professionals consider alcohol and drug abuse an important problem, and the majority categorize them both as diseases. There are private and governmental institutions that deal with education, prevention, and treatment; most of them have been active since the 1970s, with the exception of Alcoholics Anonymous, which has been in existence since the 1960s. The most important legal institution in this respect was created by the government and became active in August 1989. The Instituto Hondureño para la Prevención del Alcoholismo, Drogadicción y Farmacodependencia (Honduran Institute for the Prevention of Alcoholism, Drug Addiction and Pharmacodependence) is the state body responsible for the policy, regulation, and legal disposition of alcohol and drugs (including tobacco). There had been special interest in the subject of alcoholism due to a variety of medical, social, and psychological problems, as well as economic privation; Honduras ranks as a poor nation. In 1981 a law was passed to create a state-run institution to regulate and control the use of alcohol and other substances. Eight years later, this important agency was founded and it has since been responsible for the policies on prevention, research, treatment, and rehabilitation of substance users and abusers.

## HISTORY OF ALCOHOL USE IN HONDURAS

The first instance of use and abuse of alcohol in Mesoamerica probably dates back ten or more millennia, the likely result of humankind's inclination to experiment with the fermentation processes of plant life and its effects. Honduras, rooted in the cultures of pre-Columbian communities that still inhabit some areas, is strongly influenced by indigenous groups such as the Lencas, Chorotegas, Nahuas, Jicaques, and Tolupan in the central regions; the Payas, Garifunas, and Misquitos in the coastal regions; and the predominant Mayan tribes in the northwestern area. Their basic cultures all have a special relationship with the ceremonial intake of alcohol, where collective inebriation was sought. An important study of historical and narrative perspectives concerning alcoholism in Honduras proposes the psychological and social values of home brew as a basic food before the Spanish conquest. Fray Francisco Ximénez remarked in this respect on the importance of religion, and native cultural influences combined traditional beliefs with those introduced by the Catholic Church in such a way that Middle American Indians evolved distinctive forms of mixed religion, in which "drunkenness would become interwined with religious festivities;" this pattern persists (Sánchez O. 1984). Corn is the basic staple in their diet, as well as a special link between humankind and the earth and supernatural powers. *Chicha,* a home brew fermented from corn, is routinely drunk throughout the day by men, women, and children. Corn is also the base of a lighter home brew (*atol chuco*) that is much used to relieve hangovers. The links between food and drink deserve further ethnographic research.

Two attitudes have dominated in drinking habits. One is the ritualistic attitude before the Spanish colonization of the American continent, attached to important celebrations and festivities; the product of fermented corn (*chicha*) was the main source of alcohol. After the arrival of the Spanish, local people absorbed their ways, including new varieties of alcohol.

There are other aspects of ceremonial drinking behavior among native Middle American populations that can be considered. An example is the reference in the surviving Mayan codices to *blaché* or *balché,* a tree whose bark is used in making strong wine for ceremonial purposes. Although no longer used in Honduras, it is still part of worship among the Yucatec Maya of Mexico.

## ALCOHOL CONSUMPTION AND MAJOR DRINKING PATTERNS

In Honduras, as in many tropical regions of the Western Hemisphere, there are three basic types of alcohol ingestion. The most common one is associated with personal, family, and national celebrations. These are mostly related to religious, traditional, and community festivities. Birthdays are a frequent reason to celebrate at the workplace and within the family, as well as with friends who gather to eat, drink, talk, and dance. This pattern of behavior is a mixture of the Western and Indian ways of alcohol consumption where the young adult male is most likely to be the celebrant. There is ample evidence of the commercial value of this form of alcohol ingestion and of machismo, whereby a bottle of local beer is treated as a substitute for a female companion at any social gathering. This type of social drinking occurs in rural as well as urban communities. Local and ethnic traditions determine the drinking styles: from total abstinence in the case of a few isolated tribes (e.g., Tolupan tribes in the region of the Montaña de la Flor, in the state of Francisco Morazán) to varying degrees of intoxication on a weekly basis, especially on Sunday, when the marketing of agricultural produce and textiles takes place in a town, villagers coming together for this purpose. This may be seen in the areas where Mayan populations predominate (in the highlands of the state of Copán, close to the border of Guatemala). In general this pattern of drinking is associated with the everyday life activities when people come together in social or economic gatherings.

There is also ritualistic drinking behavior, the product of traditional belief combined with Roman Catholicism. In the past, as in the present, religious festivities that have a nationwide level of spiritual importance (such as Easter and Christmas) bring most of the population together to celebrate a time away from school and work. They spend much of their time traveling, visiting other families and friends, sightseeing, and visiting the many pilgrimage centers throughout Middle America. Drinking is part of the general behavior of the holiday period, mostly done in groups by adult males and rationalized as a means of escaping the harsh reality of everyday life. Most of the Ministry of Health statistics reveal that hospitalizations due to alcoholism and related physical effects (accidents and violent crimes), as well as emotional traumas (especially depression), are at their peak then and for a few weeks afterward.

In reference to major drinking patterns, the data of the 1980s and 1990s highlight some sociocultural traits. Most of the rural adult male population (68%) above twenty to thirty-five years of age are more involved in binge drinking; the more consistent and heavy drinkers are males forty-five and older. *Charamila, pachanga,* and *cususa* (moonshine or illegally distilled rum) are by far the most common beverages (97%). Local beer products and *guaro,* a legally distilled 90 proof rum, are the next most popular choices (Inestroza M. 1987). The profile for urban populations differs somewhat in terms of the frequency of drinking, with only half of the adult population being involved in frequent alcohol ingestion. Here, too, young and middle-aged males predominate (eight males to one female). The workforce in the large urban areas (especially Tegucigalpa, the capital) prefer beer (51%), followed by *aguardiente* (also called *guaro*), a legal distillate (38%); only a small number of urbanites drink moonshine (Zelaya 1990).

Information about drinking prior to 1975 provides little social information, but some insight can be gained from several studies on alcoholism that appeared in scientific journals. In 1967 a researcher who was invited to work in the recently founded psychiatric hospital reported evidence of past and present history of alcoholism in the psychiatric population (78% in males, 8% in females) (Hudgens 1967).

In 1974 the legal production of alcohol supported an average of one retail liquor store for every seventy-five persons over the age of fifteen years in Tegucigalpa (von Eicken 1974). A more recent study found three times as many outlets, an extreme density by international standards (Espinoza M. 1983).

Systematic research on alcohol consumption was introduced in Latin America by E. M. Jellinek. His focus-group method, used to explore the habits of alcohol ingestion in the general population, was carried out in Honduras by a group of researchers from the mental health branch of the Ministry of Health in 1979. Drinks of preference, by gender, in urban and rural settings, are quite pronounced, although "females imbibe alcohol covertly" and hence frequency is difficult to establish for them. Men drink in bars or away from home, whereas females who drink, do so in familiar settings, most likely at family celebrations or intimate friendly gatherings. It is a poor host who does not provide alcoholic beverages on social occasions. It is generally approved for the adult males to drink, even to intoxication; females are strongly discouraged from drinking at all, and those who do are generally not accepted. Women believe that men who drink in a social setting are a "real nuisance, but nevertheless must be endured" (Almendares B. 1979).

## VARIATIONS IN ALCOHOL CONSUMPTION AMONG ETHNIC MINORITIES

Honduras is a multiethnic and multi-cultural entity. It is host to a rich variety of ethnic minorities. The present estimate of the total indigenous population is about 387,500, who are distributed in groups that remain somewhat united by traditions, languages, and customs: Lencas, Garifunas, Miskitos, Tolupanes, Chortis, Pech, and Tawahkas (Chavez H. 1991). The Lencas, a group considered almost extinct, have at least one important celebration for the purpose of "unity, peace and friendship" among the tribes in the area that includes alcoholic beverages. This meeting of different tribesmen (*el Guancasco*) has been celebrated since before the coming of the Spaniards. It was, and is, an important occasion for dancing and drinking *chicha* and *chilates* (a nonalcoholic drink made from green corn). Since the Spanish colonization, this type of festivity has existed in the communities where Lenca ethnicity predominates. It even survives in combination with the celebrations of Catholic saints, whose figures are welcome guests. Other alcoholic beverages are becoming more popular due to their legal status (beer and sugarcane derivatives like *guaro* or aged rum). Clandestinely distilled beverages of sugarcane (*cususa* or *gato*) are still very popular among these groups. The Chorti Indians maintain their own cultural identity, including language, clothing, and diet. During festivities they ingest great quantities of fermented corn (a home brew called *morolonca*), as well as wines made from sugarcane, pineapple, and other fruits. Like other ethnic groups, they also ingest legal *aguardiente*.

The Afro-Honduran groups (Garifunas and Miskitos) are descendants of runaway black slaves who have very different drinking and eating habits that are strongly maintained as ritual practices. During the many rites and ceremonies dedicated to death (Digui) or fertility (La Punta), at dances and on many other symbolic occasions, eating and drinking are expressions of celebration, and intoxication is frequent. During these periods large quantities of a *chicha* fermented from the yucca plant, along with *aguardiente* and other fermented local plants, are consumed. There is a significant number of alcoholics and cigarette smokers among these populations, who mainly reside on the Atlantic coast.

## ATTITUDES AND LEARNING ABOUT ALCOHOL

Much of the information in this section comes from research by Honduran medical institutions to identify problems that may be due to excessive alcohol use. Alcohol ingestion often begins in family settings as early as eight to ten years of age, and becomes more of a habit in men fifteen to nineteen years old. One study reported sixteen as the average starting age for males diagnosed as alcoholic. The major reasons given for trying alcohol are (1) curiosity, in most cases, and (2) social and peer pressure as a facilitator. Most Hondurans continue to drink alcohol out of (1) habit, (2) friendship, and (3) desire for a leisure pastime. A study done in a rural western section of Honduras reviewed the general opinions that high school students and their teachers have about alcohol consumption. The data revealed that 72.5% of the teachers and 48.5% of the student body considered alcoholism an illness. Both groups agreed that this subject should be part of the educational curriculum. There are both similarities and differences in the drinking habits among the Honduran workforce, where 50–60% drinks at least once a month; only one in eight of them are female (Dickerman 1988). The predominantly male member of the rural workforce, the campesino (peasant), is a frequent alcohol consumer. In the major cities, his equivalent (*obrero,* or laborer) is a bachelor between twenty and twenty-nine years of age. The most frequently cited religious affiliation is Catholic, followed by several Protestant denominations (López 1990).

Beer is the most used and abused alcoholic beverage, followed by hard liquors (distillates) and home brews, according to each region's preference, availability, and price. Several important research studies covering alcohol consumption among high school students (based on a national survey conducted by the School of Medicine) report on both family and peer influences on the younger generation. Around 40% had ingested alcohol sometime during the preceding year; of these, 70% were fifteen to nineteen years old; they were 53% of the male students and 32% of the females. Also in this population, seventy admitted to having at least one alcoholic parent. The most frequent reasons given for drinking were to enjoy social interaction, and to be accepted by peers. In this population, 20% were smokers and around 3.5% used marijuana (Vittetoe B. 1990). In the adult population there were 57% smokers and up to 8.5% marijuana users, with some variations reported in other studies.

Ritual and festive drinking can frequently be excessive and even dangerous for a significant part of the population. These individuals, often called problem drinkers, who eventually may become alcoholics, are an important group. There are many of them, in rural as well as urban communities, and they produce serious socioeconomic consequences. In everyday language the term *estanco* is applied to the local bar or general store that sells alcoholic beverages; appropriately, alcoholics are referred to as *estancado,* which means "stalled" or stuck in one place."

Alcohol consumption and drunken behavior may lead to personal, familial, and more general social danger through violence or accidents. Another potential problem is economic stagnation due to unproductive activities. We also must pay attention to the whole community, and take into account the attitudes behind the drinking patterns that prevail. Among the more notorious is machismo, which, in combination with alcohol, can rapidly dominate any social interaction. Verbal and physical aggression are frequent, and result in resentment or even physical injury.

Currently Hondurans have a mixture of beer and spirits cultures of consumption (Heath 1989). Even though wines are imported for the upper classes, their ingestion is limited. Wine is preferred by women, but is not considered fit for men to drink.

In a less-developed society (such as most of the Third World), the drinking habits of the people have widespread social, economic, and political implications. This is especially noteworthy where the majority of the population suffers from tragically low family incomes, widespread unemployment, and frequent drinking. Under such conditions, drinking may be as much a symptom of problems as it is a cause. Thus, alcoholism or problem drinking becomes as much a social as an individual phenomenon that should be included in any searching discussion of public health and social welfare.

## REFERENCES

Alemán R., M. 1985. Características de los estudiantes de la Escuela Superior del Profesorado y su relación con la prevalencia del alcoholismo, uso de tabaco y drogas. Thesis. Universidad Nacional Autónoma de Honduras.

Almendares B., J. 1979. *Estudio del uso de alcohol y los problemas de alcoholismo en Honduras, usando el método de E. M. Jellinek.* Tegucigalpa: Ministerio de Salud Pública.

Amaya, D. 1990. Prevalencia del alcoholismo y tabaquismo en estudiantes de secundaria de Valle y Choluteca. Thesis. Universidad Nacional Autónoma de Honduras.

Bustamante, J. 1982. Investigación sobre alcoholismo y uso de alcohol en la ciudad de Nueva Ocotepeque. Thesis. Universidad Nacional Autónoma de Honduras.

Chávez Hernández, G. 1991. Antropología, alcoholismo, y drogadicción. Paper read at Seminario Internacional de Prevención y Tratamiento del Alcoholismo y Otras Adicciones. Tegucigalpa: Embajada de Israel.

Dickerman, A. 1988. Ingesta del alcohol y sus consecuencias en obreros de la industria manufacturera de Tegucigalpa afiliados al Instituto Hondureño de Seguridad Social. Thesis. Universidad Nacional Autónoma de Honduras.

Espinoza M., D. 1983. Algunos datos para el estudio del alcoholismo en Honduras durante la presente década. *Revista médica hondureña* 51:94–98.

Heath, D. B. 1989. Environmental factors in alcohol use and its outcomes. Pp. 312–324 in H. Werner Goedde and Dharam P. Agarwal (Eds.). *Alcoholism: Biomedical and Genetic Aspects*. New York: Pergamon Press.

Hudgens, R. 1967. *Informe de la psiquiatría en Honduras*. Tegucigalpa: Oficina Panamericana de Salud and Ministerio de Salud Pública.

Inestroza M., J. L. 1987. Bebidas alcohólicas: Aspectos medicales en la virtud. Thesis. Universidad Nacional Autónoma de Honduras.

López, J. 1990. Ingestión del alcohol y sus consecuencias en los trabajadores de la Empresa Asociativa Campesina Isletas, Departamento de Atlántida. Thesis. Universidad Nacional Autónoma de Honduras.

Sánchez, O. 1984. Aspectos históricos y psicosociales de alcoholismo en Honduras. *Revista médica hondureña* 52:210–216.

Vittetoe B., W. K. 1990. *Informe de la investigación sobre el uso y abuso de drogas en la ciudad de Tegucigalpa, D.C.* Tegucigalpa: Facultad de Medicina, Universidad Nacional Autónoma de Honduras.

Von Eicken, A. 1974. Estudio social del alcoholismo en Honduras. Thesis. Universidad Nacional Autónoma de Honduras.

Zapata M., J. W. 1985. Influencia de la destilería "El Buen Gusto" sobre la prevalencia de bebedores en la comunidad de Yuscarán. Thesis. Universidad Nacional Autónoma de Honduras.

Zelaya, M. 1990. Prevalencia de ingesta alcohólica en trabajadores de zapatería y mecánica automotriz en el Distrito Central, Departamento de Francisco Morazán. Thesis. Universidad Nacional Autónoma de Honduras.

# 12

## Iceland

### Gylfi Ásmundsson

Iceland is a large island, about the size of the state of Ohio, in the North Atlantic. It is a mountainous country with glaciers, volcanoes, and extensive lava fields. The climate is oceanic, with mild winters and cool summers. Only about a fifth of Iceland is habitable, and most of it is sparsely populated. The population was about 265,000 in 1994; the majority live in or near the capital, Reykjavík, on the southwest coast.

Iceland was settled in the 800s, mostly from Norway. Iceland was an independent nation with parliamentary rule (the Althing, established in 930) until 1262, when it came under the rule of Norway, and later of Denmark. Full sovereignty under the Danish king was granted in 1918, and Iceland became an independent republic in 1944.

Icelanders are very homogeneous with regard to ethnicity, religion, and language. They have been Christians since 1000. Since the Reformation in 1550, Lutheranism has been the national religion; very few Icelanders practice any other religion. The language, Icelandic, has changed little from that spoken all over Scandinavia in the Middle Ages, and historical, literary, and political ties have always been closest with the other Nordic countries. For centuries farming and fishing were virtually the only occupations. Literacy has long been relatively high, reading being a national pastime. This probably was mostly due to the early translation of the Bible into Icelandic and the widespread transcriptions of the Icelandic sagas.

Few European nations have experienced such rapid changes as Iceland has in the twentieth century. The population has more than tripled since 1900, and there have been revolutionary changes in both the structure of the society and the way of life, especially since World War II. At the beginning of the twentieth century, about 20% of the people lived in towns and villages and 80% in rural areas, but in the 1990s over 90% live in urban areas and nearly 60% in the capital area. The lifestyle has changed with more job opportunities and higher income, better housing, and a variety of leisure opportunities. The standard of living is similar to that of the other Scandinavian countries, among the highest in the world. Fishing is still the main source of income, but industry, commerce, and services are now the main occupations. Education and health services are good; life expectancy is among the highest in the world, and infant mortality among the lowest. A national health service has been in operation since 1936, providing almost free medical care for everybody. Old-age and disability insurance have been effective since the same time.

Alcohol has been used in Iceland since the beginning of its history, first in the form of homemade beer and since the 1400s increasingly in the form of distilled spirits. Annals of the 1700s contain the first mention that drinking was becoming a problem in Iceland, including a petition to the king of Denmark from the bishop of Skálholt asking for a total ban on the import of alcohol. In the petition it is stated that ''drinking is steadily increasing, both among learned and lay people, high and low, resulting in great damage and often serious accidents. Only in springtime, before the merchant ships arrive, is there reasonable safety from the plague of drinking in the country.'' This description may not have been an exaggeration, but it is possible that the reaction of the bishop reflected a changing attitude toward alcohol and drinking that followed the Lutheran Reformation. Lutheranism looked upon drinking as a social evil and a sin, and made people feel guilty about drinking. This view of alcohol seems to have settled in the national mind, and has characterized the alcohol policy and drinking culture in the country ever since.

In spite of heated discussions about the pros and the cons of alcohol, very few attempts have been made to provide objective analysis of the place of alcohol in Icelandic culture. Instead, arguments on both sides have been emotionally charged, and moderate evaluations have tended to be pushed aside.

## ALCOHOL CONSUMPTION AND POLICY

The registered consumption of alcohol in Iceland has always been rather low in comparison with other countries, and is still about the lowest in Europe. In the mid-1800s, it was about 5 liters per capita and almost entirely in the form of strong spirits, which were relatively inexpensive compared with wine. Beer was not brewed in the country, and imported beer was scarce.

During the last decades of the 1800s, there was a rise in the influence of the Youth Organization and the International Order of Good Templars, both of which opposed alcohol consumption. In 1910, consumption had decreased to 1.5 liters per capita for those fifteen and older. A total ban on the import of alcoholic beverages became effective in 1915 and lasted for seven years. The only exceptions were spirits for medical and industrial purposes. There was strong pressure from Spain, the main importer of Icelandic salted fish, to continue the sale of wine to Iceland in exchange for fish, and the ban was gradually lifted. In 1922, wine import was allowed again, but a stricter control was put on its sale by the establishment of a state monopoly (the State Wine, Spirits and Tobacco Authority) with a limited number of alcohol outlets. This monopoly is still in effect, and in 1928 a law was passed that banned all advertisements of alcoholic beverages in Icelandic media. The alcohol ban was further lifted in 1934 following a national referendum, and the import of spirits was resumed. The consensus did not, however, extend to the import or production of beer, and the ban on beer lasted until 1989.

Because Iceland was not a wine-drinking country and no alcoholic beer was allowed, consumption of alcohol during the period of prohibition was very low, according to sales figures. During the total ban (1915–1922), the sale of spirits for medical and industrial purposes accounted for about 0.4 liters of absolute alcohol per inhabitant, and that increased only to 0.6 liters after the wine ban was lifted. Illegal production of alcoholic beverages was, however, considerable during the ban years—naturally there are no records available. After the ban on spirits was lifted, total consumption rose to 1.31 liters per inhabitant fifteen years and older in 1935. The increase was entirely in spirits; the consumption of wine actually fell by three-fourths. Since 1935, the increase in consumption has been gradual; in 1988, the last year of the beer ban, it was 4.5 liters.

From then until the late 1960s the increase was entirely in strong spirits. In the 1970s the consumption of spirits remained stable, then dropped somewhat; at the same time the consumption of wine quadrupled.

The increase in aggregate consumption and changes in drinking habits have been affected by many factors, including tourism. Icelanders increasingly travel to other countries and experience different drinking habits. This has resulted in a general demand for the relaxation of restrictions on alcohol in Iceland, with more outlets for selling alcohol and a larger number of licensed restaurants and bars. A rapid increase in the number of tourists from abroad also has affected this demand and has led to availablity of alcoholic beverages, especially in the capital area, similar to that in most Western countries.

Alcoholic beer, which had been prohibited in Iceland for almost eighty years, was legalized in 1989. Its legalization resulted in a jump in consumption to 5.5 liters of absolute alcohol per person that year, but it has gradually decreased to its former level of 4.5 liters. The long-term effects of the addition of beer to the Icelandic drinking culture remain to be seen.

## SOCIAL NORMS AND MAJOR DRINKING PATTERNS

Since the 1890s there have been changes and fluctuations in drinking practices in Iceland, mostly influenced by better communications and relations with other countries and national restrictions. Traditional norms and attitudes toward alcohol and drinking, however, seem to be less affected by these changes and continue to mark the Icelandic drinking culture.

Prior to prohibition, spirits were the main alcoholic beverages, probably because of their quick intoxicating effects and their relatively low prices in comparison with wine and beer. The period when Spanish wines were the only imports did not alter this much, and it seems that most of those who consumed alcohol at the time preferred homemade spirits. After the ban was lifted, Icelanders returned to their former habits, and spirits constituted about 90% of their alcohol intake until the 1970s.

Since the mid-1970s there have been noteworthy changes in drinking practices in Iceland. Relatively more people drink and new groups have become consumers, notably younger people and women. Although those groups drink to a far greater extent than before, on the whole, people tend to drink more often, less at a time, and weaker drinks. During the same period, total consumption leveled off; the proportional consumption of spirits dropped from 90% to about 65%, with a corresponding increase in wine drinking. This development was probably a result of both price policy and changes in drinking habits caused by tourism and influences from abroad. The traditional drinking habits seem, however, to survive along with the new drinking patterns in Icelandic culture; during the five years prior to the legalization of beer (1984–1988), the proportion of spirits consumed increased to about 75%, probably due to a change in price policy that resulted in higher wine prices.

Legalizing beer in 1989, after almost eighty years of its being prohibited, was a very radical step in Icelandic alcohol policy, and it is still too early to estimate the long-term effects of this decision on drinking practices and culture in Iceland. In the first year, the aggregate consumption of absolute alcohol rose by 23%, but it has been gradually decreasing since then. The distribution of sales (1993) is 50% spirits, 17% wine, and 33% beer. Beer-drinking is kept in check by relatively very high prices; nevertheless, a substantial proportion of the alcohol intake is in the form of beer and seems to have resulted to a considerable degree in new drinking practices where intoxication is a less prominent feature of the drinking situation.

The most characteristic features of the twentieth-century Icelandic drinking culture have probably been the low level of aggregate consumption of alcohol per capita, and the high frequency of intoxication and even drunkenness. This reflects a typical Northern pattern of drinking, wherein extensive restrictions and high prices of alcoholic beverages keep the consumption down and result in sporadic relaxation of personal control, especially on festive occasions, when the goal is to get drunk and "have a good time." There are similar styles in Finland, Norway, Sweden, Russia, and arctic areas of America.

The general attitude toward alcohol and drinking is ambivalent. On the one hand, alcohol is considered potentially dangerous and is commonly blamed for most social problems. On the other hand, it is associated with pleasure and, for most people, is an indispensable accompaniment to festive occasions. Alcohol is valued mainly for its intoxicating effects. In an international study of Nordic drinking habits and attitudes toward alcohol, Icelanders evaluated intoxication higher than alcohol, in contrast with the other Nordic countries (Hauge and Irgens-Jensen 1987). When Icelanders buy alcoholic beverages, they look for those with the highest alcohol content relative to price. Alcohol is not a daily commodity, and wine-drinking with meals is still uncommon, although it is on the increase.

The traditional drinking habits in Iceland prescribe drinking only on well-defined occasions, where both drinking and intoxication are culturally accepted. The use of alcohol on weekends has been a characteristic of the drinking culture in Icelandic society. After a hard week's work, people feel that they are entitled to relax and have a good time. Entertainment during weekends has primarily been associated with drinking. When young people, in particular, ask each other: "Did you entertain yourself last night?" they may get the answer "No, I went to the theater." "Entertainment" means going to a dance, a restaurant, or a bar, where drinking is a major activity. Strong norms, however, keep drinking and working apart (Ásmundsson and Ólafsdóttir 1986). Drinking with daily meals is rare, and according to regular drinking surveys in Iceland, only about 2.5% drank alcohol more than once a week in 1974, increasing to 5% in 1989. In spite of a low level of aggregate consumption and infrequent drinking sessions, the frequency of intoxication is higher than that in the other Nordic countries, which have much higher aggregate consumption (Helgason 1978; Hauge and Irgens-Jensen 1987).

The Youth Organization, established in Iceland around the beginning of the twentieth century, had a great impact, especially on abstinence. The Abstinence Movement became very strong in the first half of the twentieth century and had a large membership. In the 1990s both seem to have lost their influence, as is evident in a steady decrease in the number of abstainers in the country. Its impact on Icelandic society is, however, still very evident in many respects. Many of the norms regarding alcohol that were based on the ideology of the Abstinence Movement are still highly effective.

Some of the norms and attitudes toward alcohol and drinking in Iceland that are most resistant to change probably have their roots in the Reformation of the 1500s. They are based on the teaching that alcohol is bad and that it is shameful to have it around, never mind drinking it and becoming intoxicated. Alcohol was treated with the utmost discretion by most respectable people, and this attitude is still quite prevalent. Being seen buying a bottle or carrying it around was bound to raise eyebrows and start gossip. The alcohol culture has thus been characterized by strong guilt feelings. Some of the old norms still prevail to a considerable extent, especially among middle-aged and older people.

One does not drink in the presence of children. Thus, there are strong norms against serving alcohol at christenings or confirmation parties. It is not appropriate to drink at home, the sanctuary of the family. A bottle of wine or spirits is not supposed to be visible. It is locked in a cupboard when not in use; when people are drinking at a party or in company, the bottle is placed under the table. One drinks only in well-defined situations, at special celebrations like round-number birthdays, having a special dinner at a restaurant, attending the annual ball of an organization, or celebrating New Year's Eve. On such occasions it is quite normal to become intoxicated. If a person drinks in a different fashion or under other circumstances, it produces a strong feeling of guilt and he or she becomes afraid of being an alcoholic.

There seem to be relatively more alcoholics in Iceland than in most other countries, although the aggregate alcohol consumption is about the lowest known among Western societies. Hospital admissions for alcoholism in Iceland have increased tremendously since the 1970s. At the end of 1985, 3.6% of the adult population had been admitted at least once for alcohol treatment. In the 1990s there are probably more hospital beds for alcohol treatment in Iceland than in any other country (Ólafsdóttir and Helgason 1988).

This phenomenon may have a psychological explanation. Restrictions on alcohol have been relaxed for a relatively short time, and the old, strict norms regarding drinking and alcohol are being seriously violated. These changes were particularly rapid in the 1970s, and it is hardly a coincidence that in the years immediately following, there was an explosive increase in the treatment of alcoholism in spite of no change in aggregate consumption. The guilt feeling, resulting from breaking the old norms regarding alcohol use, possibly became manifested through more and more people feeling they were becoming alcoholics. This hypothesis must, of course, remain speculative pending further research.

One of the strongest norms, still highly effective, is that alcohol and work are entirely separate. Drinking during working hours is considered a serious symptom of alcoholism. To take even a glass of wine or beer with lunch on a workday is considered a breach of this norm. When the prohibition of beer was repealed in 1989, many employers were afraid that people would start drinking during work hours, and some put up signs saying that this was forbidden. The prevailing norms were, however, probably much more effective in preventing drinking during working hours, and in the 1990s there are still no signs that drinking at work or problems in that respect are any more prominent than before.

## VARIANT DRINKING PATTERNS

As mentioned above, Iceland is an uncommonly homogeneous nation. About 98% of the population are of the same ethnic origin and adhere to the same religion. They can, however, be divided into demographic subgroups with regard to their alcohol practices, in particular according to sex, age, occupation, and residence. There is more drinking in densely populated areas than in the countryside, and people of higher education and occupation tend to drink more often, less at a time, and weaker drinks.

As in other countries, there are more abstainers among women, and those who do consume alcohol drink, on the average, much less than do men. This difference is rapidly decreasing, however. In 1974, when the first survey of alcohol practices among the population twenty to forty-nine years of age was carried out in Iceland, there were 26% women abstainers and 10% men abstainers. Ten years later, the figures were 18% and 8%, respectively.

Tourists who come to Iceland often mention the public drunkenness among youngsters. Children and youths in Iceland probably have more freedom than their peers in most other Western countries and become independent earlier. The workload of the average Icelander is quite high. A full-time job in most occupations is defined as forty hours a week, but a recent survey by the Icelandic Statistical Bureau shows that men work an average of fifty-five hours a week, and most women have at least a part-time job. Children and young people are, therefore, left very much on their own. Traditionally, they start earning their own pocket money early, doing newspaper routes or running errands, making them economically independent to a certain extent. Schools take a three-month break during the summer, and most teenagers get a summer job in the fishing, farming, or building industry. This is possible because for decades there has often been a shortage of manpower, and also because there is a greater demand for workers during the short Icelandic summer. This has made Icelandic youngsters more self-sufficient than their peers elsewhere and may partly explain their drinking behavior during their less responsible years. Survey results show high alcohol consumption among adolescence, although the legal age for buying alcohol is twenty years. Young people aged eighteen to twenty-five are the highest consumers, but most of them change their drinking habits toward more moderate and responsible use of alcohol when they settle down with a family and a permanent job.

As among the general adult population, drinking among young people is intermittent and to a great extent takes place on special occasions. The most noteworthy occasions are the Whitsun weekend in late May or early June, and especially the first weekend in August, which is followed by a national holiday on Monday. On both occasions it is traditional for youngsters to gather at camping places in the countryside with rock music, dancing, and general merrymaking. These gatherings can be rowdy with a lot of hazardous drinking, sometimes resulting in accidents. On other occasions the drinking behavior of youngsters becomes very visible in the capital area: at the end of the school year, when they gather in the city center; on National Day in June; and sometimes in the autumn, when they have their summer earnings to spend on a last spree just before school starts. The youngsters' drinking may be looked upon partly as coming of age, and at the same time it is probably a rebellion against their parents.

Traditional Icelandic drinking habits are probably most significant among the two oldest occupational groups, farmers and seamen, although in a different way. Both drink intermittently and mostly spirits; but on the average farmers drink far less than seamen, and among them there are relatively more abstainers. Farm work is not compatible with drinking, but farmers still have their special drinking occasions, mostly away from home. The farmers' major occasion for drinking is at the annual autumn roundup of sheep and horses from their summer pastures on the heaths and mountains. In some areas it is up to a week's journey to the interior for the farmers and their farmhands to gather their flock. On a certain date, thousands of sheep and horses flow into the regional corral and everybody in the area, as well as many visitors from the towns, help in getting the animals to the right owners and enjoy the major social event of the farming community. Most of the men bring a bottle of liquor with them and offer each other a sip. There is much singing and spirits are high, but major drunkenness is exceptional. In the evening there may be a dance at the local social center; until recently, people brought their own liquor and hid the bottles under the tables because these places usually were not licensed. This behavior is disappearing as restrictions on licensing disappear.

For many farmers the autumn roundup and celebration are the only drinking occasion of the year. Other occasions may be horseback riding or a fishing trip at the end of the haying period in the summer. In fact, alcohol is generally a common companion on riding and fishing trips, which are popular in Iceland. Fishing in particular is a male sport in which a group of friends spend a few days out in nature, undisturbed by their wives. At home, as in many other countries, women, as wives and mothers, have an important controlling role in family drinking.

Seamen are the occupational group in Iceland that has been most extensively studied with regard to alcohol consumption. They are most at risk for alcohol problems. Typically they drink infrequently, but large quantities at a time—sometimes for two or three days, or until it is time for another fishing trip, on which they will not touch alcohol for two to three weeks or more. Theirs is a typically Icelandic drinking pattern carried to the extreme. It is liable to result in accidents and arrests by the police for drunkenness. Fatal accidents are very frequent among seamen in Iceland, not only during their time at sea but also, and to an even greater extent, while they are on shore. These accidents are frequently alcohol-related. Investigations in the other Nordic countries have shown similar results.

A special occasion for seamen to have a good time with their peers and a bottle of liquor is the annual Seamen's Holiday in early June. This is a major festive occasion in the fishing towns and villages along the coast, and is often characterized by drunkenness into the early hours of the morning.

However, it is a very strong norm among Icelandic seamen not to drink during their fishing trips at sea. In recent years, this is probably stronger than ever, especially on the deep-sea trawlers, where crews have to operate dangerous, complicated, and expensive equipment, often in very bad weather. It has been suggested that fishing in the North Atlantic may be one of the most hazardous occupations in the world.

For that reason, seamen generally keep away from alcohol for long periods of time, although their drinking habits in between are socially evident. The same still applies on the whole to the drinking pattern of the Icelandic public in general; people drink a lot at a time, but infrequently. They keep their drinking and work entirely separate, and the traditional drinking habits are still strong enough to prevent beer-drinking from becoming a part of the workday, which many people feared would happen with the legalization of alcoholic beer.

## THE FORMATION OF DRINKING BEHAVIOR

The norms regarding alcohol do not encourage drinking at home or in the presence of children. Thus, children and adolescents do not generally learn from their parents how to handle alcoholic beverages. The message of most parents to their children is that alcohol is bad, and they should keep away from it. This means that the children have to turn elsewhere for guidance, and usually start experimenting within their own peer groups. Surveys indicate that the majority of Icelandic adolescents have their first experience with alcohol at fourteen to sixteen years of age, usually in the company of others their age. Thus drinking symbolizes an act of independence or coming of age from the outset. Later, for many adolescents drunkenness becomes a way of showing open rebellion against their parents.

The act of secret drinking with one's peers is bound to lead to closer ties and is important in establishing friendships (Pinson 1985). Under the influence of alcohol, adolescents share secrets, and this can to lead to the formation of closely knit small groups, especially of schoolmates. Drinking together seems to have played this role in boys' groups in particular, and continues into adulthood, when drinking is still an important part of get-togethers, such as fishing trips.

The typical Icelander drinks primarily to get intoxicated. The social act of lifting a glass at a marriage reception or sipping wine at a dinner party is part of a ceremony, but has little to do with enjoying the drink. Taking a glass or two before dinner without any intoxicating effects is seen as a waste of good liquor. Of course, there is the exceptional minority who have cultivated a taste for good wine and enjoy an occasional glass of whiskey or brandy. But for most people, the intoxicating effects and the associated conviviality of the group are the main functions of alcohol.

In Icelandic surveys, respondents have been asked about their main reasons for consuming alcohol. Very few mention that it is customary in their peer group or that they do not want to be different from others. Most people say they drink to have a good time, to become free of social and emotional constraints, and to get into closer contact with other people. In the alcohol survey done in four Nordic countries (Hauge and Irgens-Jensen 1987), there were also questions about the benefits of drinking. Icelanders, more often than the other groups, answered "becomes more optimistic," "can express my feelings better," and "becomes more interesting, entertaining and fluent in conversations."

Icelanders have been considered a rather closed people, difficult to get to know and apathetic to strangers at first. However, when they make friends, it is usually a lasting relationship. It is typically started over a few glasses, often followed by intoxication and an intimate personal discussion. The psychological functions of alcohol, especially as facilitating interpersonal relationships, are therefore of major importance for the typically introverted Icelander.

Although the initiation of a relationship under the influence of alcohol can lead to good friendship, especially between members of the same sex, it is also liable to have adverse effects, notably when a relationship leading to marriage is started that way. The spouses may subsequently have difficulties in an intimate relationship without the use of alcohol, which can hinder the relationship in other contexts, such as dealing with everyday problems. The most common cause for divorce in Iceland is an alcohol problem, especially the husband's. In a study of pair relationships and family life in Iceland (Júlíusdóttir and Ásmundsson 1990), the wives rated alcohol problems as the most important reason for divorce, higher than adultery or loss of love.

Most of the small minority of abstainers claim they have no need for alcohol; the second most frequent reason is setting a good example for children. A considerable proportion are afraid of becoming dependent on alcohol and fear that their work would suffer if they started to drink. Their fear of alcohol is also a reflection of the general attitude that alcohol is a dangerous substance to play with and a potential source of evil.

## RECENT DEVELOPMENTS

Iceland is probably in a transitional period with regard to drinking practices and attitudes toward alcohol. The traditional drinking habits are still strong and seem to coexist with emerging patterns reflecting a more international and liberal approach to alcohol.

The most recent surveys on drinking practices in Iceland, done after the legalization of beer in 1989, reveal two main drinking patterns that seem to be associated with education and occupational groups. On the one hand, there are people who are predominantly spirits drinkers, and the availability of beer does not affect their consumption of spirits. Beer becomes partly a substitute for wine, but to a greater extent is an addition to its consumption. This group consists mainly of skilled and unskilled workers, seamen, and farmers. Intoxication is their main reason for drinking. On the other hand, there is a smaller group dominated by white-collar professionals and administrators. Wine is a much larger proportion of their alcohol consumption, and is not affected by their beer consumption, which instead reduces their consumption of spirits. Their total consumption remains unchanged. They drink more frequently and smaller amounts at a time. They enjoy a drink before dinner and a glass of good wine with meals; their intent is not necessarily to become intoxicated.

These two patterns represent the old and the new drinking habits of Icelanders. Wine has been gaining popularity since the 1970s; the introduction of beer is a new development with uncertain results. Alcoholic beer was rarely available until 1989 and, because of its scarcity, the demand for it was great. In fact, there is not yet a beer-drinking culture in Iceland. When the ban was lifted, the main question was whether there would be a short-term beer rush while people satisfied their curiosity, followed by a gradual return to the drinking of spirits, or whether beer-drinking would become a substantial and permanent feature of Icelandic drinking culture, either as a substitute or as an addition to the other alcoholic beverages.

In fact, the legalization of beer in Iceland may affect people very differently. For some, beer is a substitute for spirits; for others, beer is a substitute for wine. But to a great extent it is an addition to the total consumption. Which pattern will survive in the coming years remains to be seen.

Icelanders are more and more becoming a part of the international community. National traditions tend to break down and fade away. There is evidence that the Nordic, Protestant attitudes toward alcohol are changing, leading to more moderate drinking practices but, at the same time, increased consumption of alcohol. Whether this is good or bad will continue to be a subject of heated controversy in the Icelandic debate on alcohol and drinking.

## REFERENCES

Ásmundsson, G., T. Helgason, and J. Bergsveinsson. 1979. Alkoholvaner i Island. *Nordisk psykiatrisk tidskrift* 33:225–234.

Ásmundsson, G., and H. Ólafsdóttir. 1986. Alcohol problems in Iceland 1930–1980: A study of medical and social problems in relation to the development of alcohol consumption. Mimeographed report.

Hauge, R., and O. Irgens-Jensen. 1987. Alkoholen i Norden (Alcohol in the Nordic countries). Supplement to *Alkoholpolitik* (Alcohol Policy) 4.

Helgason, T. 1978. Alkoholvaner i Island: Beskrivelse og sammenligning med det övrige Norden (Alcohol practices in Iceland: A description and comparison with the other Nordic countries). *Alkohol och narkotika* 72:17–27.

Helgason, T., H. Ólafsdóttir, and K. Tómasson. 1983. Nýgengi drykkjusýki og áfengismisnotkunar (The incidence of alcoholism and alcohol abuse). *Læknablaðið* (Icelandic Medical Journal) 17.

Júlíusdóttir, S., and G. Ásmundsson. 1990. Isländska par—kärlek, barn och arbete (Icelandic couples—love, children and work) Pp. 21–60 in *Kærlighed og ligestilling* (Love and equality). Copenhagen: Nordisk Ministerråd.

Ólafsdóttir, H. 1972. Unglingar og áfengi (Youth and Alcohol): Könnun á áfengisneyslu unglinga í Reykjavík árið 1972. *Félagsmálastofnun Reykjavíkurborgar.*

Ólafsdóttir, H., and T. Helgason. 1988. Innlagningar á meðferðarstofnanir vegna áfengis og annarra vímuefna 1975–1985 (Admissions to inpatient wards for alcohol and drug abuse 1975–1985). *Læknablaðið* (Icelandic medical journal) 74(4):165–167.

Pinson, Ann. 1985. The institution of friendship and drinking patterns in Iceland. *Anthropological Quarterly* 58(2):75–82.

# 13

# India

## Davinder Mohan and H. K. Sharma

### WHY ALCOHOL IS NOTEWORTHY IN INDIA

All cultures possess a set of ideal attitudes toward the consumption of, or abstention from, alcoholic beverages, and define the expected and prohibited behaviors while drinking. Pittman (1964), outlining the basis for study of attitudes toward alcohol, conceptualizes four cultural settings: (1) abstinent cultures, which condemn the use of alcoholic beverages in any form, such as Muslims and ascetic Protestants; (2) ambivalent cultures, in which sternly negative and prohibitive attitudes coexist with attitudes idealizing intoxication, such as the English-speaking and Scandinavian nations; (3) permissive cultures, which tolerate moderate consumption but condemn excessive drinking, such as Jews and Italians; (4) overly permissive cultures, in which the prevalent attitude is permissive toward drinking alcohol, and drunkenness is generally accepted in certain contexts, such as the French and the Japanese.

Western readers may be surprised that India does not neatly fit into any of the above conceptualization, inasmuch as traits of both abstinence and permissiveness toward drinking exist across the Indian population. The contemporary drinking scene reflects changes that have taken place in social, political, and economic spheres since independence in 1947. After winning independence from Great Britain, India decided on centrally planned economic development through successive five-year plans. The trends in the planning process were strongly influenced by Fabian philosophy and, in practice, by the Marxist socialist framework. The state assumed a paternalistic role, a welfare stance supporting the development of core industries. Successive five-year plans led to large-scale industrialization and vastly improved agriculture. India tripled its food grain production in the 1970s, attaining self-sufficiency, and it has been able further to diversify its industrial infrastructure. However, there have been some internal conflicts (verbal, intellectual, and sometimes even armed) and differing perceptions about these changes.

Kuppuswamy (1981) describes Indian society as having three main features. First is its ability to accommodate a wide spectrum of groups and views. There are relatively isolated tribes, and India also accepts an individual like Sannyasi (a famous Hindu religious mendicant) who opts out of the existing social framework. Second, the social structure as laid out by the semilegendary lawgiver Manu about 200 B.C. set strict rules for societal behavior and hierarchy. Despite attempts at reform from time to time, his influence has persisted and still strongly governs rural and, to a lesser extent, urban life. Manu's classification into *varnas* (castes) has survived. It has been both a source of strength and a major impediment to social change and economic development. Third, the ancient Indian concepts of life and society continue to play a vital role in the 1990s.

The processes of social change constitute what Srinivas (1966) labeled "Sanskritisation." In essence, the lower caste groups, as they gain upward mobility, will attempt progressively to adopt the norms of upper castes, the highest among whom are the Brahmans. Alongside this gradual homogenizing of culture, there has been a predominantly urban trend to modernize "untouchables" toward the higher castes. This has been broadly identified with adoption of Western lifestyles, acquisition of material goods, and growth in consumerism (Srinivas 1966). In spite of almost half a century of independence, India has not been able to shake the pull of its cultural heritage. These conflicts and changes have been reflected in the use of psychoactive substances in the following major ways:

1. The use of plant products such as marijuana and opium decreased in rural areas where agricultural advances took place. Home brewing of alcohol remained a cottage industry, and the use of commercially produced alcohol was grafted onto it (Mohan and Sharma 1983).

2. Distilled spirits (with much higher ethanol content) emerged as a major preference among consumers, attracting new drinkers from previously abstinent urban social groups who had no prior experience with home brews and could be viewed as naive with regard to all alcoholic beverages (Mohan and Sharma 1983). In both rural and urban areas, this process accelerated with a rise in disposable incomes. Although it was difficult to pinpoint specific reasons for the increasing consumption of licitly brewed and distilled alcohol in India, it may be a part of the broader social and attitudinal changes leading to a more consumeristic society that has been developing along with adoption of Western-oriented lifestyles. Alcohol has become an essential component of this change since the 1940s, and especially since the 1970s.

3. The percentage of beverage alcohol (among total alcohol produced), around 2.07% between 1951 and 1955, rose to 42.14% by the end of 1980. The increase was constant except between 1960 and 1965, when it declined by 3 percent. Explosive growth occurred between 1965 and 1980, during which there was a four-fold rise. This coincided with the emergence of regional political parties throughout the country. The

Indian National Congress Party had begun to lose sway in many of the states. Strains developed in the center-state relations, and the institutional structures of the states and the union were affected.

When the rise of potable alcohol production is examined in terms of preferred beverages, it is evident that there had been an unannounced shift in alcohol policy around 1966 on the part of the federal government. Beer production shows a linear rise from 1966 through the 1980s. Clearly, Directive Principle 47 of the national constitution of India had been ignored by the state, without any public discussion. It reads, in part: "The State shall regard the raising of the level of nutrition and the standard of living of its people and the improvement of public health as among its primary duties and in particular, the State shall endeavor to bring about prohibition of the consumption, except for medicinal purposes, of intoxicating drinks and of drugs which are injurious to health." India may be the only country that so recently had such an explicit position on alcohol and drugs written into its constitution.

The political ethos and the politicians who had strong convictions about enforcing prohibition have been claimed by the passage of time. Since politicians, administrators, and the nouveau riche are now all of the postindependence era, they do not have the moral commitment that fueled the struggle for independence, including prohibition.

## ALCOHOL IN HISTORY

Panchandikar (1965) summarized four stages of Indian civilization, based on sociocultural factors: (1) evolution from ancient history to the post-Vedic period, including Buddhism and Jainism; (2) reinterpretation of Vedic norms between about 700 and 1200; (3) trends under the impact of Moghal rule in India (about 1200–1700); (4) impact of British colonial rule (about 1800–present). Our discussion of the initial two stages explores alcohol use within the broad framework of Hinduism and its offshoots. Our discussion of the third and fourth stages examines the impact of Islam, particularly Moghal rule, and British colonial rule.

### Evolution through Ancient History, to 700

Hinduism has always stressed abstinence from alcohol through its religious scriptures (*Puranas, Sutras,* and *Smritis*). It has been described as a way of life rich in diversity, and as an amalgamation of Aryan and Dravidian cultures. Folklore and mythology provide interesting accounts of early alcoholic beverages. *Soma* and *sura* were the two common beverages in India around 2000 B.C. The experience of drinking *soma* was said to be transcendentally blissful, enlightening, and tranquilizing, creating euphoric states, stimulating both mind and body (Chand 1972). The experience of drinking *soma* (perhaps derived from the hallucinogenic mushroom fly agaric) was regarded as a high privilege, and no price was too great (Huxley 1960).

*Sura* appears to have been a strong beer produced from rice, jaggery (crude palm molasses), and blossoms of the *mahuwa* tree. Its use was common among the warriors (Kshatriyas), as a part of their fighting ethos, and among the original Dravidians in southern India, where toddy-tapping from palm trees was common. Individuals consumed two fermented variants of it, *ira* and *masura.* The effects described ranged from moderate euphoria to intoxication (Dikshitar 1951).

The two great Indian epic legends, *Ramayana* and *Mahabharata,* mention the use of alcohol. In *Ramayana,* alcohol consumption is depicted in black-and-white terms, a bad/good dichotomy. The bad faction members consumed alcohol and meat; the good faction members were abstinent vegetarians. In *Mahabharata,* the characters are not portrayed in simple black-and-white terms, but in shades of gray as well. In fact, a warrior dynasty of *Mahabharata* is said to have disintegrated because of a curse due to fighting among themselves while inebriated (Jha 1924).

In the post-Vedic era, *sura* was allowed to the warrior group, especially in time of war (Prakash 1961). The many themes and images associated with drinking then centered on rulers and courtiers. In the Sutra period (800–300 B.C.), strong alcoholic beverages were served to guests on certain occasions (Praskara 1956). There were bureaucrats who supervised alcohol sales, to check on the status and ancestry of the purchasers (Sastri 1925). The main feature of the Vedic and post-Vedic periods was ritual drinking. It was not considered to be a daily event. Although no prohibitive edicts were issued, inebriation was severely censured and abstinence was held in high esteem (Chand 1972). Brahmans (the learned men) were forbidden to use alcohol or any other intoxicant; members of other castes (Kshatriyas, Vaishyas, and Sudras) were allowed to drink. Because non-Brahmans were permitted alcohol, as well as for other reasons, they could not attain a high state of religious purity (Jha 1926).

Buddhism, another major religion, originated around 700 B.C. as an Indian offshoot from mainstream Hinduism. As a social reform movement, it spread to several neighboring Southeast Asian countries. Buddhism prohibited drinking by monks and in monasteries, and the commandments of Buddha counseled general abstention from alcohol. Emperor Ashoka (185 B.C.), a disciple of Buddha, facilitated the spread of Buddhism in India and along with it, abstinence from alcohol as one of its basic tenets. *Ahimsa* (nonviolence), utilized as a part of India's freedom struggle from 1910 to 1947, was another Buddhist tenet.

## Reinterpretation and Synthesis: 700–1100

This period in Hinduism saw an attempt to reconcile orthodox Vedic views with subsequent developments, including the emergence of Buddhism and Jainism. It was a period of synthesis among Hindus. Alcohol consumption was prevalent in a considerable section of the Hindu society, especially home-brewed, low-alcohol beers (Prakash 1961). In the tale *Sukrantisara,* fermentation of wine is described in detail as an art. Among the warrior groups, the earlier permissive attitude toward alcohol consumption continued, with additional acceptance of women's use during festive occasions (Medhatithi 1939).

### The Impact of Islam: 1100–1800

Islamic rule was preceded by a series of invasions, the primary purpose of which was to capture wealth. Only the Moghuls (from Persia) attempted to settle, and built an empire. They brought with them many aspects of Islamic culture; Persian remained the court script and the language of the elite for a long time. Although the Moghuls were initially very puritanical in their approach to alcohol, wine subsequently became a part of the court life, used by courtiers and nobles alike. In fact, the poetry of the period often alludes to the dilemma of drinking wine, which, although opposed by the edicts of the Koran, was extolled for its virtues. The Hindu society, in order to handle forcible conversion to Islam, became more introverted and rigid in following the Vedic and post-Vedic codes of behavior and attitudes toward alcohol. The introverted attitudes brought many undesirable social practices, such as child marriage and female infanticide, which were not present earlier but became part of the subsequent culture. The attitudes of Islam and of Hinduism were essentially convergent on the subject of alcohol consumption, favoring prohibition.

### British Colonial Rule and Independence: 1800–present

British colonial rule in India had a significant impact on alcohol production and consumption. The colonial government, in order to reduce import costs, set up a brewery within the country. Once the brewery was established, the Indian National Congress called on the government to take steps to discourage insobriety and even consumption. In response to this, the British set up the Indian Excise Committee (in 1905), which developed the policy aimed at controlling any rise in consumption by increasing taxation. It advised that taxation on potable beverages be at a level where consumption by regular drinkers would be decreased and few new drinkers would begin. It was assumed that this would balance out and not lead to any loss of tax revenue. The report of this committee was the guiding principle in controlling alcohol availability after 1905, persisting even after independence.

The broad alliance engaged in the struggle for independence also helped the Indian National Congress, much as had happened in the pre-prohibition period in the United States. The movement against alcohol drew strength largely from the leadership, most of whom had been educated in the United Kingdom at the turn of the century and were strongly influenced by Western ideas, including temperance and prohibition. The linkage of alcohol with the independence agenda served to give a broad base to the movement. It included the scheduled (lower) castes, who traditionally were permitted to drink, and women, who otherwise would have been left out of the struggle for freedom. Picketing of alcohol sellers was a major activity of women's groups. This alliance, although initially merely expedient, was over time consolidated, as had occurred in the early phases of the temperance movement in the United States that led to prohibition (Aaron and Musto 1981). In India there were no grounds nor historical basis for the separate evolution of a temperance movement. As a part of the struggle for independence, this focused idealism got prohibition incorporated into the constitution.

India participated willingly in World War I. This was done on an implicit understanding with the British government that after the end of war, India would be given home rule, as a preparatory step toward full independence. The war provided the opportunity for many ordinary Indians to be introduced to alcoholic beverages. The returning veterans brought a drinking tradition back with them, as a part of the fighting ethos. This was easy to sustain whether they stayed in the service or retired, because the armed forces canteen stores (PXs) sold alcohol at subsidized prices, a practice that continues today.

The opening of the Indian Civil Service (ICS) to Indians introduced alcohol to many educated Indians from higher castes. Toward the end of World War I, there was a small but growing sector among the population (from the ICS to soldiers, from commoners to royal princes, who had been in the United Kingdom to study, to fight, or to spend leisure time) to whom alcohol was a status symbol of identification with the rulers. World War II saw an even larger mobilization of Indian troops, who fought both in Asia and in Europe, where many acquired the alcohol habit. In the interim, home rule was granted in 1935, after continuing political dialogue during which the Congress legislated prohibition in all of the federated states.

After India gained independence, attempts were made to implement Article 47 of the constitution. However, a major problem was noticed in another part of the constitution. Policies on alcohol were made subject to state control, so that each state could frame its own laws. Immediately after independence the Indian National Congress, which had led the struggle for freedom, was in power at both the federal and state levels. It assumed that there would be no conflicts between the federal and state governments, and that single-party rule would continue indefinitely.

Those assumptions soon proved to be erroneous. By 1951, the states of Bombay and Madras introduced prohibition (Bombay Prohibition Act 1949; Madras Prohibition Act 1937/66 modified). Other Congress-ruled states did not feel the need for framing any laws because neither alcohol production nor its consumption was an important issue. In any case, they assumed that they would have enough time to develop policy. The purely advisory role of the federal government was handled by a standing committee that had both official and unofficial members from the federal and state governments. It had a social welfare orientation, and its recommendations were not binding on the state governments.

## MAJOR DRINKING PATTERNS

Unlike China and Japan, India essentially never accepted alcohol as a part of normal social discourse or eating behavior, nor ritualized consumption as a part of religion. Hence, there is a virtual absence of "normative patterns" of drinking alcohol and attitudes toward it. Dube (1965) strove to identify the cultural and ideological patterns of pluralistic Indian society as traditional (regional and local) and nontraditional; these categories are applicable to alcohol consumption patterns.

The traditional drinking pattern reflects the tribal drinking patterns of about 8.8% of the total Indian population (according to the 1981 census). Tribal groups in India are scattered in the northeast, the north central area, and on several southern islands. The federal government created special provisions and set aside funds to bring them into the mainstream. Almost fifty years after independence, the process is still incomplete. In Indian tribal cultures, alcohol, as a natural product, was perceived to be a gift to humankind and in turn was reverently offered to the nature gods and other sacred powers (Rao and Rao 1976). The Bondo and the Muria tribal populations traced the discovery of "mahua spirit" (made from flowers of the *madhyaka* tree) to Mahaprabhu, their supreme god. They equated alcohol with Mother Earth's milk, on which they lived and fed. To Murias, the drinking of alcohol was both a duty and a pleasure.

In Indian tribal conceptions, alcohol was also an antidote against sorcery, witchcraft, and black magic. It served as protection against attack from enemies, and could be used to attack one's enemies or to ward off spirits thought to bring drought or disease. It was also the primitive substitute for modern legal documents; a word given on drinks had the sanctity of a legal document. Among the Kondadoras of Vishakapatnam (in central India), alcohol played an important role at all stages from negotiation to solemnization of marriage. Among the Koyas, marriages were celebrated with toddy (a type of alcohol made from palm nuts). Divorce, widow remarriage, elopement, and death were occasions for alcohol use. Beyond such formal social ceremonies, alcohol served generally to strengthen tribal social bonds. It was a convention among tribal groups that no one, friend or foe, would decline any offer of alcohol (Reddy 1971). Consumption of alcohol in the tribal *panchayat* (the village decision-making body) served to ease potential frictions. Reconciliation of a quarrel by the *panchayat* was cemented by drinking together at the expense of the guilty party. This ended the dispute and restored friendships. Among the Chenchus, Yanadis Pradhans, Gonds, Bhils, and Oraons (all in northern India), alcohol played an integrative role from the cradle to the grave. Tribal people were, in one way or another, habituated to alcohol. A Chenchu, for example, could be so addicted to drinking that, in absence of alcohol, he might promise his daughter (even if she was not yet of age) in marriage to anybody in exchange for alcohol or money to buy it (Reddy 1971).

Contact with people from the plains of India has traumatized the tribal groups in many ways. One important aspect has been their introduction to distilled beverages (even while they were legally prohibited). The tribal groups have recently acquired the habit of consuming adulterated arrack (a kind of brandy), which has especially potent effects (Reddy 1971).

Usually the mean absolute alcohol content of tribal beers (of *mahuwa* or rice) and palm wines is about 3–5%. However, the alcohol content of a double-distilled spirit of tribals in North East India is much higher (70%). Tribal groups in certain areas of Madhya Pradesh and Orissa achieve 6–10% ethanol content. It is important to remember that essential nutrients—protein, calcium, vitamin B, riboflavin, and other beneficial ingredients—are found in home-brewed beers and toddies. Millet beers contain more calcium and iron than do other undistilled beverages (Roy 1978).

A ritualistic drinking pattern is found among a few Hindu sects. In the Tantric sect, drinking and all kinds of sensual indulgences are permitted and practiced during the rituals. The Shakti sect offers intoxicating drinks to propitiate their goddesses, and the devotees also consume alcohol (Chand 1972). These groups love drinking and believe strongly in using magic performed by shamans to obtain material gains and control over the lives of other individuals. Alcohol is one of various mind-altering substances that allow a priest or devotee to attain altered levels of consciousness so as to be able to cast magical spells. Since these sects are on the fringes of the Hindu religion, their adherents have always been few in number. They have never had the opportunity to spread their beliefs and attitudes toward alcohol use among the larger population.

Although availability of licit alcoholic beverages has increased in India since independence, no normative pattern of drinking has yet emerged that could be said to be valid at the national level. In general, alcohol is used only rarely for convivial purposes or taken in the evenings before dinner. The basic purpose of drinking alcohol is to get drunk as quickly as possible, and to stay drunk for as long as possible. This is more apparent in the young whose drinking careers started in mid-1970s, and is reflected in those who are now seeking treatment. Almost equal percentages of individuals between twenty-five and forty years of age and over forty years now seek assistance for their drinking. In the western and southern parts of India (states of Maharastra, Goa, Kerala, Karnataka) the legal system has loosened since the 1980s, and public bars and pubs are appearing. Yet pub drinking, as it is understood in the West, has not yet been institutionalized (in the sociological sense), and norms are only beginning to evolve.

## VARIANT DRINKING PATTERNS

The complexity of Indian culture is reflected in drinking patterns that show wide variation across regions, rural-urban location, socioeconomic status, and religious beliefs. It is difficult to provide a comprehensive picture of alcohol use, but recent cross-sectional studies show some commonalities and differences. A longitudinal multilocation study conducted in 1976 and 1986 among university students (Mohan and Sundaram 1987) shows significant correlation with a number of different factors. Gender was especially important; the prevalence rate of alcohol consumption was eight times higher among males than females (21.7% vs. 2.6%). Age was a significant factor in the alcohol consumption pattern of both males and females; students twenty years of age had higher consumption than those younger. Besides gender and age, type of institution (boarding school or day school), rural or urban background of the students, language of schooling (vernacular vs. English), and course of study helped the researchers identify relative risk factors in alcohol-using behavior.

A rural community study conducted in the economically backward and tradition-bound desert state of Rajasthan (Mohan et al. 1984) identified factors like religion, caste, family structure, and per capita income as important correlates of alcohol consumption among both youth and the adult population. Hinduism is slowly becoming more permissive with regard to alcohol, compared with Jainism, Buddhism, and Islam. Among Hindus also, there is a diversity in drinking patterns because certain castes (especially Brahmans) tend to follow the religious strictures more rigorously, whereas other castes are gradually taking on other social values, including alcohol use. In this study, other factors that favored higher levels of consumption were formation of a subcultural group of friends and relatives, close kin relationships, a good harvest, additional farm income, easy availability of local alcoholic beverages, and drinking patterns in the countryside.

Mohan and his colleagues (1983) carried out a study in four centers in different regions (east, north, south, and central India), covering both urban and rural areas, as well as specific groups (industrial workers, tea plantation workers, and tribal groups). The results of the study showed that alcohol use was higher among industrial and tea plantation workers and tribal groups in comparison with the general population. The tribal women showed the highest prevalence of alcohol use among females, reflecting norms of social acceptance. Choice of beverages differed from region to region. Home-brewed, low-ethanol beverages were popular among tribal populations and in economically backward areas of Assam. The urban and industrial workers favored factory-made spirits (whiskey, rum, brandy, or locally made specialty liquors). The urban drinking scene is moving toward Western patterns, which is not the case in the rural areas. There is also a homogenization of beverage types between urban and rural India, especially in the northern states.

In summary, contemporary India, despite a massive rise in alcohol production, remains a predominantly abstinent society. It is probable that India still consumes more home brew (which many people believe is equal in volume to licit alcohol production, thereby doubling registered consumption). India has undergone a sort of alcoholization, through entirely indigenous efforts without the influence of any significant acculturation processes (such as happened in Thailand, Japan, and Korea) and without the role of private industry. It is a licit brewer's paradise because an enormous market exists.

## LEARNING ABOUT DRINKING

In India, the drinking of alcohol, like other noninstinctual behavior, is learned by what psychologists term modeling and selective reinforcement (Bandura 1971). Drinking—both traditional and nontraditional—is a learned behavior acquired initially by imitation of a model who demonstrates and induces new behavior. In this regard, exposure to drinking situations, awareness, knowledge, opinions and beliefs, attitude toward drinking, and institutions like family, peer groups, and workplace are important. The apprenticeship years are those of adolescence and youth. The role of trainers is played by elder siblings, other relatives, peers, coworkers, and others. Role models are not readily available beyond personal networks.

### Role of the Family

As the primary socialization unit for a child, the family is often crucial. Images of the father or elder siblings drinking play an important role. A study of college students (Mohan et al. 1981) showed significant association between family members' alcohol and tobacco habits and students' alcohol-use patterns. Ahuja (1982), studying sociological factors of alcohol and drug abuse, did not find the family role to be a significant factor. He observed that more users than expected reported that their parents and/or siblings used both alcohol or tobacco, but was told that their use was not significant enough to influence children to begin using.

### Peer Groups

Rarely has a single factor been so often cited in alcohol initiation as the peer group. Ahuja (1982) indicated that students' first use of alcohol and drugs was primarily the result of peer-group pressure. Most drinking occurs at dances in social groups of peers. Early adulthood is viewed as a time for fun, but there is also exceptional stress and susceptibility. Contacts with friends are generally maintained in dormitory rooms, recreational places, or at a mutual friend's house. There are equal opportunities for nonstudent youth during festival celebrations and other life events. In northern India, open drinking of alcoholic beverages for fun and dance are doubtless additional inducements for nonuser youth.

## Coworkers

The work culture is gradually becoming another important setting for learning maladaptive drinking behavior. The workplace and work processes often form a culture conducive to alcohol and drugs. The nature of job separation, with the worker being away from a traditional lifestyle for long times, and peer pressures through colleagues, trade unions, and even supervisory staff, facilitate drinking. The social image of alcohol as a fatigue reliever, an "in thing" during leisure time, affects every level of business, service, industry, and commerce. The trend is slowly being adopted in the "unorganized (informal) sectors"—agriculture and cottage industries in the countryside.

## Caste and Class

In a few castes and other groups, the functional roles of alcohol in rituals and celebrations are integrated in their lifestyles. These groups often provide a model for initiation into alcohol consumption. In a study in the state of Rajasthan (Mohan et al. 1981), caste affiliation was observed to be a major influence on drinking patterns. The Rajputs, ex-rulers and still major landlords, had a demonstration effect on the landless laborers and other social groups. The increase in alcohol consumption by the latter is one of the reasons for the spread of alcohol in that traditional and conservative state. The Study Team on Prohibition (1964) observed that in matters of drinking, a princely Rajput individual is often viewed as the arbiter of taste.

## PROS AND CONS OF DRINKING

Some negative consequences of increased alcohol production and consumption have started emerging in the areas of health, crime, disrupted social life, increased traffic accidents, and hospital emergency-room data (overdose, suicide, etc.) (Mohan et al. 1980). Such consequences should perhaps have been anticipated by policy makers. The policy makers can claim that the consequences were unintended, only tangentially related to their unconscious association of alcohol consumption with equality and modernity. With increasing emphasis by the urban educated elite on the scientific ethos, a situation of culturally inconsistent value systems, even normlessness, has developed among the urban intelligentsia, in affluent rural areas, and among the emerging middle class. Consumption of distilled beverages and their symbolic status value have greatly increased among them.

Despite considerable industrialization, the Indian economy remains agrarian, dependent on the monsoons, and about 40% of the population remains at the subsistence level. For these reasons home brews from rice, millet, and sugarcane are still consumed, both production and consumption being limited to rural areas. Their alcohol content never reaches more than 4–5%, so that their use remains primarily nutritive, recreational, and convivial. Now that more mass-produced alcohol is available, and disposable incomes have increased, alcohol consumption has increased among farmers above the poverty line as well as among the educated elite, increasing social health and welfare consequences.

This has been particularly true in the rural contexts, as Deb and Jindal (1974) showed in their study of the utilization of increased disposable incomes that have resulted from advances in agricultural technology. They observed that instead of generating new job opportunities or creating assets, the new funds were being diverted to consumption of factory-made alcoholic beverages. This was in addition to continuing drinking of home-brewed alcohol. In Punjab state, where the study was done, farmers adopted the latest technology, high-yielding seeds, and other intensive production methods, ushering in the Green Revolution. Punjab became "the granary of India" and the country's most prosperous state. The production of home brews increased even in villages where licensed liquor stores were opened, showing clear grafting on of the new beverages with the old. Almost no economic or developmental assets emerged. Interestingly, there was a concomitant breakdown of the traditional social value system in those villages, which contributed to increased alcohol consumption, especially among the young. The upsurge in demand for Indian-made foreign-style liquors, local liquors (also made under government supervision), and home-distilled illicit liquor in the state coincided with advances in agricultural technology, compared with the previous two decades. The average head of household in Punjab spent about 1,000 times more disposable funds on alcohol than on conveniences or improvements (Mohan and Sharma 1983), a dramatic illustration of how greater wealth does not necessarily serve as a basis for further economic development. It also illustrates vividly that the widespread stereotype of India as a country of abstainers is far from accurate.

## REFERENCES

Aaron, P., and D. Musto. 1981. Temperance and prohibition in America: A historical overview. Pp. 127–181 in M. Moore and D. Gerstein (Eds.). *Alcohol and Public Policy: Beyond the Shadow of Prohibition.* Washington, D.C.: National Academy Press.

Ahuja, R. 1982. *Sociology of Youth Subculture.* Jaipur: Rawat.

Bandura, A. 1971. *Social Learning Theory.* Morristown, N.J.: General Learning Press.

Chand, T. 1972. *Liquor Menace in India.* New Delhi: Gandhi Peace Foundation.

Deb, P. C., and R. B. Jindal. 1974. *Drinking in Rural Areas: A Study in Selected Villages in Punjab in the Wake of the Green Revolution.* Ludhiana: Punjab Agricultural University.

Dikshitar, V. R. 1951. *Prehistoric South India.* Madras: N.p.

Dube, S. C. 1965. The study of complex cultures. In T. K. N. Unnithan, I. Deva, and Y. Singh (Eds.). *Towards a Sociology of Culture in India.* New Delhi: Prentice-Hall of India.

Huxley, A. 1960. *Brave New World.* Rev. ed. New York: Bantam.

Jha, G. N. 1920–1926. *Mahabarat Manusmiriti.* 5 vols. Calcutta: University of Calcutta Press.

Kuppuswamy, B. 1981. *Social Change in India.* Ghasiabad: Vikas.

Medhatithi. 1939. *On Manusmiriti.* Bibliothica India 256. Calcutta: N.p.

Mohan, D. 1980. *Pattern of Overdose in Casualty Emergency Services: A Collaborative Study of Five Delhi Hospitals.* New Delhi: ICMR.

Mohan, D., and H. K. Sharma. 1983. Alcohol: Friend or foe? *Impact of Science on Society* 133:139–140.

Mohan, D., H. K. Sharma, K. R. Sundaram, and G. B. Advani. 1981. *Prevalence and Pattern of Alcohol Abuse in Rural Community and Its Correlation with Psychosocial Sequelae.* New Delhi: Ministry of Social Welfare.

Mohan, D., H. K. Sharma, K. R. Sundaram, and J. S. Neki. 1980. Pattern of alcohol consumption of rural Punjab males. *Indian Journal of Medical Research* 72:702–711.

Mohan, D., and K. R. Sundaram. 1987. *Drug Abuse among College Students: A Replicated Study among University Students.* New Delhi: Ministry of Welfare.

Mohan, D., K. R. Sundaram, G. B. Advani, H. K. Sharma, and J. S. Bajaj. 1984. Alcohol abuse in a rural community in India, part II: Characteristics of alcohol users. *Drug and Alcohol Dependence* 14:121–128.

Mohan, D., K. R. Sundaram, and H. K. Sharma. 1983. *A Study on Health Education: Intervention on Nonmedical Drugs in the Community.* New Delhi: Indian Council of Medical Research.

National Sample Survey. 1971. *24th Round: 1970–71.* New Delhi: Yojana Bhavan.

———. 1974. *28th Round: 1973–74.* New Delhi: Yojana Bhavan.

Panchandikar, K. C. 1965. Religion, social forces and historical periods in India: An analysis of social and cultural dynamics. In T. K. N. Unnithan, I. Deva, and Y. Singh (Eds.). *Towards a Sociology of Culture in India.* New Delhi: Prentice-Hall of India.

Pittman, D. J. 1964. Social and cultural factors in drinking patterns, pathological and non-pathological. Pp. 1–13 in *Selected Papers Presented at the 27th International Congress on Alcohol and Alcoholism.* Vol. 1. Lausanne: International Council on Alcohol and Alcoholism.

Prakash, O. 1961. *Food and Drinks in Ancient India.* New Delhi: Munshi Ram Manohar Lal.

Praskara. 1956. *Grhya Sutra.* Bombay: Venkatesvara.

Rao, S. S. V. V., and C.R.P. Rao. 1976. Drinking in the tribal world: A cross cultural study in 'culture theme' approach. *Man in India* 57(2):97–102.

Reddy, G. P. 1971. Where liquor decides everything: Drinking subculture among tribes of Andhra. *Social Welfare* (New Delhi) 17:4–5.

Roy, J. K. 1978. Alcoholic beverages in tribal India and their nutritional role. *Man in India* 58(4):263–276.

Sastri, U. 1925. *Arthasastra of Kautilaya.* Lahore: N.p.

Srinivas, M. N. 1966. *Social Change in Modern India.* Bombay: N.p.

Study Team on Prohibition. 1964. *Report.* New Delhi: Government of India Planning Commission.

## ADDITIONAL REFERENCES

In an effort to make the list of readings more representative of modern work on alcohol and culture in and about India, the editor suggests the following references in addition to those cited by the authors of this chapter:

Dorschner, J. 1983a. Rajput alcohol use in India. *Journal of Studies on Alcohol* 44:538–544.

———. 1983b. *Alcohol Consumption in a Village in North India.* Ann Arbor, Mich.: UMI Research Press.

Ray, Rajat, and Roy W. Pickens (Eds.). 1989. *Proceedings of the Indo-US Symposium on Alcohol and Drug Abuse.* NIMHANS Publication 20. Bangalore: National Institute of Mental Health and Neuro Sciences.

Shukla, B.R.K. 1978. The religious and convivial use of intoxicants in a North Indian village. *Eastern Anthropologist* 31:511–520.

Singh, Gurmeet. 1989. Epidemiology of alcohol use in India. Pp. 3–11. In Ray and Pickens 1989 (q.v.).

Singh, S., and K. Preet. 1981. Drug abuse amongst school and college students in Punjab. *Child Psychiatry* 14:5–11.

Sundaram, K. R., D. Mohan, G. B. Advani, H. K. Sharma, and J. S. Bajaj. 1984. Alcohol abuse in a rural community in India. part I: Epidemiological study. *Drug and Alcohol Dependence* 14:27–36.

Thakur, C. P., R. N. Sharma, and H. S. Akhtar. 1982. Prohibition and alcohol intoxication. *British Journal of Addiction* 77:197–204.

Unithan, N. P. 1985. Cross-national perspective on the evolution of alcohol prohibition. *International Journal of the Addictions* 20:591–604.

Varma, Vijoy K. 1984. Alcohol control policy in India. Pp. 185–197 in Peter M. Miller and Ted D. Nirenberg (Eds.). *Prevention of Alcohol Abuse.* New York: Plenum.

Varma, V. K., A. Singh, S. Singh, and A. Malhorta. 1980. Extent and pattern of alcohol use and alcohol-related problems in North India. *Indian Journal of Psychiatry* 22:331–337.

# 14

## Israel

### Shoshana Weiss

**WHY ALCOHOL IS NOTEWORTHY IN ISRAEL**

The Bible praises wine as a substance that brings joy to the human heart but condemns drunkenness. Moderation in drinking is embedded in Jewish culture, within the framework of a permissive attitude toward alcohol consumption. In the course of Jewish history, drunkenness was seen as opening oneself to ridicule and bringing shame on one's family and people. The cultural norms, stemming from values encompassed in religion, oriented the individual toward moderation in the consumption of alcohol. Drinking alcohol was regulated as a part of religious practices and observances. There was a convivial type of drinking, but sanctions existed in the culture against the excessive use of alcohol. Therefore, although most Jews did not abstain from alcohol, they were relatively unlikely to develop utilitarian types of drinking, problems related to drinking, or alcoholism. Alcohol addiction was an extremely deviant form of behavior among Jews during hundreds of years in the Diaspora, in comparison to the extent of addiction among their gentile neighbors. [Ed. note: In this context, "the Diaspora" refers to the long period (about 70–1948) during which Jews were dispersed around the world rather than concentrated in what they thought of as "their homeland" (the present state of Israel).] However, despite the fact that in the Bible, beginning with Noah and Lot and ending with Proverbs, persons who drink in excess are condemned, the phenomenon of drunkenness was known in Jewish communities, and the problem of intoxication continued to occupy Jewish sages in later generations.

The opinion that Jews in the Diaspora, in comparison with other ethnic groups, possessed social and cultural traits that discouraged dependence on alcohol is well known and based on many anthropological and sociological studies. These studies have been conducted in an attempt to understand the pattern of moderate drinking among Jews within settings including a generally permissive attitude toward alcoholic drinks (e.g., Bales 1946; Keller 1970; Glassner and Berg 1980). Studies have also been carried out in order to explain the rise of alcoholism among Jews in Western society since the 1960s (e.g., Zimberg 1977; Schmidt and Popham 1976; Glatt 1970). It can safely be said that the picture we have, based on studies in the Diaspora, is not valid in the Jewish state of Israel today. Although the problem of nonritual alcohol use in Israel is less serious than in some other modern societies, alcohol abuse, drunkenness, and alcoholism have nevertheless become epidemiological problems by Jewish-Israeli standards, especially in recent years, and in some segments of the Israeli population their extent is similar to the extent of problems in some other Western societies. Even though statistics show Israel at the bottom of the international ranking of alcoholism, they are serious, if only because Israel had never before been included in the rankings.

## ALCOHOL IN HISTORY

Before the establishment of Israel as a nation-state in 1948, and under the rule of the British mandate in Palestine, the problem of alcoholism in the Jewish population was unknown (King 1961). The well-known historical and sociological factors contributing to the molding of the image of the Jew, who is moderate in drinking, operated in the early days of Jewish settlement and during the formative years of the state of Israel, with its heterogeneous population from seventy countries of origin. The sense of mission, the pioneering spirit, and austerity worked together to maintain the traditional moderate level of drinking. Social drinking habits, which were brought from countries of exile, were neglected or diminished within the context of conscious change in the lifestyle of the immigrants (Shuval and Krasilowsky 1963). Thus, in the 1950s the phenomenon of alcoholism did not exist, but it began to surface in the 1960s. Limited data were accumulated from surveys on selected groups, mainly hospitalized individuals (Krasilowsky et al. 1965). The treatment approach included psychiatric treatment of the alcoholic in a mental hospital, financial assistance to the spouse, and removal of children from the home. The presumed causes of excessive drinking leading to alcoholism among the population in this period were mainly the following (Shuval and Krasilowsky 1963; Wislicki 1967):

1. During the various waves of immigration to Israel, certain groups, especially from North Africa and the Middle East, brought with them social drinking habits acquired in their countries of origin. Adaptation difficulties, largely due to the breakdown of patriarchal traditions during the adjustment to the new and modern country, sometimes turned moderate drinking into pathologically excessive drinking. A change of status due to a redefinition of the socioeconomic standing of the head of the family, who

had to compete in a society having a far different educational and economic level than that of the society in the country of origin, caused economic difficulties.

2. The tension of day-to-day life in Israel—under pressure from hostile states—has hastened the tendency to drink as an escape mechanism.

3. Another group of alcoholics were survivors of the Holocaust, who drank in order to cope with problems of adjustment and to escape from loneliness, the horrors of the past, and its memories.

Since the beginning of the 1970s, the drinking patterns of Israelis have changed. With increased secularization, affluence, and assimilation, the movement has been away from moderation and the general negative evaluation of excessive drinking to social and routine group and individual drinking, particularly among the middle and the upper classes. For these groups, drinking has become a status symbol and a mark of being ''worldly.'' The swarming of volunteers and tourists, who brought with them the fashion of alcohol use for pleasure and fun, together with the rise in the standard of living and the quality of life, contributed to the spread of hedonistic alcohol use that promoted intoxication and led many into alcoholism (Weiss 1988a). Thus, during the 1970s, a gradual change in values and norms developed in Israel. Personal motivation became dominant at the expense of human values in which the social factor had long been predominant. As Israeli society tried to be ''like all societies,'' it seemed that it would be difficult to keep the moderate drinking pattern that had been typical of isolated Jewish communities in the Diaspora and in the period of the establishment of the state.

Several modest studies, that were carried out in the 1970s confirmed the above description. They pointed to increases in the production and consumption of alcohol per capita; the higher number of hospitalized cases; the number of young hospitalized alcoholics, of female alcoholics, and of Israel-born alcoholics; and even the number of offenses resulting from alcohol use. Alcoholism was discovered not only in large cities but also in small cities and developing towns (Eldar 1976). In 1977 the first epidemiological survey concerning alcohol use in the general adult population was launched (Kandel and Sudit 1982), and in 1979 the first epidemiological data on drinking practices of Israeli youth were collected (e.g., Adler and Kandel 1982). As far as treatment is concerned, ambulatory alcohol treatment centers were established throughout the country in the light of the negative results of treatment in mental hospitals. In 1974 the Israeli Alcoholics Anonymous movement was established, and it introduced a different kind of treatment into the system (Weiss 1990a). Also during the 1970s, regulations were initiated concerning underage drinking in public places and providing alcohol to intoxicated customers. The law prohibited the supply of alcoholic beverages to those under the age of eighteen.

At the beginning of the 1980s, the cultural climate continued to change, and Jews in Israel continued to adopt foreign types of drinking and untraditional beverages (e.g., beer). Several studies surveying the steadily growing problems of alcohol addiction and inebriation in the general adult population were carried out, as were studies among Israeli youth. Noteworthy is a national survey among adults (Bar et al. 1989) which demonstrated that alcoholism then afflicted 35% of Israeli adults. Although alcohol consumption among youth was less extensive in Israel than in other Western countries, it should be realized that by Israeli standards, a real problem was emerging (Weiss and Moore 1988). Regulations with respect to drinking and driving were initiated. A blood alcohol level greater than 0.05% is the legal definition of being under the influence of alcohol for driving-under-the-influence prosecution.

A residential treatment center for alcoholics was established in 1983, as a result of the awareness of the growing problem of alcoholism in Israel. In the 1980s, it treated about 150 alcoholics per year (Michaely et al. 1989). In the 1990s, that number doubled. The core of prevention efforts in Israel during the 1980s was an experimental school-based primary prevention interdisciplinary curricular unit, "Alcohol and Drunkenness" (Moore and Weiss 1985). When its impact was evaluated in 1984, it was deemed effective with respect to attitudinal, behavioral, and cognitive changes (Weiss and Moore 1988). Adopted by the Israeli Ministry of Education in 1987, it is the only comprehensive alcohol education curriculum in the schools today. In the early 1990s, alcohol use among youth continues to increase (Weiss and Moore 1991), especially among kibbutz-born adolescents and youth from developing towns. There are about 2,600 pubs in Israel that serve mainly beer, in comparison with some dozens of pubs a decade earlier. Beer has become an inexpensive commodity, comparable in price with soft drinks.

Immigration from the former Soviet Union has brought a relatively high proportion of alcoholics (Weiss 1993a, 1994a). Actually, what Israelis consider heavy drinking is the norm for most people from Russia and nearby republics. They drink vodka at parties, at meetings, at family get-togethers, during holidays, and/or whenever the occasion seems to suit. The immigrants with drinking problems can be divided into three groups. There are hard-core alcoholics— people who were unable to function without a drink in their home countries and can't do without it in Israel. In the second group are immigrants who were alcohol-dependent before, underwent treatment, and had stopped drinking. On arriving in Israel, the pressures of everyday life (search for housing, jobs, etc.) push them into returning to the habit. Then there are immigrants who drank, like their non-Jewish countrymen, with friends and on happy or sad occasions, but could take it or leave it. When they can't cope in Israel (e.g., with their loss of status, economic problems, and language difficulties), they use alcohol as a crutch or to run away from their problems, and may be on the way to becoming addicted.

In 1993, immigrants from the former Soviet Union constituted about 30% of patients in Israeli governmental treatment centers. Interestingly, there are some strong similarities between native Israeli and "Soviet" immigrant alcoholics. Both groups are generally male and between the ages of thirty-six and forty-five. Most members of both categories have completed at least twelve years of school, though there are relatively far more university graduates among the immigrants. Similarly, immigrants from Ethiopia who came to Israel in two waves (in the early 1980s and 1990s) have adopted excessive beer-drinking in Israel (the taste of local beer is similar to the taste of an Ethiopian beverage with a low content of alcohol), and they are expected to turn to treatment in massive numbers within the near future.

It seems obvious that the historical and sociological factors contributing to the molding of the image of the Jew who is temperate in drinking tend to disappear in present-day Israel, and the Jewish people in Israel have started to exhibit considerable remoteness from traditional "Jewish sobriety." The majority of youth do not join the Youth Movements, which have traditionally been opposed to uninhibited drinking of alcohol. It is fashionable nowadays for adolescents in Israel to sit in pubs and drink alcoholic beverages, and the enforcement of the law prohibiting the supply of alcoholic drinks to minors is lax (Weiss and Eldar 1988). The cohort of people born during the 1970s appears to be showing a higher rate of heavy frequent drinking, especially of beer, than preceding generations. More alcoholic immigrants from the former Soviet Union and from Ethiopia are expected to come to treatment in the 1990s, as well as more native Israelis. Finally, more fatal car accidents due to alcohol use are expected to occur, especially in light of the limited extent of enforcement.

## MAJOR DRINKING PATTERNS

The trends of alcohol consumption among the adult Jewish population in Israel earlier were identified on the basis of three nationwide epidemiological surveys carried out in 1982, 1983, and 1987 (Bar et al. 1990). The surveys dealt only with nonritual drinking practices. Ceremonial use of alcoholic drinks is well established in the Jewish tradition, and many Israelis drink sacramental wine frequently (at least weekly) on religious occasions. Therefore, it is essential to distinguish between the practice of drinking alcohol as part of religious ceremony and drinking for recreation. There was a decreasing trend in serving alcoholic drinks at social meetings (from 67% to 50%); a stable trend in drinking daily (3%), every two to three days (4%), or once a week (11%); and an increasing trend (from 33% to 46%) in abstaining. There was a decreasing trend (from 15% to 4%) in drinking for reasons that pose greater risk for addiction (e.g., tension, depression), but a stable number of people reporting acquaintance with alcoholics and with people who drink daily (about 26% and 35%, respectively). Furthermore, there was a stable trend observed regarding daily drinkers or alcoholics within the family. In 1983, 13% of respondents had at least one close family member drinking daily, and 8% had at least one alcoholic in their immediate family; in 1987, the percentages of respondents so reporting were 12% and 7%, respectively.

There was a decreasing trend in the percentage of respondents who worried about their drinking habits (from 10% in 1983 to 5% in 1987), and in the percentage of respondents who worried about drinking habits of family members (17% to 10%). In 1983, 40% of respondents thought that drinking alcohol was a serious problem in Israel, compared with 49% in 1987. Moreover, there was an increasing trend in the opinion that regular drinking of alcoholic beverages (at least three times a week) negatively influences a person's health (from 52% of respondents in 1983 to 62% in 1987). There was a decreasing trend in reporting noninterest in the subject of alcoholism (from 62% to 49%). Finally, two other interesting trends have emerged: an increasing trend in drinking in pubs (from 4.7% in 1983 to 11.1% in 1987) and a decreasing trend in the preference for drinking wine, the traditionally preferred drink (from 22% to 17%), and distilled spirits (from 27% to 21%), but a moderate rise in beer as the favored beverage (from 11% to 15%).

As far as adolescents are concerned, according to a 1990 study on drinking practices in the previous month (Weiss and Moore 1991a, b; Moore and Weiss 1992a), beer is the preferred alcoholic beverage among young male students (51%). The highest prevalence of beer-drinking is among kibbutz-born males (61%). The highest rate of wine-drinking is among males from developing towns (54%). These two groups of males consume more distilled spirits (39%) and report very high rates of their best friend's drinking (71%), whereas males from a large city in the north of Israel report 25% and 41%, respectively. Kibbutz-born females have the highest rates of beer, wine, and distilled spirits drinking (37%, 37%, 40%, respectively), and they report the highest rate of drinking by a best friend (58%). About 9% of kibbutz-born males consume four cans of beer or more on a single occasion, whereas 9% of males from a developing town consume four small glasses or more of distilled spirits on a drinking occasion.

According to a 1992 study (Weiss and Moore 1994), in the north of Israel most high-school students who drink (57.3%) do so with same-age friends; females drink more with older friends (24.6%) than males do (4.4%). The preferred location of female drinking is the pub (39.9%), followed by home (23.6%), whereas males drink at home (32.2%) and in pubs (30.8%) with approximately the same frequency. The proportion of drinking at pubs is the highest in small or developing towns (54.1%) and is the lowest in religious settlements (7.0%). Ethiopian students report drinking mainly beer (75%) and mostly at home (58.3%). Kibbutz dwellers are unique in their willingness to drink at "any place" (43.8%). Enjoyment is the most prevalent reason given for drinking (37.2%). However, 23.3% of drinkers report motives that may involve a risk of dependence. These include to improve a bad mood, to relax and ease tension, to forget troubles (9.9%), and to escape from boredom (13.4%). Only 3.3% of drinkers admit that peers are an important influence on alcohol use. Students from kibbutzim tend to drink in order to escape boredom (21.9%). Students from religious settlements have the highest rate of drinking in order to improve a bad mood (14%). Students choose parents more often than any other group (39.7%) as a preferred social support resource for alcohol problems. The second preferred source is a same-age friend (15.9%), and the third is the telephone hot line of a professional organization (11.5%). "Nobody" is also a frequent selection (8.9%). The kibbutz dwellers are predominant in their choice of same-age friend (33.3%). Those who live in small or developing towns are predominant in the selection of the telephone hot line (14.2%).

## VARIANT DRINKING PATTERNS

Findings concerning the adult population that indicate present trends concerning general drinking characteristics can calm fears (since 1982 there has been an increasing trend of abstaining from alcohol) may actually be "the calm before the storm" with reference to some special subgroups (Bar et al. 1990). Beer-drinking and drinking in pubs by young adults, and drunkenness among the Israeli-born second generation, have been on the increase. Furthermore, acquaintance with alcoholics was reported by religious more than nonreligious respondents in all three national surveys.

In 1983, 14% of those twenty to twenty-four years old preferred drinking beer (a nontraditional beverage), compared with 24% of the same age group studied in 1987. There was also a rise in drunkenness among Israeli-born second-generation Jews, from 4% of respondents in 1983 to 7% in 1987. The use of alcohol was found to prevail less among the religious and traditional respondents, compared with the secular respondents; and serving alcoholic drinks at social gatherings and dinners was also found to be more frequent among the secular respondents. Thus, it seems that religiosity still has a restraining effect and is a strong preventive mechanism for believers. However, in all the surveys acquaintance with alcoholics was found to be related to religiosity. The greater the religiosity, the greater the percentage of acquaintance. For example, 19% of religious respondents knew one alcoholic in 1987, versus 10% of secular respondents, and 16% of religious respondents knew two alcoholics in 1987, versus 7% of secular respondents.

As far as women are concerned, a review of the literature (Weiss 1991a) revealed that fewer women than men drink alcohol; women who drink consume less than male drinkers; and a smaller proportion of problem drinkers are females. In addition, there is a relatively low rate of alcohol dependence among women. However, treatment centers have reported an increase in the number of alcoholic women since the late 1970s; women now constitute about 10% of patients.

As far as older people are concerned, a review of the literature (Weiss 1993b) revealed that alcohol abuse is not perceived as a problem of aging in Israel. This is true despite studies showing that the proportion of drinkers who drink frequently increases around age sixty-five, and that Israeli elderly drink alone and at home more frequently than other age groups. Again, the dominant pattern seems to be one of moderate drinking, which may be more healthful than harmful.

In addition to ethnic groups discussed above (Russians, Georgians, Ukrainians, Ethiopians), it is important to mention the Arab minority in Israel (including Muslims, Druze, and Christians). The first epidemiological study on alcohol use among Muslim and Druze adolescents in Israel was carried out in 1990 (Moore and Weiss 1991a). Female students surveyed revealed little alcohol use in the previous month; Druze and Muslim females in an Arab town reported no involvement at all; in a mixed Arab-Jewish town and in Muslim villages, 1% of females reported beer-drinking, 3% reported wine-drinking, and 2% reported drinking distilled spirits. In spite of the fact that the Muslim and Druze religions forbid drinking, many male adolescents from both groups consumed alcoholic beverages. About 22% of Druze males reported beer-drinking, 11% reported wine-drinking, and 12% reported drinking distilled spirits in the last month. Among the Muslim students, the figures were 18%, 10%, and 14%. Druze males reported far more frequently that their fathers drink than did Muslim males (30% vs. 17%). The amounts of alcohol consumed by those respondents were far from negligible. About 6% of Druze males drank four cans of beer or more, or four half-glasses of wine or more, per drinking occasion. Among Muslims the figures were 5% and 1%. The greatest prevalence of alcohol use was in an Arab town, followed by Muslim villages and a mixed Arab-Jewish town.

The prevailing view has always been that Muslims and Druze do not drink alcoholic beverages. This myth is based on the Islamic and Druze religions, which prohibit drinking. When we speak of Druze and Muslim females, we cannot ignore the absence or very low rate of drinking. This is probably the result of two factors: drinking alcohol is an expression of masculinity and power in the Muslim and Druze societies, and females' behavior is under very strict control in these societies. The high involvement with alcohol among Druze students is probably due to their constant and intense contact with the Jewish secular society, and to the weakening of religious influence. Druze respondents reported a high percentage of fathers drinking. This may be the result of the above-mentioned contact, which includes the drafting of Druze males into the Israeli army together with the Jewish soldiers, and may also reflect their rapid modernization.

The Israeli way of life greatly influences the traditional way of life of the local Muslim population. The similarity in lifestyles of Jews and Muslims living in Israel is increasing, and this includes norms of drinking behavior. There is now open drinking, especially in Arab towns and in Muslim villages. This is surprising, because it would be expected that Muslim males in a mixed town will exhibit the highest prevalence of alcohol use, as a result of the presence of Jewish neighbors. However, the finding can be explained by the intention of the Muslim sector to keep its habits and not to drink like the Jews. A similar explanation was given for the low prevalence of alcoholism among Jewish people in the Diaspora (Shuval and Krasilowsky 1963).

The first epidemiological study among Arab males (including Muslims, Druze, and Christians) aged eighteen to forty was carried out in 1989 (Teichman et al. 1992). The study investigated the incidence of alcohol consumption during the last week, last month, and last year among Arab males, and compared it with that of Jewish males. It is evident from the data that the incidence of alcohol consumption among Arab males is relatively high, especially the consumption of beer and distilled spirits. Moreover, the incidence of daily drinking is higher among the Arab males than among the Jews (23.4% compared with 10.8% for beer; 9.1% and 1.6% for distilled spirits, and 6.6% and 1.4% for wine). The same patterns emerged when the data for consumption during the last month and the last year were analyzed. Those findings are crucial in regard to the overall number of Arab and Jewish men who admitted drinking alcoholic beverages. Although more Jewish than Arab men reported consuming alcoholic beverages, both daily and heavy drinking were more prevalent among Arabs. In addition, the consumption of alcohol among unemployed Arab men was higher than among employed ones, whereas among Jewish respondents, drinking was more frequent among employed subjects. Among Arabs, the percentage of young drinkers was relatively low and drinking increased with age, whereas the opposite trend was found among the Jews.

Thus, being a member of a group of people who historically belong to a religion that forbids or controls alcohol use does not by itself curb the use of alcohol. Apparently, only the close observance of Muslim and Druze religious laws can serve as a strong barrier against abusing alcoholic beverages. Nonobservant people who come into contact with an alcohol-consuming culture are not immune to drinking. Islam prohibits alcohol consumption; the Jewish religion does not, but advocates moderation and warns against intoxication. These differences may explain why the incidence of daily drinking is higher among Arab men than Jewish men. The Arab who consumes alcoholic beverages separates himself from his religion and culture, and loses his social-religious support (Teichman et al. 1992). He does not know how to drink and knows little about the nature of alcohol. These factors can contribute to his excessive drinking.

According to reports from the ambulatory centers for alcohol treatment, 8% of patients admitted during January–July 1993 were Muslims, 4% were Christians, and about 2% were Druze. At the center in Haifa (which accepts patients from the north of Israel, where most Arabs live), 16% were Muslims, 9% were Christians, and 1.5% were Druze. The percentages before recent waves of immigration were higher. It is important to note that two treatment centers in two Arab villages in the north of Israel treat alcoholics of all three religions. In early 1993, 25% were Muslim, 44% were Christian, and 31% were Druze. Thus, the belief that alcoholism does not exist among Arabs should be rejected.

## LEARNING ABOUT DRINKING

Primary prevention programs concerning alcohol abuse started functioning in Israel in 1984 (Weiss 1988b). Main efforts are focused on the implementation of the interdisciplinary curriculum "Alcohol and Drunkenness," which is aimed at high schools and was adopted by the Israeli Ministry of Education in 1986 after its evaluation (Moore and Weiss 1985; Weiss and Moore 1988). It still serves as the central theme behind the preventive program in Israel. The training of teachers and counselors is carried out in some of the universities in Israel (Weiss 1991b) and in most high schools. The unit was designed to provide high-school students with the knowledge, values, and skills necessary to prevent excessive drinking. A special kibbutz version of the program was developed in 1986 (Weiss 1988a). Both programs target all junior and senior high school students (as opposed to those identified as "high risk"), use a multiplicity of strategies, and focus on building personal and social competence.

## VOLUNTARY ORGANIZATIONS

The Israel Society for the Prevention of Alcoholism, a voluntary organization supported by the government, has a major role in prevention. Since 1976, it has distributed pamphlets for adolescents and for parents, informative leaflets aimed at youngsters and adults, a "driver card" (with information on blood alcohol levels), posters, and stickers; it also has a hot-line service. Prevention literature is available in Russian and Amharic for recent immigrants. It has been active in the Knesset (Israel's Parliament) concerning alcohol regulations, and in training professionals and parents. Israel has its own special economic problems, and the difficulty of allocating support for the prevention of problems due to alcohol is apparent.

## COMMUNITY-BASED PROJECTS

During the 1980s and 1990s, only a few attempts at community prevention have been made. A kibbutz-community model was proposed. In this model (Weiss 1990b, 1993b) all the individuals surrounding students (who are the major targets of the project) are involved in various activities in which the students also may participate, making the community mutually supportive as a whole. The kibbutz-community model encompasses education in schools, involvement of parents and the rest of the kibbutz members, changing local regulations, and providing alternatives to drinking.

Thus, schools, voluntary organizations, and community projects, as well as regulations and law enforcement, influence behavior and attitudes about drinking. (However, there are no regulations concerning the location, number, and density of pubs, nor are there taxes on alcoholic beverages.) There is no doubt that the mass media could play an important role, but very little has been done to utilize them as a preventive tool because of the expense. Alcohol-drinking appears in many imported TV programs (from Europe and the United States), and alcohol advertisements appear in newspapers, in magazines (except youth magazines), on billboards, and even on television (encouraging wine consumption). Therefore, the educational program "Alcohol and Drunkenness" relates to this issue and educates students on how to be critical about alcohol ads. In 1988, an international comparative research project was conducted simultaneously in Israel, Australia, and the United States. The purpose of the study (Weiss and Moore 1990; Moore and Weiss 1992a) was to determine the attitudes of high-school students from different nations and cultures toward alcohol advertisements. This study, which was conducted among Jewish and Arab students, can inform the creation of future prevention models. For example, it may help to exert pressure on the mass media; it can aid preventive activities by emphasizing the role of media images within the framework of alcohol education; and it can assist alcohol advertisers who are interested in responsible advertising— they can use the study both as a guide to avoiding pitfalls and as a way to find standards acceptable in various cultures. In a study that investigated sources of alcohol information among adolescents (Weiss and Moore 1994a), television was primary, with newspapers and magazines secondary.

The family is important in creating behavior and attitudes toward drinking. Jews everywhere have in common the association of drinking with religious occasions and observances, which are repeated and participated in from childhood. However, the tendency among adults in Israel to adopt foreign drinking norms has an influence on youth. When adults use alcohol as a tool for implementing self-oriented values (particularly values of fun and "the good life"), drink in excess, and use non-traditional alcoholic beverages, they tend to counter the moderation-oriented tendencies inherited from the past, and too many youngsters uncritically follow them.

## PROS AND CONS OF DRINKING

The theoretical model of prevention concerning alcohol in Israel is the "social science model" (Blane 1976). Despite the drift away from Orthodox religious practice within Israel, orthodoxy is the basis of Jewish values, encompassing traditional mechanisms of control. Of central importance is Judaism's deep-seated opposition to drunkenness—a constituent element of Jewish identity. Further, the social science model presents intoxication as being in contradiction with positive Jewish mores. Therefore, correct patterns of drinking and the issue of "responsible use" are explicitly discussed and reinforced. As far as alcohol is concerned, the main objective is to encourage moderate, controlled, and responsible drinking rather than abstinence (Weiss 1988a). In our prevention program, we like to think of the "social science model" as integrated (Weiss and Eldar 1988) within the "distribution of consumption model," which includes several regulations and enforcement (Blane 1976). The characteristics of the "social science model" resemble the Jewish normative orientation toward drinking. Therefore, there is no need in Israel to adopt foreign drinking practices in order to achieve moderate drinking. There is a need to subordinate the use of alcohol to other activities rather than making it a focal point of social activity. Light should be shed on Jewish norms concerning alcohol. The core educational program on alcohol clarifies the Jewish religious tradition and sharpens the normative structure of the Jewish nation concerning alcohol. It illustrates the place of sobriety or moderate drinking in Jewish culture, and its chapter on ''correct patterns of alcohol drinking'' is at the core of prevention efforts in Israel.

Israeli society is traditionally permissive about drinking. It is one thing to agree on the theoretical issues concerning prevention of excessive drinking among the Jewish population in Israel, but it is an entirely different matter to translate these points into a workable program. The distribution of preventive materials concerning alcohol use is still a demanding process associated with an elaborate exercise in public relations involving administrators, educational authorities, school principals, teachers, and parents. Although there is a promising beginning in the prevention of alcohol abuse, there is still a long way to go in turning it into a legitimate and acceptable component of Jewish society in Israel.

## REFERENCES

Adler, I., and D. B. Kandel. 1982. Cross cultural comparison of sociopsychological factors in alcohol use among adolescents in Israel, France and United States. *Journal of Youth and Adolescence* 11:89–113.

Bales, R. F. 1946. Cultural differences in rates of alcoholism. *Quarterly Journal of Studies on Alcohol* 6:480–499.

Bar, H., P. Eldar, and S. Weiss. 1989. Alcohol drinking habits and attitudes of the adult Jewish population in Israel 1987. *Drug and Alcohol Dependence* 23:237–245.

———. 1990. Three national surveys on nonritual alcohol drinking practices of the Israeli Jewish adult population in the 80's: What are the trends? *Israel Journal of Psychiatry and Related Sciences* 27:57–63.

Blane, H. T. 1976. Education and prevention of alcoholism. Pp. 519–578 in B. Kissin and H. Begleiter (Eds.). *The Biology of Alcoholism.* Vol. 4. New York: Plenum.

Eldar, P. 1976. Comments. Pp. 86–93 in A. Levine (Ed.). *An Israeli experiment in the treatment of Alcoholism.* Jerusalem: Ministry of Social Affairs.

Glassner, B., and B. Berg. 1980. How Jews avoid alcohol problems. *American Sociological Review* 45:647–664.

Glatt, M. M. 1970. Alcoholism and drug dependence among Jews. *British Journal of Addiction* 64:297–304.

Kandel, D. B., and M. Sudit. 1982. Drinking practices among urban adults in Israel. *Journal of Studies on Alcohol* 43:1–16.

Keller, M. 1970. The great Jewish drink mystery. *British Journal of Addiction* 64:287–296.

King, A. R. 1961. The alcohol problem in Israel. *Quarterly Journal of Studies on Alcohol* 22:321–328.

Krasilowsky, D., B. Halpern, and I. Gutman. 1965. The problem of alcoholism in Israel. *Israel Annals of Psychiatry and Related Disciplines* 3:249–257.

Michaely, N., P. Eldar, and S. Weiss. 1989. The Israeli residential Centre for Alcoholics: 1982–1987. *Journal of Substance Abuse Treatment* 6:59–65.

Moore, M., and S. Weiss. 1985. ''Alcohol and Drunkenness'': A newly developed curricular unit as a model for drug education science-oriented curricular programs. *Journal of Drug Education* 15:263–271.

———. 1991. Alcohol drinking among Moslem and Druze adolescents in Israel in 1990. *Drug and Alcohol Dependence* 28:189–193.

———. 1992a. Israeli Christian, Druze and Moslem adolescents' attitudes toward magazine alcohol advertisements. *International Journal of the Addictions* 27:735–741.

———. 1992b. Drinking among urban Jewish youth in Israel in 1990: Alcohol as the main prevention target. *Psychology of Addictive Behaviors* 6:196–199.

Schmidt, W., and R. Popham. 1976. Impressions of Jewish alcoholics. *Journal of Studies on Alcohol* 37:931–939.

Shuval, R., and D. Krasilowsky. 1963. A study of hospitalized male alcoholics. *Israel Annals of Psychiatry and Related Disciplines* 1:277–292.

Teichman, M., Z. Barnea, and G. Rahav. 1992. Alcohol consumption among non-Jewish men in Israel: A pilot study. Paper read at Kettil Bruun Society meeting.

Weiss, S. 1988a. Primary prevention of excessive drinking and the Jewish culture: Preventive efforts in Israel 1984–1985. *Journal of Primary Prevention* 8:218–225.

———. 1988b. "Alcohol and Drunkenness": An innovative curriculum for the kibbutz movement in Israel, A model for adapting general prevention programs to special populations. *Journal of Drug Education* 18:267–274.

———. 1990a. Characteristics of the Alcoholics Anonymous movement in Israel. *British Journal of Addiction* 85:1351–1352.

———. 1990b. Experiences with Israel's kibbutzim project for preventing excessive drinking. Pp. 147–151 in N. Giesbrecht et al. (Eds.). *Research Action and the Community: Experiences in the Prevention of Alcohol and Other Drug Problems.* US-OSAP Prevention Monograph 4, DHHS Pub. no. (ADM) 89-1651. Rockville, Md.: OSAP.

———. 1991a. Adult women's drinking in Israel: A review of the literature. *Alcohol and Alcoholism* 26:277–283.

———. 1991b. A course on substance abuse prevention. *Journal of College Science Teaching* 21:9.

———. 1993a. Nonritual alcohol use among Israeli Jews. *Jewish Journal of Sociology* 35:49–55.

———. 1993b. Alcohol and the elderly: An overlooked phenomenon in the literature in developing countries—the Israeli case. *Drug and Alcohol Review* 12:217–224.

———. 1994a. Prevention of alcoholism in Israel among adult immigrants from the former Soviet Union and Ethiopia. *Addiction* 89:327–373.

———. 1994b. Community policy: How a new movement for policy changes to prevent excessive drinking was built in the kibbutzim in Israel. Pp. 80–87 in T. Greenfield and R. Zimmerman (Eds.). *New Research in the Prevention of Alcohol and Other Drug Problems: Experiences with Community Action Projects.* US-CSAP Prevention Monograph 14, DHHS Pub. no. (ADM) 93-1976. Rockville, Md.: CSAP.

Weiss, S., and P. Eldar. 1988. Alcohol control policy in Israel 1986–1987: Recognizing the need for diverse primary prevention initiatives. *Alcohol and Alcoholism* 23:515–520.

Weiss, S., and M. Moore. 1988. Various characteristics of alcohol use by Israeli high school students and field test results of the innovative preventive curricular unit "Alcohol and Drunkenness." *Journal of Alcohol and Drug Education* 33:59–66.

———. 1990. Cultural differences in the perception of magazine alcohol advertisements by Israeli Jewish, Moslem, Druze and Christian high school students. *Drug and Alcohol Dependence* 26:209–215.

————. 1991a. Alcohol drinking habits of Israeli Jewish, Moslem and Druze adolescents in the north of Israel in 1990. *Israel Journal of Psychiatry and Related Sciences* 28:20–28.

————. 1991b. Nonritual alcohol drinking practices among high-school students from the kibbutz movement in Israel: Implications for prevention. *Journal of Drug Education* 21:247–254.

————. 1994. Why, where and with whom do Israeli teenagers drink? To whom do they turn for alcohol problems? *Alcohol and Alcoholism* 29:465–471.

Wislicki, L. 1967. Alcoholism and drug addiction in Israel. *British Journal of Addiction* 62:367–373.

Zimberg, S. 1977. Sociopsychiatric perspectives on Jewish alcohol abuse: Implications for the prevention of alcoholism. *The American Journal of Drug and Alcohol Abuse* 4:571–579.

# 15

# Italy

*Amedeo Cottino*

## THE IMPORTANCE OF ALCOHOL IN ITALY

### Economic Factors

Although the yearly per capita rate of consumption in liters of absolute alcohol has long been declining, alcohol production still constitutes a major industry in Italy. Trade in alcoholic beverages represents approximately 10% of the gross national product; vineyards cover fully 10% of Italy's total surface; and nearly 14,000 companies are active within this sector, according to the last industrial census. In the mid-1990s Italians spend less on alcoholic beverages than in the mid-1970s, but the figure still represents almost 2% of the family budget.

Among alcoholic beverages, wine pervades most private and public spheres of life. It constitutes a basic ingredient of the Italian material culture as much as grapevines are an omnipresent component of the landscape. This character-istic is part of a common heritage, with ancient roots in Mesopotamia, that Italy shares with many other Mediterranean countries; and it makes itself evident in many ways. There is hardly any type of human activity that does not relate, in one way or another, to wine consumption. Therefore, it is not surprising that abstainers are viewed with curiosity, as odd persons who should explain why they refuse to drink wine. In popular culture, this attitude of disapproval has been very harsh, as is expressed in the saying, "May God protect me from those who don't drink."

### Cultural Factors

Italy is a country where people do not drink pure alcohol. Rather, Italians consume wine and, to a minor extent, other alcoholic beverages. In the everyday language, to say of somebody that he or she drinks, means that he or she is a heavy drinker.

Wine is seen as nourishment. In the past, the nutritional aspects were particularly relevant in the alimentation of the lower classes, whose poor diet needed precisely those extra calories that wine could provide. Those aspects have not disappeared, and wine is still regularly drunk in connection with food.

Historically, wine and distilled beverages have always played an important part in the Italian pharmacopoeia. From the Roman era through the Renaissance, prescriptions based on alcohol were used both in popular medicine and in modern medicine to heal most types of illnesses (Cosmacini 1987). Even today, along with the widespread use of any wine to cure colds, first-class wines are recommended in moderate quantities to people recovering from illnesses and to the elderly. Moreover, it is not unusual that physicians suggest moderate wine consumption to prevent cardiovascular disease, an approach that is recently receiving significant scientific justification.

Drinking practices constitute a relevant component of social life. Wine is not only a "guest of honor" on special occasions—such as major life cycle events like birth, marriage, and entering the military—but also whenever people gather during their leisure time.

Unlike temperance countries (Levine 1992), Italy neither praises nor condemns intoxication. This is not to say that abuse does not occur, nor that the Italian drinking culture overlooks the potentially negative consequences of heavy drinking. The Italian culture has developed its own control mechanisms.

First of all, there is what is called "regulated abuse," ritual occasions where people are expected or at least encouraged to get drunk (Forni 1985). This may occur in connection with the so-called rites of passage (Van Gennep 1909), when adolescents of both sexes affirm their adult identity; it may occur when young males celebrate receiving their draft notice, or when people marry. In this last case women may be allowed to trespass what is normally considered the appropriate threshold for their gender, which is lower than for men.

Another control mechanism limiting abuse is the strong emphasis placed on the consumption of wine in connection with food. This is precisely what is meant by the very common saying, "Never drink wine between meals." This ensures that alcoholic beverages never fill an empty stomach, and it also controls the amount of drinking by relating it to eating times. Moreover, much emphasis is placed upon the negative effects that heavy drinking can have on work and sociability.

This latter emphasis discourages drinking by people who have almost lost control over their alcohol consumption. If Italian culture does not place a moral stigma upon heavy drinking as such, it does tend to blame people who have no control. These persons are said to "have bad wine." They are stigmatized not because their abuse may damage their health but because it threatens the values of sociability and manliness. According to traditional values, a man unable to master his drinking is not a real man. More important, uncontrolled heavy drinking cannot be tolerated because is not compatible with the elaborate network of social relationships based upon drinking.

The fact that alcoholic beverages in general and wine in particular represent an integrated part of Italian culture is a two-edged phenomenon. On the one hand, this integration of alcoholic beverages into everyday life prevents stigmatization of heavy drinkers, at least to the extent to which temperance cultures do. On the other hand, alcohol abuse is late to be noticed, often not until physical damage and psychological dependence are already evident.

There are no exact figures on the breadth of alcohol-related problems and alcoholism in Italy. Official statistics are not considered reliable, in particular those furnished by the Italian state agency, which is often accused of under- and overestimating the data and of changing the criteria of surveys. As a consequence, there is no agreement as to whether alcoholism has increased or decreased in recent decades, nor how consumption is distributed. If there is any unanimity, it concerns the fact that alcohol abuse is no longer a social question in the historical sense of that term. Nowadays "heavy drinking" is not a class-related phenomenon but cuts across society.

The Italian National Research Council, by adapting the parameters originally elaborated by the French Comité National de Défense contre l'Alcoolisme, has estimated an increased occurrence of cirrhosis of the liver in the 1990s.

## THE HISTORICAL PERSPECTIVE

### Vine and Wine throughout Antiquity

Viticulture was known in the Mediterranean area before 3000 B.C. and was practiced by the populations "between the rivers," as Mesopotamia was called by the Greeks. Moreover, in the epic of the Sumerian hero Gilgamesh, wine represented an important means of access to divinity.

Archaeological findings in a tomb near Syracuse attest to the use of specific containers for wine as early as the late Minoan period (2000 B.C.). Presumably wine production was widespread in Sicily long before the first Greek populations sailed over the Aegean Sea to colonize Sicily, the island they called Oenotria, "Mother of Wine."

From the Greek colonies that were established there and in southern Italy from 800 B.C., the knowledge of how to grow vineyards spread to the Romans. There is evidence, however (Johnson 1989), that the Etruscans knew how to make wine long before the Romans. A population of uncertain and very disputed origin, settled in an area corresponding to parts of what are now Tuscany and Lazio, the Etruscans produced wine for local consumption and exported it as well, in large cargo ships, to northern Italy and to Gaul (what is now eastern France). Although the evidence is scarce, there are some indications that Etruscans did influence Romans in various ways. The fact that the name Chianti, referring to a famous vine-growing area in Tuscany, is believed to derive from the Etruscan name *clante,* suggests that the Etruscans introduced viticulture in this area (Pisani 1991). Also, the Latin word *vinum* seems to come not from the Greek *oinos* but from the Etruscan *vino.*

Unlike the Etruscans, however, the early Romans held a negative attitude toward wine. According to the rigid moral standards of the Republic, drinking was associated with weak character and considered beneath the dignity of a Roman citizen. In particular, according the laws of about 500 B.C., pregnant women were forbidden to drink for fear of damage to the fetus (Pisani 1991).

Profound changes in this attitude took place after Rome, having defeated Carthage, became the dominant power in the Mediterranean area. Significantly, Cato, an early and influential Roman politician and writer, gave viticulture priority over other crops in his famous agricultural treatise *De re rustica.*

Wine became a valued drink at the tables of the rich, and viticulture proved to be a very profitable enterprise. According to the Roman historian Pliny (about A.D. 100), excellent wines had been produced in Italy since the time of Emperor Augustus (27 B.C.–A.D. 14), with a concentration of vineyards in the area between Rome and Naples, with Pompeii and Ostia as major ports for shipping.

During this period one of the few attempts in Italian history to control wine production occurred. The triggering factor was the eruption of Vesuvius in A.D. 79, which not only destroyed the town of Pompeii and killed most of its inhabitants, but also covered the surrounding vineyards with ashes. Rome's wine supplies became seriously curtailed, and in an attempt to solve this problem, vast areas that had been planted with wheat were quickly converted to vineyards. The resulting effect, less than two decades after the eruption, was wine overproduction and a serious shortage of wheat and other basic grains. Very probably these were two main factors behind the edict of Emperor Domitian that prohibited new vineyards in Italy and ordered the eradication of half of those in the outlying provinces.

Although Romans did not place all the same symbolic and mystic emphasis upon wine that the Greeks had, and they stressed its role in economic terms, wine still played an important part in the Roman religion, literature, and art. Thus wine constituted one of the main ingredients of the religious *sacrifica* (offerings), and much literature and graphic and plastic art were devoted to describing the earthly and divine joys of drinking (Pisani 1991).

In the centuries following the establishment of the Roman Empire, the wine trade spread throughout Europe. The Romans established vineyards in North Africa, Spain, Portugal, and southern France. With the decline and fall of the Roman Empire, however, viticulture started to decline. This was not only a consequence of barbarian invasions and political and administrative chaos, but also a reaction against taxes. To defend themselves against exorbitant taxation, many landowners started cutting down the vines. This became so widespread that Emperor Theodosius (about A.D. 300) proclaimed the death penalty for anyone who destroyed vineyards.

During the Middle Ages, although the land devoted to viticulture was reduced, wine maintained a central place in culture and society. Partly this was because of its role in Christian ritual, especially the Eucharist. Monasteries were not only centers of grape-growing for the church but also avenues for diffusion of the techniques of viticulture through Europe.

With the town-centered development of local society (the *comuni*), and with a relatively unsafe countryside, most agricultural activities, including viticulture, took place close to the walls of the towns. As Pisani (1991) recalled, in Bologna, until recent times, places and streets with the names Vignozi, Vinozzi, Vinazzoli, and Vinozzetti were common; in Florence there are streets named Della Vigna Vecchia and Della Vigna Nuova.

Particularly during the Renaissance, the diffusion of *mezzadria* (sharecropping), and the consequent stabilization of peasants on the land, made possible crops characterized by long biological cycles, such as grapevines. In the following centuries, increasing knowledge of the biological and physiological mechanisms that govern plants has led to modern viticulture. This ancient but modernized system is confronted with several new challenges: reduction in the availability of manpower, increasing production costs, international competition, decreased consumption, and new styles of eating and drinking.

### The Rise of the Alcohol Question

The recurring preoccupation with the potentially negative effects deriving from alcoholic beverages can be found as early as 1750 B.C., with the Code of Hammurabi. In Italy, alcohol did not become an issue of general concern until the late 1800s. However, an earlier, limited concern existed at the end of the 1700s, when scholars started warning against the consequences of excessive drinking—for example, damage "to the fetus, to the newly born and to the elderly," as it is stated in a 1774 medical treatise. However, only when the country started to be industrialized in the late 1800s did substantial shifts in public perception of alcohol consumption and abuse occur (Cottino 1985).

At first, alcohol was considered a commodity to be taxed, like salt and flour. By 1880, revenue from the production tax on spirits represented a considerable share (up to 10% in some years) of the state's annual revenue. In the 1880s, however, physicians and legal scholars started presenting an alternative view of alcohol. They sought to stress a problem orientation. The doctors spoke of a medical problem, and lawyers started to call alcohol abuse a law-and-order issue.

The state began to address the health aspects of alcohol production, especially the deleterious effects caused by poor-quality wine. However, the debate remained centered within the scientific community, and it was within this arena that scholars elaborated the theoretical framework required by the dominant political and economic forces. In general, scholars agreed that not only were alcohol abuse and poverty interwoven, but also that alcohol produced physical and moral degeneration. As Colajanni (1882), an eminent Italian social scientist, put it: "Alcohol lessens, or in some cases completely removes . . . the inhibiting moral strength which we have inherited, or learned, which holds us back from criminal or simply inappropriate actions." A fundamental disagreement arose about whether criminality was the cause of alcoholism or an effect. Obviously, depending on how one looked at the causal links, quite different measures should be adopted to fight alcohol abuse. In other words, a controversy was whether misery or alcohol abuse was the causal factor of poverty and crime.

The intense and sometimes harsh debate on the correct interpretation of this causal link ended with the defeat of those who argued that poverty lay behind social problems such as criminality and alcoholism, and, more generally, that the major responsibility fell on the social organization. On one side, it was argued that "those who have difficulty in satisfying the more urgent needs of the material life . . . find themselves yielding more easily to animal instincts" (Allevi 1906). On the other side, Lombroso and his followers successfully maintained that alcohol was the primary cause of both crime and poverty.

The identification of alcohol with criminality did not last long, however. Although the 1881 Penal Code criminalized various forms of drunkenness, the general attitude toward alcohol abuse was to an increasing extent influenced by the medical model. In turn this was due to the fact that the *grande peur* (the fear of sudden, violent, and bloody protests by the oppressed classes) gradually disappeared and was replaced by a societal order that was characterized by an improved standard of living for workers. This was achieved largely through the increasing power of trade unions. In this way, the alcohol question no longer constituted so powerful an instrument for controlling the underprivileged masses. The focus on the effects of excessive drinking on health became a main concern for the scientific community.

For a few years, a temperance movement based in Milan attempted to draw public attention to the issue of alcohol abuse. The results, however, were meager. In spite of the commitment of the Socialist Party and its leader Turati, the restrictive law passed in 1913 did not seriously curtail access to alcoholic beverages. Nevertheless, the few controls, concerning off-premises licenses and the minimum age of consumers, were considered unacceptable by retailers, who reacted with a nationwide lockout. There has never really been any serious attempt to enforce the law.

When fascism first came to power, a radical shift occurred: alcohol abuse was once again looked upon as a criminal matter. In reality, however, Mussolini's major concern was political, for it was clear to him that proletarian pubs could significantly contribute to the working class's opposition to the regime. In Italy as elsewhere, the pub not only functioned as an unemployment and insurance agency but also provided a setting for political discussion and activity. The decision to close thousands of pubs probably was an effective means of controlling subversive activity.

## MAJOR DRINKING PATTERNS

In 1990 the per capita consumption of pure alcohol in Italy was about 9.0 liters (1 liter less than 1980). The country ranked fourth in Europe on a consumption scale led by Spain (11.7 liters per inhabitant). Today Italians drink, on the average, 60 liters of wine annually. It is estimated (Rossi 1992) that the amount may decrease to 45 liters by 2000, with an expected per capita consumption of pure alcohol of 7.5 liters.

Bars today play a significant role in the life of the Italians, as pubs did until a few decades ago. However, the bar is no longer a place for people to develop political activity or to look for a job—as was the case with the old *osteria.* Now it is a place where people spend their leisure time drinking, listening to music, watching TV, and playing cards or electronic games. Unlike pubs—which, like the American saloon and the French cabaret—were largely the domain of workers (predominantly male), bars today provide a context for sociability to a much more mixed clientele.

## VARIANT DRINKING PATTERNS

When national data are disaggregated, significant differences appear in terms of geographic region, social class, gender, and age.

### Consumption Patterns: North and South

Of the four main geographical areas into which Italy is conventionally divided, the "wettest" is the northeast, followed by the center, the northwest, and the south (including islands). Traditionally, northeastern districts (the Veneto, Friuli, Trentino-Alto Adige, and Venezia Giulia) have always ranked very high in alcohol consumption. The *ombretta* (literally, "little shadow," used to indicate a glass of white wine) has been, and still is, the most frequent vehicle of sociability among a predominantly peasant culture of small vinegrowers. At the other end of the scale, alcohol consumption in the south and the islands has always been below the national average. Why this difference should exist, especially considering that the best Italian grapes come from the south, has never been satisfactorily explained.

Most puzzling is that the low level of industrialization in the south does not correspond to higher consumption. This result flies in the face of the pattern that alcohol consumption is highest in communities with fewer than 20,000 inhabitants (Rossi 1992b). Other variables, apparently unrelated to the rural/urban continuum, should be taken into consideration. First of all, the very high concentration of alcohol in most southern wines makes them less suited for everyday consumption. Unless they are mixed with water, these wines can be drunk only in small quantities. Second, the control on women exercised in the south tends to be more rigid and strict, and one therefore might expect female drinking to be rarer there than in the other parts of the country.

## Consumption and Gender

"Women get drunk much less often than men . . . their life, centered around the narrow and tranquil family world, their limited freedom of action, their shyness, in many respects more developed among them than among men, constitute perhaps the main reason for preserving them from alcohol abuse." These lines were written in the 1890s by Zerboglio, a follower of Cesare Lombroso, the Italian psychiatrist who dominated the European scene with his ideas about crime and alcoholism, both of which he thought were largely biologically determined.

Today the sparse literature on Italian female drinking patterns can hardly support Zerboglio's explanations. Women have been able to overcome some of the hindrances established by men and have acquired more freedom. Scholars are no longer prepared to relate differences in consumption to mere biological differences. Yet women do drink less than men, although their drinking is increasing.

In the traditional peasant society, gender differences in consumption were very marked. Women might drink on certain specific occasions, such as a wedding—when the bride herself was allowed to drink—but, in general, they were not even supposed to say that they enjoyed drinking. A drunken woman was considered much worse than a drunken man because, in popular culture, a woman's getting drunk was considered unnatural (Forni 1985).

Several factors converged to keep peasant women—and those of higher classes as well—away from alcoholic beverages. First of all, drinking was men's domain, and women's seclusion from it helped males to maintain their patriarchal power. Second, men were accustomed to drinking wine both to compensate for their poor diet and to quench their thirst, particularly when working in the fields. Third, drunkenness was thought to make women sexually available, easy prey for males. A fourth reason, which has been put forward in discussing the condition of working-class women, is that proletarian females have often been expected to take responsibility for their family—obliged to have less "time out," to hold the purse strings, and to control their husbands' drinking.

This argument, also known as the thesis of the responsible rationality of women, underlines the role played by external factors in controlling and limiting women's alcohol consumption. However, women's relation to alcohol has often been marked by intense, mixed feelings of fear and resignation. There is plenty of evidence for this, particularly in peasant culture, where alcohol abuse has often represented an opportunity or excuse for men to direct physical and psychological violence against their women. As it was vividly put by Forni (1985), "To women quantity is the problematic aspect of wine; to men instead quantity is good because it provides them the opportunity to show their virility: to drink much without, apparently, being affected.''

## Consumption and Occupation

In preindustrial society, a large alcohol intake was often associated with hard physical work. There were some exceptions, mainly because for many unskilled workers, as daily laborers, wine represented a rare and expensive good. Moreover, different occupations exhibited different drinking patterns. For example, ordinary pub customers were definitely not peasants (who used to visit them almost exclusively on feast days), but merchants and traveling salesmen, notorious for being heavy drinkers. In contemporary society most differences are blurred, although impressionistic data still suggest that people in certain occupations, such as bartenders, workers in the building trades, and salesmen, tend to drink more than the average.

## Drinking among Youth

If there is anything like a typical adult consumer of alcoholic beverages, one can safely state that young people in Italy today are decidedly atypical. Until recently, literature on juvenile drinking practices was scarce and generally local in focus. Because much of the work was concentrated on highly circumscribed groups, like school pupils, it has been difficult to describe general drinking patterns. Thanks to two surveys (Doxa 1992; Cottino 1990), it is now possible to indicate how young Italians, aged fifteen to twenty-four, deal with alcoholic beverages.

To start with, in the nationwide representative sample of the Doxa investigation, 26% of the respondents are abstainers. The remaining 74% have consumed one or more alcoholic drinks on least one occasion during the preceding three months. Males consume alcohol more often (84%) than females (64%) and are ''heavier'' drinkers in terms of both quantity and variety of beverages. The number of consumers increases with age, with a significant acceleration after the age of eighteen. Analogously, the number of abstainers after the age of eighteen goes down to 13% for males and 33% for females.

From a geographical viewpoint, those who consume most are young people living in northeastern Italy (drinking wine by preference) and in southern Italy (where they consume beer more often). Consumption of wine and high-proof spirits drops abruptly when going from rural to urban municipalities. Presumably, this represents the effect of traditional cultural differences rather than the result of deliberate changes in nutritional habits. Ironically, alcohol consumption is highest precisely in those areas where knowledge of nutrition is most widespread (Rossi 1992b).

Finally, depending on the type of beverage, context varies. Wine is most often drunk at home with one's family; beer is consumed outside the home with the peer group. Moreover, patterns of occasional and between-meal drinking are emerging.

### Learning about Drinking

By and large, one can safely say that Italians have their first experiences with alcoholic beverages in their early teens, with the family and the peer group as the two relevant socializing agencies.

In the past there were marked geographical differences: in the vine-growing areas, where wine was relatively easily available, small children, especially boys, were often encouraged to drink. In their fathers' opinion and in spite of their mothers' protests, wine in moderate quantities would help them to grow and to become "really men." In the districts where wine availability was limited, women and children were excluded from alcohol consumption. Today most such differences have disappeared, largely because of the rapidly declining percentage of peasants in the total population. Nevertheless, there are indications that, for young boys, moderate wine drinking is still promoted by the family.

Because longitudinal studies are lacking, and most research is carried out on school pupils, it is impossible to know whether the age of the first drinking occasion in the general population of adolescents has changed and, if so, in which direction. The national survey by Doxa (1992) found that less than 20% of the youth who now drink some type of alcoholic beverages have been consuming alcohol more or less regularly since before the age of thirteen. More than 70% start drinking between the ages of thirteen and eighteen.

Although the family is responsible for the socialization to wine, adolescents generally learn to drink beer and high-proof spirits through the peer group. This is related to the fact that wine consumption occurs in connection with meals, whereas beer is mainly drunk in other social contexts, outside of the family.

## PROS AND CONS OF DRINKING

The issue of alcohol use and abuse has been drawing increasing attention in Italy. Although no voices have been raised in favor of prohibition, both media and medical lobbies have emphasized the breadth of alcohol-related problems, particularly drunk driving and cirrhosis of the liver. Apparently, although exact figures are lacking and official statistics are rarely, if ever, reliable, the death toll caused by drunk driving is estimated at more than 2,000 persons per year, and there are about 30,000 deaths a year from cirrhosis. Estimates of the number of alcoholics, depending on the definitional criteria that individual researchers adopt, vary from half a million to several million, in a population of more than 60 million.

No matter how calculations are made and how unreliable the data may be, no one can seriously deny that alcohol abuse does occur in Italy, with all the related individual and societal effects. Moreover, the fact that drinking is well integrated into religious, nutritional, socializing, and recreational practices makes these cases of abuse less visible, their recognition more difficult, and their treatment delayed. Yet, any observer of Italian society who is free from an a priori inclination to prohibition must admit that drinking, particularly of wine, plays many important roles in both private and public spheres.

The nutritional and therapeutic aspects of alcohol have lost importance, but this has not happened with respect to sociability, which is still very much built around alcohol consumption. Moreover, wine is invested with an immense cultural capital. The loss of many ancient traditions and of their religious components notwithstanding, the prosaic and profane approach to wine characteristic of the modern era has not totally erased the deeply rooted feeling that drinking possesses a symbolic value, a means to reaffirm one's identity and continuity with the past.

In spite of the many ways justified, emphasis upon alcohol-related problems, the Italian wine-drinking culture probably will survive, particularly if the global set of traditional drinking norms is revitalized. The real threat—a measure of it is represented by the dramatic drop in wine consumption during the 1980s—comes partly from the very significant changes affecting working schedules and nutritional routines, and partly from the diffusion of new alcoholic beverages, such as beer. Obviously, when lunch breaks are shortened, no real meal (by Italian standards) is possible, and in a light meal, beer often successfully competes with wine.

## CONCLUSIONS

Italian society has undergone significant economic and social transformations that have brought profound modifications in alcohol consumption patterns. As a consequence of this, even though wine remains the essential component of sociability, in the sense that it continues to be a part of hospitality and a facilitator of social interaction at bars or at parties, greater value has been placed on alcoholic beverages that are quite a bit stronger than good wine.

Caught between alarmist campaigns against drinking and competition from other alcoholic beverages, wine's position in Italian society may be seriously endangered unless future programs of prevention of alcohol abuse and of health promotion are constructed on the recognition of the existing drinking culture and not on its rejection.

## REFERENCES

Allevi, Giovanni. 1906. *L'alcoolismo*. Milan: Hoepli.
Colajanni, Napoleone. 1882. *L'alcoolismo: Sue conseguenze morali, sue cause*. Catania: Tropea.
Cosmacini, Giorgio. 1987. *Storia della medicina e della sanità in Italia*. Bari: Laterza.

Cottino, Amedeo. 1985. Science and class structure: Notes on the formation of the alcohol question in Italy (1860–1920). *Contemporary Crises* 9:45–53.

———. 1990. Bere e sapere? Cultura e controllo sociale. *Alcoologia* 2 (2):127–131.

———. 1992. *L'ingannevole sponda.* Rome: Nuova Italia Scientifica.

Doxa. 1992. *I giovani e l'alcool: Osservatoria permanente su giovani e alcool.* Rome: Otet.

Forni, Elisabetta. 1985. *Bere e sapere.* Turin: Il Segnalibro.

Johnson, Hugh. 1989. *The Story of Wine.* London: Mitchell Beazley.

Levine, Harry. 1992. Temperance cultures: Concerns about alcohol problems in Nordic and English-speaking cultures. Pp. 15–36 in G. Edwards and M. Lader (Eds.). *The Nature of Alcohol and Drug Related Problems.* Oxford: Oxford University Press.

Pisani, P. I. 1991. Historical aspects of the vine and wine in Italy. *Alcologia* 3:21–29.

Rossi, Daniele. 1992a. *Alcool: Consumi e politiche in Europa.* Rome: Otet.

———. 1992b. Alcohol consumption of the young and territorial factor: Some outlines of analysis. *Alcoologia* 1:47–51.

Van Gennep, Arnold. 1909. *Les rites de passage.* Paris: E. Nourry.

# 16

# Malaysia

*Charles Victor Arokiasamy*

The role of alcohol in Malaysian culture cannot be adequately examined without taking into account the extremely varied and cosmopolitan nature of the Malaysian society. Malaysia, divided into East Malaysia (the states of Sabah and Sarawak, on the island of Borneo) and West Malaysia (formerly known as Malaya, comprising the remaining eleven states and the federal capital of Kuala Lumpur), is a nation of startling diversity. With a population of only 16 million in an area of 127,581 square miles, it is a country of three major ethnic groups (Malay, Chinese, and Indian), four major languages (Malay, English, Chinese, and Tamil), and four major religions (Islam, Buddhism, Hinduism, and Christianity). In addition, there are many large tribes, especially in East Malaysia, with their own languages and cultures. This broad diversity is expressed in lifestyle, nutrition, dress, values, worship, physical makeup, and almost every aspect of life. For example, more than half the population is Muslim, for whom beef is the favorite meat and pork is absolutely taboo. More than one-third of the population is Chinese, primarily of Buddhist, Confucian, Taoist, or Christian persuasion, who have no taboos regarding the consumption of meat and for whom pork is the favorite meat. Another 9% of the population is Indian, mostly Hindu but with a sprinkling of Muslims and Christians. For most of the Hindus, lamb is the favorite meat and beef is taboo; for other Hindus all meat is taboo because they are vegetarians. It is not surprising, therefore, that in a land where the same food item is for one person a delicacy and for another is taboo, perspectives on alcohol are equally varied. Malaysia's diverse population offers multiple perspectives that have some striking similarities and some equally striking differences.

## HISTORICAL NOTES

Alcohol use has been present in Malaysia primarily since the arrival of European colonialists. Prior to British rule, the population was mainly Malay Muslims who lived under the rigid strictures of Islam against alcohol (Abdalati 1975; Dawood 1986). Alcohol use was therefore almost nonexistent, except for local home brews among the indigenous non-Muslims in East Malaysia, until beer, wine, and hard liquor were imported by British colonialists. In addition, local alcoholic drinks such as toddy (fermented from shoots of the coconut palm) and *samsu* (a form of rice wine) were introduced by Indian laborers who were imported by the British to work their rubber estates and to build the nation's roads and railways. Since the early days of British rule, royal and religious leaders in many of the local states protested British tolerance or encouragement of drinking. For instance, even though the influx of Chinese and Indian immigrants in Kelantan (on the east coast of West Malaysia) was minuscule, it led to the passing of legislation in 1915 forbidding consumption of alcohol by Malays as an offense against Islamic law and as an unseemly alien cultural importation (Roff 1974).

Alcohol consumption today is considered fairly high and widespread among the non-Muslim Malaysians, although reliable statistics are not readily available. According to Denison and colleagues (1985), citing a 1980 World Health Organization survey, Malaysians drink about 200 million bottles of beer and stout yearly, making them one of the highest consumers of such beverages in the world. Malaysia now produces its own beers under international brand names such as Guinness, Tiger, Anchor, and Carlsberg. Some of these beers have won international awards and are generally of very high quality. Malaysian breweries figure prominently in the relatively small Malaysian stock market. Most of these beers are sold in quart bottles that people pour into glasses or beer mugs rather than the small bottles that are common in the United States.

Although drinking is now fairly common, relatively little attention is paid to alcohol use or abuse either officially or by the populace. Use or abuse of alcohol in Malaysia raises nowhere near the concern that the use of illicit drugs does. For instance, although alcohol consumption is much higher and more widespread than the consumption of illicit drugs, there are no government treatment centers specifically for alcohol addiction. By contrast, in 1984 the government had six drug-rehabilitation facilities with a combined capacity of 1,200 beds in addition to treatment centers in numerous government hospitals (Department of Statistics 1986). The country also has about twenty private drug-treatment facilities (at least two of which treat alcohol addicts) run by Christian churches or Muslim welfare groups. Malaysia has some of the toughest laws in the world regarding the use of illicit drugs (Arokiasamy 1991, 1992). In 1983, the use of illicit drugs was defined as a national security problem, which made the possession of drugs a treasonable offense punishable by death (Scorzelli 1986). However, there are no comparable federal laws that restrict access to alcohol, except those specifically against illicit *samsu.*

There are a number of reasons for this relative lack of attention to alcohol use. Many people drink without having problems, and most of the problems that are caused by alcohol use are not readily evident on a societal level. Problems of alcohol use or abuse tend mostly to be private concerns of individuals: disruption of family life, employment, and so forth. Of the 80,526 reported traffic accidents in 1985, only 156 (0.19%) were said to be caused by driver intoxication (Department of Statistics 1986). This percentage is the same for the 59,084 accidents that occurred in 1980, with another 0.05% (27 accidents) involving intoxicated pedestrians. Furthermore, most problem drinking is perceived to be among the Indians, and more precisely the estate laborers or plantation workers (Denison et al. 1985; Marimuthu 1979). Ethnicity (locally called "race") plays an important part in all aspects of Malaysian life, and some have speculated that the drug problem has attracted a great deal of attention because it seriously affected the dominant ethnic group (Malays), whereas alcohol is seen mostly as a problem of a small minority, the Indians. In addition, whereas drug use cuts across all economic classes, the Indian laborer, seen as the primary alcohol abuser, is marginalized by being both an ethnic minority and a member of the lowest economic class.

## MAJOR DRINKING PATTERNS

Ethnicity and religion are the most important determinants of societal patterns of drinking in Malaysia, especially inasmuch as these two factors are highly correlated (von der Mehden 1980). Islam has very strict prohibitions (*hudud*) against alcohol. Drinking among the Malays (who are almost always Muslim), although present, is therefore minimal, especially in the east coast states of West Malaysia, where the populations are more than 90% Malay and Muslim. Any drinking among Muslims is mainly by the more modern or progressive Muslims, especially those with greater exposure to the Western world, such as students who go overseas for advanced studies.

The spread of Muslim fundamentalism since the 1970s (von der Mehden 1980) has made alcohol consumption a hotly debated public issue, even without an emphasis on drinking problems as such. A great deal of criticism has been leveled against the modern Muslims, including those in high government posts, for their tolerance of alcohol consumption and for drinking themselves. Fundamentalist Muslims want Malaysia to replace its current Western-style legal system with Islamic law (*Syariah*), as is the practice in officially Islamic countries like Iran and Saudi Arabia. Such a law code would strictly prohibit alcohol. The accession to power of the Islamic political party (PAS) in the east coast state of Kelantan led to the introduction of the Syariah Criminal Code in 1993. This law, which requires changes in the Federal Constitution before it can be implemented, would prohibit all alcohol consumption among Muslims in Kelantan. Under such laws, an offender could be severely whipped for consuming alcohol. Although, technically, non-Muslims would not be bound by these laws, in practice their access to alcohol would be severely curtailed by government bans on drinking in public places (except at a few that are specially licensed by the state to serve alcohol). Non-Muslims would be allowed to drink in the privacy of their homes, but even there, probably would not be allowed to serve alcoholic beverages to Muslim guests. Whether such laws can be implemented in Malaysia remains to be determined, partly because of the multiracial and multireligious composition of the population and partly because of opposition from less conservative Muslims to various aspects of Islamic law, such as its perceived discriminatory effects on women (Nordin 1993).

Among the drinking population of Malaysia—the non-Muslim population— the main alcoholic beverages consumed are beer and stout, followed by hard liquor. Some of the ethnic groups have their own local brews. Stout is very popular among all drinking Malaysians, including indigenous tribes such as the Ibans in Sarawak and the Kadazans and Bajaus in Sabah. It is often seen as the workingman's drink and is especially popular among manual workers, such as Indian and Chinese construction workers, Indian estate laborers, and farmers in both East and West Malaysia. Stout, a dark beer, is believed by manual laborers who toil in the tropical sun to be "cooling," helping the body release stored heat. It is also believed to be a healthful drink, adding nutrients to the body and giving strength for hard manual labor. A refrain from a jingle for a popular stout says "Guinness Stout is good for you."

Different types of food and beverages are believed to have heating or cooling properties and are referred to as "heaty" or "cooling." Stout, beer, and some whiskeys are seen as "cooling"; brandy is believed to be "heaty." These beverages are believed to increase or decrease body heat according to their respective properties. Brandy is so "heaty" that drinking it in conjunction with eating durian (a pungent, extremely popular seasonal fruit that is also classified as being very "heaty") has reportedly caused deaths. Toddy is a very "cooling" drink favored by Indian laborers. It is also seen by these laborers as a healthful beverage that promotes relaxation and helps them sleep. [Editor's note: Many readers will note the similarity to concepts of "hot" and "cold" in many classical, circum-Mediterranean, and Latin American cultures. In all cases, the qualities have nothing to do with temperature, yet there is a concern to maintain a sort of equilibrium between contrasting elements, for purposes of health.]

Hard liquor, such as whiskey (especially scotch) and brandy, carries connotations of sophistication because of its higher prices and association with British colonialists. It is sometimes seen as chic and civilized to sip hard liquor, as is done at cocktail parties that are portrayed on Western television (in recent years the soap opera "Dallas" has been very popular). Just as brandy and whiskey are often favored by the upper classes, beer and stout are seen as drinks of the middle class and toddy and *samsu* the drinks of the lower class, especially Indian laborers. These associations are generalities or stereotypes; beer is fairly ubiq-

uitous among all classes, and some hard liquor is consumed by the lower economic classes. Wine is rarely drunk, although it is used in Chinese cooking and
wine tonics are occasionally recommended for women after childbirth or for
anemia. Wine is sometimes drunk as toasts at weddings. Occasionally, champagne is used instead of still wine for special festive occasions. Drinking features
prominently in social celebrations such as weddings and large family gatherings,
and cultural and religious festivities such as Christmas, Chinese New Year, or
Deepvalli (the Hindu festival of lights). Social drinking is also common in the
evenings when friends get together. Given the communitarian ethic in most
Asian cultures, friends who get together for social drinking usually buy large
(quart) bottles that they share, rather than smaller individual bottles, with each
person taking a turn to buy a round. Friends promptly fill each other's glasses,
not letting them sit empty. It is seen as inhospitable if one does not show concern
over another's empty glass, which results in much mutual encouragement of
drinking. When a group gets together, the decision of what to drink is usually
made by consensus or informal vote. It is also common to get two or more
different brands to satisfy everybody's tastes. Alcohol is heavily taxed and is
relatively expensive, so it can take a large chunk of the earnings of those who
drink often.

Many who drink beer or hard liquor like to eat spicy food with their drinks.
Hence, social groups that get together for drinks often congregate at roadside
food stalls or restaurants and share their drinks over plates of fried noodles (*mee
goreng*) or fried or boiled spicy seafood, such as mussels or oysters. When
drinking is done at home, especially by groups, it is not infrequent to have
highly spiced meat dishes, preferably chicken or lamb, as accompaniments to
alcoholic beverages. Some claim that alcoholic beverages actually ''add taste to
my food, especially hot mutton and chicken curries'' (Denison et al. 1985, 7).
The protein of the meat dishes and the oiliness of these prepared foods are
believed to reduce alcohol absorption, although they actually only slow it. The
extreme spiciness of the food, which burns the mouth, encourages more drinking, especially of cold beer. Hence, people are often able to consume larger
quantities without rapidly getting drunk.

Some Chinese, Indians, Eurasians (descendants of mixed marriages between
Europeans and Asians), and even some Malays often stop at a bar after work
or drink at home in the evenings. Most of this type of drinking, if done frequently, is by individuals who drink alone. The highest proportion of alcohol
dependence is probably among such drinkers.

Most of the drinking is done by men. Alcohol consumption by women is
often viewed, especially by the older generation, as unladylike and perhaps an
indication of lack of virtue. Two surveys of Indian estate laborers (Denison et
al. 1985) found that only 16% and 5% of women in the respective samples
drank. All of the 5% in the second survey disclaimed daily drinking, admitting
only to drinking weekly or occasionally. Drinking by women is growing among
the younger generation, who are more influenced by Western values and the

disco ambience, where modern music and alcohol go hand in hand. Among those under thirty, drinking by women is more acceptable and drinking in general has fewer of the cultural taboos of the older generation.

Alcoholics follow similar pathways to addiction as do those in heavily studied countries such as the United States. In the early stages, being able to hold a great deal of liquor is seen as a sign of manliness. However, as a person progresses to dependence and drunkenness, he loses friends, family support, and work, soon becoming an object of pity and the cause of family disgrace. Alcohol consumption largely follows family lines. Drinking is most common among those who live in families with drinking members. However, with greater exposure to the West, it has become more and more common for children of nondrinking parents to start using alcohol.

## DRINKING AMONG SPECIFIC ETHNIC GROUPS

### The Chinese

In addition to the regular beers and stout, the Chinese also favor local Chinese beers such as Tsing Tao, brewed in Singapore. Brandy is a common favorite at celebrations such as weddings and the Chinese New Year. The addition of alcohol to wedding celebrations makes these occasions of boisterous conviviality. A trademark of Chinese drinking is the distinctive toast that consists of lifting glasses and yelling "YAAAAAAAAAAA . . . M" as loudly and as long as one can hold one's breath, ending in a thunderous explosion of the last of one's breath with the word "SENG." (*Yaam Seng* is colloquially translated as "bottoms up.") At Chinese weddings, it is customary for the bride and groom to make the rounds of all the guests' tables to be toasted. This often results in competition among tables for the loudest and longest toasts. The guests at each table stand, raise their drinks, and bellow out their best "Yaam Seng," holding the "Yaam" for as long as they can.

The Chinese in Malaysia are frequently seen as entrepreneurial, self-reliant, achievement-oriented, opportunistic, avaricious, and industrious (Rabushka 1973). As a result, excessive drinking on their part is often seen as well-deserved celebration by a group who work hard and play hard. Despite heavy alcohol consumption as the norm in convivial social contexts, a Chinese derelict alcoholic is rare. However, because of the propensity of some Chinese to become red in the face when they drink, they are often teased by others as unable to hold their liquor. Apart from the alcohol use described above, some alcohol is used in Chinese cooking, usually in the form of cooking wines. Alcohol does not feature prominently in any other aspect of their life

Although the Chinese in Malaysia are not a homogeneous group and come from different clans and geographical regions in China, there is no obvious difference in their drinking patterns by clan or geographical area. Some subtle, rather tenuous differences have been suggested. For instance, the Cantonese are said to be rougher, more raucous, and louder and more vulgar in their speech compared with the more mellow Hokkien or Teo Chew. These differences perhaps do modulate their style of drinking slightly, but seem relatively minor in relation to overall patterns.

### East Malaysian Tribes

As with all the other ethnic groups, beer and stout are popular with the indigenous peoples of East Malaysia such as the Ibans in Sarawak and the Kadazans and Bajaus in Sabah. In addition to these beverages, these tribes traditionally drink a home-manufactured rice wine called *duak* in Sarawak and *tapai* in Sabah. This rice wine, reportedly very potent, features prominently in harvest celebrations and in social or communal gatherings. At such important functions, especially the harvest festival, which is of much significance for these agrarian folk, almost all are required to drink. Refusal by guests to partake of *duak* or *tapai* is a breach of etiquette. Such drinking is an integral part of the culture of these tribes.

### The Indians

Alcohol use among Indians (migrants from India) presents a special case and merits greater attention. Like the Chinese, the Indians of Malaysia are not a homogeneous group. Most of the ancestors of the present-day Indians in Malaysia arrived as immigrant labor imported in the 1800s and early 1900s by the British to work their extensive rubber estates (Gullick 1969; Hall 1955; Kennedy 1970). Paralleling this flow of laborers was a smaller but continuous flow of clerks, teachers, entrepreneurs, merchants, and such who congregated in urban areas. This latter flow continued long after the importation of laborers was discontinued. It resulted in an important division, with regard to alcohol consumption, of the Indian population between plantation or estate workers and the urban Indians. The former were more than 80% Tamils, predominantly Hindu, from south India (Denison et al. 1985); the latter included larger proportions of other Indian groups: Malayalis, Telugus, Sikhs, Punjabis, Gujeratis, Sinhalese, and Sri Lankan Tamils. In addition to Hindus, this group included many Muslims, Christians, and Sikhs. The estate Indians came to be seen as menial, prone to drink, and generally of a lower class deserving little respect, whereas the urban Indians soon formed a respected middle class (Rabushka 1973).

The drinking patterns of the middle-class Indians are similar to the general drinking patterns described earlier, perhaps with somewhat higher levels of per capita consumption and problem drinking (such as public drunkenness, disruption of family life, wife abuse, etc.) than the other groups. Perceptions of problem drinking and drunkenness are mostly centered, however, on the Indian estate population, to the extent that "the image of the Indian laborer in the eyes of the other communities of Malaya was that of an inveterate drunkard'' (Arasaratnam 1970, 70). The drinking patterns of this group of Indians, and the relatively more frequent problem drinking of Indians in general, have earned the Indians of Malaysia the social stigma of a people prone to heavy drinking and even addiction.

The imported Indian laborers were largely single males intent on making money and returning to their homeland (Arokiasamy 1991). They came from a society with very rigid familial and social supports in terms of the caste system. In fact, to leave one's area of origin was to become an outcast. Emigrating to another country without their families seriously uprooted these Indians, leaving them bereft of their familiar cultural supports. Work on the estates was as hard and thankless as slave labor. Being situated in rural areas, the estates did not offer entertainment or social amenities. In addition, the estate management soon discovered alcohol to be an easy way to keep the Indians entertained and to get money from them, so alcohol was made readily accessible (Arasaratnam 1970). Every little general store carried alcohol. Each estate had its own still or stills to manufacture *samsu,* often run by enterprising Chinese. This liquor was unsanitary and usually served under squalid conditions, but it was cheap and potent. A glass of *samsu* could be had for 10 Malaysian cents (about $U.S. .04). It is no surprise, therefore, that alcohol consumption became a central part of the lives of these Indians.

Soon *samsu* was banned by law, but spotty enforcement and the ease and inexpensiveness of manufacture led to continuation of the thriving illicit market. A study of 3 of the eleven West Malaysian states in 1979 revealed 57,197 *samsu* drinkers in those states (Marimuthu 1979). Produced carelessly, *samsu* resulted in many deaths due to poisoning. Between 1960 and 1985, whenever large numbers of people died at a still, it captured newspaper headlines and led to a flurry of enforcement activities until attention died away. In addition to these more spectacular incidents, the potent *samsu* and the unsanitary conditions in which it was prepared often led to medical complications among those who drank it. In more recent times there has been a decrease in *samsu* consumption due partly to better enforcement but mostly to improved living conditions of estate workers.

In surveys of two rubber and oil-palm estates, 68% of the males in the first sample and 44% of the males in the second sample were found to drink alcohol (Denison et al. 1985). In the second, more detailed survey, toddy was the favorite beverage of 47% of the drinkers, followed by beer for 29% and *samsu* for 6%. It is common for these estate laborers to buy hard liquor at the beginning of the month, when they receive their salary; to shift to the less expensive beer toward the middle of the month, when they have less money; and to end the month with cheap toddy or *samsu.* Many of the drinkers on these estates spend their entire income on alcohol. It is also common for them to take advances on their salary to buy liquor, resulting in virtual debt bondage.

## DRINKING AMONG THE DIFFERENT RELIGIONS

Islam, Hinduism, and Buddhism all have strictures against the use of alcohol, with Islam having the most explicit and stringent prohibitions. All the religions in Malaysia that do not have such strictures at least preach moderation. Since each of the ethnic groups tends to be identified with particular religions, the discussion on drinking among ethnic groups sufficiently describes drinking patterns of different religious groups. Christianity, being the only religion in Malaysia to use alcohol as part of the religion, is more noteworthy and is described below.

The use of wine is common among Catholics and other Christian denominations as part of their religious service. This tolerance of alcohol and the fact that Christianity is a Western religion influenced by Western values has made it more acceptable for Christians to use alcohol than for members of any of the other religions. Many of the houses of Catholics had well-stocked bars, and Catholic clergy trained in Western seminaries or by European missionaries "drank like the Europeans." With recent sensitivity to local cultures, however, this lifestyle has changed somewhat. In the days of colonial rule and early independence, it was quite common for Christian families to have a wine toast, usually with fruitcake, at Christmas and sometimes on other occasions, such as the celebration of the New Year. Families would get together after the midnight Christmas service to raise this toast. In addition, Christians tended to use wine for toasts at weddings. With the passage of time, however, the Christmas and New Year toasts have generally fallen into disuse, though wine is still used at weddings.

## REASONS FOR DRINKING

The most common reasons for drinking are for relaxation from hard labor, to induce sleep (especially true of stout and toddy drinkers), health reasons (such as for digestion or to release body heat), celebrations, and to avoid problems. Among estate Indians, convivial drinking ranked low because most of the drinking was done at home and usually individually (Denison et al. 1985). Only 18% of their sample sought company when drinking. Alcohol provides a temporary escape for these laborers and other low-income groups from the daily grind of a very difficult life (Marimuthu 1979).

Within drinking groups, there is a great deal of peer pressure to imbibe. However, one must be careful in understanding this peer pressure. Instead of being pressure to be like others or to act like them, encouragement for drinking appears to be an extension of the hospitable nature of the Malaysian people. People are pressured to drink by hosts at any gathering. In groups that get together to drink, the role of host shifts, with everyone being solicitous of the others' well-being, taking turns encouraging the others to drink or filling their glasses. Often the "host" will not take no for an answer. One can see the same type of behavior when invited to eat.

Celebrations provide suitable occasions and legitimate excuses to drink. Sometimes those who do not serve alcohol, especially at weddings or religious celebrations, are considered miserly. To avoid such designations, hosts at these celebrations make sure there is ample liquor available. The free-flowing alcohol, the spirit of celebration, and the legitimating of overindulgence on these special occasions lead to much drunkenness.

## CONCLUSIONS

Despite the widespread use of alcohol in Malaysia, it cannot really be seen as an important cultural component of any of the three largest Malaysian cultures. It is not an integral part of traditional meals as it is with the French or Italians. Nor is it part of cooking, save for the minimal use of wines in Chinese cooking. Except for Christianity, a Western religion, it does not play any integral role in religion or religious ceremonies. Although it is widely used in wedding celebrations, it is not part of the wedding ceremony proper. When it does figure in folklore, literature, or drama, it is usually as a danger to be avoided. Only among the East Malaysian tribes is alcohol, in the form of *duak* or *tapai,* an integral feature that permeates traditional culture. In all other cases, its presence is due to the incorporation of Western lifestyles, or it is drunk for social and psychological reasons that may remain outside the core of the cultural realm.

Malaysia can be expected to continue to experience the tension between the assimilation of the drinking styles of the West and the strict prohibition of the fundamental Muslims. For now it appears that both will coexist for a long time, with abstinence being common, not prescribed by law but a purely personal or religious choice. Far more common is social drinking, in various ways and on various occasions, among the ethnic groups who comprise the diverse population.

## REFERENCES

Abdalati, H. 1975. *Islam in Focus.* Indianapolis: American Trust Publications.

Arasaratnam, S. 1970. *Indians in Malaya and Singapore.* Kuala Lumpur: Oxford University Press.

Arokiasamy, C. V. 1991. *The History of Rehabilitation Services in West Malaysia from 1957–1982.* Ann Arbor; Mich.: UMI.

———. 1992. Drug rehabilitation in West Malaysia: An overview of its history and development. *International Journal of the Addictions* 27:1301–1311.

Dawood, N. J. (Trans.). 1986. *The Koran.* New York: Penguin Books.

Denison, J. J., G. Sundram, E. Rajasooria, J. Selvamany, D. B. Lawrence, S. Maniam, J. Jayaseelan, and S. Selvaraj. 1985. Alcoholism among plantation workers in Malaysia. Paper presented at the First National Conference on Alcoholism, Pusat Seri Putra Anti-Alcoholism Centre, Ipoh, Malaysia.

178       *International Handbook on Alcohol and Culture*

Department of Statistics, Malaysia. 1986. *Social Statistics Bulletin.* Kuala Lumpur: Department of Statistics.

Gullick, J. M. 1969. *Malaysia.* New York: Frederick A. Praeger.

Hall, D.G.E. 1955. *A History of South-East Asia.* London: Macmillan.

Kennedy, J. 1970. *A History of Malaya.* 2nd ed. London: Macmillan.

Marimuthu, T. 1979. The illicit *samsu* problem in Malaysia. Paper presented at the Seminar on Health, Food and Nutrition, Consumer Association of Penang, Penang, Malaysia.

Nordin, M. 1993. (Nov. 19). Many questions on *hudud* laws still unanswered. *New Straits Times.*

Rabushka, A. 1973. *Race and Politics in Urban Malaya.* Stanford: Hoover Institution Press.

Roff, W. R. 1974. The origin and early years of the Majilis Ugama. Pp. 101–152 in William R. Roff (Ed.). *Kelantan: Religion, Society and Politics in a Malay State.* Kuala Lumpur: Oxford University Press.

Scorzelli, J. F. 1986. Malaysia's rehabilitation system: A challenge to the drug problem. *Journal of Applied Rehabilitation Counseling* 17(2):21–24.

Von der Mehden, F. 1980. Islamic resurgence in Malaysia. Pp. 163–249 in John L. Esposito (Ed.). *Islam and Development: Religion and Sociopolitical Change.* Syracuse, N.Y.: Syracuse University Press.

# 17

## Mexico

### Guillermina Natera Rey

**ALCOHOL IN MEXICAN HISTORY**

Maguey, or American agave (a sort of century plant), has been fundamental in Mexico's history. It is the source of pulque as well as other beverages, such as tequila and mescal. Pulque is made from *aguamiel,* the sugary liquid extracted from the maguey's heart and later fermented. Chili pepper, unrefined sugar, cooked corn, fruit pulp, or spices are sometimes added; many of these additions strengthen its alcoholic and irritating effects. Tequila is the liquor obtained by fermenting and then distilling cooked and minced maguey. Mescal is a liquor obtained by braising, fermenting, and distilling the maguey heads or yolks. Each of these drinks is made from different varieties of maguey (Peregrina R. 1993).

Although tequila and mescal are considered national beverages, they made their appearance only after the Conquest, when the Spaniards brought the knowledge of distillation processes they had learned from the Moors. Pulque is the beverage most deeply embedded in customs and rituals, because its use was closely associated with the religious beliefs of pre-Hispanic civilizations.

Archaeological findings suggest that pulque was present some 1,500 years before the next significant finding: the Toltec legend (about A.D. 50) claiming the discovery of *aguamiel* and other maguey by-products.

Although drunkards did exist in pre-Hispanic times, legitimate drinking was mostly ceremonial, confined to the upper classes, the old, and the wise. Commoners were allowed to drink only in certain situations: women after giving birth, to "strengthen their blood"; men and youths after exhausting work, to "restore their strength." Ceremonial drinking occurred as offerings to honor or placate the gods, to bless gatherings and collective tasks, to signal calendrical cycles, and to promote fertility in the fields (Celis R. 1985). Nevertheless, drunkenness was a grave misdemeanor. Illustrations in the Mendocino Codex indicate that habitual drunkards were considered unworthy neighbors and had their homes torn down. There were other punishments for drunkenness; for some, such as priests and maidens, being drunk meant a sentence of death.

It is significant that the destruction of a civilization was associated with the effects of alcohol. According to legend, Quetzalcoatl, a white and luminous god, bestowed upon the Toltec people such extraordinary benefits that they made him their main divinity, thus leading to the jealousy of his opposite, Tezcaltlipoca, a god as dark as night. In revenge Tezcaltlipoca got Quetzalcoatl drunk and had him dance about shamelessly, tear off his clothes, and finally fall down in complete inebriation. Such was his shame upon awakening that Quetzalcoatl decided to go away, leaving his people to themselves. This is the story of how the Toltecs, one of Mexico's greatest civilizations, were destroyed, having lost their god of light through alcohol.

During the colonial period, as early as 1524, Philip II of Spain prohibited the sale of liquor to Indians and the introduction of it into Indian towns. However, the crown controlled alcohol production and distribution for its own benefit. Throughout the colonial period royal permission was required to make wine and beer, to plant vineyards, to plant barley fields for beer, or to import black slaves to work them. One-third of all profits went to the royal treasury. As well as being a source of royal revenue, alcohol was used by the colonizers as an instrument of control of the native population (Celis R. 1985). Pre-Hispanic rituals were continued as in the ancient tradition. The Indians attributed the effects of drinking to the gods and to the pulque, not to the drinker.

The first large-scale vineyard was planted in northern Mexico around 1717, and various prohibitions were decreed thereafter in order to secure the Spanish wine monopoly. None of them were fully obeyed, however, and as a result vineyards extended throughout Mexico. As with wine and tequila, mescal production was allowed, banned, or ignored, depending on royal interests at the time. Mescal was frequently given to Indians to buffer the effects of fatigue and miserable working conditions. Prohibitions were decreed and enforced mainly for economic reasons, although they were phrased in terms of morality and decorum. They were largely enforced only with respect to Indians and plebeians.

After independence, alcohol policies became more openly economic. The change started with the 1822 taxing of pulque, wine, and hard liquor. This was followed by the 1833 suppression of prior regulations that had "proven unable to stop the excess of drinking" and the creation of others. The main beneficiary was the treasury, because it "was not possible to ban from us the abuse of liquor, source of so much disgrace and degradation among our people." From then on, there were numerous decrees, prohibitions, rulings, and administrative regulations concerning, for example, the regulation of conditions in bars and liquor sales outlets, taxation, licenses, restrictions on alcohol sales, but no special dispositions to fight alcoholism.

The Porfirio Díaz government at the end of the 1800s seemed to favor alcohol.

During this period pulque haciendas, vineyards, tequila production, and the beer industry all flourished. A tolerant 1878 decree ordered police to have a stretcher available to carry drunkards and to "put them away . . . only if unable to walk by themselves, if their living quarters are unknown or if disposed to cause or suffer damage." The situation was such that in the early 1900s, a study on alcohol pointed out the government's tolerance and questioned its policy because alcoholism was already labeled "an enemy that, if not destroyed or at least stopped, will end up demolishing our social structure" (Celis R. 1985).

Although the Mexican Revolution seemed to reverse this situation with a "dry law" for the Federal District passed in 1915, no important change came about until the 1932 anti-alcohol campaign. In the 1940s there was an Assembly Against Vice to determine new regulations regarding the sale of alcohol. In the 1960s there was a five-year ban on new liquor outlets and the closing of many already in operation on the grounds of hygiene. In the 1970s, President Echeverría preached by example, serving only fruit drinks at official receptions, and in the 1980s a National Anti-alcoholic Council was formed to coordinate efforts, study proposals, and bring together the initiatives of different organizations.

## MODERN ATTITUDES AND BEHAVIORS

In Mexico, knowing how to drink is a source of admiration and respect. Whoever can take the most is the most macho, since not drinking much is a trait of women. A man learns from childhood that if he doesn't drink, society will censure him; he will be thought of as a victim of nagging, or lacking in masculinity. Among the population as a whole, the attitudes of both men (62.8%) and women (53.8%) are favorable to "having a drink as one of the pleasure-giving activities of life" (ENA 1988); they also think that "it does some people good to get drunk now and again," and they endow alcohol with a quality that facilitates "a way of expressing friendship." Although these attitudes are common among young people, it is thought quite intolerable that they show any signs of drunkenness.

In general, it is believed that a man is obliged to drink, although nowadays it is more acceptable that a woman drink, as long as she doesn't get drunk. Alcoholism is still widely regarded as a mental illness. The person fails to "get well" because he or she lacks the willpower to stop drinking.

Alcohol persists as a very important element in Mexican culture. Although there are variations according to gender, alcoholic beverages taken as a whole affect urban, rural, and indigenous families, even though there are significant differences with respect to attitudes, myths, and attributions. The availability of alcohol in Mexico, as much as the amount of liquor—whether legally manufactured by large companies or the result of clandestine or domestic production—generates problems. At least forty mixtures of alcohol with regional herbs and fruits are sold. The clandestine production of alcohol has been estimated to

**Table 17.1**
**Consumption Patterns in the Population Aged 18–65**

| Type of Consumption | Male | Female | Total |
|---|---|---|---|
| Heavy drinker (at least weekly, with 5 or more drinks per occasion, over various years) | 14.2% | 0.6% | 6.8% |
| Frequent high (at least weekly, with 5 or more drinks per occasion, during past year) | 13.1% | 1.4% | 6.8% |
| Frequent low (at least weekly, but less than 5 drinks per occasion) | 3.8% | 3.1% | 3.4% |
| Moderate high (1-3 times monthly, with 5 or more drinks per occasion) | 20.9% | 2.7% | 11.1 % |
| Infrequent (less than once a month, regardless of quantity) | 14.5% | 21.5% | 18.3% |
| Moderate low (1-3 times monthly but less than 5 drinks per occasion) | 6.9% | 7.2% | 7.1% |
| Abstains (once a year or less) | 26.6% | 63.3% | 46.5% |

*Source*: Encuesta Nacional de Adicciones, 1991.

be almost as large as that of legal manufacture. The consumption of pure alcohol distilled from sugarcane has increased in recent years; it is drunk by the poor because of its low price.

The availability of alcohol is related to profit. This is the case both for legally manufactured and distributed alcohol that meets the dispositions of the General Law of Health, and for illegal alcohol. For example, licenses are often authorized even when requirements are not met, be they concerned with prices, quality, or location of sales outlets. Some critics complain that advertising uses values that tend to promote and legitimate alcohol consumption. The continuous presence of alcohol in the everyday life of Mexicans is the result. On the other hand, the typical consumption pattern consists of a low frequency of drinking but the consumption of large quantities on each occasion. All this has aggravated the situation in Mexico, turning alcohol into a very serious public health problem.

The National Survey of Addiction (ENA 1988) provides the first data on the distribution of alcohol consumption by region and sex for the urban population aged twelve to sixty-five (Table 17.1). The Central South region (states of Guerrero, Michoacán, Oaxaca, Veracruz) showed the lowest prevalence of dependency (4.7%); the highest was found in the Central region (7.2%). There were marked differences between the sexes. Drunkenness was uncommon in women, whereas 18% of the men reported getting drunk once a month or more frequently, and in the year preceding the survey, only 32% had not been drunk at least once. Only 17% of the women surveyed reported an episode of drunkenness.

For those twelve to seventeen years old, the differences between males and females were observed. Consumption of alcohol once a week or more was 7.2% for males and 1.4% for females. A far higher percentage of males than females fulfilled the criteria of dependency in this population: 12.5% versus 0.6%.

One-fourth of the drinkers consume 75% of the available alcohol. The male heavy drinkers are in the group aged thirty to forty-nine; the female heavy drinkers are aged thirty to thirty-nine (Medina Mora et al. 1991).

Both sexes drink all types of alcoholic beverage, even pure cane alcohol, no matter what their consumption pattern. The consumption of beer is high; in 1989, it accounted for 89% of the volume consumed. Beer is consumed in the greatest quantities in northern Mexico, and pulque is more common in the center of the country. The consumption of spirits is equally distributed throughout Mexico. Wine is consumed more by women. Cider and liqueurs are consumed relatively little.

The problematic consequences of consumption are illustrated by the following figures: deaths caused by alcohol-related liver cirrhosis have risen from 8 per 100,000 inhabitants in 1970 to 12.5 in 1990. Car accidents caused by drunk drivers reached 14.1% of the total in 1987 and continue to rise. Crimes committed while under the influence of alcohol have been rising since 1975. In 1986, 22% of admissions to hospital emergency rooms registered positive for alcohol. In 1989, the coroner's office reported that 29% of the corpses handled showed indications of alcohol consumption. It should also be noted that the number of sales outlets grew 25% between 1980 and 1986.

Alcohol consumption per capita in the population over fifteen years old rose from 3.8 liters of pure ethanol in 1970 to 5.1 liters in 1991. These figures may give the impression that Mexico is a relatively "dry" country. However, low per capita consumption, high rates of mortality caused by liver cirrhosis, the number of accidents, and the social consequences, together with the typical consumption pattern, put Mexico in the category of "mixed" (neither "dry" nor "wet" in the international perspective).

The importation of alcoholic beverages has increased enormously since 1987. These are frequently sold more cheaply than domestically produced drinks. In this sense the North American Free Trade Agreement promises to pose new problems.

In six of the thirty-two states of Mexico, the preliminary results of the National Survey of Addictions with respect to children between the ages of fourteen and eighteen show consumption in school of between 14.5% and 24%. The same source indicates that between 7% and 13% occasionally arrive at school drunk. The Federal District has the highest prevalence. Between 20% and 30%

of teachers say they try to help the children by giving them advice. The prevalence of alcohol is greater than any other drug and is the cause of a larger number of problems (Rojas et al. 1940).

## VARIANT PATTERNS IN RURAL AREAS

Alcohol consumption during work is still very common in rural areas. And peasants often drink with the boss after the day's work is over. In southern Mexico, Bunzel (1946) reports consumption practices linked with the exploitation of the peasant. First he is invited for a drink; then he is accused of drunkenness; then the overseer pays the fine in exchange for commitment on the part of the peasant not to leave the job; and finally his wage is reduced.

The role played by alcohol in rural communities is not always the same. Viqueira and Palerm (1954) described the behavior of the drinker in two ways, according to whether, when drunk, he was "like Apollo" (serene and controlled) or "like Dionysus" (wild and violent). In rural areas, the reasons for greater consumption levels are often religious or regional fiestas, the latter related to the harvest. In Milpa Alta, a semirural area near Mexico City, there are 12 villages that have a total of 300 fiestas a year. After each one it is common to find drunken men lying in the street. However, there is usually only one sales outlet for alcohol in the village. This suggests that many are drinking alcohol produced clandestinely, or a popular mixture of alum and pure cane alcohol (the alum supposedly enhances the effect).

In rural areas the reason for drunkenness usually given is that "life in the pueblo is very dull," so "the most attractive activity is drinking." In a Mazahua Indian community the weekly per capita consumption of pulque was calculated at 14.5 liters per adult and 1.5 per child. Besides pulque, the adults drink "pearls of ether and pure alcohol" and *teporochas,* a mixture of a soft drink with pure cane alcohol. Every week 3,000 beers are drunk. Good drinking water is less easily accessible than alcohol for these people. In a rural area of the state of Puebla, a per capita consumption of 24 liters of liquor and 237 liters of beer per year was found. However, since the women consume much less than the men, the per capita consumption for the latter is much higher. The liquor is legally produced by two factories with production reaching fifty liters a day. In addition, there are known to be at least six clandestine manufacturing facilities nearby (Berruecos and Velasco 1977).

In one rural area, the way of drinking serves to distinguish the mestizo from the Indian. There are two ways of drinking: one is accepted as legitimate and consists of drinking two or three times a week out in the fields, for comfort and not in order to get drunk; the other is alcoholism, which is understood as a form of drinking in excess and with greater frequency. In this area, the mestizo exploits the Indian by buying *piloncillo,* a type of raw sugar produced by Indians, and selling it to the liquor manufacturers at a great profit (Lomnitz 1987).

In general, alcohol consumption in rural and Indian areas follows ancestral custom mixed with modern elements. Some festivities are full of religious syn-cretism where alcohol plays an important role. The patterns of consumption in rural areas are similar to those of the urban environment, in that women drink much less and generally do not drink in the same places as men. They usually start to drink after reaching eighteen years, whereas men start earlier. Men may drink inside and outside the home. Women may drink only at home, and only once they come of age or are married. Some older women, depending on the role they play in the community, are allowed to get drunk or even to drink with the men. On other occasions, the women prepare the drink for the men. Usually parents accept a son's drinking but not that of a daughter. The population is disposed to become involved and help when someone has had too much to drink—for example, by helping someone in the street. They will not, however, defend a woman whose drunken husband is beating her.

## FAMILY, GENDER, AND ALCOHOL

In Mexico alcohol consumption is present in all areas of family and social life, including work in both rural and urban areas. Each moment of the life cycle, from birth to death—passing through baptism, wedding, and funeral—is marked by the use of alcohol. The same occurs in the agricultural cycle; alcohol is used to celebrate the completion of the various stages of the cycle. It is found in working life at all levels, and when birthdays, saint's days, and other com-munity festivities are celebrated. In effect, it is difficult not to learn to drink in Mexico. There is great freedom to drink. In some rural areas the ancient custom of feeding children pulque or other local alcoholic drinks still persists. Although in both town and country the men separate from the women to drink, neither the fact of drinking nor its effects are hidden. Consumption frequently occurs in the street, the most public of places. Children cannot fail to observe this behavior. Furthermore, parents often give the children a drop "to try."

Various studies show that more than 50% of alcoholics have a close relative (father, mother, brother, or sister) with the same problem. This does not mean there is genetic transmission, but rather socialization in a culture of alcohol (Natera et al. 1993). Behaviors that imply masculine dominance and feminine subordination in Mexican families affect the learning of attitudes toward alcohol. The man "should be a macho" who learns to hold his drink; the woman should not try to control the man and should relieve the discomfort of his hangovers. There is evidence that women "protect" the men, keeping them from knowing about problems in the family, to the extent that they are closer to what happens in the family. If a woman tries to control a man's drinking, she generates re-sistance. This sometimes triggers violence, so it is often assumed that alcohol causes fights.

The fate of the woman is to remain married. She feels needed; "although he hits me, I can't leave him" is a common sentiment. Only fierce violence leads women to ask for help. When a woman has a problem with alcohol, it is attributed especially to internal psychological problems. Women alcoholics frequently are abandoned by husband and children.

With respect to attributions of causality, the wife points to the husband's family: lack of affection, considerable authoritarianism, or overprotection. "Feeling a man," making a good impression, and feeling superior or brave are effects of alcohol that are mentioned as reinforcing. Much influence is attributed to work and friends. Mothers feel guilty if a child is an alcoholic: "I didn't give him (her) all he (she) needed" or "I was selfish and only looked out for myself," they will often say. They are also ashamed and prefer to hide the child's problem. Although they are held responsible for finding a solution, shame prevents them from looking for outside help in a timely manner. However, it is common for them to look to traditional resources, such as prayer or native curers, as ways of facing the problem of alcohol consumption and of finding relief from it.

The alcoholic may deal with the problem in various ways: by submission to divine will—for example, by swearing to the Virgin Mary or vowing to stop drinking for a given period. Or he or she may become resigned to being such a person, unable to change: "Thus was I born, drunk." Or he or she may challenge and defy the family: "No one will change me" or "While I live, I'm the boss." Some simply say, "My fate is to die drinking" or "Thus I was born and thus I will die."

Nowadays the family feels more threatened by the spread of psychoactive drugs in Mexico: "He's also been a drinker, but the most worrying thing now is that he's started to mix it with the weed [marijuana]" or some other drug.

## MAJOR POLICIES ON ALCOHOLISM

The traditional position has been to emphasize the treatment of the alcoholic. Current policy, however, recognizes that this is only part of the problem, and the focus is now on alcoholism as a public health problem. More effort is made in the area of prevention than before.

The General Health Law is very clear and precise as to how the problem should be dealt with at a national level. Every bottle or advertisement must carry a warning label: "Abuse in the consumption of this product is bad for the health." Persons under the age of eighteen cannot legally be served alcoholic beverages. Advertising should aim to foster moderate consumption, to induce and promote values, activities, and behavior that benefit the health of the individual and of society. The Penal Code requires that every person who commits a crime and is diagnosed as alcohol-dependent receive treatment.

Although all hospitals and clinics are required to provide preventive and curative treatment, there is a lack of trained personnel in this area. How to treat alcoholism is a subject much discussed today, because the reigning concept of alcoholism as an illness means that the hospitals receive the patients. The federal government's interests are currently represented by the National Council Against

Addiction, which is responsible for coordinating all the institutions involved in that area, be they public or private. The instrument is the revised Program Against Alcoholism (1992–1994), which synthesizes the objectives, strategies, and actions aimed at reducing the problem.

## REFERENCES

Berruecos, L., and P. Velasco. 1977. Patrones de ingestión de alcohol en una comunidad indígena de la Sierra Norte de Puebla. Mexico City: Centro Mexicano de Salud Mental.

Bunzel, R. 1940. The role of alcoholism in two Central American cultures. *Psychiatry* 3:361–387.

Celis, R. 1985. *El alcoholismo en México.* Vol. 4. Mexico City: Fundación de Investigaciones Sociales.

*Encuesta Nacional de Adicciones.* 1988– . Mexico City: Dirección de Epidemiología, Instituto Mexicano de Psiquiatría.

Lomnitz, D. 1987. Alcohol y etnicidad en la Huasteca Potosina, 1985. *Revista de salud mental* 10(4):183–192.

Medina-Mora, M. E., R. Tapia-Conyer, J. Villatoro, J. Sepúlveda, M. C. Mariño, and M. L. Rascón. 1991. Patterns of alcohol use in Mexican urban population: Results from a national survey. Paper read at Keitil Bruun Society.

Natera, G. 1987. El consumo de alcohol en zonas rurales de México. *Revista de salud mental* 10(4):163–182.

Natera, G., M. Casco, M. E. Herrejón, and J. Mora. 1993. Interacción entre parejas con diferente patrón de consumo de alcohol y su relación con antecedentes familiares de consumo en México. *Revista de salud mental* 16(2):33–43.

Peregrina Robles, Rodolfo. 1983. Aspectos agrícolas, industriales y comerciales. In P. Molina, C. Román, L. Berruecos, and M. Sánchez (Eds.). *El alcoholismo en México* Vol. 3. Mexico City: Fundación de Investigaciones Sociales.

Rojas, G. E., et al. 1993. Prevalencia del consumo de drogas en la población escolar. *Anales del Instituto Mexicano de Psiquiatría 13:* 192–197.

Viqueira, C., and A. Palerm. 1954. Alcoholismo, brujería y homicidio en dos comunidades rurales de México. *América indígena* 14:7–36.

## FURTHER READINGS

Almada-Bay, I. 1985. La crisis y la salud. Pp. 87–116 in P. González Casanova and H. Aguilar Camín (Eds.). *México ante la crisis.* Mexico City: Siglo XXI.

Bernal Díaz de Sahagún. 1938. *Historia general de las cosas de la Nueva España.* Vol. 5. Mexico City: Pedro Robledo.

Berruecos, V. L. 1984. El consumo de alcohol en algunos grupos indígenas de México. In L. B. Bernal Sahagún, Bernardo Navarro, and Arturo Márquez Selser (Eds.). *El alcoholismo en México: Negocio o manipulación.* Mexico City: Nueva Imagen.

Borges, G. 1987. El consumo en cuatro facultades de Ciudad Universitaria (UNAM). *Revista de salud mental* 10(2):85–96.

———. 1989. Prevalencia de bebedores consuetudinarios en México: Un análisis ecológico. *Revista de salud pública de México* 31(4):503–518.

Borges, G., H. Rosovsky, E. Rodríguez, and E. López-Lugo. 1990. Alcohol consumption and its impact in Mexico, 1970–1983: Mortality and crime. *New Trends in Experimental and Clinical Psychiatry* 4(3):228–239.

Calderón, G., C. Campillo, and G. Suárez. 1981. *Respuestas de la comunidad entre los problemas relacionados con el alcohol.* Mexico City: Instituto Mexicano de Psiquiatría.

Campillo, C., R. Díaz, M. Romero, and G. P. Padilla. 1988. El médico general frente al bebedor problema. *Revista de salud mental* 11(2):4–12.

Casco, M., and G. Natera. 1993. El alcoholismo en la mujer: La explicación que ellas mismas dan. *Revista de salud mental* 16(6):24–32.

De la Fuente, J. R. 1986. *Estudio internacional coordinado por la OMS sobre identificación y tratamiento de personas cuyo consumo de alcohol pone en peligro su salud. Fase 1.* Mexico City: Instituto Mexicano de Psiquiatría.

De la Fuente, J. R., and M. E. Medina-Mora. 1987. Las adicciones en México: El abuso del alcohol y los problemas relacionados. *Revista de salud mental* 10(2).

Díaz, G. R. 1982. *Psicología del mexicano.* 4th ed. Mexico City: Trillas.

*Encuesta Nacional de Adicciones.* 1988. Mexico City: Dirección de Epidemiología, Instituto Mexicano de Psiquiatría.

Fromm, E., and M. Maccoby. 1973. *Sociopsicoanálisis del campesino mexicano.* Mexico City: Fondo de Cultura Económica.

García, Z. G., and G. Borges. 1990. Problemas relacionados con el consumo de alcohol: Regencias hospitalarias, su evaluación y registro. Pp. 53–63 in *Anales V reunión de investigación.* Mexico City: Instituto Mexicano de Psiquiatría.

Gilbert, J. (Ed.). 1988. *Alcohol Consumption among Mexicans and Mexican Americans. A Binational Perspective.* Los Angeles: UCLA.

León, P. M. 1958. La mujer en la cultura indígena. *Nicaragua indígena* 21:6–8.

López Acuna, D. 1980. *La salud disigual en México.* Mexico City: Siglo XXI.

Medina-Mora, M. E., Z. García, M. L. Rascón, and B. R. Otero. 1986. Variables culturales relacionadas con las prácticas de consumo de bebidas alcohólicas. Pp. 167–172 in *Memorias III reunión de investigación y Enseñanza.* Mexica City: Instituto Mexicano de Psiquiatría.

Mendieta, L. N. 1939. Ensayo sobre el alcoholismo entre las razas indígenas de México. *Revista mexicana de psicología* 1(3):7–93.

Menéndez, E. 1992. *Prácticas e ideologías "científicas" y "populares" respecto del "alcoholismo" en México.* Mexico City: Miguel Othón de Mendizábal.

Menéndez, E., R. Di Pardo, P. Ravelo, P. S. Lerín, and E. Ríos. 1988. *Aportes metodológicos y bibliográficos para la investigación del proceso de alcoholización de América Latina.* Mexico City: Casa Chata.

Molina, V., C. Román, L. Berruecos, and L. Sánchez. 1983. *El alcoholismo en México.* Vol. 3. Mexico City: Fundación de Investigaciones Sociales.

Natera, G. 1987. El consumo de alcohol en zonas rurales de México. *Revista de salud mental* 10(4):59–66.

Natera, G., and M. Casco. 1991. Actitudes hacia la enfermedad mental en población general y en un grupo de profesionales de la salud. *Anales del Instituto Mexicano de Psiquiatría* 1991:176–182.

Natera, G., and M. Holmila. 1990. El papel de los roles sexuales en la familia y el consumo de alcohol. Una comparación entre México y Finlandia. *Revista de salud mental* 13(3):20–26.

Natera, G., and J. Orford. 1992. Research on the development of family abilities for the treatment of problems of alcohol abuse. Pp. 353–359 in J. Cohén-Yañez, J.J.L. Amezcua-Gastelum, J. Villareal, and L. Salazar Zavala (Eds.). *Drug Dependence: From the Molecular to the Social Level.* London: Elsevier Science Publishers.

Natera, G., and C. Orozco. 1981. Opiniones sobre el consumo de alcohol en una comunidad semirural. *Revista de salud pública de México* 23(5):473–482.

Natera, G., C. Orozco, C. Mas, and E. Rojas. 1985. Comparative analysis of two methods for the study of alcohol intake in Mexico. *Journal of Drug and Alcohol Dependence* 15(1–2):165–177.

Natera, G., and G. G. Terroba. 1982. Prevalencia de consumo y variables demográficas asociadas en la ciudad de Monterrey, N. L. *Revista de salud mental* 5(1):82–86.

Negrete, J. C. 1976. Alcoholism in Latin America. *Annals of the New York Academy of Sciences* 273:9–23.

Orford, J., G. Natera, M. Casco, A. Nava, and E. Ollinger. 1990. Coping with alcohol and drug use in the family. In *Report of a Mexican Feasibility Study.* Geneva: WHO, Division of Mental Health.

Rojas, G. E. 1942. Estudio histórico-etnográfico del alcoholismo entre los indios de México. *Revista mexicana de sociología* 4:111–120.

Rosovsky, H., G. Borges, L. Casanova, and J. Villatoro. 1990. Alcohol consumption and its impact in Mexico, 1970–1984: Socioeconomical variables. *New Trends in Experimental and Clinical Psychiatry* 6(3):127–136.

Secretaría de Salud, Consejo Nacional contra las Adicciones. 1992. *Programa contra el alcoholismo y el abuso de bebidas alcohólicas.* Mexico City: Instituto Mexicano de Psiquiatría.

Smart, R., G. Natera, and J. Almendares. 1981. A trial of a new method for studying drinking and drinking problems in three countries of the Americas. *Bulletin of the Pan American Health Organization* 14(4):318–326.

# 18

# The Netherlands

*Henk F. L. Garretsen and Ien van de Goor*

Alcohol has always played an important role in the Netherlands, although the per capita consumption has never been very high compared with other European countries. Consumption is much higher in southern European countries, as well as in neighboring countries like Germany, Belgium, and Luxembourg. Lower consumption rates exist in such Scandinavian countries as Norway and Sweden (De Zwart 1989).

The Netherlands cannot be characterized as a country with one predominant type of beverage; it does not have a "beer culture" or a "wine culture." Beer, wine, and spirits are drunk in relatively large amounts. The same holds true with regard to the norms and attitudes toward drinking: there is no predominant norm. In many aspects the Netherlands can be seen as a country with varied drinking habits and drinking norms. There have been many changes in those habits and norms over time. Also, the influence of the temperance movement has varied from very strong to very weak.

The consumption of alcohol in the Netherlands has been integrated into everyday life for quite a long time. The next section of this chapter discusses the role of alcohol in Dutch history. Then we present general information on drinking behavior and attitudes today. Variant drinking patterns and drinking behaviors of specific populations are then discussed. A later section deals with learning about drinking, how behavior and attitudes of young people are influenced by family, friends and others. Finally, a general overview and future concerns are mentioned.

## ALCOHOL IN HISTORY

### Early Use

The use of alcohol has been common in the Netherlands for centuries. Until the Middle Ages, wine was made of fruit and beer of barley or honey. The alcohol content of these products was low, and their availability depended on the season. Since about 1200, distilled liquor has been produced, and is available all through the year. However, these products were expensive. Geneva (gin), made of the juniper berry, was first produced in the second half of the 1600s. In the second half of the 1700s, the production of brandy from potatoes and sugar beets started. Since that time strong alcoholic drink has been within economic reach of everyone (Van Iwaarden 1992). Around 1880, the use of alcohol had increased to 7 liters (of 100% alcohol) per capita. Gin and beer were consumed most frequently.

### Temperance Movement

In the Netherlands, temperance advocates have been active since the first half of the 1800s. The Maatschappij tot Nut van't Algemeen (Society of Public Welfare) published a little book titled *Het morgenslokjen* (The Morning Drink) in 1804 (Maas 1982). Others followed. In 1842, the Dutch Association for Abolition of Spirits was founded. Around 1880, together with increased use of alcohol, a decrease in the number of members of the temperance movement occurred. However, the period from the end of the 1800s until after World War I was characterized by a newly strong and very active temperance movement. The abolition of spirits (but not the abolition of all alcoholic beverages) was pursued. Together with Christian temperance advocates, the socialist movement was very active. Alcohol was seen as an obstacle to reaching a better society (Maas 1982; Brijder 1979). The temperance advocates scored many successes and had considerable political influence. At the beginning of the 1900s, alcohol use per capita drastically decreased and health centers for alcoholics were founded. However, after this period a constant—at first gradual but later increasing—decline of the temperance movement occurred.

### Alcohol Use after World War II

A marked increase in per capita alcohol consumption took place in the period following World War II, especially between 1960 and 1975. Of all countries reporting to the World Health Organization, the Netherlands experienced the sharpest increase in per capita consumption (population fifteen years and older) in this period, from 2.5 liters in 1960 to 8.6 liters in 1975. After 1975 a stabilization (followed by a light decrease) became noticeable (Garretsen 1985). It is difficult to explain the increase in consumption. Different factors may be responsible: the increase in leisure time, the increase in income, a tendency to catch up with the drinking habits of neighboring countries (consumption has always been higher in Germany and Belgium), and perhaps the fact that as a consequence of secularization, Calvinistic attitudes have become less influential (Garretsen and Knibbe 1985). The twentieth century shows a constant accumulation of drinking habits and drinking environments in the Netherlands (Dekker 1978). Up to 1940, most drinking took place in pubs. After 1940, drinking at home became common. Since 1960, people still drink in the pub and at home, but also in other surroundings (like canteens of sport clubs, community centers, etc.). Around 1980, some studies revealed that alcohol was being consumed at work and in schools, although this was not common. Attitudes toward alcohol use have been changing along with the increase in consumption.

## DRINKING BEHAVIOR AND ATTITUDES

### Drinking Patterns

Since 1958 several major surveys of alcohol use have been conducted in the Netherlands. These surveys show no marked shift in the proportions of drinkers and abstainers. About 80% of the population over twenty years drink. However, since 1958, alcohol consumption appears to have increased, to varying degrees, among all subgroups of society. Drinkers on average consume more glasses a day than they used to (Garretsen 1989; Garretsen and Knibbe 1985). In 1958, the large majority of the population drank only occasionally and rather small amounts. Knibbe noted in 1984 that the variations in individual drinking habits could be summarized as "incidental moderate drinking" and "drinking at home almost every day." A third current drinking pattern (especially for younger people in the southern part of the Netherlands) is periodic excessive drinking (a comparatively high level of consumption during the weekend).

About half of the total alcohol consumed in the Netherlands is beer; about a quarter is spirits, and somewhat less is wine (De Zwart 1989). Males drink more beer and gin and other spirits; females drink more wine. The type of beverage also differs by region. For example, in Limburg (the most southern province of the Netherlands) considerably more men and women drink beer than in the larger cities in the western part of the Netherlands. And more gin and other spirits are consumed in the cities, especially by men.

### Drinking Norms

Various surveys indicate that new attitudes toward alcohol consumption have changed. It appears that there has been a change in attitude toward the consequences of drinking, such as against "being drunk every week," in favor of "not drinking on principle," and permissive about "becoming tipsy or intoxicated." Respondents in Rotterdam and Limburg in 1980/81 were less concerned about a family member's being tipsy occasionally than the respondents in the national survey of 1958. There were also regional differences: people in Limburg are more tolerant than in Rotterdam. This could be related to the traditionally more Calvinistic culture of Rotterdam compared with the traditionally more Catholic culture in Limburg. In general, the population at large seems to be more tolerant or more indifferent about the use of alcohol, compared with 1958. Still, there is no clearly dominant attitude. This can also be illustrated by the opinion of Rotterdam people in 1991: 39% think that alcohol use in the Netherlands is "much too high," but 23% think "not too high (or low)" (Reelick 1992). In general, males are more tolerant (or indifferent) than females, and the young are more tolerant than older age groups.

Not only are the norms for drinking and drunkenness important but so are attitudes toward alcoholism. How is alcoholism defined by the population? Most people in the Netherlands see being under treatment as the most defining characteristic of alcoholism—irrespective of the amount consumed and the presence or absence of any specific symptoms of alcoholism. This seems to illustrate the stigmatizing effect of having to get help and being a client (Garretsen 1985). Escape drinking (drinking to forget problems, to fight depression, etc.) is rarely considered to be a characteristic of alcoholism (Garretsen and Knibbe 1983).

To a certain extent, the attitude toward drinking is also reflected in the attitude toward measures to restrict consumption that have been laid down by the government. When Davies and Walsh (1983) compared the number of alcohol measures of fifteen European countries, they classified the Netherlands as a "low control country." Several studies show that there are no strong feelings one way or the other in the Netherlands about consumption-restricting measures. A substantial part of the population favors restrictive measures; a substantial part is against; and a substantial part have no definite opinion (Garretsen and Knibbe 1985; Reelick and Lamers 1991).

## DRINKING PATTERNS

The percentage of drinkers and abstainers has not substantially changed since the 1960s, whereas the amount of alcohol consumed per "average" drinker has almost tripled in the same period. This increase, however, is not spread equally over the various drinker categories. Females and younger adults have shown a larger increase in alcohol consumption than other drinkers.

### Drinking Habits by Sex and Age

Like most other countries the Netherlands has more male than female drinkers. At present, 90% of the adult males and 76% of the adult females say they drink alcoholic beverages. Traditionally, males drink more frequently and larger amounts per occasion compared with females. However, the amount drunk by women has been increasing more rapidly (De Zwart 1989). A similar trend can be found among the young drinkers. Whereas among those eleven to eighteen years old, about 25% do not (yet) drink alcoholic beverages, the amounts drunk by the 75% who do drink have shown an above-average increase since the 1960s (Van Dam and Driessen 1988; Sijlbing 1984).

Although the above information suggests that women have developed heavier drinking patterns, it appears that very few women tend to become problem drinkers (in terms of excessive alcohol use in combination with certain alcohol-related health consequences). The percentage of male problem drinkers is at least four times higher than that of females (Garretsen and Knibbe 1983). Partly this may be caused by stricter social norms regarding excessive drinking among women. Also, problem drinking among women may still be developing as a pattern. With respect to young people, it is important to mention that the legal drinking age in the Netherlands is sixteen. The drinking patterns of young people in the Netherlands differ considerably from those of the adult population. Their drinking can be characterized by three main aspects: (1) drinking almost exclusively in groups of peers; (2) infrequent drinking, concentrated on the weekends, often outside the home, in public drinking places; and (3) moderate or even low average consumption, but large quantities per occasion.

Most of the under-25 drinkers, especially males, can be characterized as periodic excessive drinkers—they infrequently drink large quantities. As in adults, young males in general exceed young females in frequency and number of drinks consumed. Recent research, however, shows diminishing differences in adolescents' drinking habits, especially between males and females aged sixteen and seventeen (Plomp et al. 1991). Compared with neighboring countries, drinking habits of the Dutch youth can be described as moderate. In Belgium a higher percentage of young people drink alcoholic beverages and drink large quantities on average. Only in Germany (as in the United States) is the frequency of drinking among young people slightly higher (Casselman et al. 1982; Schippers and Kwakman 1988).

### Drinking Habits by Region and Religious Affiliation

The statements about drinking patterns by sex and age should be understood as information concerning the "average" person in the Netherlands. Even in a country as small as the Netherlands, geographical areas sometimes show fairly large variations in drinking habits of the people living there. Religious affiliation is one of the stronger factors that influence these differences. Degree of urbanization is another. The southern provinces (except for Zeeland) are known for their relatively high average alcohol consumption, whereas the provinces of Zeeland and Friesland are known for their low average consumption levels. These geographical differences are closely associated with the religious affiliation of the majority of the inhabitants. The consumption of large quantities in public drinking places is more frequent among Roman Catholics and nonaffiliated than among Protestants (Garretsen and Knibbe 1983; Sijlbing 1984). Most of the Dutch Roman Catholics live in the southern part of the Netherlands.

### Drinking Habits in Specific Populations

In addition to differences in drinking habits by sex, age, and geographical region, other meaningful distinctions can be made. In general, the laboring population shows a considerably higher alcohol consumption than white-collar workers. This is not surprising because the Dutch labor force consists mainly of males aged twenty to fifty. As in all countries, that is the drinker category with the highest alcohol consumption. Certain professions, however, appear to be associated with heavier alcohol consumption. Those working in construction, transport, the hospitality industry, and commerce show a higher average alcohol consumption compared with the general working population. Workers in banking, insurance, and the hospitality field show the highest frequency of drinking at the workplace. Absenteeism due to sickness (frequency as well as duration) appears to be most common among both abstainers and those with excessive alcohol consumption. Interestingly, light and moderate drinkers show the least absenteeism due to sickness (Gründemann 1988).

Another category is formed by people from ethnic minorities. In the Netherlands, people from the former colonies (Suriname and some of Antilles), and people from Turkey and Morocco, constitute the largest ethnic groups. Unfortunately there are very few data on the drinking behaviors of these groups. This may be a consequence of the relatively small numbers of ethnic minorities in the Netherlands, or it may indicate that they are not yet well integrated into Dutch society. The little information available indicates that the people from Suriname and the Antilles may have considerable drinking problems. Most of these problem drinkers, however, are not treated or even recognized as such in the regular health care system. Huge cultural differences between the predominantly Caucasian Dutch health care workers and the darker-skinned problem drinkers result in difficult communication and limited recognition of alcohol-related problems among such drinkers. However, only further research can answer such questions (Ramlal-Körmeling and Rolsma 1989). The second large ethnic minority in the Netherlands, people from Turkey and Morocco, are predominantly Muslim. Islam does not allow the drinking of alcoholic beverages. The (again limited) information available from research among Turkish and Moroccan people living in the Netherlands supports this only partly. Problem drinkers are found among Turkish and Moroccan males, though the percentage is considerably lower compared with Dutch males (Gorissen et al. 1988). The drinking habits of the second generation of Turkish and Moroccan adolescents and young adults (those born in the Netherlands) appear to be more similar to those of the Dutch young people, which seems to be a normal consequence of cultural integration.

Because these second-generation youth encounter many problems—being raised between two cultures (the culture their parents were raised in and that of Dutch society, where they live), language, unemployment, being less educated, and so forth—they run a fairly high risk of developing addictive problems, among which drinking, using (hard) drugs, and gambling appear to be the most serious.

## LEARNING ABOUT DRINKING

In the Netherlands, as is the case in most European countries, alcohol is by far the most commonly used psychoactive substance in all age groups. The sharp increase in alcohol consumption in Dutch society, with a stabilization since 1985, has been accompanied by progressively stronger integration of alcohol use into everyday life. Drinking has become more accepted and more common for all groups, especially for women and young people. Norms regarding where to drink and how much one is allowed to drink in certain situations, and on certain occasions, have become less strict. The increase of accepted drinking places can be seen as a result of these changing norms toward drinking. Besides the home and public drinking places, youth centers, social centers, and even the office and the sports canteen have become places where alcohol use is not unusual. Consequently, young people encounter many more different situations in their everyday life activities where alcohol is being used.

### Age at Onset of Drinking

It should not be surprising that in the Netherlands, young people generally drink their first alcoholic beverage when they are quite young. Research has shown that among ten-year-olds, 42% have drunk an alcoholic beverage at least once (Plomp et al. 1991). Most of these teenagers are introduced to drinking at home by their parents, at around age eleven. This appears to be different from other countries, such as the Nordic countries, where teenagers rarely take their first alcoholic drink at home with their parents present. This introduction of teenagers to alcohol within the nuclear family might be seen as an indication of the relatively high level of integration of alcohol use in Dutch society. They do not drink much at home with their parents, though. The age at which adolescents start adopting more regular, adult drinking patterns is closer to the legal drinking age, fifteen or sixteen. The age of onset of drinking is almost the same in all west European countries. In earlier days the Nordic countries and Ireland were known for a higher age of onset of drinking (Ahlström 1988).

Until the age of fifteen, adolescents' drinking behavior appears to be influenced mostly by their parents' attitudes toward drinking. Whereas 15% of the fourteen-year-olds claim to have been drunk at least once, this percentage rises to 61% for the seventeen-year-olds (Plomp et al. 1991). At the age of fifteen, adolescents, especially males, expand their action radius, often visiting public drinking places and starting to adopt adult drinking patterns. From then on, when they start dating and going out, adolescents' drinking habits become more and more influenced by their friends' attitudes. Alcohol use becomes more important, not only because this peer influence increases but also because many of the occasions where young people meet are customarily associated with alcohol consumption.

This culture of drinking in public places is most common among adolescents and young adults in the south of the Netherlands and (generally speaking) in the smaller towns. Research showed that, especially for young males in the smaller towns in the south of the Netherlands, drinking—often periodically excessive drinking—is an important part of male status role (Knibbe 1984).

Group pressures and peer influences tend to be very strong among young drinkers. Observational research in this "wet" area in the south of the Netherlands showed that male heavy drinkers concentrate in same-sex groups of four or more. Drinking rates in such groups may go to more than five drinks an hour (mostly beer, in glasses of 25 cl., containing 12 g. of alcohol each) (Van de Goor 1990).

This way of drinking brings higher risks of several alcohol-related problems: drunken driving, serious hangovers resulting in absenteeism from school or work, and vandalism or group aggressive behavior. Besides legal controls and public health preventive activities at the local and national levels, alcohol education (especially in secondary schools) is implemented in an effort to change young people's attitudes toward drinking in such a way that they drink in moderation.

## Alcohol Education

Since 1985, primary and secondary schools in the Netherlands have paid attention to alcohol use (and smoking and, in secondary schools, sometimes drug use) in courses of health education. Besides facts about drinking, young people in these courses discuss norms, attitudes, and behaviors they see around them. Sometimes this includes the development of social skills to avoid social pressure when in a drinking group, by practicing these situations in role-playing. The aim of these courses is not to keep young people from drinking. In a society where about 83% of the adults drink alcohol and where alcohol consumption is not only accepted but also highly appreciated in many situations, aiming at developing a large percentage of abstainers is naive and unrealistic. The aim is to get young people to drink moderately and, most of all, responsibly. Another area that is quite important with respect to the development of responsible drinking habits in young people is traffic. In the Netherlands, young people can get a driving license when they are eighteen. The percentage of drunken-driving accidents in which an under-25 male driver was involved is nearly 50%, meaning that about 250 traffic deaths a year are accounted for by young people's drunken driving (VVN 1987; SWOV 1987). At present this problem is addressed by a more intensified control on drunken driving and harsher treatment of drunken drivers, in combination with compulsory education and treatment for repeat offenders. Apart from health education courses in schools, responsible drinking is encouraged in mass media campaigns. These campaigns mainly focus on young adult males (between twenty and thirty years of age).

## GENERAL OVERVIEW AND FUTURE CONCERNS

Alcohol use has been common in the Netherlands for some centuries. A steep increase of alcohol consumption—since 1960 the per capita consumption has almost tripled—coupled with stabilization on a high consumption level followed by a slight decline, marked the stronger integration of alcohol use into Dutch society. Average consumption now almost matches that of neighboring countries. Although gin was the favored drink in the first half of the twentieth century, it is no longer the typical drink. Norms and attitudes toward drinking have changed; overall, they are less strict. Male drinkers, but especially young people and females, now drink more alcohol per occasion (and are allowed to) than before.

Probably this more tolerant attitude toward drinking is the result of the general decline of the influence of the strongly moralistic religions. The influence of Protestantism and Roman Catholicism became much less strong during this period. Whereas cultural, economic, and sociological influences might be held responsible for the increase in alcohol consumption in the Netherlands, the stabilization and slight decline in the last few years may be the result of changes in Dutch alcohol policy, which has become more restrictive since the 1980s. More attention is being paid to specific areas where preventive activities are developed and implemented. National mass media campaigns, as well as courses for alcohol education in schools, have been implemented. Control of drunken driving is intensified, and in situations where alcohol may have serious effects (as at soccer matches), the sale of alcoholic beverages has been prohibited. A positive development is the introduction of low-alcohol and nonalcoholic beers. It is not yet clear whether these beers are added to regular consumption of alcohol or are being used as substitutes in situations where alcohol use is to be avoided (as when one has to drive or work afterward). In opposition to this introduction of low-alcohol beer is the trend of young adults' drinking liquors and distilled spirits. The alcohol industries are promoting distilled spirits for young people quite strongly, and they seem to be successful.

In addition to the drinking habits of young people, women drinkers require more attention. There are too few data available on women's drinking. The number of problem drinkers found in general research is usually too small to form a specific category (only one in five problem drinkers is female), so specific research on female problem drinking should be carried out. Moreover, data from treatment show that female problem drinkers in therapy profit from a different approach. Another major future concern is the development of drinking habits of the second generation of ethnic minorities. These young people now encounter many problems. Besides the conflicting drinking norms in the culture their parents lived in and the modern Western culture they grow up in, they may be a high-risk category for problem drinking because of difficulties they encounter in a society that has traditionally been quite homogeneous, and is slow to develop facilities for minorities.

## REFERENCES

Ahlström, S. 1988. A comparative study of adolescent drinking habits. Paper presented at Kettil Bruun Society, Berkeley, California.

Brijder, K. 1979. De hulpverlening aan verslaafden in de historie. Pp. 13–31 in R. Van Amerongen (Ed.). *Min of meer alcohol*. Alphen aan den Rijn: Samson Uitgeverij.

Casselman, J., G. Cooreman, O. Deraeck, O. De Wijs-Koppen, and W. Prové. 1982. *Jongeren en alcohol*. Deventer: Van Longhum Slaterus.

Dam, G. van, and F. M. H. M. Driessen. 1988. *Inventarisatie van alcohol en drugsstudies bij jongeren sinds 1969*. Amsterdam: Vrije Universiteit.

Davies, P., and D. Walsh. 1983. *Alcohol Problems and Alcohol Control in Europe*. London: Croom Helm.

Dekker, E. 1978. Elementen van een beleid met betrekking tot de preventie van alcoholmisbruik. *Tijdschrift sociale geneeskunde* 56:226–234.

Garretsen, Henk F. L. 1983. *Probleemdrinken*. Lisse: Swets en Zeitlinger.

———. 1985. *Developments with Regard to Alcohol Consumption and Alcohol-Related Problems*. Rotterdam: Municipal Health Service.

———. 1989. The Netherlands. Pp. 81–90 in World Health Organization. *Alcohol-Related Problems in High-risk Groups*. EURO Reports and Studies 109. Copenhagen: World Health Organization.

Garretsen, Henk F. L., and Ronald A. Knibbe. 1983. *Alkoholprevalentie Onderzoek Rotterdam/Limburg*. Leidschendam: Ministerie van WVC.

———. 1985. Alcohol consumption and alcohol control policy: The case of The Netherlands. *Health Policy* 5:151–158.

Goor, L. A. M. van de 1990. Situational aspects of adolescent drinking behavior. Dissertation, University of Maastricht.

Gorissen, W.H.M., P.C.M. Ticheler, R.P.M. van Kessel, and C. R. Souverein. 1988. *Gezondheidspeiling Utrecht: Resultaten van de gezondheidspeiling Utrecht 1986–1987*. Utrecht: GG. en GD.

Gründemann, R.W.M. 1988. Alcoholgebruik onder de Nederlandse beroepsbevolking. *Vervolg onderzoek alcohol en werk*. Vol. 1. Leiden: NIPG/TNO.

Iwaarden, M. J. van (Ed.). 1992. *Feiten over alcohol: Projectgroep Alcohol Voorlichtings Plan*. Rijswijk: Ministerie van Welzijn, Volkgezondheid en Cultuur.

Knibbe, Ronald A. 1984. Van gangbaar tot problematies drankgebruik Ph.D., Rijksuniversiteit Limberg.

Maas, M. J. 1982. In de spiegel der historie: Drankbestrijding in Nederland. Pp. 39–43 in G. M. Schippers (Ed.). *Alcohol en het menselijk tekort*. Amersfoort: De Horstink.

Plomp, H. N., H. Kuipers, and M. L. van Oers. 1991. *Smoking, alcohol consumption and the use of drugs by schoolchildren from the age of 10*. Amsterdam: Amsterdam University Press.

Ramlal-Körmeling, A., and G. J. J. Rolsma. 1989. *Onderzoek naar de aard en omvang van alcoholproblematiek bij Surinamers in de gemeente's-Gravenhage en randgemeenten.* Gravenhage: Stichting Surinaams Regionaal Steunpunt.

Reelick, N. F., and L. M. Lamers. 1991. *Gezondheidsenquête Rotterdam 1991: Gezondheid, gezondheidszorg en leefgewoonten.* Rotterdam: Gemeentelijke Gezondheidsdienst.

Schippers G., and A. Kwakman. 1988. Alcohol-, drugs- en medicijngebruik van jongeren. *Jeugh en samenleving* 10:527–546.

Sijbing, G. 1984. *Het gebruik van drugs, alcohol en tabak: Resultaten van een onderzoek onder Nederlandse jongeren van 15–24 jaar.* Amsterdam: SWOAD.

Stichting Wetenschatpelijk Onderzoek Verkeersveiligheid. 1987. *Alcohol en verkeer, een dodelijke combinatie.* Leidschendam: SWOV.

Veilig Verkeer Nederlands. 1987. *Alcohol en verkeer, dat kun je niet maken: Achtergrondinformatie over het rijden onder invloed.* Hilversum: VVN.

Zwart, W. M. de. 1989. *Alcohol, tabak en drugs in cijfers.* Utrecht: NIAD.

# 19

# New Zealand

## *Julie Park*

## THE SETTING

Aotearoa and New Zealand are two names for the same land. Aotearoa evokes a Maori and Polynesian history and the rights of the indigenous people. To the Polynesian ancestors of the Maori, the land, seen from a great voyaging canoe, resembled a ''long white cloud'' and became their southernmost settlement in Te Moana a Kiwa, the Pacific Ocean. For the Dutch explorer Abel Tasman, the rediscovery of these islands in 1642 provided an opportunity to name them for an area of the Netherlands. However, New Zealand was ultimately colonized not by the Dutch but by Britain. Although sustained contact between Europe and Aotearoa began in the late 1700s, only toward the middle of the 1800s did appreciable numbers of settlers arrive.

Two peoples with different traditions share one land: the Maori, alienated from much of their land and resources, struggling to claim their place as equal partners; and the Pakeha (New Zealanders of mainly European extraction), who brought with them their institutions and the trappings of modernity. The complexities of the relationship between the two limit the generalizations that can be made about any aspect of national cultural or social life.

In addition to these two peoples—the Pakeha, numbering 2.6 million, and the Maori, numbering over 400,000—New Zealanders include around 160,000 people of Pacific Island heritage who arrived or were born there, mainly after 1950, and substantial numbers of people of Chinese and Indian heritage, as well as small numbers of people from many other countries. The total population in 1991 was close to 3.4 million.

The land of New Zealand consists of two large islands and several smaller ones that are roughly the size of the British Isles or Japan (268,110 sq. km.).

Over two-thirds of the people live on North Island, nearly 1 million residing in the Auckland urban area.

## ALCOHOL IN NEW ZEALAND CULTURE

Aotearoa/New Zealand has been noted for its startling contrasts in the physical landscape—this is what brings the tourists—but for much of its history the country has been dominantly monocultural. There are many aspects to this image, and alcohol is one. Many of the alcohol-related images are both white (in racial terms) and male: the hard-drinking colonist; the man enamored of rugby, racing, and beer; the man who can hold his liquor; and, more recently, the man who knows his wine. National identities or stereotypes expressed in terms of alcohol are dominating images, obliterating diversity. As such, they are accurate symbols for what Jock Phillips (1987) termed *A Man's Country?* Phillips examined the beginnings of the Pakeha (white) "kiwi bloke" in the male-dominated society of colonists, and analyzed changes and continuity of this stereotypical masculinity in wartime, in peacetime, on the rugby field, and in the pub. He found that the costs of this stereotype were high for both men and women. Mateship (friendship) between physically tough, emotionally inhibited men, whose family role was mainly that of economic provider, epitomized the "kiwi bloke." Drinking large amounts of beer in all-male groups was, like sharing the experience of war or the experience of playing or supporting rugby, a central practice of this dominant type of masculinity. For these reasons, both gender and ethnicity are crucial in understanding the relevance of alcohol in New Zealand.

Having a drink in an accepted part of social intercourse for many New Zealanders. In home-based entertaining, relaxing with family and friends, celebrating or commiserating after a game, thanking people and giving gifts, meeting new people and saying farewell to old friends, there is no doubt that alcohol has a special place in the lives of many New Zealanders.

In recent years, with increasingly export-oriented wine and brewing industries, New Zealanders have been encouraged to take pride in the success of these products overseas, especially in countries that are the classic sources of these alcoholic beverages. The wine-growing regions of the country vie with each other in attracting a loyal following of drinkers, and both microbreweries and the national brewing giants tap into regionalism and patriotism in selling their products. The alcohol industry is an important employer and economic force in the country. Over the years, alcoholic beverages and the industries that manufacture, distribute, advertise, and sell them have received an enormous amount of attention, in terms of setting limits on their activities, thus indicating the importance society attaches to alcohol and its regulation.

Many New Zealanders' lives are adversely affected by alcohol: alcohol-related road crashes and other forms of violence leave few people completely unscathed, and there are groups active at all levels of society working to separate drinking

from driving. The misery of alcohol addiction and the suffering caused by alcohol-related problems of all sorts touch many: those involved in alcohol treatment and other forms of health care and their clients, those involved in alcohol
education and health promotion, and those involved at the policy levels.

## ALCOHOL IN NEW ZEALAND HISTORY

Alcohol was unknown in Aotearoa prior to the rediscovery of these islands
by explorers from Europe. In the late 1700s and the early 1800s, several navi-
gators and explorers, such as Marion du Fresne (in 1772), noted that the indigenous people, the Maori, were not fond of liquor and reacted in surprise and
disgust when they tasted it.

Many of the European visitors to New Zealand were, by contrast, extremely
fond of drinking alcoholic spirits. Sailors, whalers, traders, and escaped convicts
from the penal colonies of Australia were by and large hard-drinking and hard-
living men. Public drunkenness and brawling were clearly recognized as social
problems from the earliest days of European settlement.

This style of drinking was not immediately adopted by the Maori. Even by
the 1820s, the artist-explorer Ralph Earle noted that very few Maori were addicted to alcohol and even fewer became drunk. However, from the 1830s on,
observers began to remark on drinking and drunkenness among the Maori as
well as among Europeans. In 1835, five years before the Treaty of Waitangi
was signed between the British crown and the chiefs of many Maori tribes,
concern about the effects of liquor on both Europeans and Maoris led to the
first temperance society's being formed in one of the most populous areas, the
Bay of Islands.

Heavy drinking of spirits by men in public places was the predominant mode
of the time, but from the earliest days of missionary and governmental activity,
grapevines were planted and wine was made to be drunk with meals and offered
to guests. Indeed, one of the early winemakers was also president of that first
temperance society, indicating that unlike so-called temperance societies in
many other countries, sobriety rather than prohibition was its aim. Within European society, even at this time, there were at least two main styles of drinking.

Concerns about the negative effects of alcohol on the community eventually
led to legislative measures aimed at controlling the sale of alcohol. The 1974
Royal Commission of Inquiry into the Sale of Liquor in New Zealand divided
the 130 years after 1840 into five periods:

1. A laissez-faire period until 1873

2. Some efforts at regulation until 1893

3. A rising tide of prohibition and restriction until 1918

4. A long stalemate between prohibition and liberalization until 1948

5. Gradual liberalization until 1960, with rapidly increasing liberalization and normalization of alcohol after that date.

An important outcome of the 1974 commission was the establishment of the Alcoholic Liquor Advisory Council (ALAC), which was charged with promoting moderation in the use of alcohol and with minimizing the negative consequences of misuse.

Between 1974 and the mid-1980s, reform proceeded on a piecemeal basis, leading to an unwieldy legislative situation with highly centralized licensing control. Following intense public and governmental activity, a new Sale of Liquor Act was enacted in 1989; among other things, it simplified the licensing system and handed over some of the controls on the sale of liquor to local authorities. It kept the public drinking minimum age at twenty years, but allowed alcohol to be sold at a much wider range of outlets. Two years later, brand advertising of liquor, which had previously been banned, was permitted on electronic media, and ALAC was reviewed and redirected somewhat away from its public health stance.

Drinking practices have changed quite dramatically over the 200 years of European contact with New Zealand, and these practices have been both cause and effect in relation to liquor legislation. Public reaction to public drunkenness, violence, and road accidents (at that time, injuries sustained through falling off horses) brought about the 1873 Licensing Act; the efforts of the temperance movement to make drinking less attractive, coupled with the financial benefits to liquor retailers of providing only the most basic drinking conditions, gave rise to what are now regarded as the barbaric public drinking conditions of the first half of the twentieth century. Public reaction to these conditions led to amended legislation, upgrading of hotels, permission for bars to open in the evening, and the provision of entertainment and food in bars, as well as liquor licenses for restaurants.

The roles of men and women, both Maori and Pakeha, were different in relation to liquor legislation, as they were in relation to drinking practices. The Woman's Christian Temperance Movement (WCTU), established in New Zealand in 1885, was one of the pressure groups that favored prohibition. Its members, drawn mainly from the urban middle class, responded eagerly, in the belief that alcohol was the enemy of their domain, the home. Although both men and women worked hard for prohibition, the brewers and hoteliers took the women so seriously that they organized a petition and used an array of dirty tricks to try to prevent women from obtaining the vote. Their efforts probably delayed women's franchise, which was eventually achieved in 1893. Despite the fears of the liquor interests, votes by women did not lead to national prohibition. However, from 1894, a series of local-option no-license areas began to be voted in, and restrictions on the circumstances of the sale of liquor were put in place, such as no barmaids in hotels (1912), no sales after 6 P.M. (a 1917 "temporary war measure" that lasted until 1967), and no liquor at dances (1939). There was never any legislative attempt to ban Pakeha women from licensed premises, but the vast majority of customers were men.

In contrast, all North Island Maori women (except those married to Europeans) were barred from licensed premises and could not drink alcohol except on doctor's orders. North Island Maori men could legally drink only on licensed premises (and, by custom, were permitted only in certain bars); even after the laws were lifted in 1948, informal bans remained in some areas. South Island Maori men and women and all Pacific Islanders in New Zealand suffered no such legislative discrimination.

In the last thirty years of the 1800s, there were a number of petitions from Maori groups and individuals requesting local-option prohibition areas to protect their people from the ravages of alcohol and its agents. At the same time, contemporary observers noted that existing laws governing the sale of liquor were frequently broken by Maori people as a sign of defiance against the government. The situation was complex, and the operation of the Land Court (which brought Maori into towns for long periods and gave them cash), coupled with the use of alcohol as part of the process of persuading people to sell their tribal lands, is another factor that cannot be ignored. It is significant that many of the Maori prophetic or messianic religiopolitical movements and communities that sprang up in the late nineteenth and early twentieth centuries made an issue of community control of alcoholic beverages, often in defiance of the law of the land (Park 1984).

## DRINKING PATTERNS

As a review of the history suggests, there have been important changes in drinking patterns in New Zealand. In the early years of settlement, spirits were the mainstay of the drinking spree, but by 1870 beer had overtaken spirits in popularity, a situation that has continued to the present day for male drinkers. The stereotypical image of the Kiwi (New Zealander) male as being obsessed with "rugby, racing and beer" had its heyday until the middle of the twentieth century. From the 1960s, a new trend, wine-drinking, became significant. It was also around this time that middle-class women report beginning to drink on a regular or semiregular basis, rather than only on special occasions. The New Zealand wine industry started to grow; as well as being something to drink, local wines became an important source of national pride and a valued export item.

Although there have been annual fluctuations in the amount of alcohol that adult New Zealanders have drunk since the 1970s, the average adult has consumed ten to twelve liters of pure alcohol a year, over 50% of that being beer, 25% or 20% being wine, and the rest, spirits. Wine consumption has increased during this time, and beer and spirits consumption has generally decreased.

Of course an "average adult" is difficult to define in real life. New Zealand men drink about three times as much as women; younger men and women drink more than older men and women; women drink more wine than do men; men drink much more beer than do women. Drinking is such a gendered practice that it is hardly meaningful to talk in terms of an average New Zealand adult, even when describing overall consumption. It is even less meaningful to talk in these terms in describing drinking practices. Within these gender categories there is a wide range of variation, with class, ethnicity, occupation, and age being some of the important considerations in drinking patterns.

The most obvious drinking in any country is public drinking. In New Zealand this has changed remarkably from being a predominantly male preserve in the 1970s to being extremely diverse. In addition to the traditional hotel bars, large and small restaurants, licensed cafes, nightclubs, and bars cater to men and women of all classes, ages, ethnic backgrounds, and sexual orientations. Many workplaces have social clubs that cater to after-work drinking, and sports clubs are also a very important drinking venue.

Despite the popularity of drinking on licensed premises, the majority of alcoholic beverages are consumed in private homes. Women, except those in their teens and early twenties, are very likely to drink primarily at home.

Drinking patterns, types of drinkers, and drinking contexts are diverse. Wyllie and Casswell (1989) performed a cluster analysis on alcohol survey data obtained from a sample of New Zealanders aged fourteen to sixty-five and identified five clusters of types of drinkers for women and for men. The following text is based on their work; ethnographic research has been included where it is available.

Nondrinkers or abstainers comprised 8% of the men surveyed and 11% of the women. At the other end of the spectrum, 10,000 New Zealanders present themselves for the first time each year for help with alcohol-related problems (unpublished statistics from Alcohol Liquor Advisory Council).

The largest cluster of women comprised light drinkers. They represented 30% of female drinkers and accounted for 11% of women's consumption. On average, they drank the equivalent of just under half a bottle of wine at a time, about three times a month. These women drank mainly wine and some beer; they drank mainly at home; and they came from a wide range of socioeconomic backgrounds. In group discussions they were described by others as careful or sensible or special-occasion drinkers (Banwell 1991).

The second cluster were also light drinkers, but they differed from the first cluster in that they lived in situations where alcohol was readily available and felt under some pressure to drink. Many of them reported that they were reducing the amount they drank. These women comprised 18% of women drinkers and consumed 6% of the alcohol drunk by women. In the amounts they drank and their socioeconomic characteristics, they were similar to the other light-drinking women.

A third cluster, frequent at-home drinkers, contained 30% of women drinkers and accounted for 48% of women's alcohol consumption. These women were a little older than average and more of them were married. They tended to drink mostly wine or spirits and to have less than a half bottle of wine at a time, every couple of days. They tended to see alcohol as part of their lives and to like a drink with their meals. Such women would describe themselves as moderate drinkers, and their main drinking occurred at dinner (Banwell 1991).

Clusters four and five both comprised heavy-drinking women: the young and the very young. In cluster four were 12% of women surveyed. They drank 30% of the alcohol; had an average age of twenty-six; about half were single; and they tended to be of lower socioeconomic status. They drank on average twice a week and consumed the equivalent of three bottles of beer when they drank. As well as beer, they drank wine and spirits, often in their homes but also in hotel bars. The fifth cluster members had an average age of nineteen, and most were single. This cluster contained 2% of women drinkers and accounted for 5% of the alcohol that women consumed. These young women drank more spirits and some wine and beer; they drank on average twice a week, consuming about 5 double nips of spirits or a bottle of wine on a drinking occasion. They drank mainly away from home in a range of licensed and unlicensed premises.

The contrasts between the slightly older married women and the younger single women is well exemplified by an ethnographic study conducted by Marivee McMath on an army base (Banwell 1991). There the army wives drank mainly wine and spirits on two or three days a week, drinking a couple of glasses per occasion. The enlisted women drank mainly beer and spirits once or twice a week, but drank about seven glasses per occasion.

The five segments of male drinkers also ranged from light drinkers to very young heavy drinkers, but there were important differences between these clusters and the women's clusters in their use of alcohol. The first cluster of light-drinking men comprised 59% of the sample and consumed 28% of the alcohol. These men averaged about one and two-thirds bottles of beer every four days. They drank mainly beer but also some wine, and drank mainly at home.

The second cluster was of spirits-drinking men who were also light drinkers, but who had deliberately reduced their drinking. They accounted for 7% of the men and 4% of men's consumption. These men were different from the rest in that they drank spirits approximately twice a week, mostly at home, and averaged several glasses per occasion. They tended to be a little older than average.

Cluster three, the frequent at-home drinkers, drank daily, averaging a couple of bottles of beer at a sitting. They drank at home and in other people's homes, and drank with their meals as well as without food. These men were also older, and tended to be married and highly educated. This cluster accounted for 12% of the men and 26% of the alcohol.

Cluster four, younger heavy-drinking men, made up 20% of the male sample and drank 36% of the alcohol. They drank on average every two days and consumed three and a half bottles of beer when they drank. Home was the most common place to drink, but considerable numbers drank frequently in pubs, in clubs, and at the workplace. Over half of this cluster were single, and they were mainly under thirty-five years.

The very young heavy drinkers, cluster five, were mainly under twenty-three years, and nearly all were single. Only 2% of the men fell into this cluster, but they drank 6% of the alcohol—mainly beer, averaging five bottles a couple of times a week. They drank often in nightclubs and at work.

Young men in this last cluster are similar to those described in Hodges's ethnographic reports on young heavy-drinking men from the Otago area. These young men play competitive drinking games and enjoy much horseplay and dangerous use of motor vehicles. Hodges (1985) interprets their heavy drinking as attempts to explore the limits of power and control in the context of Kiwi male social relationships.

To these pictures of types of drinkers can be added information from other research about drinking situations and drinking patterns. Drinking in public bars and sports clubs is more associated with men than with women, with younger people than with older people. This is not to say that these settings are the exclusive preserve of younger males, but rather that young men predominate there. Some bars and clubs have gone to considerable lengths to make their environment more attractive to women patrons.

Rural and working-class pubs are especially likely to be primarily identified with male patrons. Recent studies of rural public drinking (Fairweather and Campbell 1990) stress the interpretation, well supported by research evidence, that the pub and the men in it are clearly opposed to the world of women and the home. This contrast has existed for a long time and has been dwelt upon by a succession of novelists, such as Ian Cross, who wrote in *The Good Boy* (1958, 12): "You'll probably find all the decency in life you can find is in a bar, drinking with a few friends, real friends." This is said by the hero's father, walking home with his son and bracing himself to meet his disapproving wife. The strong link between drinking together and mateship (or friendship) between men, and the opposition between mateship and men's relationship with women and the domestic sphere, is a recurring theme in Pakeha culture (Phillips 1987; Park 1990).

Maori writers have often commented that the pub is one of the few places where Maori can feel they are on "eyeball to eyeball" level with the rest of New Zealand society (e.g., Rangihau 1977). At the same time Maori drinking occasions can be times for reinforcing ties with kin or for creating quasi-kin relationships in an urban setting where few real kin are present. Although some *marae* (Maori meeting places) make provision for the serving of alcohol on appropriate occasions, alcohol is banned from others (National Council of Maori Nurses 1988). In such cases, a nearby pub, sports club, or converted garage may be used as a bar for family or community.

People from the different ethnic categories in the New Zealand population have a variety of ways of drinking. In the 1970s, an observational study of pub drinking indicated that Maori were more likely to drink in mixed-gender groups than either Pakeha or Pacific Island people (Graves et al. 1982). Since that time, more mixed-gender groups have been noticeable in the pubs overall, but the earlier findings could probably still be replicated today. Despite, or perhaps because of, Maori women's being banned from bars until 1948, Maori drinking in public is now most likely to involve groups of family and friends of both sexes.

In studies of women's relationship to alcohol, it was noticeable that Pacific Island and Maori women tended toward a pattern of infrequent drinking, although on drinking occasions they would usually consume several drinks. This contrasted with the predominant Pakeha women's pattern of drinking small amounts on a more or less frequent basis (Banwell 1991). Among Pacific Island and Maori people, in contrast with Pakeha, there are more abstainers and more people who stop drinking for lengthy periods. Surveys of alcohol consumption also find that Maori men and women report drinking less frequently than Pakeha, but they may consume twice as much during a drinking session. Maori and Pacific Island populations in New Zealand are young populations compared with the Pakeha, and part of the difference in drinking behavior can be accounted for by this fact. Similarly, part of the difference can be accounted for by socioeconomic status—drinking small amounts frequently is closely related to higher socioeconomic status and older age groups. However, even when these factors are considered, there is still some difference that in part may be attributable to patterns of sociability characteristic of Maori and Pacific Island groups, such as getting together in medium-to-large groups for periods of several hours, or even days, rather than meeting frequently in small groups for shorter periods, as Pakeha tend to do.

## LEARNING ABOUT DRINKING

Children learn about drinking and about alcohol, as they learn about most things, from watching the people around them, from what people tell them, and from reading, television, or other sources. But learning drinking is different from learning to ride a bike. Around drinking behavior there is a great deal of emotion and conflict of norms; in addition, beverage alcohol is a highly commodified and aggressively marketed product. Although children are somewhat protected by law from direct appeals by alcohol advertisers, they are still aware of alcohol advertising. For example, even before brand advertising was permitted on TV, many New Zealand children said they had seen alcohol advertised on TV. Usually they described various sorts of sports sponsorship, but quite often they talked about drama programs where alcohol was used extensively, or advertisements for other products that featured alcohol as part of the lifestyle portrayed.

New Zealand parents, particularly mothers, are concerned about their children's learning about alcohol. Many hope that by good example children will learn to use it sensibly or not at all. Other parents are concerned that they are setting their children a bad example, or that their children are learning about drinking behavior from undesirable sources.

There is a plethora of independent alcohol educational agencies operating at all levels of the school system, and alcohol education is part of the health curriculum. However, the effectiveness of such education is, as elsewhere, very much in question.

A particular focus in recent years has been in relation to driver education; and in combination with enforcement of regulations on drinking and driving and appropriate penalties, community health promotion programs and individual driver education would seem to have some chance of reducing alcohol-related crashes. There is a clear need for such improvement; alcohol-related fatalities amount to about 360 avoidable deaths each year (Bailey and Carpinter 1991).

## THE PROS AND CONS OF DRINKING

About 90% of adult New Zealanders have at least an occasional glass of wine, beer, or spirits. Drinking alcohol has wide acceptance in the society, and although it has been increasingly normalized as part of everyday life, many New Zealanders see it as something special: something with which it is especially appropriate to signal a special occasion, to mark a period of relaxation, or to transform an ordinary occasion into something special. Opening a bottle of champagne, bringing out that special bottle of wine or whiskey, "shouting" (i.e., paying for) a round of drinks, or having a party is the way to celebrate and mark life-cycle events, career moves, special times such as New Year's Eve, and the comings and goings of family and friends. This type of use of alcohol, when not carried to excess, is the sort of use that most New Zealanders refer to when asked "What's good about alcohol?" (Banwell 1991).

When asked "What's bad about alcohol?" New Zealanders—Maori, Pakeha, Pacific Island and others—have little difficulty developing quite a long list. Basing analysis on just what women said when asked this question, the answers can broadly be classified as either direct health problems or social problems. The health problems include liver complaints, problems resulting from alcohol use during pregnancy, and a range of "accidents," including car crashes and falls, that result from a person's being impaired by alcohol. The social problems include conflict and violence associated with the use of alcohol, loss of family income due to its being spent on alcohol, irresponsible behavior of all types, and problems in human relationships, especially family relationships (Banwell 1991). The cost of these problems has been estimated in monetary terms to be around 3% of gross national product, or around NZ$900 million a year, about U.S.$504 million, (unpublished statistics from Alcohol Liquor Advisory Council).

From a societal level rather than an individual level of analysis, it is clear that different categories of people bear the costs of alcohol disproportionately. For example, Maori people fare much worse in the mortality and morbidity statistics than do Pakeha, and this is related to their position vis-à-vis the dominant Pakeha society (Awatere et al. 1984). Lesbian women researching alcohol use in their own community noted that, like other oppressed groups, they had a tradition of using alcohol as an escape from some of the harsher realities of their lives (Lesbian Alcohol Research Project 1988). Young people, especially young men, are overrepresented in alcohol-related fatalities on the roads (Bailey and Carpinter 1991).

Some debates about alcohol have particular salience in Aotearoa/New Zealand because of national characteristics, such as an obsession with sport. Sponsorship of sporting activities by liquor companies gives the impression that drinking is a healthful activity for young people, a controversial issue. Closely tied to this is a debate about sport, alcohol, and violence. In an incident in July 1992, the entertainment provided in a hotel consisted of fights between untrained young men who fought for money and were not restrained by any sporting code. One young man among the patrons said that he thought it was good entertainment— no more violent than a soccer match. The reinforcement of negative features of gender stereotypical behavior by the alcohol-sport-violence convergence at a time when male violence is increasingly being identified as a major social problem is indeed socially problematic.

In reviewing alcohol problems and costs, one moves into a highly politicized sphere of argument over whether these costs derive from the product itself or from the characteristics of the individuals who (mis)use it. There is also debate about which harms alcohol use actually causes and what positive effects it may have (Casswell and Stewart 1988; Park 1992). These debates take place in a context in which the alcohol industry is big business, and taxes collected on alcohol are a significant source of government revenue, both of which have major implications for alcohol control policy.

At local and community levels, there are a number of initiatives being taken by Maori and non-Maori to try and minimize the ill effects of alcohol. These range from activities relating to the granting of commercial alcohol licenses to informal controls in one's own group. However, at present, despite the efforts of a strong public health lobby, the individualizing neoliberal philosophy favored by government and the normalizing of alcohol as part of everyday life mean that the public health perspective has a reduced impact on national alcohol policy.

## ACKNOWLEDGMENT

I would like to thank Dr. Fay Wouk of the Department of Anthropology, University of Auckland, for commenting on this chapter.

## REFERENCES

Awatere, Donna, Sally Casswell, H. Cullen, L. Gilmore, and D. Kupenga. 1984. *Alcohol and the Maori People.* Auckland: Alcohol Research Unit.
Bailey, John, and Adele Carpinter. 1991. *Beyond the Limit: Drinking and Driving in New Zealand.* Petone: DSIR Chemistry.

Banwell, Cathy. 1991. I'm not a drinker really: Women and alcohol. Pp. 173–205 in Julie Park (Ed.). *Ladies a Plate: Change and Continuity in the Lives of New Zealand Women.* Auckland: Auckland University Press.

Casswell, Sally, and Liz Stewart. 1988. Persuading parliamentarians: Advocacy and lobbying on alcohol-related issues. *Community Health Studies* 12:273–281.

Fairweather, John, and Hugh Campbell. 1990. *Public Drinking and Social Organisation in Methven and Mt. Somers.* Lincoln: Agribusiness and Economics Research Unit.

Graves T. D, N. B. Graves, V. N. Semu, and I. Ah Sam. 1982. Patterns of public drinking in a multiethnic society. *Journal of Studies on Alcohol* 43:990–1009.

Hodges, Ian. 1985. Drinking vernacular and the negotiation of intimacy. *SITES* 11:13–20.

Lesbian Alcohol Research Project. 1988. *Lesbians like Us.* The Place of Alcohol in the Lives of New Zealand Women 8. Auckland: Department of Anthropology, Auckland University.

National Council of Maori Nurses. 1988. *Te Hunga Wahine Te Waipiro.* The Place of Alcohol in the Lives of New Zealand Women 14. Auckland: Department of Anthropology, University of Auckland.

Park, Julie. 1984. *Towards an Ethnography of Alcohol in New Zealand.* Department of Anthropology Working Papers 66. Auckland: University of Auckland.

———. 1990. Only ''those'' women: Women and the control of alcohol in New Zealand. *Contemporary Drug Problems* 17:221–250.

———. 1992. Interested parties: A discussion of public statements in the alcohol arena in New Zealand. *Australian and New Zealand Journal of Sociology* 28:351–368.

Phillips, Jock. 1987. *A Man's Country? The Image of the Pakeha Male: A History.* Auckland: Penguin Books.

Rangihau, John. 1977. Being Maori. Pp. 165–176 in Michael King (Ed.). *Te Ao Hurihuri: The World Moves on.* Wellington: Methuen.

Wyllie, Allan, and Sally Casswell. 1989. *Drinking in New Zealand: A Survey.* Auckland: Alcohol Research Unit.

# 20

# Nigeria

## *O. G. Oshodin*

### DOMINANT PATTERNS OF ALCOHOL USE

In Nigeria, as in most African countries, alcohol is considered food, a necessary nutrient rich in vitamins, a stimulant, a disinfectant necessary to the body to fight against cold, fear, weariness and intrusive microbes (Inter-African Anti-Alcohol Conference 1956). Alcohol is justifiedly considered a nutrient because Nigerian palm wine is reported to contain 145 milligrams of ascorbic acid and 100 grams of vitamin C per serving (Platt 1956). These beliefs about alcohol prevail among all segments of the Nigerian population. Social customs encourage such beliefs, and the use of alcohol in Nigeria is often a reflection of cultural traditions and interpretations by parents and peers. If parents drink alcohol, the probability of their children's drinking is high; while if parents abstain from alcohol, the probability of their children's abstaining is high. However, the children are often exposed to faulty reasons for drinking alcohol. Such reasons include failing school examinations or the need to relieve feelings of stress.

Alcohols that are commonly used in Nigeria include native gin (popularly called *ogogoro*), palm wine, and Western gin, wine, and beer. Alcohol is very commonly used (Asuni 1975; Nevadomsky 1981; Odejide and Sanda 1976). Palm gin is a distillate of palm wine; locally brewed beers are made from various grains, and beer is also brewed in large factories; some alcohol is imported. Alcohol is readily available and is commonly used on both joyful and sorrowful occasions. With the recent increase in the number of breweries in Nigeria, alcohol problems appear to be increasing.

Alcohol is a central nervous system depressant; [I still believe that] the intoxication produced by alcohol which appears to be a stimulation of the brain is due to the fact that it depresses one's inhibitions. The consumption of small amounts usually produces mild relaxation; large amounts can cause loss of control of emotions, and impairment in decision-making and in problem-solving. Excessive drinking can, in extreme cases, result in respiratory depression, coma, and death.

Alcohol studies have often neglected early childhood, disregarding children up to the age of twelve. However, a study done in Nigeria on alcohol poisoning among children revealed the existence of a problem (Anumonye 1980). It was discovered that younger ones, including babies from a few days to several months old, sometimes suffered alcohol poisoning. Many of their parents indicated that they had administered alcohol, mixed with herbs, "to kill germs in the stomach" or "to cure malaria." There were also reports that some of the children drank the alcohol independently; often it was readily available at home because the parents sold alcohol.

The use and abuse of alcohol in Nigeria are both on the increase (Anumonye et al. 1977). Studies on alcohol use among secondary school students show that most are drinkers (Asuni 1975; Oshodin 1981 a, b; Nevadomsky 1985). More males than females indicate that they use alcohol. This could be a result of the fact that Nigeria is a male-dominated society. It is generally believed that males should drink more than females. Psychological and social reasons are often indicated for using alcohol among this group. The psychological reasons are to feel better, to reduce pressure or problems, reaction to peer-pressure, and confusion of self-image. Among the social reasons are that alcohol is a means of seeking a good time or a means to celebrate. Others cite the availability of alcohol. In Nigeria, alcohol is known to be consumed by teenagers on traditional festive occasions. The teenagers often take advantage of these occasions to use or abuse alcohol in an attempt to emulate adults. Often the main activities connected with the occasions overshadow the drinking, so an alcohol problem is not recognized.

The effects of economic development on the drinking patterns in Nigeria are obvious in the changes in the cost of alcoholic beverages. As the Nigerian economy changed due to the "oil boom," more breweries were built, alcohol became readily available, and more teenagers became involved in alcohol consumption. On many festive occasions, teenagers serve drinks, and have the opportunity to save some for themselves, to consume later. Studies show that students are drinking at an earlier age than previously. This could be as a result of the fact that children are sent to purchase alcohol, and they serve it during parties. Their access to alcohol gives them opportunities to try it earlier than young people in many other countries.

All the published studies done on alcohol in Nigeria agree that there are alcohol-related problems among students, including teenagers, and that there is a need to prevent or eliminate such problems. It is also the view of most researchers that if drinking problems were controlled or eliminated among this group, they might not long persist among adults.

As is typical in most African communities, alcohol plays a major role in social, political, economic, religious, and ideological relationships among adults in Nigeria. For example, in Nigeria, the bride-price and gifts to the bride's relatives can be alcohol. An analysis of a typical community best describes the situation of drinking patterns in Nigeria (Umunna 1967). Frequent occasions for drinking alcohol are engagement parties, marriage ceremonies, meetings, funerals, title-taking, festivals, worship of local gods, weekends, holidays, and gatherings of friends. Drinking usually is a sign of hospitality, functioning to strengthen bonds of friendship or kinship. During such occasions, there is no explicit segregation on the basis of age or sex. However, elders tend to drink more, and women generally are expected to drink less.

Even though Nigerians drink a great deal of alcohol, it is generally believed that it is bad to drink too much. For the prestige of a family, relatives make sure that an intoxicated person is not a nuisance. Occasionally, women may be excluded from drinking, though generally everyone participates. The youngest person present, usually a teenager, pours drinks from a container or bottle, handing the first cup to the oldest person and then to the others, in descending order of age. All males are usually served before the oldest female. Often only a single cup is used; hence it is regarded as a sort of communion, and social unity is reinforced. Unfortunately, that method of distribution of alcohol can promote the spread of communicable diseases.

The presence of teenagers during the consumption of alcohol enables them to emulate the adults; they probably feel that the consumption of alcohol is a way of achieving adulthood. In a typical Nigerian community, the more a man consumes alcohol and remains sober, the more respect he gains. This is now also a practice among teenagers, who hold secret drinking contests. Usually among Nigerian students, being able to drink and remain sober makes one a hero.

Some Nigerians feel that drinking is a means of emulating Europeans. A study on alcohol in primitive societies observed demoralizing effects of alcohol on primitive people (Horton 1943). Alcohol was found often to play a role in the acculturation process. Another study on a group in northern Nigeria found that beer plays a part in a great variety of social, political, economic, religious, and conceptual relationships (Netting 1964). A newly married man or one who has paid his taxes is entitled to a jar of beer from whoever brews it. In such economic situations as the cultivation of land or communal farming, beer parties are usually a form of payment for helping out. Beer is often given in exchange for services, for rent, and for wages. However, group drinking is always emphasized to promote unity. It is an occasion to talk freely, a time to weigh arguments, to release tensions, and a means of exposing areas of friction to public review. There is sometimes verbal aggression, but no physical violence, and the elders often arbitrate whatever quarrels may arise. Sexual approaches are acceptable as long as they do not lead to hostile acts. These practices are nowadays more common among rural than urban populations.

More city people use alcohol than do rural dwellers (Oshodin 1981a, 1981b).

More males than females drink, and more young people than their elders. Teachers in cities drink more than those in the country (Oshodin 1985). The concept of alcoholism as a disease is not accepted by teachers. Nigerian students studying in New York said that they drink alcohol when troubled with problems of urbanization, acculturation, or other social and personal problems (Oshodin 1982).

The pattern of alcohol use in Nigeria are related to family structure. A study on the dynamics of drug use found that most of the patients in a psychiatric hospital were from single-parent homes (Pela 1982). In addition, most of the patients were from polygamous or large monogamous families. This suggests parental deprivation, a finding in agreement with another study done in a hospital in a different part of Nigeria (Odejide and Sanda 1976).

## HISTORICAL DEVELOPMENT OF ALCOHOL POLICIES

The use of alcohol in Nigeria almost certainly began long before Europeans came to Africa. Palm wine and home-brewed beer from grains were the indigenous alcoholic beverages of importance. Palm wine still plays an important role in ceremonies like marriage, death, festivals, and naming ceremonies. However, the drinking of palm wine and local beer was controlled and moderate until the Europeans arrived in Africa.

When the Africans were introduced to European trade in the 1400s, foreign liquor, especially distilled spirits, was exchanged for native products. This increased the use of alcohol among Nigerians. The anti-slavery movement of the 1800s criticized a link between the slave trade and alcohol. The Europeans who were benefiting economically from this cheap spirits trade acted to bar the anti-slavery people's attempt to stop the alcohol trade. No concrete steps to curb the trade in alcohol came out of the Berlin Conference of 1884. A further effort to suppress the alcohol trade in Nigeria was the 1889–90 Brussels Conference Act, prohibiting the importation or indigenous distillation of alcohol in colonial Africa. This was further reinforced in 1895 at Abeokuta and Lagos, where similar resolutions were signed by a group of Africans. In 1899, 1906, and 1912, other conferences were held to examine revision of the alcohol provisions.

However, such efforts failed and commercial trade interests prevailed. Efforts to protect Nigerians and other African peoples from imported alcohol continued. When World War I ended, the Brussels Act was succeeded by the only international treaty concerned with alcohol until then. In September 1919, the United States, Belgium, Britain, France, Italy, Japan, and Portugal signed a treaty, and the League of Nations, through its commission, supervised the application of decisions reached at the convention.

When the International Council on Alcohol and Addiction convened an international conference in 1925 to examine the problem of alcohol and try to persuade the League of Nations to regard alcoholism as a health problem, there was strong opposition from wine-producing countries in Europe. However, in

1947, the World Health Organization (WHO) included alcoholism in its health program, and action that gave birth to a variety of treatment and prevention services.

The effects of treatment and prevention services in Nigeria are hardly felt even today. In the Muslim areas, religion forbids consumption of alcohol. But elsewhere, Nigerians generally believe that both palm wine and home-brewed beer are beneficial, although foreign alcohol might be dangerous to health.

During the sixth International Congress on Alcohol Abuse (held in Brussels in 1897), Bishop Oluwole, representing Nigeria, pointed out the dangers that imported alcohol was creating in Lagos, the capital. Although there were no statistical figures to back his claims, he assumed that the situation had increased crime. Bishop H. H. Trigwell, also from Lagos, stated that the trade in alcohol had prevented the trade in more useful articles, which was creating a serious handicap to the development of Nigeria (Anumonye 1980). In 1917, the governor general of Nigeria, addressing the Nigerian Legislative Council, implied that Nigeria would benefit if its foreign imports of alcohol were replaced by articles that would raise the standard of living and the comfort of Nigerians, or articles that would increase the output of the industries from which they derived their wealth.

In 1920, the government formulated a policy to control alcohol:

1. The extinction of the traffic in alcohol, of whatever origin, as an article of private trade with Africans and the restriction of importation of alcohol by levying heavy duties on alcohol.
2. The control of the sale of imported liquor by a licensing system in areas where its application was feasible.
3. Enforcement of prohibition in specific zones, and the extension of such areas where possible. The implementation of prohibition was most effective in the northern part of Nigeria; this was a result of Muslim religious beliefs that forbid the consumption of alcohol.
4. The substitution of light beer for imported alcohol. This policy was established because many of the imported drinks were found to contain a great deal of alcohol and the policy makers felt that substitution of a drink with minimal alcohol could help to reduce problems.
5. The control of the sale of local fermented liquor and the prohibition of tapping oil-palm trees, the source of palm wine.
6. The prohibition of local distillation except by special permit.

After World War II it became legal to distill or sell alcohol locally when the Nigerian Brewery Company was established in 1949.

## RECENT DEVELOPMENTS

In Nigeria today, the policy on prohibition of alcohol has become tempered in comparison with years ago, when tapping oil-palm trees to make wine and distilling alcohol except by special permit was prohibited. For some time, the country has experienced considerable economic strain, which has affected the production of alcohol in many breweries. The government may have succeeded in indirectly discouraging the consumption of alcohol by not providing import licenses for purchasing raw materials that are necessary for the large-scale production of alcohol. However, alcohol is freely purchased.

In southern Nigeria, prohibition for religious reasons is minimal, since most of the southerners are either Christians or practice traditional tribal religions. It is therefore evident that alcohol use is less prohibited in southern Nigeria than in Islamic northern Nigeria.

There are prohibitions on the sale of certain foods, cosmetics, and services as well as of drugs. It is forbidden to sell any drug (including alcohol) that is adulterated or was manufactured, prepared, preserved, packaged, or stored under unsanitary conditions (Food and Drugs Decree 1974). The implementation of this latter prohibition leaves much to be desired. Native gin (*ogogoro*) is still being produced under unsanitary conditions. Even the beer from the modern breweries is questionable, because there are no effective mechanisms by which its manufacture can be monitored.

It is also forbidden to prescribe or give alcohol as a treatment, preventive, or cure for any disease, disorder, or abnormal physical state. This prohibition is often ignored, since there is a general belief that alcohol can relieve stomach problems (Oshodin and Goyea 1983). Specifically, it is generally believed that Guinness stout (an Irish beer) can cure dysentery.

### Rationing

The rationing of alcohol occurs more frequently during some periods of the year. Large amounts of beer are produced by the breweries, both modern and local, and people have plenty of choices. However, during the Christmas and New Year period there is often a shortage of alcohol, whether real or artificially created. It could be real, because more people consume alcohol during this period. It could also be artificial because production and supplies are often controlled by middlemen or distributors in order to increase prices temporarily. Generally, alcohol is manufactured in all states of Nigeria, so that under normal circumstances rationing should not be necessary.

### Indexing of Prices

There are usually different price categories for alcohol. Factory prices are relatively low. After purchase from the factory, often by distributors, the price increases. The distributors often sell their alcohol at exorbitant prices, ignoring the government-stipulated prices. Retailers sell to consumers at still higher prices. On the average, a bottle of beer costs 1 naira, 30 kobo (N1.30) at retail, instead of the government-specified factory price of about 70 kobo (70k, less than U.S. $.10). This trend results from lack of enforcement of the prices set by the government. The percentage of alcohol and the month and year of manufacture, together with the price, all of which are supposed to be displayed on the bottle labels, are virtually never shown. The availability of alcohol in the market (which can be manipulated) determines the price of alcohol, especially beer. Often the price of beer will go up sharply if enough is not available in the market, whereas it will go down if enough beer is available.

## Taxation

There are taxes on both the production and the sale of alcohol in Nigeria. The breweries pay taxes to the government, though some of the breweries are owned by the government. The retailers (the restaurants, beer parlors, and bars) pay taxes for running their business. The taxes for selling beer or alcohol are usually imbedded in the total taxes paid by these enterprises. Consumers do not pay taxes directly for the purchase of alcohol or beer. However, the taxes are included in the price that consumers pay for meals and drinks. Home-brewed alcohol does not generate taxes even though those who make it are supposed to pay taxes for running such businesses. Again, this is a problem with the enforcement of the laws governing taxation generally.

## Regulation of Time and Place of Sale

Although there are laws stipulating that alcohol can be purchased only in restaurants, bars, beer parlors, and hostels, their enforcement is lax. In Nigeria, it is possible to purchase alcohol anywhere, because people continually ignore the regulations. For example, people sell alcohol from their bedrooms or turn their living rooms into beer parlors.

Government efforts to control the time of sale of alcohol have not succeeded. Although places selling alcohol officially are not supposed to be in business before noon on any day, many people wash down their breakfasts with beer. This is just one indication that alcohol is readily available at any time of day. The time at which alcohol sales must stop is ignored by both retailers and consumers. Although it is stipulated that alcohol sales must stop by 2 A.M., most beer parlors are open until 4 A.M. and may open early as 6 A.M.

## Age Restrictions

There is no age restriction for purchasing or consuming alcohol. In Nigeria, it is possible to see a five-year-old child purchasing alcohol for his parents or other elders. This has raised great alarm among researchers, who are calling on the government to come up with guidelines. Studies have shown that the problems of alcohol are more often associated with young children. The fault in this case could be attributed to the adults who send them to purchase alcohol.

## Controls on Advertising

There are basically no controls on advertising of alcohol in Nigeria. Alcohol is advertised freely on television, radio, or billboards, or in newspapers. One advertisement for Guinness stout emphasizes strength. It is therefore generally believed that by consuming Guinness stout, one will increase his or her strength or power. There is a law prohibiting the sale or advertisement to the general public of alcohol as a treatment, preventive, or cure for any disease or disorder. In addition, it is against the law in Nigeria to label, package, treat, process, sell, or advertise alcohol in a manner that is false or misleading, or is likely to create a wrong impression as to its quality, character, value, composition, merit, or safety.

## Public Education and Voluntary Groups

Private organizations and institutions, as well as the government, have been making efforts to highlight the effects of alcohol on society. Experts in drug use and abuse have, through seminars, research, and workshops, made contributions to public education regarding alcohol.

Voluntary groups in Nigeria also have contributed to public education. They have been able to educate the public on alcohol's effects on health through seminars and workshops, or launching campaigns against the use and abuse of alcohol and other drugs.

## INSTITUTIONAL AND LEGAL FRAMEWORK

The enactment and implementation of the institutional and legal framework of alcohol are often carried out by government. The laws prohibit the sale of adulterated alcohol and the advertisement or importation, exportation, or distribution of alcohol, especially if it is manufactured in a foreign country. There are also prohibitions of misleading practices. These regulations are applicable at both the national and state levels. The regulations determine what constitutes adulterated alcohol. They prescribe the type and level of additive or contaminant that may be present in alcohol offered for sale; standards of composition, potency, and purity; and methods of preparing, manufacturing, preserving, and testing alcohol. Any person who contravenes any of the regulations and is found guilty is liable, on conviction, to a fine or imprisonment. The same holds when an offense is committed by a corporate body or by an official of a corporation.

Violations of the alcohol regulations are identified through inspection of production, processing, and preparation establishments, and retail outlets; import control; investigations of product complaints; sampling; and laboratory testing (Federal Ministry of Health n.d). Prosecution is usually a last resort. The purpose of a court action is to gain compliance. Prosecution is seen as a punitive action for past violations.

Alcohol may be rendered unusable through denaturation or destroying it (in the containers) by crushing, burning, or burying. Sometimes the owner or dealer will voluntarily destroy the product. Recalling may be done to stop the distribution of alcohol the government believes is in violation of the laws.

## FUTURE CONCERNS AND IMPLICATIONS

Many studies claim to have identified the problems of alcohol in Nigeria, although none actually documents them. Drinking is mistakenly equated with abuse, so there is a clamor to eliminate even moderate drinking. However, any such policy should consider the sociocultural approach if any progress is to be made.

Alcohol education programs should probably be initiated at an early age. They could be aimed at prevention and counseling, which would help to eliminate some of the psychological and sociological reasons for misusing alcohol. There is probably also a need to incorporate some discussion of alcohol in the school curriculum. Subjects as diverse as chemistry, social studies, health sciences, biology, and history could incorporate these discussions. This would educate the children about alcohol and presumably lessen problem drinking in the future.

## REFERENCES

Adomakoh, C. C. 1976. Alcoholism: The African scene. *Annals of the New York Academy of Sciences* 172:39–46.

Anumonye, A. 1980. Drug use among people in Lagos, Nigeria. *Narcotic Bulletin* 32(4): 39–45.

Anumonye, A., N. Omoniwa, and N. Adaramijo. 1977. Excessive alcohol use and related problems in Nigeria. *Drug and Alcohol Dependence* 2:23–30.

Asuni, T. 1975. Pattern of alcohol problems seen in the Neuro-Psychiatric Hospital, Aro, Abeokuta, 1963–73. In *Proceedings of the 1974 Workshop of the Association of Psychiatrists in Africa.* N.p.: International Council on Alcohol and Alcoholism.

Ebie, J. C., and O. A. Pela. 1981. Some sociocultural aspects of the problem of drug abuse in Nigeria. *Drug and Alcohol Dependence* 8:301–306.

Federal Ministry of Health. N.d. *Type of sanctions taken on misbranded products or against violation firms.* Information Series 1. Lagos: Food and Drug Administration and Laboratory Services.

Food and Drugs Decree. 1974. *Federal Government Officials' Gazette* 55(61):A191–A195.

Horton, D. 1943. The functions of alcohol in primitive societies: A cross-cultural study. *Quarterly Journal of Studies on Alcohol* 4:199–230.

Inter-African Anti-Alcohol Conference. 1956. *Report of the I.A.A.A.C.* New York: United Nations.

Netting, R. M. 1964. Beer as a locus of value among the west African Kofyar. *American Anthropologist* 66:575–584.

Nevadomsky, J. J. 1981. Patterns of self-reported drug use among secondary school students in Bendel State, Nigeria. *Bulletin on Narcotics* 33(1):9–19.

————. 1985. Drug use among Nigerian university students: Prevalence of self-reported use and attitudes to use. *Bulletin on Narcotics* 37(2–3) : 31–42.

Odejide, A. C. 1978. Alcoholism: A major health hazard in Nigeria. *Nigerian Medical Journal* 8:230–232.

Odejide, A. C., and M. O. Olatawura. 1977. Alcohol use in a rural Nigerian community. *African Journal of Psychiatry* 3(1–2):69–74.

Odejide, A. C., and A. O. Sanda. 1976. Observations on drug abuse in western Nigeria. *African Journal of Psychiatry* 2:303–309.

Oshodin, O. G. 1981a. Alcohol abuse among high school students in Benin City, Nigeria. *Drug and Alcohol Dependence* 7:141–145.

————. 1981b. Alcohol abuse: A case study of secondary school students in a rural area of Benin District, Nigeria. *Drug and Alcohol Dependence* 8:207–213.

————. 1982. Alcohol abuse among Nigerian college students in the New York area of the United States. *College Student Journal* 16:40–47.

————. 1985. Attitudes toward alcoholism: A comparative study of secondary school teachers in urban and rural areas of Benin District, Nigeria. *Journal of Alcohol and Drug Education* 30(2):63–69.

Platt, B. S. 1955. Some traditional alcoholic beverages and their importance in indigenous African communities. *Proceedings of the Nutritional Society* 14:115–124.

Umunna, I. 1967. The drinking culture of a Nigerian community: Onitsha. *Quarterly Journal of Studies on Alcohol* 28:529–237.

## ADDITIONAL REFERENCES

In an effort to make the list of readings more representative of modern work on alcohol and culture in and about Nigeria, the editor suggests the following references in addition to those cited by the author of this chapter:

Adelakan, M. L., O. A. Abiodun, A. O. Imouokhome-Obayan, G. A. Oni, and O. O. Ogunremi. 1993. Psychosocial correlates of alcohol, tobacco, and cannabis use: Findings from a Nigerian university. *Drug and Alcohol Dependence* 33:247–256.

Anumonye, A. 1984. Alcohol control policy in Nigeria. Pp. 227–233 in P. M. Miller and T. D. Nirenberg (Eds.). *Prevention of Alcohol Abuse.* New York: Plenum.

Ebie, J. C. 1990. The use of different alcoholic beverages in two urban areas of Nigeria. Pp. 168–184 in J. Maula, M. Lindblad, and C. Tigerstedt (Eds.). *Alcohol in Developing Countries.* NAD Publication 18. Helsinki: Nordic Council for Alcohol and Drug Research.

Gureje, O., and D. Olley. 1992. Alcohol and drug abuse in Nigeria: A review of the literature. *Contemporary Drug Problems* 19:491–504.

International Council on Alcohol and Addictions. N.d. [ca. 1988]. *Report of a research project on substance abuse in some urban and rural areas of Nigeria.* [Lausanne[?]: ICAA[?]].

Obot, I. S. 1990. Substance abuse, health, and social welfare in Africa: An analysis of the Nigerian experience. *Social Science and Medicine* 31:699–704.

Odejide, A. O. 1986. Alkohol i Nigeria: Produktion, bruksmönster och hälsoeffekter. *Alkoholpolitik* 3(1):4–18.

Odejide, A. O., J. U. Ohaeri, M. L. Adelekan, and B. A. Ikuesan. 1987. Drinking behavior and social change among youths in Nigeria: A study of two cities. *Drug and Alcohol Dependence* 20:227–233.

―――. 1988a. Alcohol use among Nigerian youths: The need for drug education and alcohol policy. Pp. 441–450 in R. B. Waahlberg (Ed.). *Proceedings of the 35th International Congress on Alcoholism and Drug Dependence.* Vol. 3. Oslo: N.p.

―――. 1988b. Problems of alcohol epidemiology data collection in a developing country—Nigeria. Pp. 451–463 in R. B. Waahlberg (Ed.). *Proceedings of the 35th International Congress on Alcoholism and Drug Dependence.* Vol. 3. Oslo: N.p.

―――. 1990. Need for cross-cultural collaborative research activities: Promotion of alcohol research in Nigeria. Pp. 59–69 in J. Maula, M. Lindblad, and C. Tigerstedt (Eds.), *Alcohol in Developing Countries.* NAD Publication 18. Helsinki: Nordic Council for Alcohol and Drug Research.

Olukoju, Ayodeji. 1991. Prohibition and paternalism: The state and the clandestine liquor traffic in northern Nigeria, c. 1898–1918. *International Journal of African Historical Studies* 24:349–368.

Pela, O. A. 1986. Adolescent alcoholism in Benin City, Nigeria. *Adolescence* 21:487–492.

# 21

# Poland

## Jacek Moskalewicz and Antoni Zieliński

### DRUNK AS A POLE?

The stereotype of being "drunk as a Pole" seems to be widespread in western Europe and North America. It refers to heavy drinking that ends in loss of self-control, often with aggressive behavior. "Drunk as a Pole" came to symbolize wild drinking bouts that are in sharp contrast with the temperance tradition of Protestant cultures. Lack of temperance as a virtue and personal irresponsibility as far as drinking is concerned, have been generalized to impact on a more general picture of Polish culture.

According to a common belief in Poland, the origins of this expression reach back to Napoleonic times. After a heroic, victorious charge of Polish cavalry in the Spanish canyon of Sammossiera, the emperor of France supposedly said "drunk as a Pole" ironically, to express his appreciation of their courage and high morale in battle, as well as their moderation in drinking. Unlike French troops, whose drinking often had a demoralizing effect and weakened their capacity to fight, Polish soldiers, according to Napoleon, knew how and when to drink (Falewicz 1978). Over the years, this appraisal became transformed so that it now sounds like an affront rather than a compliment.

A history of this anecdote shows that there are often strong links between alcohol, culture, and politics, and changing configurations in their mutual relationships. On the following pages, we will give a nonanecdotal perspective on the changing roles of alcohol in Polish culture and politics.

### ALCOHOL IN HISTORY

For centuries, alcohol production and distribution in Poland were controlled by its rulers. As early as the Middle Ages, an alcohol monopoly was held by kings, who exercised almost absolute power. From the end of the 1300s, however, a growing class of noblemen, representing about 10 percent of the population, increased its power at the expense of the royal families. Unlike other countries, Poland's gentry elected consecutive kings. Becoming increasingly aware of their political power, the nobles became more and more influential and were able to win a variety of privileges, including economic benefits (Bardach et al. 1993). One of them was the propination privilege, which granted a monopoly of alcohol production and distribution within an estate (Kieiewicz 1984). The role of this privilege in the economy increased, especially in the 1600s, when, because of the numerous wars, Polish grain could not be exported to western Europe. The surplus production had to be utilized on the domestic market. Development of a cheap technology of distillation stimulated the production of grain-based spirits (Bielewicz and Moskalewicz 1986a). Serfs could drink only in a local inn (which was owned by their landlord), and this helped to secure his income (Bystroń 1976). This mechanism of forced alcohol consumption was expanded in the 1800s. Polish feudal agriculture was no longer competitive in Western markets. On many estates, alcohol represented nearly half of all income. By the 1800s, consumption varied from 9.6 to 38 liters of ethanol per capita (Święcicki 1977). A peak of 48 liters of aqua vitae annually was recorded in the Wielun district (Rożenowa 1961).

Propination is strongly associated with "the Jewish question" in Poland. Because of legal and customary restrictions, one of the few careers open to Jews was to lease an inn from a local landlord. The feudal serf perceived the Jewish innkeeper as an oppressor who benefited directly from his drinking (Baranowski 1979). In anti-feudal riots, the burning of inns became a symbol of anger and determination.

The mid-1800s witnessed the birth of the first temperance movement in Poland. A specific feature of Polish temperance was its combined religious and national character. First, sobriety fraternities were animated and framed by Catholic parishes (Korża 1973; Moczarski 1983), and spread to 30–50 percent of them (Bielewicz 1985). They were especially active in the Russian Partition. In some parishes half of the people took a sobriety oath (Chodźko 1937). In temperance rhetoric, freedom from alcohol was strongly associated with national independence. Such a message had a special appeal in a country that was, at that time, partitioned among three powerful neighbors. This great wave of temperance sentiment declined in the second half of the 1800s. It survived, however, in Socialist political and trade-union movements. For them, the fight against alcohol was part of a struggle for the emancipation of the working class (Moskalewicz and Sierosławski 1985).

It can be argued that a sudden and short eruption of temperance activities changed the social climate around alcohol in a way that lasted much longer (Zieliński 1993b). Alcohol became an issue of broad concern. Its consumption, as in most European countries, tended to decrease; in Poland it fell to 3.7 liters of pure alcohol just before World War I.

Shortly after Poland regained its independence in 1918, the alcohol question was given a new priority. In 1920, despite the war with Soviet Russia and a great variety of other political and economic problems, a law on limitation of alcohol sales was passed by Parliament, and a state alcohol monopoly was established. The alcohol law introduced many restrictions, including minimum drinking age and a limit on the number of outlets. Provisions for dry zones existed; by 1930, alcohol sales were prohibited in 10 percent of the communities (Zieliński 1993b). In spite of extremely low consumption levels, compared with other European countries, Polish temperance at that time was open to a wide range of patterns. The American idea of total prohibition seemed to be an ultimate goal (Szymański 1939). In temperance journals, enthusiastic articles were published on anti-alcohol experiences in Italy and Germany (Łuniewski 1935; Szymański 1935). During the 1930s, the anti-alcohol lobby became much weaker. Alcohol control was liberalized to satisfy a need for increasing revenues to support the state budget. This liberalization did not immediately affect consumption. Because of the Great Depression, it remained low, about 1 liter of ethanol per capita until 1933, then rose to 1.5 liters in 1938.

The interwar era of moderation was eventually broken; during World War II, a black market flourished in Poland. Its expansion was reinforced by a rationing system, feelings of instability, and a sudden drop in buying power through inflation. The black-market economy was actively supported and even approved by a majority of the population. It symbolized civil disobedience and collective resourcefulness. Thus, moonshining was not condemned, and developed at enormous scale (Moskalewicz 1985). A free market for alcohol did not exist. Coupons for spirits were given in exchange for agricultural products delivered to the authorities and as bonuses to outstanding employees. This system, introduced by the Nazis, was perceived as a policy promoting alcohol (Moczarski 1978). Toward the end of the war, however, alcohol became an issue of special concern to the Polish resistance fighters. In 1944, an order was given by the Home Army Headquarters to destroy illegal distilleries. Members of the Home Army who were found drunk while on duty could be sentenced to death (Falewicz 1978).

A new chapter in the social history of alcohol opened just after the war. As early as 1944, the state alcohol monopoly was restored. Under nationalization, the state was in full control of production, trade, and distribution. The general trend of centralization and state control overwhelmed temperance activities that were reinvigorated in the first years after liberation. Numerous temperance associations were banned and replaced by one organization, the Polish National Anti-alcohol Committee. Its activities were fully controlled by the state apparatus (Rogowski 1983). In the beginning, new authorities presented alcoholism as a relic of capitalism that would vanish as the building of socialism progressed. Reality did not fit with these ideological presumptions. Contrary to expectations, drunkenness increased, especially among the working class, who were highly visible on huge construction projects that were a hallmark of the new system (Malanowski 1981).

All these problems became public issues during a short period of political liberalization in the mid-1950s, "the political thaw." The disease concept of alcoholism, popularized in America, was a convenient explanation of the growing wave of alcohol problems in a socialist society. Among new alcohol legislation of that time, compulsory treatment was introduced, replacing repressive criminal approaches that had predominated in previous decades. Public drunkenness became decriminalized, and "sobering-up stations" were established, as in the Soviet Union. These measures were meant to show that an alcoholic is an ill person who should be cared for, even against his or her will (Wald and Moskalewicz 1987). Nobody could be blamed for his or her illness (Moskalewicz and Światkięwicz 1989).

Medicalization of the alcohol problem led to its reduction from a social to an individual level. During the years that followed, the alcohol question gradually lost its status as a public issue. Censorship about alcohol as a social problem could be legitimized on the basis of its new medical definition.

In the late summer of 1980, after a series of strikes that gave birth to the Solidarity movement, the alcohol question resurfaced alongside many other social problems, and became part of the political game (Bielewicz and Moskalewicz 1982). The regime was blamed for pushing alcohol in order to manipulate a "drunken society" more easily and to maximize its revenues. Sources of the problem were thus located at the structural level. Alcoholism seemed to be product of the system (Moskalewicz and Sierosławski 1985). This interpretation was legitimized by epidemiological evidence. The trend of increasing consumption in the postwar period, which was observed in most European countries and in North America, was presented as if it were specific to the socialist system.

To respond to this challenge, the government suddenly increased alcohol control and reduced production. On the one hand, these measures could be seen as an effort to find a common field of cooperation with the opposition. On the other hand, they were an attempt to regain the moral high ground. Widespread drunkenness was suggested as an explanation for low productivity, crime, and general anarchy (Moskalewicz 1981a, b).

The social history of alcohol in Poland shows that cultural definitions of social problems not only evolve gradually within a culture but also change rapidly in response to political challenges. No matter how great a problem there may be in epidemiological terms, it can be presented as a major issue or totally neglected. Its sources can also be located according to current political requirements. Scientific definitions are often invented or adopted in response to political demands.

## MAJOR DRINKING PATTERNS

The long waves of change in alcohol consumption that were observed throughout Europe and North America have flowed over Poland. According to early statistical sources and estimates, consumption reached its peak of 12 or so liters of pure alcohol per capita by the mid-1800s, then fell to about 4 liters on the eve of World War I. A very low consumption level, below 2 liters per capita, was a typical feature of the interwar period. It started to grow again after World War II, from 3.0 liters per capita in 1950 to 8.4 liters in 1980. In 1981–82 consumption decreased to 6.4, then 6.1 liters, before leveling off at about 7 liters (Wald et al. 1992). The introduction of a free-market economy brought a sudden growth of alcohol consumption at the beginning of the 1990s (Moskalewicz 1991; Sierosławski 1992).

Traditionally, Poland belongs among the spirit-drinking cultures. In 1938, spirits constituted fully 88% of overall alcohol consumption; in 1950, 78%; in 1960, 60%. Traditional drinking revived in the 1970s, when this share increased to about 70% (Wald et al. 1981). The proportions of wine and beer long remained equal and low. At the beginning of the 1990s, beer consumption dramatically increased. Its share grew to one-third, at the expense of vodka and wine (Sierosławski 1992). The dominant position of vodka is reflected in popular culture and perceptions. For over 30 percent of Poles, an abstainer is a person who may consume beer or wine but does not drink vodka (Zieliński 1987).

Frequency of drinking is relatively low. In the 1980s, Poles drank not more often than once a month, on average. However, between 34 and 40% of men and about 20% of women consumed alcohol once a week or more frequently. Even that was twice as often as twenty years earlier (Moskalewicz and Sierosławski 1991).

The stereotyped pattern consisted of rare drinking bouts that ended in severe drunkenness. For centuries, Polish culture has been predominantly a rural one (Czerwiński 1974). The bourgeoisie, with its values of temperance, moderation, self-control, work, and responsibility, was practically nonexistent. Among the gentry, drinking was a manifestation of an idle lifestyle and wealth. Heavy drinking seemed to be not only a right but almost a duty of a nobleman. A host used to urge his guests to drink heavily and felt offended if they refused (Bystroń 1976). Traces of these customs can be found in popular songs and sayings. Even today, Poles sing while drinking: "And who will not drink to the bottom of the glass should be beaten with two sticks" or "He has drunk, he has drunk to the bottom; may God bless him" (Tuwim 1991, 181, 184). In the 1700s, special wine cups without a foot were invented, to force a guest to drink a full cup in one gulp. A winner of drinking contests became famous and often was awarded high state positions in recognition of his "strong head." There are anecdotes that Polish King August II offered the Order of the White Eagle as a prize to brave drunkards (Bystroń 1976). For peasants, drinking happened to be the only way in which the lifestyle of their lords could be imitated.

This pattern has tended to weaken over the years. A comparison of surveys from the beginning of the 1960s (Święcicki 1964) and the 1980s (Jasiński 1989) shows that in spite of a twofold increase in per capita consumption, the proportion of men who drink more than 200 grams of vodka at a time decreased from over 60% to about 30% (Zieliński 1988).

## VARIANT DRINKING PATTERNS

Changes in drinking patterns in Poland have been associated with industrialization and urbanization. In the prewar period, two-thirds of the population lived in rural areas, whereas in the 1990s, close to 70% are town dwellers. This urbanization, especially rapid in the 1950s, which was a period of extensive industrialization, had a peculiar impact on cultural patterns. To describe this impact, Polish anthropologists developed a concept of "ruralization" of the society (Czerwiński 1974). Traditional rural patterns were not replaced by urban ones; rather, as happened in many countries at that time to varying extents, the reverse was true. Later a distinctive blend of urban and rural traits emerged.

Rural migrants brought with them a traditional drinking pattern of rare bouts of heavy alcohol intake. An urban environment, however, offered new opportunities for drinking, as well as new constraints (Bielewicz and Moskalewicz 1986). In contrast with agriculture, working hours in industry were well established. Young migrant workers who received their wages regularly every week or every month had more and more leisure time, which had not existed in rural life except on Sundays. For them, leisure time was associated with Sunday festivities and the local inn, where they dropped in after attending mass. In the city, every afternoon seemed to have time for festivity and drinking. The anonymity of the urban environment weakened social control and encouraged alcohol consumption and heavy drinking.

One of the factors that had influenced ruralization of towns was the institution of workers' hostels, which were very popular in the period of industrialization. Every year, thousands of migrants from the countryside moved to these hostels, hoping to improve their lives and waiting to get a regular apartment. Standards of life were very low: one room for several persons, one kitchen and one bathroom for several dozen. Workers' hostels developed a reputation as centers of drunkenness, violence, and crime (Kozicki 1970).

On the other hand, urban life modified rural patterns. Long drinking sessions and celebrations that could last for several days in the countryside had to be shortened because of an industrial work regimen that required punctuality and high productivity. Traditional conviviality had to vanish in the small urban apartments.

At the beginning of industrialization, a blending of rural and urban drinking patterns occurred (Moskalewicz 1981b). Frequency of drinking increased, and per-session consumption remained very high. Normal alcohol intake per adult male was between 250 and 500 grams of vodka. Later, urban patterns became increasingly predominant.

Traditionally, women participated in convivial gatherings but were not supposed to drink to excess. Even in times of particularly heavy drinking in the 1700s, when men were not supposed to refuse any amount of alcohol, "ladies had to demonstrate moderation and only touched full cups with their mouths to mark that they joined a toast" (Bystroń 1976, 186). Unlike men, they were allowed to discard a drink, under the table or on their plates. According to the first Polish alcohol surveys of the 1960s, women drank seven times less than men (Święcicki 1964). In recent years, this ratio is one to four or five (Jasiński 1989). Between the 1960s and the 1980s, alcohol consumption among the female population increased 300%, whereas among males it increased by 75%. In that period, female drinking accounted for one-third of the growth of average consumption (Moskalewicz 1986).

These changes can be attributed to the rapid emancipation of women in the postwar era. Between 1950 and 1990, the proportion of women in the labor force grew from 30 to 46%. In some professions, such as doctors and teachers, women surpassed 80%. Equality of the sexes on the job was a rallying cry of socialism. Especially in the 1950s, women were encouraged to perform what had been thought of as male jobs. Posters with a women on a tractor symbolized emancipation in the spirit of those times. While undertaking gainful employment and new duties, women demanded privileges that had previously been accessible only to men. Entertainment, sexual liberalization, smoking, and drinking became hallmarks of the new position of woman.

Nevertheless, social norms regarding female drinking are still more restrictive, a double standard that occurs in many other countries. According to recent surveys, about one-third of respondents believe that women should abstain from vodka and beer (Zieliński 1991). Drunkenness on the part of a woman is not acceptable, and a woman who drinks alone in public may be regarded a prostitute.

### Adolescent Drinking

The postwar era was marked by the "emancipation" of ethnic minorities, underprivileged social classes, women, and youth. Unlike women, who were glad to imitate patterns of the opposite sex, young people questioned the existing system and looked for alternative values. In Poland, a counterculture was born in the late 1960s and blossomed in large urban centers. A turning point in the self-identification of youth as a separate social force was a student revolt in March 1968. Polish students protested against hypocrisy, the discrepancy between values of social justice, equality, and freedom that were officially promoted by the Communist Party but absent in real life. Strikes that started at Warsaw University spread to university centers all over the country. They lasted more than a month and proved the solidarity of young people. Youth emerged as a separate social category. To distinguish themselves from adults, they used a variety of symbols. New fashions, sexual freedom, drug use, and different drinking patterns formed parts of a distinctive youth culture. In the decades that followed, this culture became institutionalized and commercialized. The cult of youth that dominates in popular culture and fashion, even affecting other generations, is largely a product of the market.

The generation that came of age in the late 1960s was particularly "wet."

Unlike their parents, whose beverage of choice was vodka, those young people chose to drink wine and beer. Consumption of low-alcohol beverages was meant to underscore the peaceful, nonviolent character of their culture. In surveys carried out in the 1960s and 1980s, the cohort of 1960s teenagers always had high consumption levels and the lowest proportion of abstainers (Falewicz 1972; Moskalewicz and Sierosławski 1991).

Youth seem always to be those most willing to adopt new cultural patterns. Especially in recent decades, when a youth culture has been crossing national, ethnic, and class boundaries, young people tend to drink in a similar way. In the Polish context, Western cultural patterns were particulary attractive. After twenty postwar years of political and cultural isolation, Poland was open, uncritically and nonselectively, to everything that originated in western Europe and North America.

The pattern of consuming dilute alcohol, or frequent drinking of small quantities, has become prevalent, especially among students and university-educated people in urban centers. In recent years, the best-seller among students is canned beer that constitutes part of a package of American popular culture, alongside fast food, movies, and fiction.

Does a visible increase in drinking among teenagers suggest that this generation initiates a new ''wet'' wave? This question cannot yet be answered. From a longer historical perspective, it should be noted that adolescent drinking has been of concern to adults since the 1890s. At the beginning of the twentieth century, as well as in the interwar period, children started drinking as early as they do today, or even earlier, and there were similar proportions of abstainers (Ciembroniewicz 1913; Gnoiński 1938; Neczaj-Hruzewicz 1937).

Polish tradition clearly defines age thresholds below which drinking is not socially approved. Since the 1960s, the opinion has prevailed among adults that beer should not be drunk by those below fifteen, wine below eighteen, and vodka below twenty. These thresholds are higher for females as far as vodka and beer are concerned (Malanowski 1963; Zieliński 1991).

The norms are not fully respected on the behavioral level. Young people begin to drink much earlier. No significant difference exists between boys and girls, which may reflect both growing gender equality and the general discrepancy between norms and behavior that is typical for sudden cultural transitions (Zieliński 1991).

The eighteen-year threshold is enforced by the state and the church. The legal drinking age in Poland is eighteen for all alcoholic beverages. Since the 1970s, the Catholic Church has required a sobriety oath (to abstain until eighteen) from all children before they receive their first Communion. Thus, on the normative level, adulthood is strongly associated with alcohol. In traditional Polish child raising there are no positive norms that regulate alcohol consumption among children. They are simply told not to drink. Nobody tells them what, when, or how to drink. Parents and teachers may discuss the bad aspects of drinking but are careful not to describe the favorable ones.

According to the drinking survey of 1984, in 40% of families, parents did not talk about alcohol with their children; in only 20% were positive norms concerning drinking presented. The latter approach was mostly adopted in families of white-collar background, especially those with university education; it was virtually absent in workers' and farmers' families (Bielewicz 1984; Zieliński 1993b).

In such a situation, youngsters experiment with alcohol on their own. Alcohol education mostly takes place among peers. Parents, as potentially important agents of social control, have little or no influence. Experimentation with alcohol, using a trial-and-error approach, may lead to many problems related to adolescent drinking. The adult pattern is sometimes imitated at the behavioral level but lacks the complete normative context. The lack of parental impact on socialization about alcohol leaves children open to the influence of popular culture, which often emphasizes "wet" patterns.

### Alcohol and Occupational Status

Popular opinion formulates different expectations for different occupational groups. Some professions are expected to be moderate, and others are permitted to drink more. According to national surveys in 1984 and 1989, moderation was especially expected of priests, policemen, doctors, teachers, judges, employees of the Communist Party apparatus, army officers, and (to a lesser extent) journalists and clerks. Very seldom is moderation expected from laborers and farmers. It seems that drinking is strongly related to occupational role, and especially to the values associated with given occupation. To some extent this is also linked with a ladder of occupational prestige. The breakdown of the political system in 1989 was followed by a significant decrease in social expectations of moderation among employees of the Communist Party apparatus: in 1984, 53% of respondents expected them to be moderate; in 1989 this decreased to 39% (Zieliński 1991).

There is a link between social norms and levels of drinking. Highest consumption is among blue-collar employees, especially unskilled workers; farmers are next highest. White-collar employees and professionals with university education drink less. Lower classes have the highest proportion of both heavy drinkers and abstainers. The opposite is true among people with university education, where abstaining is rare as is heavy drinking (Zieliński 1991). People with a university education are those most open to Western culture, including drinking. They tend to drink less per session but much more frequently. They do not need a special occasion to drink. Alcohol consumption becomes a question of individual choice rather than of tradition. The traditional social obligation to drink as much as others is more and more frequently rejected. At the same time, they are more liberal as far as drinking by women and teenagers is concerned (Zieliński 1991).

## PROS AND CONS OF DRINKING

Benefits and problems associated with alcohol use are part of the life experience of most drinkers. Both can be attributed to consumption levels, drinking patterns, and norms that regulate drinking behavior, as much as to general norms prevailing in the society.

Compared with other countries, Poland's drinking patterns produce more acute problems like mental disorders, violence, and public drunkenness; chronic complications seem to be less prevalent. According to drinking surveys carried out in the 1980s, temporary health disturbances like hangover, headache, and stomach disorders predominated; they were suffered by more than one-third of respondents in the twelve months preceding the interview. Around 10% experienced other, perhaps more harmful, effects of alcohol, including family brawls, being robbed, or other financial losses.

Quantitatively, benefits were much more frequent. More than 60% of respondents enjoyed improvements in mood; more than 50% felt less constrained in chatting; 25% got closer to coworkers, and, for about 12% alcohol helped in getting closer to a person of the opposite sex. Many Poles think alcohol can be good for a cold (20%), headache (8%), or stomach disorders (13%).

It appears that the higher the level of drinking, the more benefits and the more problems are experienced. Drinking seems to be perpetuated by an interplay of rewards and punishments in which the former are far more numerous and frequent (Światkięwicz 1986, 1990).

## CONCLUDING REMARKS

For most people in Poland, a majority of traditional and individual life events are associated with drinking. Even those who abstain cannot imagine a wedding party without alcohol. Alcohol illuminates almost all significant values of the society: health, friendship, frankness, respect for the elderly. It increases the importance of social gatherings and, in important ways, helps to integrate family, groups of friends, neighborhood, and coworkers. Most people drink primarily for social reasons; solitary drinking is exceptionally rare.

Polish culture is traditionally a "wet" culture. Since the 1840s, however, the seeds of temperance sentiment have been planted, and they have influenced cultural patterns. This is reflected by the high position accorded alcoholism in discussions of social problems. Some traditionally "wet" celebrations have become alcohol-free. Fewer people serve alcoholic beverages at baptism or first Communion parties that were declared "dry" by the Catholic Church. May Day celebrations, which used to be quite "wet" in the 1950s, became dry due to the ban on alcohol declared by the state. For that matter, the tradition of public festivities on May Day and on many other occasions has vanished. Public drinking is less and less accepted.

A new drinking culture, combining "dry" and "wet" traditions, and comprising both urban and rural patterns, is emerging. In the 1990s, a great variety of drinking practices, opinions, and attitudes coexist at the social and the individual levels.

## REFERENCES

Baranowski, B. 1979. *Polska karczma: Restauracja: Kawiarnia.* Wrocław, Warsaw, Kraków, and Gdansk: Narodowy Zakład im. Ossolińskich.

Bardach, J., B. Leśnodorski, and M. Pietrzak. 1993. *Historia ustroju i prawa polskiego.* Warsaw: Państwowe Wydawnictwo Naukowe.

Bielewicz, A. 1984. Socjalizacja alkoholowa w rodzinie. Warsaw: Instytut Psychiatrii i Neurologii. Manuscript.

———. 1985. Bractwa Trzeźwości. *Przegląd katolicki* 26:1–2; 27:2; 28:1–2.

Bielewicz, A., and J. Moskalewicz. 1982. Temporary prohibition: The Gdansk experience. *Contemporary Drug Problems* 11(3):331–335.

———. 1986a. Alkohol a współczesne procesy makrospołeczne. Pp. 35–45 in I. Wald (Ed.). *Alkohol i związane z nim problemy zdrowotne i społeczne.* Warsaw: Państwowe Wydawnictwo Naukowe.

———. 1986b. Historia społeczno-kulturowa alkoholu. Pp. 11–34 in I. Wald (Ed.). *Alkohol i związane z nim problemy zdrowotne i społeczne.* Warsaw: Państwowe Wydawnictwo Naukowe.

Bystroń, J. S. 1976. *Dzieje obyczaju w dawnej Polsce: Wiek XVI–XVII.* Warsaw: Państwowy Instytut Wydawniczy.

Chodźko, W. 1937. Stulecie zorganiżowanej walki z alkoholizmem w Polsce. *Treźwość* 11–12:641–646.

Ciembroniewicz, J. 1913. Młodzież szkolna a alkohol: Badania statystyczne. *Walka z alkoholizmem* 2(3/4):

Czerwiński, M. 1974. *Zycie po miejsku.* Warsaw. Państwowe Wydawnictwo Naukowe.

Falewicz, J. K. 1972. *Spożycie alkoholu w Polsce i jego uwarunkowania.* Warsaw: Ośrodek Badania Opinii Publicznej RTV.

———. 1978. Rzecz o pijaństwie. *Kultura i społeczeństwo* 3:307–322.

Gnoiński, S. 1938. To alkoholiźmie wśród dzieci szkół powszechnych m. Wilna (badania stystyczne). *Trzeźwość* 11–12:478–483.

Jasiński, J. 1989. Spożycie napojów alkoholowych w Polsce w 1985. *Archiwum kryminologii* 16:7–100.

Kieniewicz, J. 1984. Moment otrzeźwienia. *Przegląd powszechny* 755/756: 157–170.

Korża, H. 1973. Abstynencki ruch. Pp. 43–47 in *Encyklopedia katolicka.* Vol. 1. Lublin: Katolicki Uniwersytet Lubelski.

Kozicki, S. 1970. Z reporterskiego notatnika. *Problemy alkoholizmu* 7/8:13–15.

Łuniewski, W. 1935. Prawo niemieckie o zapobieganiu potomstwu obciążonemu chorobami dziedzicznymi. *Trzeźwość* 5:185–190.

Malanowski, J. 1963. *Niektóre zagadnienia konsumpcji napojów alkoholowych w Polsce: Wyniki badania ankietowego z jesieni 1962.* Warsaw: Ośrodek Badania Opinii Publicznej RTV.

———. 1981. *Robotnicy polscy.* Warsaw: Książka i Wiedza.

Moczarski, K. 1978. *Rozmowy z katem.* Warsaw: Państwowy Instytut Wydawniczy.

———. 1983. *Historia alkoholizmu i Walki z Nim.* Warsaw: Społeczny Komitet Przeciwalkoholowy.

Moskalewicz, J. 1981a. Alcohol as a public issue. Recent developments in alcohol control in Poland. *Contemporary Drug Problems* 8(1):11–21.

———. 1981b. Alcohol: Commodity and symbol in Polish society. Pp. 9–30 in E. Single, P. Morgan, and J. de Lint (Eds.). *Alcohol, society, and the state.* Toronto: Addiction Research Foundation.

———. 1985. Monopolization of the alcohol arena by the state. *Contemporary Drug Problems* 12(1):117–128.

———. 1986. Obecne tendencje w zróżnicowaniu spożycia alkoholu w Polsce. Pp. 90–95 in I. Wald (Ed.). *Alkohol i zwiazane z nim problemy zdrowotne i społeczne.* Warsaw: Państwowe Wydawnictwo Naukowe.

———. 1991. Alcohol as an economic issue. *Contemporary Drug Problems* 18(3):407–416.

Moskalewicz, J., and J. Sierosławski. 1985. Alkohol a robotnicy. Pp. 257–344 in P. Wójcik (Ed.). *Położenie klasy robotniczej w Polsce.* Tom 4, *Problemy patologii i przestępczości.* Warsaw: Akademia Nauk Społecznych.

———. 1991. Zmiany w konsumpcji alkoholu w Polsce w latach 1984–1989. *Alkoholizm i narkomania* Lato: 137–152.

Moskalewicz, J., and G. Świątkiewicz. 1989. Deviants in a deviant institution. *Contemporary Drug Problems* 16(2):157–176.

Neczaj-Hruzewicz, J. 1937. Alkoholizm wśród dzieci szkół powszechnych ujęty liczbowo. *Trzeźwość* 1–3:24–39.

Rogowski, E. 1983. Społeczny Komitet Przeciwalkoholowy. Warsaw: Społeczny Komitet Przeciwalkoholowy. Manuscript.

Rożenowa, H. 1961. *Produkcja wódki i sprawa pijaństwa w Królestwie Polskim: 1815–1863.* Warsaw: Państwowe Wydawnictwo Naukowe.

Sierosławski, J. 1992. *Spożycie alkoholu i polityka wobec alkoholu w ocenie społecznej.* Warsaw: Ministerstwo Zdrowia i Opieki Społecznej.

Świątkiewicz, G. 1986. Pozytywne i negatywne konsekwencje spożywania alkoholu w indywidualnych doświadczeniach Polaków. *Problemy medycyny społecznej* 8:81–97.

———. 1990. Pozytywne i negatywne doś wiadczenia zwiazane z piciem. Warsaw: Instytut Psychiatrii i Neurologii. Manuscript.

Święcicki, A. 1964. *Spożycie alkoholu w Polsce.* Warsaw: Ośrodek Badania Opinii Publicznej RTV.

———. 1977. *Alkohol; Zagadnienia polityki społecznej.* Warsaw: Społeczny Komitet Przeciwalkoholowy.

Szymański, J. 1935. Kilka uwag w sprawie projektu ustawy sterlizacyjnej. *Trzeźwość* 5: 190–192.

———. 1939. Wytyczne i osiągnięcia XX lat pracy. *Trzeźwość* 7–8: 421–426.

Tuwim, J. 1991. *Polski słownik pijacki i antologia bachiczna.* Warsaw: Wydawnictwo Oskar.

Wald, I., T. Kulisiewicz, J. Morawski, and A. Boguslawski. 1981. *Raport o problemach polityki w zakresie alkoholu.* Warsaw: Instytut Wydawniczy Związków Zawodowych.

Wald, I., J. Morawski, J. Moskalewicz, and T. Szydłowska. 1992. *II Raport o polityce wobec alkoholu* Warsaw: Ministerstwo Zdrowia i Opieki Społecznej.

Wald, I., and J. Moskalewicz. 1987. From compulsory treatment to the obligation to undertake treatment: Conceptual evolution in Poland. *Contemporary Drug Problems* 14(1):39–50.

Zieliński, A. 1987. Social attitudes towards abstinence in the light of 1987 survey. Pp. 398–404 in *Alcoholism Symposium Proceedings*. Warsaw: N.p.

———. 1988. Wzory picia alkoholu w Polsce. *Alkoholizm i narkomania* Jesień:16–42.

———. 1991. Normy obyczajowe regulujące stosunek do alkoholu. *Alkoholizm i narkomania*. Wiosna:36–53.

———. 1994. Polish culture: Wet or dry? *Contemporary Drug Problems* 21:329–340.

———. 1995. Abstynencja, umiar i samokontrola w piciu alkoholu. *Alkoholizm i narkomania:* in press.

# 22

# Russia

*Pavel I. Sidorov*

## THE HISTORY OF RUSSIAN ALCOHOL CULTURE

In old Russia, traditional alcohol drinks were home brews, especially mead and beer; all were taxed (the "revel tax"). When vodka appeared in Russia in the 1500s, the government monopolized its sale, immediately abolishing private taverns and establishing "tsar pubs." Two main systems sold alcohol drinks: state and private (farmed out). In the first the profits were collected by publicans who were officials in the state employ; in the second, pubs were farmed out to private persons in exchange for a licensing fee. In the 1600s, profits from the alcohol trade formed a considerable part of the government budget. In the mid-1600s, the private system replaced the state trade. Every four years the government organized auctions for the right to sell vodka. Tavernkeepers collected far more from the population than they had to pay to the state. In 1859–1863, annual profits of tavernkeepers were 220 million silver rubles—ten to eleven times greater than those of all the other trades serving the domestic market.

Tavernkeepers' abuses aroused great hatred among the ordinary people and gave rise to riots and the appearance of a temperance movement. In 1863, the system was replaced by taxes levied on all stages of alcohol production and trade. In 1894, a state alcohol monopoly was introduced. The government alcohol policy is well illustrated by a quotation from a circular of the Ministry of Finance in 1904: "rapid increase of alcohol consumption is not a misfortune but an indication of the people's well-being."

To visualize the Russian alcohol culture, let us consider consumption by peasants and workers, clergymen and monks, soldiers and military officers, landlords and aristocrats. The peasants usually drank alcohol on holidays and wedding days, during fairs and funeral feasts, *mirshchina* (collective drinking by the whole village), and *pomochi* (joint work, such as a barn-raising, to help a neighbor). In one of the agricultural districts in 1875, with 1 pub per 350 peasants, expenses for vodka were 36 rubles per peasant household, that is, 7 pails of 40% (80 proof) vodka a year (1 pail = 12.3 liters = 20 bottles = 80 glasses of vodka). The traditions of spending leisure time with other people and the supposed need to relax after hard work were connected with the formation of class-consciousness among the Russian peasantry. The need for social interaction was satisfied in organized holidays. Being half-starved and eating only bread and *shchi* (cabbage soup without meat) for months, peasants tried to have great celebrations on holidays. It was their only means of self-affirmation.

Ethnic minorities in the Far North, Siberia, and Far East often succumbed to a predatory alcohol policy of the tsarist government during colonization of the remoter parts of Russia. Native populations soon became accustomed to hard drinking and being cheated by local authorities. *Voivodes* (provincial governors) bought valuable furs for trifles and soon bought out northern aboriginals with the help of vodka. For example, at the beginning of the 1900s, in any nomad encampment a bottle of liquor cost 4 rubles and a sable pelt of the best quality sold for 3, whereas elsewhere the prices were many times the reverse. What should have been government care for minorities was little more than exploitation through alcohol.

Workers had many more occasions and reasons for drunkenness. There were 196 official nonworking days in the Russian calendar. In the working-class neighborhoods, there appeared a tradition of "wets" on paydays. Having received money, workers lingered at the pub after work. Taking a job, graduation of apprentices, welcomes and farewells, new appointments and purchases were celebrated with "wets." Traditionally entire working groups drank together. Significantly, it was in towns that the demand for alcohol in bigger (3- and 6-liter) bottles arose. In 1912 the Arkhangelsk district ordered vodka exclusively in 3-liter bottles. Twenty years earlier, the "democratic" bottles (100-gram and 200-gram bottles, called *merzavchik* and *zhulik*) had been used.

If the heavy drinking of peasants and workers was due to poverty, then the heavy drinking of the privileged classes was due to surfeit and a display of excess. In the Russian alcohol culture, the part played by the clergy was contradictory. According to Orthodox interpretation, Holy Scripture approved of moderate alcohol consumption, and wine was used in many church ceremonies, rites, and sacraments (Eucharist, marriage, etc.). The spread of drunkenness among clergy whose mission was to serve as an example of morals contributed to the propagation of alcohol customs. In 1697 Emperor Peter I ordered the Moscow patriarch "to forbid priests to go to the pubs [so as] not to tempt ordinary people." However, drunkenness among the clergy flourished. According to the newspaper *Eparkhialny novositiÿ*, in the Novgorod bishopric alone, fifteen clergymen were brought to trial for misdemeanors committed while intoxicated in 1880. And there were sixty-two bishoprics in Russia.

In monasteries, things were still worse. From ancient times they had had special privileges for vodka production and trade. Monks were thought to drink round the clock. Orgies were so great that the synod had to establish special prison wards for drunkards in some monasteries, with "fetters and shackles," and with whipping "to inculcate abstinence."

Landlords also contributed to the propagation of alcohol customs. Here is a fragment from a story told by a Siberian landlord about his life: "In summer I usually get up at 4 o'clock in the morning, drink a glass [200 g.] of vodka and ride round the fields. Then at 6 o'clock I drink a glass of vodka and go round my estate. At 8 o'clock I drink a glass of vodka, have a bite and lie down for a while to have some rest." During the day a glass of vodka was taken every two hours.

Drunkenness in the Russian army was maintained by the official alcohol rations. During the war soldiers were given a glass of vodka (0.16 liter), three times a week for combatants and twice a week for noncombatants; in peacetime, troops were authorized vodka fifteen times a year, at the discretion of local commanders (e.g., in nasty weather, during maneuvers, to celebrate troop reviews, etc.). Abstinent soldiers could decline vodka and get six kopecs instead. According to navy regulations under Peter I, sailors were given four glasses of vodka a week, increased to one a day in 1761. Half to three-quarters of sailors refused the vodka and took the money. Unlike drafted or enlisted soldiers and sailors, regular officers were obliged to drink under the threat of dismissal. Distribution of vodka in the army and its sale in soldiers' shops were forbidden in 1908.

There are numerous examples of drunkenness among aristocrats and tsars. The last tsar, Nicholas II, is said to have spent his youth in orgies and binges. As heir to the throne, he undertook a course of practical study as a junior officer in the Bodyguard Hussar regiment, and was drawn into traditions of "guards' drinking." These included games like "*arshin* drinking" (each person having vodka glasses lined up against each other for the distance of 1 *arshin*, 28 inches) and "staircase drinking" (a person climbing from the ground floor to the first floor had to drink a glass on each step). Such excessive drinking was obligatory among young officers.

Thus, the basic features of Russian alcohol culture were a rigid frame of traditions and customs that required drinking wine and vodka on fixed occasions, and alcohol was an integral attribute of everyday life.

Traditionally consumption of liquor predominated (in 1911, vodka accounted for 89.3% of the total alcohol consumption); the pattern of alcohol consumption was notable for bingeing, taking large amounts at a time, rather than sipping beer or wine throughout the day. Asocial and criminal behavior while intoxicated was frequent. Alcohol can be treated as a cultural phenomenon only in the frame of customs and traditions adopted in the society.

When World War I broke out in 1914, trade in spirituous drinks was stopped. Winemakers and brewers received governmental compensation for loss of profits. However, the nation did not become sober. By 1916, the making of illicit spirits and home brew, and the consumption of nonbeverage alcohols had developed greatly. By the October Revolution of 1917, alcohol warehouses were full, and alcohol abuse encouraged the lumpen proletariat to massacre their foes. The Bolsheviks, having come to power, tried to stop the spread of moonshining by drastic measures: five years' imprisonment and confiscation of property. However, only the introduction of official sale of vodka in 1925 relieved a growing alcohol shortage. Starvation and devastation in 1920–30, World War II, and restoration of the country relegated alcohol and related problems to the background for a long time. In 1958, 1972, and 1978 the Central Committee of the Communist Party of the Soviet Union and the Council of Ministers (cabinet) passed resolutions fostering moderate alcohol consumption. As a result, alcohol became an inevitable element of official and leisure intercourse, an integral part of public life and human relations. Negative consequences of drunkenness started to appear at a rapid rate. For twenty years the per capita alcohol consumption of the population increased 2.2 times (from 3.6 liters of alcohol in 1960 to 8.7 in 1980); the number of misdemeanors due to alcohol abuse increased 5.7 times and the number of alcoholics, 7 times. These increases to a great extent stimulated the drastic anti-alcohol campaign of 1985. The failures of that ill-fated temperance campaign resulted from the danger of ignoring bureaucratic channels; the need to increase and improve scientific and social examination of alcohol use and policy; the importance of economic factors in political decisions (in 1985, the alcohol trade had brought 53 million rubles [nearly $U.S. 96 million] to the budget); and the need to adhere to democratic principles in the formation of an effective social movement.

Alcohol vividly demonstrated its illusive-compensatory functions, the need for which can be displayed both by individuals and by social systems devised to manipulate public consciousness. Divergence between Communist ideas and human practice required greater support of social welfare illusions, including alcohol. The removal of alcohol as a narcotic agent increased the abrupt effect of social sobering.

## FORMS OF ALCOHOL CONSUMPTION

In the progression from one's first acquaintance with alcohol to the last stage of alcoholism it is possible to distinguish several periods having qualitatively different sociopsychological content. The starting point is abstinence from alcohol.

Abstinents [or abstainers] refrain from taking alcohol for any reason. There are absolute and relative abstinents. Absolute abstinents never take alcohol, or at most, once a year for some symbolic celebration. Relative abstinents take alcohol very seldom (two to three times a year) and in small doses (50–100 ml. of wine), and drink it without any special pleasure, mainly under pressure from people around them. More people take alcoholic drinks from time to time— once a month or once in two to three months. They usually prefer light wine and try to take not more than 50–150 milliliters. Intoxication is absent or slight. They drink alcohol during family celebrations at home or at their friends', seldom at restaurants, and only on festive occasions. The psychological content of drinking from time to time is, first, conformity to drinking customs that prevail in the given setting and, second, reaction to any specific provocative stimulus associated with intoxication. Still more people are moderate in drinking, taking 100–200 milliliters of vodka or an equivalent dose of wine on the average of one to four times a month. Intoxication is usually slight, control over the dose of alcohol and critical appreciation of behavior being present. In cases where such people drink too much at any given time, pronounced intoxication with subsequent aversion for alcohol is observed.

Then there are people who abuse alcohol but have no symptoms of alcoholism, those we call drunkards take alcohol two to four times a week until they reach extreme intoxication (more than 200 ml. of vodka or more than 500 ml. of fortified wine). The psychological content of such drunkenness is the loss of sobriety on specific occasions that are determined by alcohol customs. The behavior does not depend upon external stimuli. Such a person drinks in any situation, regardless of ethical standards of the social environment. Simultaneously with the development of drunkenness, conflicts are almost certain to appear at home and at work, and the reputation of such a person is damaged. The motive does not influence behavior in the state of intoxication. Euphoria increases up to a state of complete comfort. Drinking acquires special importance; the desire ''to have a hard drink'' becomes a dominant motive of behavior. Stereotypes of emotions and speech appear in the course of intoxication. In this state a person does not need anyone to talk to, and dealings with people are supplanted by a set of monologues. Remembrance of the comfort achieved in the state of intoxication remains for some days.

The first stage of alcoholism is characterized by the appearance of obsessive attraction to alcohol and places of its consumption; an increase of alcohol tolerance by two or three times in regard to low doses; and loss of the defensive vomiting reflex that normally occurs with overdosage of alcohol. Simultaneously with the beginning of alcoholism there emerges a distinctive alcoholic mode of life, destroying the psychological nucleus of a person and his or her chief moral and ethical values. The chief vital aim or felt need is drinking alcohol. The alcoholic mode of life is a way of satisfying a pathological need for alcohol over and over, in the most diverse situations. In the state of intoxication an alcoholic experiences full-scale psychological comfort, acquiring features of unmatched bliss.

The second stage of alcoholism is characterized by the coming of biological mechanisms of the disease to the fore, and the psychological peculiarities of an individual's alcoholic mode of life is dissolved in them. The flattening and deformation of an alcoholic's personality is observed. Attraction to alcohol is both obsessive and compulsive, reflecting the formation of physical dependence. A patient does not try to resist the rising desire. Control over the amount of alcohol and the context of drinking is lost. Alcohol tolerance reaches its maximum, and drinking sprees last for days. The leading criterion of the second stage of alcoholism is the appearance of the withdrawal syndrome: shakes, cold sweats, and other somatic and psychic disturbances in the period of waning intoxication, which can be relieved by taking another dose of alcohol ("hair of the dog").

The third stage of alcoholism is characterized by a sharp decrease of alcohol tolerance, so that even small doses are enough to make a patient drunk. Alcohol dependence acquires a compelling, vital character; the need for ethanol is felt with the same urgency as the need for food and sleep. Normal vital activity is impossible without alcohol. The state of intoxication is devoid of excited mood or stimulating effects; intoxication only stabilizes psychosomatic functions at a low level. Ironically, in such a state of intoxication, disinhibition and aggressiveness decrease, and behavior becomes more bearable. The withdrawal syndrome is accompanied by pronounced somatic and psychic disturbances. A patient must have a drink for brief relief of a hangover—"so as not to die," one may say, or "not to let his heart stop."

Thus, with the development of drunkenness and alcoholism profound changes are observed in the person and his or her mode of life. The first general characteristic of the alcoholic culture or way of life is an orientation toward an illusive way of reaching goals, by shifting one's aims from objective achievements to subjective emotions affected by alcohol. Next is orientation toward satisfaction of any goal with minimal efforts, development of passive ways of ego defense when encountering difficulties (for example, willingness to respond to any obstacle or intricate situation by drinking). There is also a desire to avoid responsibility for one's actions in the state of intoxication, and a preference for egocentric motivations over altruistic ones. Activity occurs according to a primitive pattern, avoiding difficulties in regularizing one's efforts and accepting delay in the realization of any desired aim. There is a willingness to be satisfied with temporary results of an activity that do not correspond exactly to what one had hoped for. One settles for temporary illusions of happiness and the realization of any aim in the state of intoxication, accepting temporary work and inadequate housing. All of these shortcomings are typical of a drunkard, and are closely interconnected with each other, the alcoholic mode of life, and traditions of alcoholic culture.

## ETHNOCULTURAL PECULIARITIES OF ALCOHOLIZATION

Russia is home to numerous nationalities and ethnic groups who have a great variety of cultures. Ethnonarcology is a branch of ethnopsychiatry dealing with alcohol and narcotics in different nationalities, ways of their production, forms of use according to rites and customs, and medicosocial complications and consequences. Ethnonarcology can be defined as a field of cooperation between ethnography and anthropology, folkloristics and religious doctrines, sociology, and psychology, on the one hand, and social, clinical, and toxicological narcology, on the other. Five main directions can be distinguished in ethnonarcological research in Russia.

Transcultural narcology studies forms and ways of narcotization and alcoholization in connection with social and ethnocultural factors. An example is the use of tinctures made of hallucinogenic mushrooms was a traditional way of drug-taking among several minority populations in the Far North of Russia. It may be related to the progressive development of alcoholization among northern nationalities, whose alcohol-metabolizing capacities may be different.

Cross-cultural narcology comprises studies comparing aspects of narcotism and alcoholism in different cultures. The occurrence of alcoholism among northern aboriginals in Russia is three to six times higher than among the general Russian population. Nearly half of northern aboriginals, who were traditionally known to be skillful herdsmen and fishermen, suffer now from eye and ear diseases. Every fourth inhabitant of the Far North has an immune deficiency. Tuberculosis mobidity there is seven times higher than in central Russia; child mortality is four times higher, and malignant tumors are two times higher. In the native population of Nenets Autonomous District, traumas and poisoning due to drunkenness have increased 65.6 times since the 1970s. Alcoholism, conditioned by closely interrelated ethnoecological and sociopsychological factors, is the most common (40–50%) psychic morbidity of small northern nationalities. It is the chief symptom of stress from acculturation, which develops during the abolition of the traditional mode of life and national culture. A rapid transition from one level to the another in the system of production relations, a change of life tempo, and of nutrition (from predominantly protein to carbohydrate, which affects metabolism), and the expansion of the Russian culture and mode of life have resulted in serious disturbances of psychic health among northern nationalities. Inhabitants of the most geographically isolated settlements show a lower frequency of alcoholism and psychic disturbances.

This constitutes an interesting case study of culturally bound disturbances occurring in an ethnic group. The main form of alcoholic psychosis among the Nenets minority is hallucinosis (90.5%), compared with only 44.6% in the Russian population. Narrowing of interests, weakness, and stereotyping of psychotic forms of alcoholism are characteristic of native inhabitants of the Far North. The absence of alcoholic delirium in the clinical picture of alcoholism may reflect the specific structure of the language and different ways of thinking. About 1980 we put forward a hypothesis about the existence of ethnic peculiarities of brain morphofunction and personality structure among northern aboriginals that manifested themselves in severe forms of alcoholism and the specific character of alcoholic psychosis. Nowadays we can speak freely about it without being accused of racism and sedition. Moreover, today morphofunctional distinctions between Europeans and northern aboriginals are taken into consideration in special vaccination schemes for the native population of the Far North.

Treating psychic and somatic diseases with alcohol-containing remedies can be a branch of ethnography and history of medicine. Practically all founders of medical science in Russia and elsewhere regarded alcohol as a drug; the external effects produced by alcoholic drinks were vivid and visible to doctors and patients. Alcohol and the tradition of its use in medicine constitute an integral part of the professional medical culture. The amount of wine used for therapeutic purposes in the hospitals of pre-Revolutionary Russia exceeded its consumption per capita in the healthy population. The problems of alcohol therapy were most dramatic in pediatric practice; often was the doctor who gave children their first wine. Thus, according to the generalized data of a number of investigations at the end of the 1800s, it was a doctor who initiated children's acquaintance with wine in 45–55% of cases. I quote from the *Manual on Children's Diseases* by A. Komb (1904): "Alcohol is a valuable and very useful remedy for children that can be used from the age of six."

At that time, there was a branch of Russian science called enotherapy, using alcohol as a therapeutic drug. Traditions of that science survive today. All modern Russian medical and pharmaceutical reference books contain instructions for using alcoholic drinks in treating patients. The most frequent indications for alcohol therapy are loss of appetite and depression of the digestive function, shock and faintness (syncope), vascular weakness and cooling, traumas with blood loss and pain, pulmonary edema, and postoperative pains. There are even modern instructions to use vodka for anesthesia in outpatient stomatological practice more frequently. Doctors in Georgia worked out indications and contraindications for using dry wines (tsinandali, tsolikouri, kindzamarauli, saperavi) in a number of diseases. Of all the "positive effects of alcohol," they especially emphasize increase of appetite, vasodilation and warming, and tranquilizing and sedative effects that surpass the analogous effects produced by other standard drugs in quality and safety.

A number of researchers have emphasized the role of alcohol in improving life for elderly people, mentioning that it is possible to speak about positive effects of ethanol when its doses are not more than 80–100 grams a day for males and 40–60 grams for females. However, the prices of alcohol in Russia today are beyond the means of the majority of pensioners who may need tranquilizing remedies in the period of "perestroika stress." According to generalized data in the 1990s, 8% of surgeons, 7% of stomatologists, and 6% of ambulance doctors are alcoholics. Also, 36% of anesthesiologists, 27.4% of surgeons, and 14.3% of X-ray technicians take alcohol more frequently than once a week.

Socionarcological aspects of culture are connected with religious rites, magic and occultism, shamanism, and folk art. Ethnonarcology, based upon the understanding of alcohol customs as phenomena of ancient culture, touches not just on religion but also on folk medicine; the dialectical unity of cultural types and subsistence modes of life, structural and functional foundations, and even sociopsychological characteristics of individuals within ethnic groups are reflected in traditional ways of alcoholization and narcotization.

## REASONS FOR ALCOHOLIZATION

Social, individual, and biochemical factors interact to promote alcohol abuse and the development of alcoholism. Alcohol consumption correlates with specific historical conditions and manifests itself in public attitudes toward alcohol, both normal use and drunkenness. Peculiarities of the person (emotional instability, suggestibility, immaturity, etc.) and individual characteristics of the body (hereditary predisposition to alcoholism, nervous disturbances, liver diseases, etc.) play an important part in the development of alcoholism. Consequently, when studying the reasons for alcohol consumption, abuse, drunkenness, and alcoholism, it is necessary to consider the whole complex of causes and conditions forming the "alcoholic person" in dynamic interplay. With age, the motivational and moral spheres of an individual and his or her relations and place in the social environment change. Therefore, in reference to Russian culture, I have singled out five main groups of factors that together form an indivisible chain of alcohol consumption and abuse: (1) factors contributing to the development of alcohol consumption in the first place; (2) factors maintaining alcohol consumption; (3) factors contributing to the development of alcohol abuse; (4) factors maintaining alcohol abuse; and (5) factors contributing to the development of alcoholism.

The influence of these factors at different ages or stages of development is not the same. Factors of group 1 (such as absence of one of the parents, alcoholism of one or both parents, negative psychological climate, low educational and cultural level of parents, poor upbringing, asocial company, and troubles in school) affect a child before the age of fifteen, when the behavioral basis of alcohol consumption is being formed. At this young age, children create their own alcohol orientation, actively assimilating and revising the alcohol customs of their surroundings. Alcohol orientation of others helps guide the behavior of a person in regard to drinking. Factors of group 1 compose the initial element in the genesis of alcohol abuse, but for many individuals do not necessarily result in it.

Factors of group 2 (such as alcohol traditions of the youth subculture, uncertainty in professional orientation, reluctance to work, failure to achieve specific ambitions, unawareness of individual development, deficiency of behavioral motivation, escape from crucial situations and decisions, too narrow a range or instability of interests, lack of hobbies and spiritual requirements) affect young people to the age of nineteen, forming both systematic and conscious alcohol consumption and the chief characteristics of the "prealcoholic person." Therefore it is possible to regard this group of factors as a determining element in the genesis of alcohol abuse.

Factors of group 3 (such as economic independence, absence of control, drinking behavior of coworkers, increase of alcohol intake and frequency of drinking, formation of an alcoholic lifestyle, and habitual drinking) affect a person to age twenty-five. This can be considered the beginning of alcohol abuse. At this age the majority of patients were in social surroundings with widespread and harmful drinking behavior. Living in this environment and observance of its alcoholic customs led in the long run to frequent and sustained intoxication. This conclusion is confirmed by subjective opinions of those who abuse alcohol and their spouses: 89% of drinkers and 96% of their spouses claimed that it was "friends" who were primarily to blame for their hard drinking.

Factors of group 4 (such as conflicts in the family, poor job skills, lack of public activity and socially significant orientation, and high wages) maintain alcohol abuse and secure a high level of intoxication. This set of factors is vividly expressed in the groups of workers whose jobs are relatively simple (physical labor, low qualification) but well paid.

Factors of group 5 (such as hereditary predisposition to alcoholism, nervous and psychic anomalies of the person, morphofunctional peculiarities of the body) are the biological background against which social stereotypes of drinking are realized.

This sequence of factors suggests the integrated and successive action of social, biological, and psychological factors that contribute to the development of drunkenness. In detail, it is linked to the local situation and cannot pretend to universality. At the same time, it accurately reflects the main stages of a Russian pattern of alcohol abuse. Thus, drunkenness is, in many respects, a nonspecific marker of the sociopsychological failure of a person and an indicator of the harmfulness of the micro environment and a largely passive role in social relations.

Any attempt to find the causes of alcoholism only in the peculiarities of a person and his or her body, or in the specific character of one's surroundings and external circumstances, is doomed as one-sided and oversimplified. If amnesia of an alcoholic or a person abusing alcohol is thoroughly studied, one always finds both external reasons for drunkenness and causes within the person.

Alcohol, drunkenness, and alcoholism are complex phenomena having many levels belonging equally to world culture and civilization, social and colonial policy, family and individual. Every level of generalization has its own reasons and conditions for alcoholization. Alcohol can be an appropriate and helpful component of culture, but only insofar as its consumption is restricted by traditions and customs that fulfill control-regulating functions.

On the average, normal human blood contains 0.1–0.3% endogenous ethanol, secreted by the intestinal microflora and providing 10% of human energy. Endogenous ethanol is the product of metabolism, without which human vital activity is impossible, so alcohol is native to the human body. A decrease of such natural ethanol levels, due to excessive drinking, reflects one of the components of the dependence syndrome. With the development of drunkenness, the form of consumption changes the requirement content: endogenous ethanol is indispensable to metabolic processes, reflecting the existence of a normative requirement, whereas exogenous ethanol abuse is a form of autoaggressive behavior that destroys the normal requirement and forms a pathological quasi requirement. Clearly, alcoholism can be defined as a chronic disease characterized by a pathologic need for alcohol.

## THE COSTS OF ALCOHOLIZATION

Having discussed some of the merits and features of intoxication that attract people, we will now analyze briefly the price of such satisfactions for an individual, his or her family, and society. Because a drunkard lives and works with people, the damage caused by drunkenness becomes linked to a wide range of medical, social, moral, and economic problems. Traditionally, in Russia as in other countries, these problems are in three large groups.

The problems of a drunkard include the consequences of acute alcohol intoxication (such as a rapid decrease of the capacity for acting and self-control, aggressiveness and accidents, breaking the law, and alcohol poisoning). They also include the consequences of prolonged alcohol abuse (risk of various diseases, decrease of mental abilities, progressive worsening of capacity for acting and self-control, disturbances of nutrition and digestion, traumas and accidents, decrease of physical and working activity, development of alcohol dependence and degradation, alcoholic psychosis, death at the age of forty-five to fifty-five, deviant behavior, and suicide). Other negative consequences include the loss of friends and family, self-respect, work, fortune, freedom. But problems do not occur only for the drinker. His or her family is likely to experience internal conflicts, bad treatment of the children, lack of respect, psychic disturbances, birth defects (fetal alcohol syndrome [FAS] or fetal alcohol effects [FAE]), children's arrested development, and neglect of the children's education and development of their character. The children's early acquaintance with alcohol is likely to draw them into a deviant mode of life.

Society in a larger sense also suffers. Such broader problems include breaking of the law (aggressiveness, hooliganism, crimes), accidents at work and on the road that result in injuries, more sick days and days off, lower productivity, material loss, and additional expenditures for health maintenance, organization of special narcological services, and compulsory treatment of alcoholics.

It is very important to single out a universal mechanism of cross-cultural unification of consequences and complications due to drunkenness and alcoholism. At the stage of moderate alcohol consumption in different cultures, we encounter a great variety of forms and ways of alcoholization. With the development of drunkenness and alcoholism in subpopulations, we observe the increase of psychic degradation and asocial behavior, and the loss of originality of alcohol customs and alcohol culture. The long-term consequences of alcoholism are the same throughout the world.

According to a survey by the popular Russian magazine *Family* (1990, no. 16), 30% of parents consider physical punishment the most effective method of discipline; 10% of them spank their children and 20% give them an occasional flogging. Very often a child is a victim of alcoholic abuse when, in the state of intoxication, a parent gives a terrible beating, inflicting serious damage. Each year 2,000 children are admitted to the surgical department of the Children's Clinic, and 20 of them are officially declared to have been crippled by their parents. In reality this number is probably much higher, but there are no precise statistical data because of problems in reporting. The role of alcohol in the disturbance of the family structure and function is significant. By the age of fifteen, 25% of children are fatherless. Among 65 million families, 10 million have only one parent; 15 million children have no father; and 1 million have no living parents. Further, 300,000 children live in children's homes or orphanages, and 700,000 in foster homes. It is wives who insist on divorce in two cases out of three. The main reason is the husband's drunkenness. By the age of forty, 25% of women suffer neurotic disturbances associated with the husband's drunkenness. Alcohol is a universal indicator of unsolved family problems, a catalyst of conflict relations, and a generator of outrages due to alcohol abuse or excess.

Although no statistics can cover this problem as a whole, I'd like to give one example from my work as the head of the Expert Commission on Forensic Psychiatry. In June 1992, Natasha M., a schoolgirl aged fifteen, was directed for inpatient examination by a public prosecutor of one of the districts of the Arkhangelsk region. A preliminary investigator had doubts about her mental health because she had killed her father. He was a chronic alcoholic, drank practically every day, and abused her mother in the children's presence. There were three children in the family: the eldest, Natasha, had been born before her father became an alcoholic; the second child, a ten-year-old boy, had a slight degree of oligophrenia and attended a special school for children with mental retardation; and the youngest, a boy aged four, was profoundly retarded and lived in a special boarding clinic.

The father's alcoholism resulted in ruined lives for his three children. Tormented and worn out by her husband, the unhappy mother had to endure abuse every day. After the murder, the commission found that the victim had had chronic alcoholic delusions linked with jealousy. Abusing his wife, he tried to make her confess adultery. She suffered many beatings silently, having been brought up in the Russian tradition that "there is no love without jealousy." One day he beat his wife especially cruelly; when he fell asleep, drunk on the floor in his own vomit, his daughter took an ax and cut off his head. Examining the girl, we found ourselves in a trying situation. Humanely, we understood the impulsive act of a teenager driven to despair. Professionally, we couldn't find any serious psychic disturbance that could exempt her from prosecution. The girl was sentenced to many years' imprisonment for premeditated murder. I give this example to illustrate that consequences of drunkenness are more vividly expressed by human tears and suffering than by abstract and cold statistics.

Statistics on alcohol were concealed from the public during almost all the years of the socialist experiment. From 1930 to 1985, moral statistics (including crimes due to alcohol, suicides, etc.) were not given in official reports of the USSR Central Statistical Board. In 1928, for every 10,000 population in Moscow, there were 1.5 schools, 0.58 clubs, 0.38 libraries, 0.13 theaters, 0.22 cinemas, 1.64 churches, and 4.5 pubs selling alcoholic drinks. This vividly shows the part of alcohol in the socialist culture. In the 1990s, after the failure of the last anti-alcohol campaign, alcoholic drinks are sold everywhere; in contrast, cultural institutions are frequently closed due to rise in prices. Therefore, by limiting aesthetic culture, alcohol creates its own parallel culture fulfilling defense-compensatory social functions.

## APPENDIX: A PSYCHOSOCIAL THEORY ABOUT THE UNIVERSALITY OF ALCOHOL, BASED ON THE RUSSIAN EXPERIENCE

The need for alcohol is not a vital physical requirement like the need for oxygen or food. The "need" arises because society produces the product and gives birth to habits and prejudices connected with its consumption. Mark Twain compared civilization to a machine producing needs for which there is no real need.

But there has always existed, in all cultures, an objective need for a universal relaxant to relieve anxiety and reduce strain, smoothing national and interpersonal conflicts, even serving as a "social lubricant" in terms of relations among individuals. Traditionally in Russian culture this role has been played by alcohol, the consumption of which is regulated by customs.

Alcohol customs, historically established and passed from one generation to another, include ways of drinking that correspond to each society's spiritual makeup and world outlook. Alcohol customs have two social functions: stabilizing the forms and relations of alcohol consumption established in a given social environment, and reproducing these relations in the life of new generations.

The learning and acceptance of alcohol customs begins long before the need for alcohol arises, long before one's first acquaintance with alcohol itself, its taste, and its effects. A small child sitting at a holiday table expects to be given "children's [i.e., watered] wine" and, encouraged by adults, clinks glasses with them, thus imitating the formal rite of toasting while actually drinking. Experiments carried out in kindergarten showed that if children are invited to play "birthday" or "wedding party," they tend to reproduce many of the attributes of such an event among adults, not only imitating the raising and clinking of glasses, but also drinking and even the staggering of drunken guests. A view of alcohol as an indispensable accompaniment to celebration and an attractive symbol of adult life is formed by the age of four or five.

It is largely the alcohol customs of the family that determine the alcohol orientation of the children and the stereotypes of alcohol consumption. According to our data, schoolchildren who are allowed to drink alcohol with their parents on festive occasions have already drunk alcohol in the company of their friends nine times more often than those who were forbidden to do so. However, an individual is not only a product of culture: one does not simply reproduce the alcohol customs of the social surroundings but also works out his or her own attitudes toward such customs while increasing the experience of drinking alcohol. In other words, it is necessary to turn from the description of outer cultural determinants of alcoholization to the analysis of inner psychophysiological effects that instill the attractiveness of alcohol.

Certainly, the psychophysiological effects of alcohol are not always the same; they change depending upon the age and general state of health, as well as peculiarities of the constitution and the nervous system. On the whole, the most general pattern of alcohol's effect on the body includes two phases: the first usually manifests itself by excitement and a surge of strength, and the second is accompanied by relaxation and sleep.

Let us consider whether such psychophysiological conditions are attractive to a person and whether it is possible to explain the popularity of alcohol in this way. Obviously it is not. The attractiveness of alcohol, increasing with the increase of alcohol experience, is based on the psychological motivation for its use, in those wishes and requirements that a person tries to satisfy with its help. Primarily, having a good time at a celebration is anticipated, and people put themselves in a frame of mind that creates an excited emotional atmosphere. Subsequent consumption of alcohol creates a specific psychophysiological background on which all preceding psychophysiological expectations are powerfully projected, like the screen on which a film is projected. A person is usually unaware of this mechanism, which leads to the generally accepted notion of the specific heartening or cheering properties of alcohol.

Euphoria due to alcohol is not a direct consequence of intoxication per se. It is a psychic state formed to a great extent by mechanisms of self-induction and interinduction, the essence of which is determined by the situation and depends upon the general level of the person's culture. We carried out experiments with medical students who were given intravenous injections of 33% alcohol under the pretense of a functional test. The injections caused slight excitement and tonus increase, followed by relaxation, without any emotional component. In cases when a student was warned that he or she would be injected with alcohol, there appeared speech and behavior reactions like those caused by intoxication and directly related to the prior alcohol experience of the person involved. That is, the normal euphoria of drinking is an inner and dependent derivative of outer sociopsychological characteristics of the situation.

The following is an extract from the diary of the Russian writer Fyodor Abramov: "How did we live during the war? Worked, ate moss and celebrated holidays. Poured water into the bottle, put it on the table and sang songs." This vividly illustrates the great role of formal cultural features in a holiday rite or any festive occasion.

Thus, it is not alcohol as such but the projection of psychological expectations that causes the subjective image a person holds concerning the effects of alcohol. It is from this objectification of conditions, primarily unformed in terms of content, that the attractiveness of alcohol arises. It is from this that inattention and distortion of perception appear: a person begins to see in alcohol the main source of the condition that attracts him or her.

Other properties and functions of alcoholic drinks that come to be considered important to the drinker have the same origin. Thus, alcohol consumption is related not only to happy but also to sad occasions, such as a funeral feast or wake. People who feel a death keenly are sad and do not experience any cheering effect from alcohol. Alcohol has occupied such a place both in Russian and world culture because its effect creates a suitable and quickly achieved background for almost any psychological projection. It is the content vagueness of the effect that makes it a universal means of achieving various psychical conditions. And one may choose either of the two contrasting phases of intoxication: excitement or depression. If the first one creates the background necessary for happy events, the second can be the basis for suffering. An additional physiological effect of alcohol is to diminish perception, which makes it possible for a person to think he or she can reduce the difficulty of problems in life.

Of course, the subjective picture of intoxication is not created by a momentary act of projection of psychological expectation and actual requirements on the background of alcohol intoxication. This picture is produced in the course of specific activities of a drunkard, which can be called illusive-compensatory; they are aimed at creation of a desirable emotional state, specific alcohol-based satisfaction (even if illusory) of some actual requirement.

In order to understand the specific character of this activity, it is sufficient to compare it with the activity of a healthy person. Let us consider a very important universal need, self-satisfaction. A healthy person tries to set goals whose achievement will be highly appreciated by him or her and by others, and that will lead to the increase and maintenance of self-esteem. But there is quite a different way for drunkards to achieve self-respect. The achievement of real aims in life is replaced by subjective emotions in the state of intoxication that, to the drinker, are similar to the emotions of a healthy person realizing his or her intentions. For example, the question "Do you respect me?," addressed to a companion, is very typical of a Russian drinker in the state of intoxication. An affirmative answer is sufficient to reinforce the questioner's feeling of self-respect. Gradually a larger range of a person's requirements can be satisfied by means of intoxication. It is very important to emphasize that this satisfaction is based not on real activity but on the image and imitation of it by creating subjective emotions in the state of intoxication. As a rule, desirable subjective conditions are not attained when a drinker is alone. Illusive-compensatory activity demands extensive "dramatization" of these states that implies company: an interlocutor, listener, and spectator. Therefore it is more precise to discuss not the attractiveness of alcohol in itself but the influence of the rite of alcohol consumption in a particular group.

Everything said above testifies to the groundlessness of widespread attempts to explain psychological addiction to alcohol solely by a conditioned-reflex connection between the event (alcohol drinking) and confirmation (euphoria). A person expects a greater effect from alcohol than euphoria. The "principle of gratification" is too trivial to explain this widespread phenomenon. Psychological causes are deeper: first they lie in the (illusive) possibilities of at least temporarily satisfying desires and settling conflicts, because the state of intoxication makes it possible to objectify different requirements in this state. Second, they also lie in the social, psychological, and cultural conditions that predetermine the broad diffusion of alcohol customs.

## REFERENCES

The author is aware that specialized Russian publications are hard to find outside of Russia, and that few non-Russians can read them. For this reason, he did not include the usual list of references. However, the editor would like to draw to the attention of readers a few sources in English that, although strongly colored by political sentiment, offer fairly accurate assessments of many historical and cultural aspects of alcohol in Russian culture.

Christian, David. 1990. *Living water: Vodka and Russian society on the eve of emancipation.* New York: Oxford University Press.

Herlihy, Patricia. 1991. Joy of the Rus' [*sic*]: Rites and rituals of Russian drinking. *The Russian Review* 50:131–147.

Hutchinson, J. F. 1980. Science, politics, and the alcohol problem in post-1905 Russia. *Slavonic and East European Review* 58:232–254.

Ivanets, N. N., I. P. Anokhina, V. F. Egorov, Y. V. Valentik, and S. B. Shesterneva. 1992. Present state and prospects of treatment of alcoholism in the Soviet Union. Pp. 87–112 in H. Klingemann, J.-P. Takala, and G. Hunt (Eds.). *Cure, care, or control: Alcoholism treatment in sixteen countries.* Albany: State University of New York Press.

Segal, Boris M. 1987. *Russian drinking: Use and abuse of alcohol in pre-Revolutionary Russia.* New Brunswick, N.J.: Rutgers Center of Alcohol Studies.

———. 1990. *The drunken society: Alcohol abuse and alcoholism in the Soviet Union.* New York: Hippocrane Books.

Segal, R.E.F. 1980. Drink in old Russia. Pp. 42–54 in E. J. Hobsbawm, W. Kule, A. Mitra, K. N. Raj, and I. Sachs (Eds.). *Peasants in history: Essays in honor of David Thorner.* Calcutta: Oxford University Press.

Snow, George E. 1991. Socialism, alcoholism, and the Russian working classes before

1917. Pp. 243–264 in S. Barrows and R. Room (Eds.). *Drinking behavior and belief in modern history*. Berkeley: University of California Press.

Treml, Vladimir G. 1985. *Alcohol in the U.S.S.R.: A statistical study*. Durham, N.C.: Duke University Press.

# 23

# Spain

## *Juan F. Gamella*

In Spain, alcoholic beverages are woven into the cultural fabric of everyday life. Traditions that have for centuries sanctioned alcohol consumption have merged with more recent customs. Alcohol has always been the main social lubricant, and its consumption is a source of sociability and conviviality. In every region some form of drinking is positively sanctioned as a medium for "social participation and for relating to friends" (Rooney 1991, 390). Social drinking peaks at festive times, usually marked by drinking in varied forms. Alcohol is associated with most public and private rites and celebrations, such as those concerning birth, marriage, and death, as well as the religious festivities of Easter, Christmas, and Corpus Christi, and with local fiestas, of which every village or neighborhood has its own. In public rituals, drinking in common is an expression of group solidarity and even of ethnic identification. For instance, in the Basque country, Ramírez Goicoechea (1990) sees alcohol use as a trait of militant Basque identity. Whereas illicit drugs are thought of as foreign and a threat to nationalist ideals, alcohol is viewed as inherently "Basque."

Moreover, alcoholic beverages are integrated with food consumption to the extent that a meal is often judged incomplete without wine (or cider or beer, in some places). As the old refrain goes: *Comer sin vino, comer mezquino*—a meal without wine is mean. As nourishment, alcoholic drinks are not perceived differently from other beverages, such as juices, tea, or coffee. As Rooney (1991, 382–383) states: "Alcohol is not placed in a separate moral category in the Spanish cognitive map but rather constitutes one class of beverages among others, all of which are sold in the same establishment and generally have some degree of association with food consumption." This integration is evident in the system of distribution. Alcoholic beverages are sold in every grocery store and supermarket along with other beverages and foodstuffs; no special permit or license is required to sell them.

Furthermore, alcohol production is a vital economic activity for Spain, one of the leading wine-producing countries in the world, which dedicates about 10% of its cultivated land to vineyards. All sorts of wines are produced here. For some regions, such as Rioja, Jerez, Penedés, and Valdepeñas, wine is their foremost product and a source of local pride. Surplus wine of inferior quality is distilled and used to make spirits, such as brandy, anisette, gin, or even vodka. Beer is also produced in great quantities, Spain being one of the ten major beer producers in the world. Alcohol provides many jobs in agriculture, manufacturing, transportation, and commerce; it is also important as an adjunct to the tourist trade, one of the major national industries.

Thus, in Spain, even for those who do not drink, alcoholic beverages are a "natural" fact of life, something that has always been there, neither good nor bad in themselves but only in the use that is made of them. Drinking in Spain has been moderate by international standards, and until recently drunkenness was despised in all but exceptional circumstances.

## PROBLEMATIZATION OF ALCOHOL USE

Rapid social and cultural change, accelerated in recent decades, has modified standard expectations and behaviors toward alcohol. New patterns of drinking that conflict with old rules and conventions have spread. For instance, beer and spirits such as whisky and gin have become very popular, surpassing wine as the drinks of choice among young drinkers. Many young Spaniards now concentrate their excess drinking in weekends and even drink to get drunk, a pattern of drinking alien to traditional standards. At the same time, young women are drinking more, and more often, than their mothers and grandmothers, becoming more similar to men in their drinking habits. Alcohol is thus increasingly used as a psychoactive drug, ingested primarily for its effects on behavior, mood, or perception. Hence, the standards of the older generations increasingly disagree with those of the younger ones.

Some of those changes have increased the awareness of the extent of drinking problems beyond drunkenness and alcoholism. Alcohol plays an important role in a high proportion of the more than 8,000 deaths caused every year by road accidents, as well as in many home and on-the-job accidents, civil and criminal cases, fights, homicides, rapes, spouse abuse, and unwanted pregnancies. Frequent heavy drinking leads to diseases and mental problems.

Moreover, after more than a decade of intense social alarm about illicit drug use and addiction, there is an increasing realization that misuse of alcohol is often combined with and worsened by the use of drugs. This favors the new perception of alcohol abuse as a drug problem and, together with tobacco, a source of addiction.

Hence alcohol in Spain today is an equivocal symbol that means different things to different people in different circumstances. It is seen as a socializing agent, a pleasant beverage to combine with food, even a foodstuff with some distinctly beneficial effects; but it is also seen as a hazardous and habit-forming psychoactive drug, and a source of disease, injury, and economic loss in an increasingly mechanized society. This may explain the incoherence and inconsistency of individual and collective perceptions and judgments, especially when measured by opinion surveys.

Many experts complain that Anglo-Saxon patterns of drinking, foreign to Spanish traditions, are at the root of the new problems, and rightly point to the acculturation experienced in many spheres of Spanish life in the twentieth century. They do not recognize, however, how the perception of "alcoholic beverages" as a separate, homogeneous category, defined by the presence of ethanol, is also an innovation, foreign to Spanish perceptions until recently. Traditionally more attention was paid to the ways in which beverages were used than to the psychoactive compound that some contain. Hence, no significant group in Spain felt the American horror of alcohol and no one organized to further its prohibition. For over 2,000 years, alcoholic beverages were a staple of the diet of Spaniards that they took with them wherever they went, from Cape Horn to California.

## ALCOHOL IN SPANISH HISTORY

Alcoholic beverages have been widely used in Spain since ancient times. Strabo, the Greek geographer (63 B.C.–ca. A.D.) who described the Iberian peninsula at the time of Augustus, refers to a form of beer known to Iberians as *zythos,* which they drank combined with fruits and plants (García Bellido 1945). From the archaeological record, we know that wine was imported by Phoenicians "in their own amphoras" from their colonies along the Mediterranean coast at least from 775 B.C. (Harrison 1988, 52). Greeks may have introduced vineyard cultivation to Spain; certainly they incorporated Spanish wines in their active wine trade from Gibraltar to the Black Sea. Roman conquest spread and encouraged wine production throughout the country.

After the fall of the Roman Empire, the monastic orders preserved and cared for vineyards in some of the major wine-producing areas that were neglected by the Visigoths and the Arabs. The Visigoths, a Germanic people who ruled most of Spain and southern France from the end of Roman hegemony until 711, when they were ousted by the Arabs, originally were beer drinkers. With the arrival of the Arabs, wine production and trade were abandoned for some time in many areas of southern and central Spain. Thus, in medieval Spain vineyards were first connected with monasteries and monks, and later were a visible marker of the Christians' movement from the north to the lands controlled by Islam.

In Muslim Spain, vineyards were increasingly grown as well, both because of the high demand for grapes and raisins by a population of eager fruit eaters and—contrary to what would be expected from the Koranic prohibition—because Muslims were avid wine drinkers. It is documented that wine was popularized in the kingdom of Abd al-Rahman II (822–852), and large areas of Andalusia were planted with vineyards (Glick 1991). Thus, even if the data point to a higher per capita consumption of wine by Christians, the best wines were often produced in lands ruled by Islam (Glick 1991).

## Alcohol in Classic Spain

From the 1400s to the 1800s, wine remained one of the staffs of life for Spaniards, together with olive oil and bread. Wine was also used for cooking, to preserve food, as a medicine mixed with herbal remedies, and often as a substitute for unsafe water. The majority of those wines were unstable, low in alcohol, and drunk within the year of their production. Most wines were sold locally, but some that were resistant to spoilage were exported and became very popular, such as wines from the Canary Islands and from the Jerez district in Andalusia, which came to be known in the English world as ''sherry'' (a mispronunciation of Jerez) and were enjoyed by people such as Shakespeare, who sang its virtues:

> A good sherris-sack hath a two-fold operation in it.
> It ascends me into the brain; dries me there all the
> foolish and dull and crudy vapours which eviron
> it. . . . The second property of your excellent sherris is,
> the warming of the blood; which, before cold and
> settled, left the liver white and pale. . . . this valour
> comes of sherris.
>
> (*Henry IV, Part 2:* Act IV, scene 3)

In sum, to Spaniards grape wine was a symbol of civilization and Catholic heritage, and a culturally essential part of the diet in all lands they controlled. A Mexican friar called it ''a most noble, useful, and necessary drink in these kingdoms; a drink venerated and honored by Christ; and . . . the most noble of drinks. He chose to transform it into His most precious blood'' (Taylor 1979, 41).

## Temperate Use

For centuries wine was used for sustenance rather than intoxication, for food rather than drunkenness. Moderation in drinking was a deeply ingrained value in Spanish culture; ''Spaniards generally valued a Mediterranean ideal of drinking mostly at mealtimes and being able to 'hold' their liquor without losing control of their dignified demeanor and 'natural reason.' Drunkenness to the point of passing out was considered barbarous, disgusting, ridiculous, and a blot on a man's honor'' (Taylor 1979, 41).

A historian of the classic period noted that Spanish temperance was ''all the more remarkable because the provinces of Spain produced excellent wines,'' and quotes the astonishment of a French traveler who toured the country in 1679 and found that Spaniards were ''surprisingly abstemious as regards wine. . . . The women never drink it, and the men use so little that half a *setier* [about a quarter of a liter] is enough for a day. One could not outrage them more than to accuse them of being drunk'' (Defourneaux 1970, 152–153). Similar observations on drinking are found in many other sources, both local and foreign.

Like other Mediterranean groups, Spaniards hold a cultural prejudice against intoxication, drunkenness being a sort of ethnic boundary marker attributed to outsiders. In fact, Spaniards derived a sense of superiority over northern Europeans and over the natives they ruled in their colonies because of their ''civilized'' attitude toward drinking. In colonial Mexico, for instance, Taylor has shown how local Spanish officials saw excessive drinking as a custom that supported their view of native Mexicans as ''perpetual minors,'' incapable of conforming to Spanish standards of moderation: ''If the Indians drank pulque the way Spaniards drink wine (which is not the case, nor has it been, nor is there any hope of their ever doing so) it could be permitted . . . but these are Indians and it is proven that their custom is to get drunk, and it is for that reason that they drink'' (Taylor 1979, 2).

## Industrial Production of Alcoholic Beverages

Beginning in the late 1600s, more and more alcohol was produced for sale and export. New technologies for the preservation of wine and the introduction of large-scale commercial distillation facilitated the transportation of larger quantities of alcohol and the consolidation of an interregional market for alcoholic beverages. Ringrose (1985), who has studied Madrid's economy in the 1800s and 1900s, states that since about 1850, better wines were brought to Madrid from the south-central regions.

The Spanish empire in America and the Philippines offered a huge market for alcohol exports, and distillation enlarged the range of beverages available. The most popular spirits were brandy, anise liquor, and *aguardiente,* a strong liquor made from either sugarcane or mashed grapes. In the late 1700s, regulatory measures were relaxed, exempting liquors and *aguardiente* from most tariffs and taxes. The ensuing opening of colonial markets to all Spanish regions in 1765 encouraged the production of alcoholic beverages in Catalonia, where they played an important role in the industrial growth of the region. Thus, in the late colonial period, spirits were massively exported to the cities, mining zones, and major plantation areas of Spanish America. According to Taylor (1979), in 1778, in the mining areas of Mexico alone, 20,000 barrels of Spanish brandy were consumed, in addition to many more barrels of cheap local *aguardiente.*

Industrial production of alcoholic beverages led to new forms of drinking, different in type and scale from traditional customs. The use of spirits increased in frequency and quantity, together with greater use of alcohol apart from meals, and sometimes even as a cheap substitute for food among laborers and working men. When most American colonies were lost after the Napoleonic wars, the resulting oversupply of alcoholic beverages in Spain was diverted to the national market, encouraging local consumption. Hence, during the 1800s, there was an increase in heavy drinking in urban and industrial centers. In this period there was "an important inflection from a relatively abstemious national culture to new patterns of use" (Comas 1985, 47). The traditional role of alcohol as nourishment served to legitimate and justify the use of wine and other alcoholic beverages for their euphoric effects.

A second push for the Spanish alcohol industry came from the disaster experienced by European vineyards in the late 1800s. In 1863 a mite called phylloxera, which feeds on the roots of grapevines, was introduced, and in a few years it devastated many of the wine-growing areas throughout Europe. In France, the plague destroyed more than 2.5 million acres and created a huge demand for imported wine. Tariffs for Spanish wines were lowered in France, and the Spanish regions in which some vineyards were temporarily spared took advantage. Large tracts of land that had been used for growing grain but were abandoned because of competition from cheap grain imported from the United States, Argentina, and Russia, were planted with vines. When the ravages of phylloxera were checked in France by the grafting of European vines with mite-resistant stocks from America, Spain again found itself with an oversupply of alcohol, which was again directed to the local market. This new turn of the world economic system induced further important changes in local consumption.

In the following decades there was a serious increase in excessive drinking and alcoholism, which became a social and public health problem for the first time, particularly among wage earners. The first Spanish trade unions demanded measures against alcoholism, and several medical and charitable organizations tried to promote public awareness of alcohol-related problems. Still, use of alcohol in Spain was lower than in many other European countries, such as England and France.

In this period there was also a growing emphasis on status-conscious drinking and class-oriented public drinking establishments. In the taverns of working-class neighborhoods and villages, laborers drank cheap wine or *aguardiente;* in the cafés or casinos of middle-class professionals and the elites, the preferred beverages were vintage wines and expensive brandies. In their drinking customs, the new generations paralleled the preferences of their elders. In taverns and cafés, young workers drank mostly wine, while middle- and upper-class young people drank more expensive spirits.

More recently there has been an increase in cosmopolitan patterns of drinking involving beer and liquors. Whiskey, for instance, was a status drink rarely consumed by lower-income groups until the 1960s, when its use started to spread as a sign of social mobility and sophistication, and a local firm produced a Spanish version, named Wisky [*sic*] Dick. Today Spain is one of the world's main importers of whiskey. Since World War II, American influence has been strong in drinking customs as well as in other realms of life. For example, the first cafeterias opened in Madrid in the 1950s, attended by waitresses (rather than traditional waiters). They served a variety of showy foods and drinks, and had such names as Nebraska, Montana, Iowa, and California.

Mass industrial production of alcohol has "democratized" some of what had been upper-class drinks. It has also supported an increase in per capita consumption of alcohol, which rose in Spain beginning in the 1940s and is now among the highest in the world (over 20 liters per capita in 1985). This is associated with high rates of death from cirrhosis of the liver and other alcohol-related diseases. It should be noted, however, that the total alcohol consumed in Spain includes not only that drunk by Spaniards but also that consumed by the millions of tourists who visit the country every year (their numbers exceed the population of Spain). Together with movies and television, tourists have helped to popularize foreign drinks, customs, and attitudes.

## MAIN DRINKING PATTERNS TODAY

According to recent surveys of the Spanish population, over two-thirds of adult Spaniards drink regularly, and most people over sixteen have tried alcoholic beverages at some point in their life. The proportion of drinkers decreases with age. Over 83% of those between sixteen and twenty-five years of age declare that they drink, compared with only 64% of those in the forty-six to sixty-five age range, and 45% of those over sixty-six. Women drink less frequently than men; three times more women than men abstain. Younger women, however, drink more, and more often, than their mothers and grandmothers. Thus, in the age group sixteen to twenty-five, over 77% of women drink, compared with 51% of those in the range forty-six to sixty-five (Ministerio de Sanidad 1992).

The majority of Spaniards drink moderately, and apparently without suffering from their drinking. Drinking small amounts on many occasions is the typical consumption pattern; around half of all adult males conform to it throughout the country. Nevertheless, over 6% of adults confess they drink heavily (over 75 cc. of pure alcohol per day), and another 4% that they drink very heavily (over 100 cc.). Thus, it is reckoned that over 1 million adults are classifiable as heavy drinkers, and another 1.5 million drink in ways that put them at risk of hurting themselves and others. Twelve times more men than women appear to drink in excess. Female homemakers appear to be the group of adults who drink least.

Spaniards still drink much wine, but also a lot of beer and spirits. The increase in beer consumption has been massive; annual per capita consumption rose from 2 liters in 1950 to 59 in 1985. In the same period, wine drinking increased much less, from about 52 to 85 liters (Rooney 1990). Beer has also replaced wine as the beverage young Spaniards first drink. A 1983 survey among high school students in Valencia found that the beverage of initiation was 60% beer, 25% wine, and 15% a liquor.

## Dimensions of "Proper" Drinking

Alcohol use in Spain is highly institutionalized. Proper drinking (*saber beber*) includes the ability to know when and how to drink, avoiding inebriation, and behaving correctly even if slightly inebriated (*alegre:* merry or high). To be blatantly drunk in public is still a breech of major norms, because under such circumstances, people lose control, make fools of themselves, and "become unable to participate in the social interaction" (Rooney 1991, 392). Inebriation is especially degrading for women. Standards of proper drinking, however, are changing rapidly, mainly among the young.

Of the key factors that determine the patterns and expectations of alcohol use in Spanish society, the most important are the association of drink with food, the gender and generational composition of the group of drinkers, and the time and place where alcohol is consumed. Their combination defines proper use with respect to acceptable occasions, the amount and type of alcohol considered appropriate, and the tolerance for showing signs of intoxication.

In Spain it is assumed that drinking at meals and drinking outside meals are different forms of drinking. With a meal, inebriation is made more difficult, and the psychoactive effects become secondary. As Rooney points out, "settings in which food consumption is more salient involve lesser focus upon alcohol and generally include a greater proportion of women as customers" (1991, 383). Therefore, at certain hours, not to drink on an empty stomach is a tacit cultural prescription, and food, even a morsel, will be included with the drinking.

The generational and gender composition of the group also influences the general ambience and the norms of behavior operating in any particular setting where alcohol is consumed. The presence of elders and women usually exerts a moderating effect on drinking comportment. Nevertheless, young people are developing different attitudes and behaviors toward alcohol.

The temporal dimension of drinking is also important. Beyond the seasonal patterns related to climate and to the festive calendar, the day of the week and the time of the day at which the drinking is done are important dimensions in the social pressure to drink or not to drink. Thus, drinking may be perceived as acceptable at one time and negatively perceived at another, even in the same social setting.

Winter and summer produce differences in drinking patterns. In summer, thirst quenchers such as cold beer, diluted wine, or wine punches (such as sangria) are preferred to straight brandy or whiskey. Holidays and celebrations are major periods of celebratory drinking. Weekends and holidays are festive times in which the daily norms of workdays are altered.

### Patterns of Drinking by Time of the Day

Daily schedules in Spain are different from those predominant in the United States and in other European countries. Social life starts and ends later, and is divided by a rest period (siesta) after lunch, particularly in summer. Ideally a day consists of different periods that define proper drinking routines. I distinguish eight of those periods, which, with small regional and local variations, can be found throughout the country:

*Breakfast Time (7–10 A.M.)*

In Spain adults start their day with a light breakfast that they often eat away from home, especially on workdays. Bars and cafeterias serve coffee or tea with rolls or toast. Some men complement their coffee with a glass of liquor, especially in winter. They are following a popular custom among their parents and grandparents, when it was common for workingmen to start their day in the early morning with one or more glasses of strong liquor (*aguardiente,* dry anisette, or brandy), with or without coffee or tea. This working-class breakfast, less usual today, is traditionally understood as energizing for the physical work ahead, and hence is more common in winter, on days of hard labor, and in rural areas.

*Morning (about 10 A.M.–1 P.M.)*

Many people eat a second, more substantial breakfast (*almuerzo*), ideally around 11 A.M. It usually consists of a sandwich or a snack (a *racion* or *tapa*) and a drink that, if alcoholic, will be beer or a glass of wine. Increasingly, people on different time schedules eat at this time, and it is common to see patrons at bars having their first breakfast together with those who are having a more substantial meal. Nevertheless, alcoholic beverages at this time are considered a complement of food, and are secondary to it.

*Aperitif Time (1–2 P.M.)*

This is the time before lunch during which people will have a glass of wine or beer with colleagues and friends in a relaxed and convivial atmosphere. Perhaps the closest to the American "happy hour" (although prices remain the same), it is most popular on weekends and holidays, when the number of drinkers at this time of day doubles (Alvira Martín 1986). Vermouth is very popular at aperitif time, which it defines in some areas—*la hora del vermú* (vermouth hour) or *tomar el vermú* (to drink vermouth).

A snack (*tapa*) of variable size and content is usually included with the drink. In some areas, such as Andalusia, *tapas* may be treats that enhance the experience of the aperitif, and three or four of them make a satisfying meal. At aperitif time, however, drink is the primary activity and food is a complement.

### Lunchtime (2–3:30 P.M.)

Lunch is usually the main meal in Spain. It usually starts between 2 and 3 P.M. and lasts longer than in other European countries. Ideally a two-course meal plus dessert, it usually includes table wine. This is the time of the day at which more people drink an alcoholic beverage; over 40% of adults say they drink with lunch. Wine is the preferred drink at this time, often diluted with soda water. For the middle and upper classes, it is the time when the whole family will meet around the table. Main newscasts are aired between 2:30 and 3 P.M. by radio and television stations. Manual laborers generally have their lunches earlier, around 1 P.M., and working schedules in the service economy are increasingly packed into a shorter workday (8 A.M.–3 P.M.). Thus, families eat lunch together less frequently.

### Coffee or Siesta Time (3:30–6 P.M.)

In Spain it is common to have strong coffee after meals. With their coffee, many people will have a glass of liquor, particularly on holidays. A trickle of liquor may also be dropped in the cup of coffee to make the popular *carajillo*. Coffee and liquor are often considered part of the meal, particularly on formal occasions. After lunch, especially in summer, comes siesta time, a period of up to an hour for having a nap or relaxing quietly. This is the period of the day when bars will be most empty.

### Evening (6–9 P.M.)

At this time of day, drinking becomes more independent of food. It is also a favorite time for young people to drink, particularly on weekends. Over 50% of those eighteen to twenty-four years of age drink at this time. However, when people go out for dinner, some of the midday patterns may be reenacted, including aperitifs, wine, and postdinner drinks.

This is also the most frequent time for *tapeo* or *chiquiteo* (barhopping), a ritualized form of drinking in which several bars are visited regularly by a group of friends. Again most of the expectations and practices described for aperitif time apply. Snacks, for instance, are normally added to drinks. Sometimes the *tapeo* is prolonged and becomes a substitute for the evening meal, or the group of drinkers may go to have dinner together.

### Dinnertime (9–11 P.M.)

At dinner most of the patterns of lunch are repeated, but it is rare today that people have the time for two large and extended meals in a day. Hence, if lunch is an elaborate family occasion, dinner is often shorter and simpler, and vice versa. Dinners at home are becoming less formal and familial, and the proportion of people drinking at this time has decreased (Alvira Martín 1986). Nevertheless, dinner is the preferred meal for eating out in a restaurant with family or friends.

*Night (11 P.M.–7 A.M.)*

At this time of day, drinks are not associated with food, but are consumed as a means for relaxation, recreation, and social and sexual interaction. Going out at this time is often referred to as *alternar* (alternate), because it is understood as time for shifting gears toward a less concerned, less hierarchical, and more individualistic mood. Alcohol is perceived as facilitating that emotional transition. Thus, drinking at this time increases on weekends, particularly among young people and couples.

**Places to Drink: The Bar as a Core Institution**

In Spain there is an imposing array of places where drinks are served and consumed. It has as many alcohol outlets as all the other European Economic Community countries together. Some are modest, such as the *bodegas* (warehouses) where drinks and refreshments are sold wholesale, often adjoining grocery stores. Others are very status-conscious, such as the fancy new cafeterias or the old casinos where in the past local elites ruled the towns, others are sexually exclusive, such as the increasingly obsolete male-only taverns; and some cater to specific age groups, such as the bars or pubs for the young that have sprouted in the last decades. Most of them offer tobacco, coffee, snacks, and even full meals, and satisfy many needs beyond drinking.

In any of their various forms, bars are a central institution of Spanish social life. They play a vital role "in mediating human contacts" (Hansen 1977, 122), as well as in the gathering and distribution of news, in networking, and in political activities. People go to bars to meet friends, smoke, eat, chat, play cards or dominoes, gossip, gather information, and drink. Hence, for many people, the bar, tavern, or café "constitutes their principal sphere of social activity and focus of community" in their neighborhood (Rooney 1991, 389).

Popular bars teem with social life in multifaceted forms, and offer a haven from and an alternative to the economic, cultural, and social shortcomings of villages and poor neighborhoods. In a study of a rural district of Catalonia during the late Francoist period, the anthropologist Edward Hansen observed the dynamics of the main bars in town as they served their multiple functions as centers of communications, as well as for the building up of instrumental coalitions in an atmosphere of political repression where most public meetings were forbidden: "On weekdays, there is a continuous trickle of people from early morning to late afternoon, and by seven in the evening there is a veritable avalanche of patrons, who stay until just before the evening meal at ten. On Saturdays and Sundays the flow of humanity is so great at all hours of the day that there is barely elbow room indoors and standing room only at the outdoor tables" (Hansen 1977, 121).

Today there is a growing generation gap in the use of bars by teenagers, especially in working-class neighborhoods; they rarely go to the taverns and bars that are preferred by their parents and grandparents. Apart from having their own bars or discos, teenagers often drink in parks or in the streets around bars and discos, a behavior that their elders disapprove.

## VARIANT DRINKING PATTERNS

Regional differences are the main source of ethnic feelings in Spain today. Regional cultures such as those of Catalonia, the Basque country, Castille, and Andalusia still have contrasting drinking traditions, and attachment to local beverages is intense. Yet widespread intranational migration and commercial standardization have blunted regional uniqueness. For instance, Asturias, on the north Cantabrian coast, is the main producer of cider, which in its processed form is exported and drunk all over Spain, but is drunk fresh only in the region. Asturians are proud that only there can you drink "the real thing"; to appreciate cider and to know how to drink it may be a marker of regional affiliation. The same is true of more delicate beverages, such as Manzanilla, a dry white wine produced in the southern province of Cádiz, and *ribeiro,* a Galician wine.

Consumption of alcoholic beverages is higher, both in amount and in frequency, in northern regions such as the Basque country, the Cantabrian coast, and Rioja, and lower in the south and the Mediterranean regions (Gili et al. 1989; Elzo 1987; Martínez and Martín 1987). Nevertheless, patterns of drinking today differ more by age group than by class or ethnic group.

### Drinking Patterns of the Young

The young now drink more than their parents and grandparents. Surveys consistently show that males eighteen to twenty-five years old drink more than any other group in the population. They are also developing patterns of drinking that have few precedents in Spanish culture. The most important have to do with the ways in which the young begin to drink, as well as what, how, and where they drink.

*Initiation*

Teenagers today start drinking regularly at an earlier age, and learn to drink in peer groups rather than in the family. Systematic surveys indicate a persistent reduction in the onset of drinking age. On average, the generations born in the 1930s and 1940s started to drink regularly at around eighteen years of age. But each new generation since has begun to drink a little earlier. Nowadays, mean age for onset of regular drinking is near fifteen. Thus, in a recent survey of high school students, over 96% of boys and 90% of girls were found to have started drinking alcohol at that age (DGPND 1990; Alvira Martín 1986).

Traditionally one learned to drink in one's family. A sip of weak or diluted wine was given to children in rural areas beginning when they were small, and traditionally many infants' paps included wine. Moreover, until recently, there were fortified wines that were supposed to help children grow strong. However, a more formal initiation into drinking usually took place in the context of rituals and celebrations at which the extended family came together: a wedding, a first Communion, a baptism, or on Christmas Eve. However, teenagers drank only rarely until they were old enough to enter the tavern and drink in the company of adult men.

Today young Spaniards are learning to drink among their peers, without elders being present, and are keeping their drinking apart from their family and home. This process often involves inebriation, and a feeling of rule-breaking resembling initial tobacco and illicit drug use. Thus drinking is still part of a rite of passage to adulthood and independence, but done with equals rather than adults.

*Why, When, How*

Teenagers drink increasingly apart from meals, seeking primarily the euphoric, intoxicating, or social properties of alcohol. It seems that "each generation drinks more often outside meals than the previous one" (Rooney 1990, 216). Alcohol is increasingly associated with leisure, and leisure with alcohol. Most young people drink only on weekends and holidays, when they will start drinking in the evening and often go on until the early morning. Alcohol consumption helps to make weekends a culturally exceptional period removed from the routine and drudgery of workdays. This time of leisure and freedom has become so important for young people that they have mobilized violently against adult measures to control it.

In recent decades, a new type of establishment, catering only to the young, has prospered. These youth bars and discos are very different from the taverns and bars where their elders started to drink. Old local taverns were located in one's neighborhood, more sexually exclusive, and multigenerational. They were less restricted in hours and comportment than the noisy, hyperactive pubs or discos of today. In bars and taverns, patrons could sit alone and drink, or read the newspaper, or chat peacefully. By contrast, youth bars, pubs, and discos tend to be concentrated in specific areas of cities and towns. On Friday night, hundreds and even thousands of youth of both sexes soon fill them to the point of spilling into the adjacent streets, creating a "special territory" that is now emblematic of youths' independence; its main attraction is "the presence of a multitude of people of the same age in an environment free of adult control" (Rooney 1990, 215). Those areas are often a source of friction with neighbors and passersby. But young people have shown an intense attachment to them, and have rioted in several cities when laws were enacted to make the areas less noisy or to close the establishments earlier—by 3 A.M.

*Inebriation*

Often young people drink to get drunk, and they experience frequent episodes of intoxication. Weekend binges have become common and alarming, with many teenagers drinking to the point of losing motor control or even consciousness. Today, it is common to see youngsters vomiting, crawling, or even unconscious on Friday and Saturday nights near discos or youth bars, and also on buses or subways. In a national high school survey in 1990, over 50% of boys and girls in the tenth grade (sixteen years of age) admitted to having been drunk at least once; 12% confessed to having been drunk at least ten times. The average age of first intoxication was 13.4 years of age (Delegación del Gobierno para el Plan Naciona de Drogas 1990).

The frequency of drunkenness and its deliberate character are a departure from the customs of their elders. In a survey of the Madrid population, over 70% of those between twenty and twenty-nine years of age admitted to having been inebriated, while in their parents' age group (forty-five to sixty-four), the proportion was only 34% (Alvira y Comas 1990).

This increase in the number of drunks may prove to be a passing fad without serious consequences for most youngsters. If that is so, the resulting culture of alcohol in Spain would institutionalize the bimodal pattern of drinking by age that we see today, in which alcohol is used differently in different stages of the life cycle. But if a substantial group of youngsters continue with their excessive drinking in later years, there could be an important shift in the dominant forms of alcoholism and problem drinking in the country. Unproblematic heavy drinking could give way to quicker and more self-destructive forms of dependence.

### Problem Drinking by the Young

Drinking among the young is primarily a means of interacting with friends and relating to people of the opposite sex. There are, however, alarming signs of serious misuse of alcohol by an important minority of teenagers and young adults. It's likely that most will reduce their drinking in later life, and grow out of those age-specific drinking patterns. But many may develop dependence or other enduring problems from their excessive drinking, there are already some disturbing cases in the form of alcohol-related diseases and accidents.

Moreover, in this age group, alcohol is often used in combination with other drugs, especially by those who get drunk often. Since the late 1970s, there has been a great expansion in the use of illicit drugs, such as hashish, heroin, and cocaine, as well as of designer drugs. So far, the most destructive consequence of the popularization of new forms of drug use has been a massive growth of heroin addiction, which has contributed to the spread of AIDS among heroin users who inject, and among their partners and children.

Being so visible and dramatic, such a drug crisis has diverted attention and resources from the less spectacular prevention and treatment of alcohol problems. Today it is still easier to generate political and moral consensus by fighting drugs rather than alcohol use. There is, however, an increasing realization that alcohol—and tobacco—although legal, are subject to abuse and claim lives, as do illegal drugs.

In this sense, a growing number of professionals, public officials, and ordinary citizens now reject the traditionally tolerant attitudes toward excessive alcohol use, which they perceive as a major social and public health problem requiring urgent collective action. They are demanding and sometimes securing sterner measures against drunk driving and against the advertisement of alcoholic beverages, and for strict enforcement of the law that forbids the sale of alcoholic beverages to minors under sixteen.

However, it is still easy for a child of ten or twelve to buy alcoholic beverages at a grocery store. Besides, many parents who would scold their adolescent sons and daughters for coming home drunk would just as easily show some relief because their children were not involved with "hard drugs." The public approach to alcohol use and misuse in Spain is still marked by ambivalence and contradictions.

### Drinking by Young Women

Patterns of alcohol use are becoming less differentiated by gender, so that adolescent and young women are closer to men in their drinking habits than were their mothers and grandmothers. This is a major cultural change. Still, girls drink less and less frequently than boys, and get drunk less often. Drinking was traditionally considered men's business, and women rarely drank, especially in public; and when they did drink, they were in the company of their men or of other women.

By drinking to excess, women were considered to put their virtue at risk— and thus, the honor of their family. Inebriated women were thought to be sexually accessible; as in other cultures, it was understood that seducing a woman could made be "easier" by giving her drinks. Until recently, even in medical and scientific environments, it was widely accepted that drinking by women was ugly, female alcoholism more shameful, and its prognosis more grave. Excess drinking by women was despised, and their inebriation was particularly intolerable. Hence, alcoholism or problem drinking carried more stigma for women, who would rarely seek help; those few who had problems hid their drinking from their neighbors and families.

Since the 1960s and 1970s, women have developed more conspicuous drinking and smoking habits associated with their increased education and work opportunities. Today the available statistics show that men drink less in better-educated groups; women, by contrast, tend to drink more as their educational level increases (de Miguel 1992).

In sum, the changes in drinking patterns by women and young people highlight the growing departure of present customs and attitudes about alcohol from traditional forms. As secular customs and beliefs are combined with new ideas and practices, the culture of alcohol in Spain is being radically altered, and becoming less and less different from that in other Western nations.

### REFERENCES

Alvira Martín, Francisco. 1986. Cambios en el consumo de bebidas alcohólicas en España. *Revista española de investigaciones sociológicas* 34:111–130.

Comas, Domingo. 1985. *El uso de drogas en la juventud.* Madrid: Instituto de la Juventud, Ministerio de Cultura.

Defourneaux, Marcelin. 1970. *Daily Life in Spain in the Golden Age.* Stanford, Calif.: Stanford University Press.

Delegación del Gobierno para el Plan Nacional de Drogas. 1990. *Encuesta sobre consumo de alcohol.* Madrid: Ministerio de Sanidad y Consumo.

de Miguel, Armando. 1992. *La sociedad española, 1992–93.* Madrid: Alianza Editorial.

Elzo, Javier. 1987. La investigación epidemiológica y sociológica de la drogadicción en Euskadi (1978–1986). Pp. 71–89 in Gobierno Vasco, *Libro blanco de las drogodependencias en Euskadi (1978–1986).* Vitoria: Servicio Central de Publicaciones.

García Bellido, Antonio. 1945. *España y los españoles hace dos mil años, según la "Geografía" de Strabon.* Madrid: Espasa Calpe.

Gili, M., J. Giner, J. R. Lacalle, D. Franco, E. Perea, and J. Dieguez. 1989. Patterns of consumption of alcohol in Seville, Spain. Results of a general population survey. *British Journal of Addictions* 84:277–285.

Glick, Thomas F. 1991. *Cristianos y musulmanes en la España medieval (711–1250).* Madrid: Alianza Universidad.

Hansen, Edward C. 1977. *Rural Catalonia under the Franco Regime: The Fate of Regional Culture since the Spanish Civil War.* Cambridge: Cambridge University Press.

Harrison, Richard J. 1988. *Spain at the Dawn of History: Iberians, Phoenicians and Greeks.* London: Thames and Hudson.

Martínez, R. N., and L. Martín. 1987. Patrones de consumo de alcohol en la comunidad de Madrid. *Comunidad y drogas* 5–6:39–62.

Ministerio de Sanidad y Consumo. 1992. *Encuesta sobre estilos de vida de la población adulta española.* Madrid: MSC.

Ramírez Goicoechea, E. 1990. Drogues au Pays Basque: Une analyse socio-anthropologique. *Psychotropes* 6(2):29–45.

Ringrose, David R. 1985. *Madrid y la economía española, 1560–1850.* Madrid: Alianza Universidad.

Rooney, James F. 1990. Funciones sociales de los bares para la juventud en España. *Adicciones* 2(3):209–220.

———. 1991. Patterns of alcohol use in Spanish society. Pp. 381–397 in David J. Pittman and Helene R. White (Eds.). *Society, Culture and Drinking Patterns Reexamined.* New Brunswick, N.J.: Rutgers Center for Alcohol Studies.

Taylor, William B. 1979. *Drinking, Homicide, and Rebellion in Colonial Mexican Villages.* Stanford, Calif.: Stanford University Press.

# 24

# Sri Lanka

## *Diyanath Samarasinghe*

Sri Lanka is a country populated by significant numbers of people who speak different languages; each language group adheres to different religious faiths, pursues a vastly different lifestyle, and demonstrates large variations in degree of urbanization and Westernization. The influence of each of these variables on individual and group drinking habits is fascinating.

The large majority speak either Sinhalese or Tamil as their mother tongue; a few speak English. A very small pocket of indigenous people constitutes a negligible proportion of the population, and is gradually becoming integrated into the mainstream. Among the Sinhalese, most are adherents of Buddhism and the others of various Christian denominations. Tamil speakers are generally Hindus, Christians, and Muslims. Attitudes and lifestyles are dictated perhaps even more strongly than religious affiliation by the degree of closeness to what could be termed Western values. The more highly educated, affluent, and urban groups have more access to technology, are aware of fashions and tastes in the affluent countries, and seek to emulate them as a definition of their class and sophistication. They provide the model for the less affluent aspirants to higher social status.

Strong commitment to what are regarded as Buddhist or Hindu values, although not overtly denigrated, is seen as a mark of the less sophisticated, and clearly a sign of not belonging to the elite. The position of the adherents of Islam is less clear. Religious commitment or identification is probably less of a handicap for Muslims than for Buddhists and Hindus. Being identified as a practicing Christian is no impediment to achieving high social status.

Attitudes toward alcohol use, the meanings and values attached to it, and ways of consumption can serve as indicators of the influence or power of different imperatives upon the individual. The Buddhist and Hindu attitude to alcohol use is generally understood to be disapproving but not strongly proscriptive (de Silva 1983; Samarasinghe 1990), whereas the Islamic view is seen as strongly proscriptive (Baasher 1983). Where strong adherence to Buddhism, Hinduism, or Islam could be perceived subtly as a social handicap, alcohol use becomes a necessary marker for high social status. Interesting cognitive and social acrobatics are called for when social aspirations toward Westernization have to be reconciled with genuine allegiance to one of these faiths.

## HISTORY OF ALCOHOL CONSUMPTION

Alcohol receives scant attention in early historical records and literature. This is probably a reflection of the negligible importance it held in the social life of early Sri Lanka. In the very few instances that it is mentioned, the reference is not in positive terms. Before the advent of European colonialists, the dominant religious influences were those of Buddhism and Hinduism, and social practice seems to have left alcohol use outside the mainstream.

In the early 1500s the Portuguese took control of parts of coastal Sri Lanka, followed by the Dutch and then the British, who in the early 1800s conquered the entire island. These invaders promoted the production and sale of alcohol in order to raise revenue. It was also an element in the conversion of the indigenous population to the lifestyle of the invaders. The anticolonial sentiment soon incorporated a strong temperance component.

During the latter stages of British occupation, the increasing strength of the temperance lobby led to the adoption of some control policies, such as the closure of retail outlets or taverns. But the alcohol habit was firmly and widely established by the time Sri Lanka obtained independence from the British in 1948.

## MAJOR DRINKING PATTERNS

Buddhism, Hinduism, and Islam are not entirely without impact on alcohol use. The need to identify with the more affluent elite weakens the influence of religion. Perhaps more important now is the fact that alcohol use has become a routine part of many social events and rituals. But some drinkers belonging to those religious denominations have a negative evaluation of alcohol use, notwithstanding their own practice. Thus we have a situation where a large part of the drinking population, if pushed to confront the issue, concedes that their alcohol use runs contrary to their innermost values and religious beliefs. This is a fundamental contradiction, and has bearing on the way alcohol is perceived and used. Alcohol use varies considerably in different groups, depending on the mix of these influences operating in each.

The strength of religious faith is not the only factor that determines the extent of control a religious admonition holds. Religious authority is also tempered by the degree to which various groups feel they can transgress socially conveyed and enforced religious proscriptions. Thus, in a society where women have much less power than men, they are less likely to challenge or flout the religious tenet that alcohol should not be consumed. This is certainly true for much of Sri Lanka's population, where alcohol use is overwhelmingly a male activity. In subgroups where women drink in significant numbers, the women are more independent in other ways, or they do not subscribe strongly to Buddhist, Hindu, or Islamic values.

Among men in general, alcohol use and dependence are very high despite the influence of the predominant religions (Samarasinghe et al. 1987). In urban and strongly Western-oriented circles, alcohol use often starts in the late teens, on special occasions and celebrations connected with school life. For most subgroups in this culture, alcohol is an effective and readily available marker of fun, freedom to flout social norms, and passage to adulthood. Nevertheless, there is an undertone of disapproval of drinking in this age group alongside a tendency by some parents to turn a blind eye. The undertone of disapproval contributes greatly to the desirability of alcohol use, with the drinkers often displaying exaggerated behavior as supposed signs of drunkenness wherever they can do so without incurring too great a risk of serious repercussions later. In this young group, religious and presumably cultural constraints to alcohol use are not paramount, and may even provide an impetus to use.

What the children of the rich and successful urbanites do provides a model for those who admire and aspire to this class. As a result, youthful revelries and special festivities among boys from different backgrounds have begun to include alcohol, which serves as a symbol not only of fun, disinhibition, and adulthood but also of identity with the upper classes. For the rich youths, alcohol is merely a symbolic addition to a fun occasion, whereas the poor have to be content with the symbol alone. As a result, alcohol eventually assumes much greater power over the poor than over the rich. This discrepancy is reflected in adult drinking patterns. The urban affluent consume alcohol while enjoying many of the pleasures of life, and for them alcohol is an incidental accompaniment to a pleasurable activity. It is not central to the experience, which would be enjoyable even in the absence of alcohol. For the poor, too, alcohol acquires a conditioned mood-altering capability through repeated use in the right circumstances. But in a life that offers little variety and few avenues of pleasure, the conditioned experience soon becomes central. Thus one sees among the less affluent a tendency for occasional use to rapidly progress to daily use, and for drinking to be not for fun so much as for intoxication.

Public displays of aggression and violence, loud ribaldry, and alleged disinhibition after drinking alcohol are common among the poor, both urban and rural. Such displays are exceedingly rare among the affluent, especially those considered "more refined." It is generally agreed, however, that domestic violence after alcohol use, directed at women, is found even among the "refined" classes. This happens only in private, because public misbehavior after alcohol use is not tolerated in these circles.

## VARIANT DRINKING PATTERNS

As everywhere, there are many patterns of drinking, and much variation in the meanings attributed to alcohol use, in different subgroups and communities within the broad cultures that prevail in Sri Lanka.

A pecking order of socially stratified castes was important until recently, and did not disappear during Western colonization. Caste was defined by family occupation. In early times people were restricted to the traditional occupation of the family they were born into. Despite this restriction's being gradually eroded, a person's caste continued to be that of the parents, irrespective of his or her present occupation. Variant or atypical drinking patterns were associated with this caste system. People belonging to the castes considered socially lower tended not to consume alcohol with those of the higher castes. Nor were they permitted to display drunken behavior in the presence of the higher castes. The restriction on women's drinking seemed not to apply to a few of the socially most underprivileged groups.

A carryover of this system is still seen, even though the concept of caste is far less powerful. Those belonging to the caste that has fishing as its occupation—found mainly in the Roman Catholic areas—are well known as heavy consumers and allow their women many of the privileges that are traditionally allowed only to men in other castes. In this community, women may drink and be even abusive and ribald. But they are not allowed to assault men or other women when drunk, even though society now permits men a greater level of disinhibition, on the ground that they do not know what they do when drunk.

Even though the caste system has weakened, rules once applied between castes now apply between different levels of social status. Thus drunken misbehavior tends to settle down rapidly when a higher-ranking person or a clergyman appears—to be replaced by cringing and obeisance. Cigarettes are instantly tucked out of sight should a person of higher status be confronted.

Lower-status occupations are associated with almost ritual alcohol use. For example, morticians, gravediggers, and those working in foul environs such as sewers tend almost always to consume alcohol before starting work. A man's status is determined, in a caste-governed society, by the level of job he is willing to undertake. Where the work involved is considered degrading or disgusting, alcohol provides one means of countenancing the work or reducing personal stigma. Doing something degrading is more easy to explain if one has the excuse that it is done in an altered state, thus not entirely as if one were doing it oneself. A drink before cleaning the sewers gives the message that this is not something one would be willing to undertake in one's normal state. Some self-esteem is thereby salvaged.

Alcohol use among the minority who adhere to the Roman Catholic religion is believed to be more than that of those who profess other faiths. Those living in the "Roman Catholic belt" (the coastal areas that were first colonized by the Portuguese) are considered to be more hedonistic and are known to have more festivities and celebrations than those in other areas, where the more austere religions predominate. The frequent festivals of the Catholics are nearly always associated with alcohol use. Many Catholics would find it difficult to conceive of fun and celebration in the absence of alcohol. And the close association of alcohol with the lifestyle of those reputed to be fun-loving promotes the image, among the others as well, of alcohol as a social stimulant.

Another area where alcohol use is at variance is among the labor force on tea plantations. Workers in these plantations are usually provided family living quarters on the estate. They are thus bound within the confines of one location for work, family life, and leisure. Even special events and occasions are confined, for most, to similar estates and locations within the tea-growing area. The labor force on these estates came mostly from southern India, and were originally brought by the British. They are generally Tamil-speaking Hindus.

Alcohol use among the estate Tamil population is different from that of the Tamil Hindu population elsewhere. Consumption is high and women drink, but alcohol-induced violence and aggression are not prominent. Alcohol use is frowned upon in Hindu culture. But the Tamil workforce brought to the plantations were initially under the control of British planters, for whom alcohol was an integral part of ordinary life. The values of the landlords were probably influential in overcoming the religious barriers. Good workers were rewarded with alcohol. The influence of the Hindu culture was overturned by the Christian through a mechanism very different from that seen among the more affluent classes. The workers acquired Christian values through their social proximity to the ruling groups. Among the estate labor force, there was no thought of or aspiration to social proximity, yet they acquired the drinking habit across a social chasm.

Social class influences probably account for the lack of violence and aggression. Those lower on the scale of power are not at liberty to stand up to their masters. Thus the estate workers were not allowed to be rude after consuming alcohol. This original learning seems to have carried over to the present day, even though class and social differences have ceased to evoke subservience.

## LEARNING ABOUT DRINKING

Nearly all young people first use alcohol outside of the family, but much of the learning about drinking still takes place within it. Even in circles where families have relatively positive attitudes toward alcohol, use by young people is not often viewed positively. For young people in the social group that approves of alcohol use, it is presented as something that is good for adults but not for young people, with the point of transition being unclear.

In less Westernized families, the confusion is not about the age at which alcohol use becomes acceptable but whether it is acceptable at all. In many families where there is genuine allegiance to Buddhism, Hinduism, or Islam, the official position of the adults is that alcohol use is not sanctioned, even though a parent, usually the father, consumes alcohol. Mothers almost invariably hold this position; most fathers agree, even though they themselves do not necessarily feel obliged to abstain.

Thus children in the majority of families learn that alcohol use is bad, and usually say that they would abstain as adults. As they grow older, drinking, and many other activities disapproved by parents, become attractive, with connotations of forbidden enjoyment. This shared perception among youth from very dissimilar backgrounds leads to the majority of males drinking, regardless of warnings not to. For young men, abstinence carries the implication of being unwilling or unable to break away from parental authority.

Special occasions and celebrations among older boys are the contexts in which most start to use alcohol. The powerful symbolic meanings attached to drinking ensure that the experience is rewarding. There is no social penalty for young people known to be drinking, even though it is not socially approved. Youth who drink need only be concerned about repercussions if their parents or teachers find out. Alcohol has the attraction of "forbidden fruit" while being easily available without any real risk of sanctions.

Young men who do not drink with friends at school or soon after, are influenced to start when they enter university or take a job. Newcomers to university, for instance, are "ragged" (or hazed) by their seniors during their early days. Graduation from this novitiate stage to full-fledged identity as an undergrad takes place at a ritual fellowship where the "freshers" and their seniors fraternize. This event invariably calls for consumption of alcohol by all the men. Whatever attitudes may have prevailed in their homes, freshmen do not wish to have such a coming-of-age party that is symbolically incomplete.

Acceptance of a new member by senior employees at a workplace, or of recruits in a military group, or a newcomer to a communal or shared residence, often involves an event similar or equivalent to that described for the university. An extended "rag" for newcomers, as part of the social ritual for accepting newcomers, was transplanted from the British public schools [private schools in the United States] during the time that Sri Lanka was under colonial rule. This ritual is growing stronger in Sri Lanka even as it is diminishing in Britain.

Attitudes among the young show a sharp change with the advent of drinking. Negative attitudes are the commonest finding among youthful abstainers, who often reevaluate the issue as soon as they feel strong peer pressure, in situations such as those described above, to drink. It appears that drinking is not the result of slow erosion of negative attitudes but of powerful inducements to drink that result in attitudes being redefined. Pressures within a social group can be highly compelling on young people.

There is an interesting transition in adult life among some of those who still subscribe to traditional values but began to drink as a result of the various forces operative during youth. In middle age a few begin to recognize the dissonance between their drinking and their worldview based on a religion other than Christianity. Resolution of this dissonance calls for a certain amount of psychological skill. These individuals may not be particularly attached to alcohol, but continue to drink because of the difficulty in making the transition from occasional use to abstinence. Refusing a drink involves a socially embarrassing admission of a move toward becoming religious or traditional in outlook, unless a more acceptable reason (such as medical advice against further drinking) can be offered. As a result, many men continue to use alcohol against their innermost convictions but overcome discomfiture by making suitable adjustments to their interpretation of the doctrine. In short, they rationalize that abstinence is not really so important. Others, less flexible in ideology, continue to drink but handle nagging concerns about religious transgression by promising themselves that they will soon stop alcohol use.

Those who eventually do stop drinking because religious and other considerations overcome the imperatives to continue drinking socially, provide an example of an unusual kind of learning about alcohol. They do not stop drinking as a result of a sudden religious awakening. What happens instead is the gradual reassertion of an attitude that was submerged for many years due to other obligations.

A quiet and undramatic move from drinking to abstinence is not an uncommon phenomenon, in Sri Lanka or elsewhere. The significant numbers regularly making this move probably make Sri Lankan society unique. The presence of pressure to drink during youth, together with an underlying resilience of anti-alcohol sentiment, explains this unusual occurrence.

## BEHAVIORAL AND SUBJECTIVE EFFECTS

Not only does a culture teach individuals how to behave after consuming alcohol; it also trains them in what the chemical experience of alcohol should feel like. Although the importance of social factors in determining what people do after taking alcohol is well recognized in scientific circles, the importance of nonpharmacological factors in determining what people feel after drinking (Wilmot 1985) is not as widely acknowledged among the general public.

Determinants of what people feel like when intoxicated include their expectations, the meanings attached to use, the associated rituals, and how they are permitted to behave after using the drug. Perhaps most important is the influence, during early experimentation, of the experienced users who, intentionally or not, train the the novices in how to label and to evaluate experiences as exciting or pleasurable.

The factors that persuade new users to repeat the experiment are remarkably similar in the different subgroups in Sri Lanka. Newcomers are introduced to drinking at a celebration, party, or other leisure or recreational occasion. Often the amount of alcohol consumed is not adequate to produce a noticeable subjective change, but a good feeling is nonetheless attributed to the alcohol consumed. When the quantity consumed is adequate to produce a subjectively experienced change, the new user does not pay much heed to what the alcohol itself makes him feel, unless there is significant discomfort. If this is noticed, a great deal of fun is made of the novice's discomfort, which is dismissed as being due to inexperience.

There are standard expressions, jokes, and other strategies to dismiss the element of discomfort in alcohol use and to define the experience as fun even when the true subjective experience is decidedly unpleasant. The novice sufferer is obliged to subjugate the real experience and go along with the collective wisdom that some inadequacy on his part prevents him enjoying the experience. The slightest indication that he does not completely acquiesce in this interpretation is met with much more than lighthearted banter. Thus the social practice surrounding initiation ensures that the novice either feels good after drinking or accepts that something is the matter with him, if he doesn't.

## CHANGING THE SOCIAL LEARNING

An experimental effort now under way in Sri Lanka is worth reporting here. This is an effort to change the positive social attributions to alcohol as a means of reducing consumption and, thereby, alcohol-related problems.

Primary prevention activities usually take the form of educating target groups about the potential ill effects of alcohol use. These all presume that alcohol use in itself is pleasurable and rewarding, and that countervailing arguments about the harm related to use, or some forms of use, or at least some forms of excessive use, are the most appropriate method for minimizing this harm. The new prevention program in Sri Lanka attempts instead to institute social changes that question and reverse the various elements that make alcohol use such a positive experience.

The underlying premise is that the alcohol experience itself is generally slightly unpleasant for the beginner, and that various social rituals, attributions, and sanctions for transgressing norms are really the factors that contribute to making the experience rewarding. The objective of the program is to bring about changes in the social environment that will expose the drinking experience for what it is, in the hope that new recruits will be discouraged from use, resulting eventually in reduced consumption and fewer problems.

The activities undertaken include helping groups and communities to recognize the ways in which they speak, act, and think, based on a set of beliefs and assumptions about the effects of alcohol, that serve to make the chemical experience so desirable and pleasurable. This is followed by encouraging them to reexamine their subsequent experiences with alcohol in this light and to determine whether the subjective experience remained the same. The next step is to encourage them to determine whether it is worthwhile to continue the social facade if the drinking experience is not really significant in terms of pleasure.

Informal reports of the results of these efforts in some locations are very interesting (Fekjaer 1992). They suggest that groups of people can look at their own perceptions and socially conditioned experiences, and opt to change these deliberately. The result of doing this is, for some, a complete change in what seems to happen to their behavior after drinking, and to what they ''feel inside'' after they drink.

Whether a similar conditioning is possible in other cultures is doubtful. Although Western assumptions about alcohol effects have effectively superseded all others even in Sri Lankan culture, there is still a remnant of the anticolonial perception of alcohol as part of an alien intrusion. There is, as a result, a readiness to reexamine from a different standpoint the various assumptions derived from the West and still propagated through the Western media. It is ironic that the scientific evidence describing negative subjective experiences with drinking, thereby contradicting the experience of most Westerners, may have more impact in a country such as Sri Lanka, far removed from the cultures in which the studies were conducted.

## OPINIONS ABOUT DRINKING

What is special about the different cultural settings in Sri Lanka, compared with the West, is that alcohol use falls, at least officially, into the category of something ''bad.'' Not everybody shares this opinion, but people concede that the majority religions in the country have a strongly negative evaluation of alcohol use. Many of the positive connotations of alcohol use are derived from this perception. Being a handy symbol of the rejection of what are considered by some to be traditional and hidebound values gives alcohol a special aura it does not hold to this extent in settings where the underlying negative social evaluation does not exist.

The nuances of meaning attached to use by women, men, youths, and adults, in different social situations and different contexts, along with a variety of other variables, make any one instance of use very different in moral tone from another. Sri Lankan society provides such a wide array of cultures that, whatever an individual's opinion about alcohol, a sizable social group holding similar beliefs and attitudes can easily be found.

## REFERENCES

Baasher, T. A. 1983. The use of drugs in the Islamic world. Pp. 21–32 in G. A. Edwards, A. Arif, and J. Jaffe (Eds.). *Drug use and misuse: Cultural perspectives.* London: Croom Helm.

de Silva, P. 1983. The Buddhist attitude to alcoholism. Pp. 33–41 in G. A. Edwards, A. Arif, and J. Jaffe (Eds.). *Drug use and misuse: Cultural perspectives.* London: Croom Helm.

Fekjaer, H. O. 1992. *Alcohol and illicit drugs—Myths and realities.* Colombo: Alcohol and Drug Information Centre.

Samarasinghe, Diyanath. 1990. The Buddhist, Hindu and Islamic influence on alcohol. Pp. 231–233 in J. Maula, M. Lindblad, and C. Tigerstedt (Eds.). *Alcohol in developing countries.* Helsinki: Nordic Council for Alcohol and Drug Research.

Samarasinghe, D., S.A.W. Dissanayake, and C. P. Wijesinghe. 1987. Alcoholism in Sri Lanka: An epidemiological survey. *British Journal of Addiction* 82:1149–1156.

Wilmot, R. 1985. Euphoria. *Journal of Drug Issues* 15:155–191.

# 25

# Sweden

## Karin Nyberg and Peter Allebeck

### ALCOHOL CONSUMPTION IN SWEDEN

The Swedes are reputed to be heavy drinkers. Sweden is known as one of the countries in the "vodka belt" across northeastern Europe. However, when looking at the total consumption of alcohol in Sweden in 1990, and comparing it with thirty other countries, Sweden is number 28. Because the statistics reflect only the amounts of legally sold alcohol, it is sometimes argued that illegally distilled alcohol and private importation might serve to explain the apparently high alcohol consumption (drunken men often seen in the streets) in spite of the low national figures. However, indicators of alcohol-related harm, such as liver cirrhosis and alcohol related-accidents, are on a moderate level in Sweden. Thus, it seems likely that the overall alcohol consumption in Sweden is indeed lower than in many other countries.

How is it, then, that Swedes are known for being heavy drinkers, and that this view is shared by most Swedes? The most likely reason is the pattern of consumption; Swedes often binge-drink on occasions like weekend parties, holiday festivities, and vacations. In this respect the Swedish consumption pattern can be considered similar to what is found throughout the "vodka belt"—heavy drinking on rare occasions.

The immediate, intoxicating effects of alcohol consumption are thus more visible in Sweden than in the southern European countries (where people drink much more often but in smaller quantities), even more than in the neighboring country of Denmark. In Sweden, drinking frequently takes place outside of the home, and alcohol is consumed in such quantities that people frequently are drunk. This pattern often occurs on holidays. The Swedish drinking pattern has ancient cultural roots.

The second noteworthy aspect of Swedish alcohol consumption is that it is surrounded by a well-developed regulatory system. This phenomenon is now viewed in most countries as being an effect of industrialization and urbanization. Regulation of drinking with regard to driving is the best-known example of this. Laws regulating the alcohol level in the blood permitted while driving were first introduced in Scandinavia: in Norway this was done in 1936, and in Sweden in 1941. Since then, Scandinavia has often been looked upon as a model when regulations on alcohol consumption are being considered in other areas of the world.

One of the first major alcohol regulations was passed in 1855, when home distilling of liquor was prohibited. Before that, there had been a long period when people were allowed to distill liquor for personal use, or, as it was formulated, "for the needs of the household." Around 1830, though, the consumption is estimated to have been about 46 liters of hard liquor per person per year—numbers indicating that the "needs of the household" were far greater than what was reasonable, and home distilling was consequently prohibited. From then on, only licensed "royal" distilleries (those with permission granted by the king) were permitted. Besides the social and humanitarian aspects of this (which may have been an important component), the regulation was the first major step to impose taxes on production and distribution of alcohol.

Since 1905, all selling of liquor has been controlled and monopolized. All distribution is handled by the company Systembolaget, which is owned by the state. Consequently the profits, as well as the high taxes, return to the state. The amount may seem large, but is still minor compared with the amount the Swedish state spends on alcohol-related medical treatment, sick leave, early retirement, and alcohol-related accidents. Most economists consider taxes as a means of transferring resources between groups in society, not as income for society. Nevertheless, if public finances (of which taxes are an important part) are considered as such, the final bill to the state for alcohol consumption is still important because the costs of alcohol-related treatment, damage, and so on outweigh the income from both taxes and sales of alcoholic beverages.

## ALCOHOL IN SWEDISH HISTORY

The regulations on alcohol consumption in Sweden have derived from long experience of the consequences of heavy alcohol use and abuse. Alcohol consumption was high in the 1800s and 1700s. There are considerable difficulties in estimating the exact amount of consumption during that time, but according to historical sources, there were about 700 inns that served alcoholic beverages in Stockholm in 1754. This meant one inn per 88 citizens, which can be compared with today's one restaurant per 700 citizens. With such a density of public drinking places, there was undoubtedly heavy drinking during certain periods in Swedish history, especially during the first half of the 1800s. The annual consumption of 40–50 liters of hard liquor per person per year is hard to imagine today.

There was at that time widespread poverty, and the housing conditions of the urban working class were extremely harsh. Large families occupied small apartments or shared an apartment, kitchen, and toilet with other families. Hygienic facilities were few, and infectious diseases like tuberculosis were widespread. Living conditions among farm laborers were also very hard. Such laborers often had heavy workloads, and their small wages were paid partly in food. Some farm owners "helped" the contracted family to buy food and liquor on credit, putting them in constant debt so that they had no possibility to pay off their debts at the company store. This was an extreme example of a broad range of conditions that kept laborers tied to their contracts, especially because liquor was viewed as providing a way to escape the difficult times that so many of them experienced.

By contrast, it was expected that a thoughtful landlord would offer his laborers a glass of liquor on specific occasions that varied in time and place. It was a sign of appreciation and generosity, and in older cookbooks or housekeeping manuals there are descriptions of how many glasses "the good master" should offer at Christmas and New Year's. Even housemaids could have a glass "in case of cold weather."

Among craftsmen there was a tradition that a newcomer to the workplace, usually a very young and inexperienced person, should offer the work team a bottle of liquor on his first day on the job.

Evidence of a high alcohol consumption in earlier centuries is supported by literature, songs, and paintings. One of the most famous poets and composers of the 1700s, Carl Michael Bellman, vividly and at length described life in his time. In his lyrics there are continuous reminders of both the huge consumption of alcohol and the difficult living conditions. One of his songs tells of the use of alcohol as an anxiety reliever, and is still often used as a drinking song:

> Does the grave to you seem far too deep?
> Well, then take a drink, and then another one,
> And then a second one, and then a third one,
> and you will die with more peace.

Thanks to the prohibition on home distilling and other actions resulting from the temperance movement, there was an important decrease in consumption during the latter half of the 1800s that continued into the 1920s. From the very low level of around 3.5 liters of absolute alcohol per person per year, the trend then reversed. Although the increase in consumption was relatively moderate, an important movement, initiated by the temperance societies, called for complete prohibition of alcohol. After a referendum in 1920, an internationally unique regulation was implemented; the buying of alcohol was limited to a certain amount per month, which was recorded in a book (the *motbok*). Under such rationing, the husband or father in the family was in charge of the book. Single women were not routinely issued such a book, and if they requested one, they were allowed to buy less alcohol than were men. Young people under twenty-five years of age were practically excluded from alcohol consumption because they had no *motbok*. Hence, availability was limited, and the heads of the households were generally reluctant to share their limited rations with the young and with women. During the last year of the "*motbok* era," 1954, annual alcohol consumption per person was 4.9 liters. It has been debated to what extent this regulation contributed to the low consumption level between 1920 and 1954. The Great Depression and World War II may very well also have been important factors.

During the postwar era, consumption continued to rise, probably due to a combination of deregulation of sales and increasing economic wealth. Consumption increased to a peak of 7.7 liters per person per year in 1976; since then the trend has reversed again, having reached a rather stable level around 6 to 6.5 liters per person per year in the 1990s.

The major change during recent decades is in the types of alcoholic beverages that are consumed. Swedes drink less hard liquor and more wine and beer than before. The alcohol culture from the European "wine belt" has had an important influence since World War II. The two main reasons for this are significant immigration from southern and southeastern European countries during recent decades and increased traveling by Swedes to the Mediterranean area.

The temperance movement had a relatively strong impact on Swedish society at the end of the 1800s and beginning of the 1900s. One reason for this was its link to both religious and political movements. There were strong links between the temperance movement and the Liberal and Social Democratic parties. Throughout the twentieth century, teetotalers have been overrepresented in the Swedish parliament, compared with the general population. This phenomenon is probably one reason for the strongly restrictive Swedish alcohol policy. The position of the temperance movement has been somewhat paradoxical. It was, for example, against rationing by the *motbok* because it preferred prohibition. Clearly, some of the Swedish alcohol regulations have been compromises between the extremist temperance positions and the more moderate popular opinion; such compromises generally have been in favor of a highly restrictive alcohol policy but short of full prohibition.

## MAJOR DRINKING PATTERNS

As mentioned above, there is a tradition of binge drinking in Sweden, which also means a rather permissive attitude toward being drunk. It is acceptable among men, but the general attitude toward a woman "in her cups" is rather condemning. Getting deliberately intoxicated is strongly associated with masculinity, and there are numerous jokes about men in general, and especially male friends, who have committed errors or caused embarrassment while "pickled."

These alcohol jokes have many similarities to popular Swedish jokes about sex or death. These topics are still surrounded by certain taboos, and jokes make it easier for people to talk about them. A classic example is the following sign often posted in kitchens, bars, and pubs: "All alcohol consumption is strictly prohibited in this room, except when fish is served. All food except sausage is considered to be fish. Should sausage be served—God forbid this—it might also be considered fish."

The attitude that heavy drinking is a sign of masculinity still prevails among Swedes who otherwise have a comparatively egalitarian view of the genders, and is hard to combat, especially in certain environments. Furthermore, getting drunk is thought to be often associated with violence. In fact, violent acts and crimes are frequently committed under the influence of alcohol, although sociability is more common. Family life is sometimes compromised; some divorces are associated with increased alcohol consumption. These stresses form a vicious circle, prompting a saddened drinker to drink even more.

Despite general acceptance of social drinking, there is a tendency rather quickly to condemn and exclude individuals with persistent alcohol problems. These problems are generally considered to be caused by the individual, and less by the family and workplace. Hence, many alcoholics find themselves without social support from the family or at work, so that help is more often sought in the health care system and from various self-help groups. There is a growing interest in alcohol policies in the workplace, with the aim to stimulate early recognition of and intervention in alcohol-related problems, and to prevent exclusion and isolation leading to further deterioration (like employee assistance programs in the United States).

Finally, there is a "gray zone" of alcohol misusers who are taken care of by the family or other close persons from their social network. Some of these stop drinking on their own, so they are never entered into the statistics on alcohol abusers. But, compared with the south European view that everyone has to contribute to solving a family member's alcohol problem in order to preserve the family's dignity or honor, the Swedish view is more that this is a medical problem that has to be handled by professionals. There is among Swedes a deeply rooted general view regarding the overall responsibility of the society at large, which means that each person is entitled to receive help for such problems. Health care and social services are available to everyone, even if the problems are related to alcohol abuse and might be thought to be the drinker's own fault.

## VARIANT DRINKING PATTERNS

We have described the "typical"/stereotyped drinking pattern in Sweden, but of course there are large differences both between groups of people and among individuals in the same group. First of all, there is a large difference in consumption between the two genders. This difference seems to have diminished during the postwar period, in that women drink more than before. Recent epidemiological data show that the lifetime prevalence of alcohol dependence is around 3.5% in women, and the prevalence of high consumption is around 7%. Corresponding figures for males are about four times as high, but the differences between males and females seem to have diminished. There is increasing consumption among women in spite of the widespread knowledge that heavy drinking during pregnancy may have deleterious effects on the child. Most women abstain during both pregnancy and breast-feeding. However, alcohol use is increasing among the elderly, and this may be one of the explanations of increased consumption by women in general, because elderly women constitute a rapidly growing segment of the population. Data on younger people's alcohol consumption show that the differences between the genders in this age group are attenuating; still, consumption among males is about twice as high as among women.

When looking separately at the distribution of alcohol consumption, a great similarity between the sexes can be observed. About 15% of Swedish men are responsible for 50% of the total consumption. The corresponding number among women is that 15% of the women account for 60% of the total female consumption. That is, for men as well as for women, a small part of the population is responsible for a large part of the alcohol consumption.

The proportion of teetotalers is much larger among women than among men. Approximately 10% of Swedish men and 25% of the women advocate and practice abstinence from alcoholic drinks. The statistics on teetotalers exclude individuals who do not consider themselves such but drink alcohol to a very small extent. There are, for example, people who have one or two drinks a year on festive occasions and who are against banning alcohol even though they practically don't drink. This group of low consumers is much more common among women.

Another noteworthy group of the population is the youth. Unfortunately, contrary to the overall stable or slight decrease in alcohol consumption, there has been a rise in total consumption among young people. In 1991–92, the average consumption among Swedes aged sixteen to twenty-four was 3.3 liters of alcohol. It is mainly the stronger beer (4.5 vol% alcohol) that has had a renaissance since the 1980s. The youth are now specifically targeted in preventive actions through community work in schools, social services, and sport associations.

Religion does not have a very large impact on the attitudes toward alcohol in Sweden. Some churches advocate total abstinence from alcohol, but the size of the population that abstains on religious grounds is probably rather small. It is a pattern among people belonging to a few churches that impose a nondrinking culture, a kind of peer pressure for abstinence (instead of the more common peer pressure to drink).

The Swedish population was long considered to be very homogeneous, but around 5% are now immigrants. Among them are Muslims, a religious group most of whom are teetotalers. Little is written about drinking patterns among immigrants, but it can be assumed that the first generation brings the habits from their own cultures, and that these tend to attenuate in subsequent generations, as their offspring assimilate into the Swedish society. The largest group of immigrants in Sweden are Finns, who, like Swedes, have a well-documented pattern of binge drinking. In addition, they often come to Sweden on a temporary basis to work, and return home frequently to their families. This "bachelor's life" of long periods away from home, in combination with binge drinking, contributes to a risk of developing alcohol problems among Finnish men living and working in Sweden.

The highest socioeconomic class has the largest proportion of alcohol consumers; the proportion decreases with decreasing social status. Regional differences also are important, with alcohol consumption higher in the cities than in rural areas.

## LEARNING ABOUT DRINKING

The importance of the family's attitude to drinking is an often-debated topic in Sweden. The position of the teetotalers is that parents should educate their children by information and by serving as abstinent models. In groups with more liberal attitudes but still moderate consumption, there has been a tendency to let youngsters "taste" alcohol, that is, get acquainted with alcohol under controlled and supervised conditions—for example, during dinners at home. Recent studies, however, have demonstrated that children from families with this more liberal attitude on alcohol are still at risk for drinking in an uncontrolled way outside their homes.

The temperance movement no longer has the same impact on young people that it did years ago. To a large extent, sports clubs and youth organizations focused on music, outdoor activities, and so forth have replaced its function of fostering group activities. Sports are undoubtedly the most important activities, but music also plays an important role as a spare-time activity in Sweden. In a country of 8 million people, there are about 20,000 active choirs.

When it comes to sports, there is a broad spectrum of involvement. It could be twelve-year-old girls going to a horseback-riding club and ending up with their friends, drinking hot chocolate and giggling. It could also be membership in a group of soccer fans who regularly drink before and after watching matches—and may indulge in binge drinking and hooliganism. Drinking in relation to sports has recently been debated and given much attention in the Swedish mass media.

General attitudes reflect patterns of learned behavior that have reached the majority of people. An example of this is the rather new phenomenon that hosts at parties and official festivities almost always offer an alcohol-free alternative for guests to drink. A common question is "Do you want a sherry, or are you driving?" It is so accepted that abstaining alcoholics often say they are driving, because this relieves them of the social pressure that otherwise would certainly be exerted by the host to convince the guest to have a drink.

## PROS AND CONS OF SWEDISH DRINKING

Assessing positive and negative aspects of the Swedish alcohol culture is a matter of judgment and personal values. But, from the public health point of view, it is apparent that the restrictive alcohol policy has contributed to the comparatively low levels of alcohol-related disease and harm, at least compared with many other Western countries. The negative side of these restrictions is that they sometimes give people a feeling of being controlled too much and not allowed to take responsibility for their alcohol consumption. These are arguments that frequently arise in the current discussion on how to adapt Swedish regulations to the much more liberal ones of the European Common Market. It is an understandable reaction, but scientific research suggests that the price would be high in terms of increased deaths, medical complications, and so on. The debate is not yet over, and political decisions will show which arguments are considered the most important.

It is also important to consider the methods that are used to implement such a restrictive alcohol policy. Several previously used methods have been abolished as incompatible with the integrity and responsibility of the individual: for example, the limit on the number of bottles that each individual could buy for "personal use" and the use of community "blacklists" to exclude persons with records of alcohol abuse from buying alcohol.

Furthermore, a majority of Swedes regard the trend toward more continental drinking patterns to be a positive change. Hard liquor is often replaced by wine and beer, and more often consumed in the context of tasty food and socializing environments such as pubs and pizzerias. The use of alcohol to overcome shyness and embarrassment when trying to socialize is still common, but at least the alcohol is more often consumed with others, instead of being quickly gulped in private before going out.

A negative aspect of these permissive attitudes toward social drinking is that many young people are favorably impressed by the jovial type of alcohol consumption, which probably has contributed to their increased consumption, particularly of strong beer.

In conclusion, from being a heavy-drinking population in the 1700s and 1800s, Swedes now consume alcohol to a lower extent than people in most other Western countries. The tradition of binge drinking on weekends and vacations remains, but takes place now in large groups and is being gradually replaced by a more continental type of drinking, with wine and beer predominating over spirits, and consumption mainly in conjunction with food and social gatherings.

In response to severe medical and social consequences from excessive alcohol consumption in the 1800s, well-developed systems for regulation of drinking have been in place throughout the twentieth century, although the specific methods have varied over time. To what extent such restrictive systems can and will be maintained in the face of continuous adaption to the European Common Market is hard to tell. Ironically, under prompting from the World Health Organization, many other countries have adopted or are in process of adopting regulatory policies similar to those of the Nordic countries, so there will probably be a convergence of drinking patterns and of systems for regulation of drinking throughout Europe, perhaps more strict than liberal.

## REFERENCES

Andréasson, S., P. Allebeck, and L. Brandt. 1993. Predictors of alcoholism in Swedish men. *American Journal of Public Health* 83:845–850.

Bruun, K., G. Edwards, M. Lumio, K. Mäkelä, L. Pan, R. Popham, R. Room, W. Schmidt, O. Skog, P. Sulkunen, and E. Österberg. 1975. *Alcohol control policies in the public health perspective*. Helsinki: Finnish Foundation for Alcohol Studies.

Centralforbundet for alkohol- och narkotikaupplysning (CAN). 1990. *Trends in alcohol and drug use in Sweden* Rapportserie 11. Stockholm: Gotab.

Horverak O., and E. Österberg. 1992. The prices of alcoholic beverages in the Nordic countries. *British Journal of Addiction* 87:1393–1408.

Leifman, H. 1992 Alcohol and other social problems in Sweden: Domestic and global issues. In *Social problems around the Baltic Sea*. NAD Publication 21. Helsinki: Nordic Council for Alcohol Research.

Norstrom, T. 1987a. The impact of per capita consumption on Swedish cirrhosis mortality. *British Journal of Addiction* 82:67–75.

———. 1987b. The abolition of the Swedish alcohol rationing system: Effects on consumption distribution and cirrhosis mortality. *British Journal of Addiction* 82: 633–641.

# 26

# The United Kingdom

## *Martin A. Plant*

The United Kingdom (UK) consists of England, Wales, Scotland, and Northern Ireland (Ulster). Its population is approximately 55.4 million, of whom 46 million reside in England. Scotland has a population of just under 5 million. The populations of Wales and Northern Ireland are roughly 2.8 million and 1.6 million, respectively. The UK has a single government, based in London. Even so, the four main component parts of the UK have long-established, highly distinctive national traditions and cultural identities. Moreover, within the individual countries that make up the UK there exists a profusion of local and regional social and cultural variations. In some areas of Wales the Welsh language still thrives, as does Gaelic in certain parts of northwestern Scotland. The cultural diversity of the UK has been further enriched by postwar immigration, most notably from the Caribbean and from the Indian subcontinent.

Alcohol has long been established in the UK as a whole. Its entrenchment is so great that, as Mandelbaum (1967) noted, the word "drink" is frequently assumed to imply an alcoholic beverage. The importance of alcohol in the UK is emphasized by the fact that approximately 750,000 people are engaged in its production, distribution, and sale. In spite of the widespread use and general (but not total) acceptance of alcohol, the UK may be grouped with those mainly Protestant cultures in which there is considerable ambivalence about drinking. As this chapter will elaborate, the UK, like several northern European countries, the United States, Canada, Australia, and New Zealand, is a country in which per capita alcohol consumption is not especially high but alcohol misuse has long been regarded as a major national problem. In spite of this, "the alcohol debate" in the UK is probably less polarized than that in most countries in which a large proportion of the population refrains from alcohol consumption and temperance movements exert greater influence.

## A BRIEF HISTORY

The earliest records of human presence in the British Isles date back to Paleolithic times. Human expansion was limited by glaciation. The northern areas were settled later than those in the south. Murray (1973) notes that human settlement in Scotland was not in evidence until the postglacial period, around 6400 B.C. Ireland also was uninhabited during the Ice Age. Neolithic people arrived in Britain from continental Europe. Subsequent waves of immigrants followed. These included Picts, Celts, Saxons, Romans, Vikings, and Normans.

The Romans established a network of strategically placed *tabernae* along their roads in Britain. These buildings, primarily designed to provide food and shelter, also sold wine. By the Middle Ages, alehouses or taverns were commonplace. Such establishments provided little more than ale for travelers.

Alcohol use was well established in the Middle Ages, as noted by Spring and Buss (1979, 22): "Ale has been drunk in England since Celtic times and hopped beer since the fifteenth century." Alcohol consumption in medieval Britain was, by modern standards, very high. However, much of the ale and wine then available was probably weak, and alcoholic drinks were often safer to consume than water or milk, given the sanitary conditions of the times. The latter became relatively safe to drink only in the late 1800s, with purification and pasteurization. There is clear evidence that in Britain of the 1300s, the daily consumption by adult males of one or two gallons of ale per day was not uncommon. Warner (1992, 8) notes:

about all of the sources say that the heaviest drinking occurred in northern Europe, that is in those regions where Protestantism and the various temperance movements later scored their biggest successes. The English were by far the heaviest drinkers, or so our sources, most of them French, would have us believe.

She also reports that although women in medieval England commonly drank alcohol, they rarely did so in taverns.

Williams and Brake (1982) have commented that alehouses gradually evolved into small pubs (public houses) that largely catered to local residents. Inns, too, were widespread in England in the Middle Ages. These were distinguished from taverns by the fact that taverns initially provided sleeping facilities but no food. The difference between inns and alehouses (or taverns) became blurred by the 1500s. The same authors commented that "better class inns" were numerous in English towns by the 1600s. Such establishments reflected an increase in travel. Inns were numerous between the 1500s and 1700s, especially in towns along the major routes of travel and trade. Inns became social centers after the emergence of the country gentry as a leisured class.

The image of the urban inn changed for the worse during the 1700s and 1800s. The "gin epidemic" of the 1700s, associated with rapid urbanization and the Industrial Revolution, did much to bring the popular image of the urban public drinking place into disrepute. It was a notorious example of unrestrained alcohol sale and consumption. During the reign of Queen Anne, the monopoly of the Worshipful Company of Distillers was ended. This was followed by unrestricted production of often low-grade gin. In consequence, gin consumption soared, in association with widespread problems. A system of retail licensing was introduced in 1729. This curbed consumption but was repealed four years later. New legislation restricted the selling of spirits outside dwelling houses. The effect of this was to foster the spread of "gin shops." As noted by Spring and Buss (1979, 25), "Thus gin and other crude spirits were both cheap and readily available at a time when the social conditions of the urban poor were extremely hard with little hope of escape other than intoxication." Legislation was introduced in 1751 and 1792 that increased duty on spirits and controlled the number of public houses in England. Significantly, the latter legislation was entitled The Disorderly Houses Act.

The consumption of spirits rose considerably during the 1800s, reaching a peak around 1880. Wine consumption was more stable, but also rose between 1860 and the 1870s. Tea and coffee consumption also rose, but were modest in comparison with that of alcoholic drinks. Harrison (1971, 69) reported that per capita consumption in England and Wales was as follows in 1834: "Only 1.41 lb. of tea and 0.96 lb. of coffee per year, as opposed to 23.1 gallons [about 27.7 U.S. gal.] of beer and 1.13 proof gallons of spirits [equivalent to about .775 U.S. gal. or 3.41 liters of pure alcohol].

Increasing alcohol consumption and a proliferation of licensed premises were accompanied by widespread alcohol misuse. Concern about drunkenness in Britain had periodically been expressed since before medieval times. Even so, only during the 1800s did an influential movement favoring total abstinence emerge. It has been described in detail by Harrison (1971). This movement was greatly influenced by Anglicans and Nonconformists. It was also encouraged by American temperance campaigners. Initially an anti-spirits movement, the temperance campaign was closely allied with the anti-slavery movement. Alcohol and slavery were seen as parallel evils.

Concern about alcohol problems reached high levels during the 1800s. One of the first major scientific essays on this topic was produced by the British physician Thomas Trotter in 1804. Trotter suggested that chronic drunkenness was a disease. By the 1850s, an active prohibitionist movement, the Alliance, was urging the end of alcohol production and consumption in Britain. Legislation was introduced in 1872. This made magistrates the sole licensing authority and limited the hours licensed premises could be open. The effects of this act, together with vigorous public campaigning, are uncertain. Even so, the number of licensed premises declined after 1870 and per capita alcohol consumption began to fall around 1876. Many of the problems associated with urban public houses were simply reflections of the social conditions endemic in towns during the Industrial Revolution. Widespread prostitution and cruelty to animals (in the form of dog fights for gambling) were both associated with the Victorian pub, which came to be an extremely important social center for the poor, whose living places were miserable.

After this period the temperance movement lost much, but by no means all, of its influence. Developments in the UK during the 1900s were far less dramatic than was the introduction of total prohibition in the United States. Other laws were introduced during the twentieth century. They limited public bar opening hours and (in 1908) forbade entry into bars by children under the age of fourteen. During World War I, public house opening hours were further restricted, and the alcohol content of beer was reduced. These and other measures were ostensibly introduced to prevent the war effort from being impeded by heavy drinking. In 1923, it became an offense to sell alcoholic beverages to those below the age of eighteen, which remains the minimum age for purchase in the UK. However, it is not illegal for those aged five and above to drink outside licensed premises.

National differences in drinking styles and cultures have always been evident within the UK. As late as 1982, two of the thirty-seven licensing areas of Wales did not allow public houses to sell alcohol on Sundays. Until 1976, public houses in Scotland closed earlier than in England and Wales, and were closed on Sundays. Public bar standard measures of spirits still vary in different parts of the UK. Two committees have examined licensing arrangements in Britain. One of these related to England and Wales (Errol 1971); the second, to Scotland (Clayson 1972). Both reports adopted a social integrationist position and recommended relaxing the current system of licensing, which had largely been established during World War I. The Licensing (Scotland) Act of 1976 allowed public houses to stay open after 10 P.M. and to open on Sundays. Flexible opening hours have been permitted since 1977. The impact of these changes on health appears to have been neutral (Duffy and Plant 1980). Licensing arrangements in England and Wales were slightly relaxed during 1988. Further minor changes in Scottish licensing were introduced in 1990. These extended the permitted weekday afternoon opening hours.

Other legislation has been introduced in response to public concern about alcohol problems. The Road Safety Act (1967) introduced breath-testing for drivers who had been involved in accidents, who had committed a moving traffic offense, or who were suspected of having consumed alcohol. Recently drunken driving in Britain has decreased, and there is strong public support for the introduction of random breath-testing to detect intoxicated drivers. The Criminal Justice (Scotland) Act of 1980 banned the taking of alcoholic beverages into sports grounds and restricted the carrying of alcohol on public transport associated with sport. Similar restrictions for England and Wales were introduced under the Sporting Events (Control of Alcohol etc.) Act (1985), largely in reaction to hooliganism by crowds at sporting events. More recently several towns, including Coventry, Dundee, and Motherwell, have introduced bylaws banning the consumption of alcoholic beverages on the streets in certain defined areas.

## ALCOHOL CONSUMPTION PATTERNS

Trends in alcohol consumption in the UK since 1700 have been described by Spring and Buss (1979). There have, over time, been major changes in levels of per capita consumption. Beer consumption was vastly higher during the early 1700s than it has been since, and spirit consumption reached a peak during the notorious "gin epidemic." More recent alcohol consumption reached a low point after World War I and during the Great Depression of the 1930s. After World War II per capita consumption increased, virtually doubling by its peak year, 1979. The level of per capita alcohol consumption in the UK is much lower than that of France, Spain, Italy, Belgium, Denmark, and Germany. In 1989, UK per capita consumption of absolute alcohol was 7.3 liters. This was similar to that of New Zealand, Canada, and the United States, but higher than that in Eire and the Nordic countries (Brewers Society 1991). In spite of its middle-of-the-road level of alcohol consumption, concern about alcohol problems is higher in Britain than in many countries where per capita alcohol consumption is much higher. This concern reflects a variety of social, religious, and cultural factors. It also reflects the commonplace nature of drinking to intoxication, which particularly involves young males.

The postwar increase in alcohol consumption in the UK was accompanied by a considerable rise in alcohol-related problems. These, in turn, provided the stimulus for extensive research into various aspects of alcohol use and misuse. This research, in terms of quantity, reached a peak during the 1980s (Royal College of Psychiatrists 1986; May 1992a). A number of surveys of drinking habits have been carried out in various parts of the UK. These provide an excellent description of the ways in which different subgroups of the population use, or do not use, alcohol. Significantly, they have generally failed to support the well-established and pejorative stereotypes of the drunken Scots and Irish.

Studies suggest that people in Northern Ireland are much more likely than their counterparts in Britain (England, Wales, and Scotland) to be nondrinkers. Over half the women and nearly a third of the men in Northern Ireland are abstainers (Wilson 1970). In comparison, only 12% of females and 7% of males aged eighteen and over in Britain do not drink alcohol (Foster et al. 1990).

Northern Ireland is very different from Britain in relation to a broad constellation of social attitudes and mores. For example, people in Northern Ireland are far more likely than those in Britain to attend church or to hold a variety of "conservative" views (Stringer and Robinson 1991). In many ways social attitudes in Northern Ireland appear closer to those of Eire, the Irish Republic (which was established in 1922) than to the rest of the UK (O'Connor 1978). Even those in Northern Ireland who do drink consume, on average, rather less than do their counterparts in England, Wales, or Scotland (Wilson 1970).

Conventional wisdom has long suggested that the Scots imbibe greater quantities of alcohol than do their English or Welsh counterparts. This image probably owes much to the fact that Scots and Irish have been conspicuous among the Skid Row populations in London and other English cities. The image of the drunken Scot has also been popularized by comedians such as Harry Lauder, Billy Connolly, and the contemporary television character Rab C. Nesbitt. A number of surveys have permitted a comparison of the drinking habits of the Scots and their southern neighbors. These have generally failed to confirm the conventional view that heavy drinking is more common in Scotland than in England and Wales. One of the most recent studies (Foster et al. 1990) indicated that higher levels of alcohol consumption among adult males were most common in the north (Yorkshire, Humberside, the northwest) and the Midlands of England, and in Wales. Among females, the lowest proportions of heavier drinkers were evident in Scotland, East Anglia, and Wales. It is clear that regional variations in alcohol consumption do exist and that these are quite marked (M. A. Plant and Pirie 1979; Crawford et al. 1984; Breeze 1985a). Even though adult Scots have not emerged from recent surveys as Britain's heaviest drinkers, two surveys of teenagers have indicated that young Scots are more likely than their English peers to drink less often but to drink more heavily (Marsh et al. 1986; M. A. Plant and Foster 1991).

It is clear from UK survey data that males above the age of seventeen generally consume significantly greater quantities of alcohol than do females. Males are also less likely than females to be nondrinkers. Surveys typically suggest that three-quarters of adult males and around half of adult females in England, Wales, and Scotland drink during most weeks. The corresponding proportions for Northern Ireland are 50% of males and only 8% of females. Typical survey data suggest that British males who drink regularly consume about twenty units; female regular drinkers consume around six or seven units. (A "unit" is equivalent to half a pint of normal-strength beer, cider, lager, or stout; a single glass of wine; or a single bar measure [jigger or shot] of spirits. Each unit is approximately equivalent to 1 cl. or 7.9 g. of absolute alcohol.)

There has been considerable attention paid to the use of alcohol by women in the UK (e.g., Camberwell Council on Alcoholism 1980; M. L. Plant 1985; Breeze 1985b). There is no doubt that alcohol consumption by women is far more widespread than it was a few decades ago. Even so, there is no evidence of a recent convergence of the drinking habits of the sexes. Females continue to drink smaller quantities and to drink less often than males (M. L. Plant 1990). The sexes do, however, differ in their beverage preferences. Females consume only a minority of their alcohol in the form of beer, lager, or cider. Females in Scotland and Northern Ireland are more likely to drink spirits than other forms of alcohol, whereas those in England and Wales are more inclined to drink wines or fortified wines. In contrast, males in all parts of the UK drink around two-thirds of their alcohol in the form of beer, lager, stout, and cider. Men in Scotland and Northern Ireland consume a much higher proportion of their alcohol in the form of spirits, notably whisky (as spelled by the Scots). This is not surprising, because scotch whisky is Scotland's most famous export.

Males who drink typically do so on three or four days a week, whereas females do so on two to three days. Males in Northern Ireland drink on average on two days and females less (Wilson 1970). There is evidence of a more concentrated drinking style in Scotland and Northern Ireland. This was a major factor motivating the liberalization of Scottish liquor-licensing arrangements in 1976. The change, it was hoped, might ease the pressure to beat the clock by drinking rapidly during the few hours when bars were open.

## ALCOHOL AND SOCIETY

Alcohol consumption has long been an important aspect of social life in most areas of the UK. The British public house remains a key focus for recreation and leisure activity. Since Roman times taverns, inns, hotels, and other licensed premises have been conspicuous features of the British (and Irish) landscape, and have exhibited many of the virtues and flaws of contemporary society. Most adults in the UK drink at least occasionally. Recent research indicates that although some regional variations do exist in UK drinking habits, vast differences are not evident. As in many countries, drinking repertoires have widened during recent years to include imported drinks such as wines and spirits. Many people may have first encountered some of these while on holiday abroad.

The number of licensed premises (public house, hotels, etc.) in the UK fell from 126,707 in 1926 to 121,931 in 1945. By 1989, the number of such establishments had risen to 199,500. In contrast to the general increase in licensed drinking places in the rest of the UK, the number of such establishments in Northern Ireland (2,999) was lower in 1990 than it had been in 1945 (Brewers Society 1976, 1991).

Drinking, whether at home, in bars, or in restaurants, is normal behavior for most people in the UK. Alcohol, as in many other countries, not only is a beverage but also is widely regarded as a token of celebration and of conviviality.

## LEARNING TO DRINK

Most children in the UK learn about alcohol at an early age. Alcohol is legal, widely available, and extensively advertised. Most adults drink, so most children are exposed to alcohol consumption in their homes. A considerable minority of young people in Northern Ireland, as well as areas of Scotland such as Glasgow and the Western Isles, are reared in Protestant homes in which alcohol use is disapproved on religious principle. In addition, drinking is commonly discouraged by parents who are Muslim. Most of them reside in urban areas in England, but there are also Muslim communities in other areas of the UK.

A classic study of young children's orientations to alcohol was conducted in Glasgow by Jahoda and Cramond (1972). This exercise employed a series of gamelike tests to examine what children aged between five and ten years knew and believed about alcohol use. This investigation revealed that even at an early age, most of the children had formed a clear concept that alcoholic drinks were distinctive. Approximately 40% of six-year-olds could identify alcoholic drinks by smell, and 60% of ten-year-olds were able to do so. Most of the children were able to connect drunken behavior shown to them in a film with alcohol. The study also indicated that boys were more likely than girls to have been encouraged to drink by their parents or other adults. The authors concluded that as children became older, they developed more negative attitudes to drinking, possibly in response to warnings from authority figures about alcohol misuse. A modified version of the Jahoda and Cramond investigation was conducted by Fossey (1994) in Birmingham and Edinburgh. This study confirmed the earlier conclusion that older children in the age group 5–10 have more negative attitudes toward alcohol. In spite of the increase in alcohol use that had occurred since the earlier study, she found a persisting double standard, in that female drinking was viewed more harshly than that by males. Fossey concluded "That alcohol is primarily a male prerogative is a concept that is continually reinforced in British culture" (1994, 6).

A study of children ten to fourteen years old in the Central Region of Scotland was conducted by Aitken (1978). This investigation revealed that the proportion of children who had tried alcohol rose from 62% at ten years of age to 81% at the age of fourteen. Boys were more likely than girls to report earlier use of alcohol. Three-quarters of the children in this study had first consumed alcoholic beverages in their homes. In contrast with the increasing negative attitudes to drinking noted with age among those five to ten years old, the opposite was evident among those ten to fourteen years old. Among the latter, older children reported less disapproval of drinking. Aitken, like Fossey, noted the existence of sexist attitudes; most children were more disapproving of drinking by girls than by boys.

## TEENAGE DRINKING

Particular attention has been paid to the use and misuse of alcohol by teenagers. Several reasons explain this concern. First, it is apparent that most "regular" or "serious" drinking begins among this age group. Second, teenage drinking has periodically received widespread attention due to its alleged links with public disorder or other adverse consequences. The mass media in Britain periodically highlight youthful alcohol misuse, often in a sensationalist and distorted way. Such concern has sometimes been justified, even though the role of alcohol in relation to specific offenses is frequently unclear (Tuck 1989).

A Scottish study by Davies and Stacey (1972) indicated that most teenagers begin to drink out of curiosity and to be sociable. Moreover, teenagers who drink are often viewed by their peers as more attractive than those who do not drink.

Several studies of teenage drinking in Britain have been conducted since the 1970s (e.g., Hawker 1978; M. A. Plant et al. 1985; Marsh et al. 1986; M. A. Plant, Bagnall, and Foster 1990; M. A. Plant, Bagnall, Foster, and Sales 1990;

M. A. Plant and Foster 1991; Bagnall 1991). These studies show that the great majority of teenagers in Britain drink alcohol. At the age of thirteen only 6–7% of boys and 9–16% of girls have not tasted it. By the age of seventeen, only 3–4% of girls and 4–6% of boys have not done so (Marsh et al. 1986). By the age of seventeen, approximately 90% of British teenagers are described as drinkers, though the proportion of teenage nondrinkers in Northern Ireland, on the basis of sparse evidence, appears to be higher.

Younger teenagers do most of their drinking at home, whereas older teenagers are much more likely to drink with friends and to do so illegally in bars. There is clearly strong social support for alcohol consumption among British teenagers, and a minority of them drink heavily. Most teenagers who drink sometimes experience intoxication or other adverse consequences, such as nausea. Even so, as emphasized by several commentators, the great majority of teenage drinkers normally consume only moderate quantities of alcohol. Available evidence also indicates that during the 1980s alcohol consumption among teenagers and other young adults in Britain did not increase; it may even have declined slightly (Goddard 1991; May 1992b; Plant and Plant 1992). Many, and probably most, older teenagers drink in bars before the legal age for alcohol purchase (eighteen years). Very few publicans, hoteliers, or bar staff are prosecuted for selling alcohol to minors, a practice that is widely tolerated or ignored.

Two studies have monitored the changing drinking habits of study groups of young people from their teenage years into their twenties. Both investigations indicate that there is little continuity between teenage drinking and that of several years later. Even so, the authors of one study concluded that those who drank the most at sixteen were also the heaviest drinkers at the age of twenty-three (M. A. Plant et al. 1985; Ghodsian and Power 1987).

Young people who drink most heavily are particularly likely to engage in other risky or health-threatening behaviors. These include smoking, illicit drug use, and unprotected sex (Plant and Plant 1992). A degree of risk-taking is normal among adolescents from all socioeconomic backgrounds. Even so, those from low-income backgrounds are, in a variety of ways, additionally at risk in relation to ill health, smoking, and illicit drug use. The apparent stability of trends in youthful drinking habits in Britain contrasts with a decrease in tobacco smoking and an increase in illicit drug use among young people (M. A. Plant 1987; Plant and Plant 1992).

## CONCLUSION

Drinking has long been an integral part of social life in the UK. The popularity of alcohol is combined with a widespread perception of alcohol misuse as a chronic national problem. In this respect the UK resembles a number of other countries in which popular attitudes toward alcohol are ambivalent. Temperance movements gained considerable influence during the nineteenth century. At that time alcohol consumption was high, and the urban bar was associated, rightly or wrongly, with many of the social problems of rapid industrialization. Since World War II, rising alcohol consumption has heightened concern about alcohol misuse. Even so, British attitudes are generally favorable to drinking in itself while disapproving of heavy or problematic drinking. The drinking scene in the UK has undergone marked changes during recent decades. Public bars are now far more congenial and attractive to drinkers of both genders. In addition, British drinking habits have been influenced by the availability of new alcoholic beverages. The British generally enjoy drinking, and recent legislation has attempted to increase the social integration of alcohol use and to discourage alcohol-related problems, but not drinking in itself.

## ACKNOWLEDGMENT

Mrs. Janis Nichol is thanked for processing an illegible manuscript with amazing humor and efficiency.

## REFERENCES

Aitken, P. P. 1978. *Ten-to-Fourteen-Year Olds and Alcohol.* Edinburgh: HMSO.

Bagnall, G. 1991. *Educating Young Drinkers.* London: Tavistock/Routledge.

Breeze, E. 1985a. *Differences in Drinking Patterns Between Selected Regions.* London: HMSO.

———. 1985b. *Women and Drinking.* London: HMSO.

Brewers Society. 1976. *Statistical Handbook.* London: Brewers Society.

———. 1991. *Statistical Handbook.* London: Brewers Society.

Camberwell Council on Alcoholism (Ed.). 1980. *Women and Alcohol.* London: Tavistock.

Clayson, C. 1972. *Report of the Departmental Committee on Scottish Licensing Law.* Edinburgh: HMSO.

Crawford, A., M. A. Plant, N. Kreitman, and R. Latcham. 1984. Regional variations in alcohol-related morbidity in Britain: A myth uncovered? II. Population surveys. *British Medical Journal* 289:1343–1349.

Davies, J. B., and B. Stacey. 1972. *Teenagers and Alcohol: A Developmental Study in Glasgow.* London: HMSO.

Duffy, J., and M. A. Plant. 1980. Scotland's liquor licensing changes: An assessment. *British Medical Journal* 292:86–89.

Errol of Hale. 1971. *Report of the Departmental Committee on Liquor Licensing.* London: HMSO.

Fossey, E. 1994. *Growing up with Alcohol.* London: Tavistock/Routledge.

Foster, K., A. Wilmot, and J. Dobbs. 1990. *General Household Survey 1988.* London: HMSO.

Ghodsian, M., and G. Power. 1987. Alcohol consumption between the ages of 16 and 23 in Britain: A longitudinal study. *British Journal of Addiction* 82:175–180.

Goddard, E. 1991. *Drinking in England and Wales in the Late 1980s.* London: HMSO.

Harrison, B. 1971. *Drink and the Victorians.* London: Faber and Faber.

Hawker, A. 1978. *Adolescents and Alcohol.* London: Edsall.

Jahoda, G., and J. Cramond. 1972. *Children and Alcohol: A Developmental Study in Glasgow.* London: HMSO.

Mandelbaum, D. G. 1967. Alcohol and culture. *Current Anthropology* 6:281.

Marsh, A., J. Dobbs, and A. White. 1986. *Adolescent Drinking.* London: HMSO.

May, C. 1992a. *Register of United Kingdom Alcohol Register 1991–1992.* Edinburgh: The Portman Group.

———. 1992b. A burning issue? Adolescent alcohol use in Britain 1970–1991. *Alcohol and Alcoholism* 27:109–116.

Murray, W. H. 1973. *The Islands of Western Scotland.* London: Eyre Methuen.

O'Connor, J. 1978. *The Young Drinkers.* London: Tavistock.

Plant, M. A. 1987. *Drugs in Perspective.* London: Hodder and Stoughton.

———. 1985. *Women, Drinking and Pregnancy.* London: Tavistock.

———. 1990. *Women and Alcohol.* Copenhagen: World Health Organization.

Plant, M. A., G. Bagnall, and J. Foster. 1990. Teenage heavy drinkers: Alcohol-related knowledge, beliefs, experiences, motivation and the social context of drinking. *Alcohol and Alcoholism* 25:691–698.

Plant, M. A., G. Bagnall, J. Foster, and J. Sales. 1990. Young people and drinking: Results of an English national survey. *Alcohol and Alcoholism* 25:685–690.

Plant, M. A., and J. Foster. 1991. Teenagers and alcohol: Results of a Scottish national survey. *Drug and Alcohol Dependence* 28:203–210.

Plant, M. A., D. F. Peck, and E. Samuel. 1985. *Alcohol, Drugs and School-leavers.* London: Tavistock.

Plant, M. A., and F. Pirie. 1979. Self-reported alcohol consumption and alcohol-related problems: A study in four Scottish towns. *Social Psychiatry* 14:65–73.

Plant, M. A., and M. L. Plant. 1992. *Risk-Takers: Alcohol, Drugs, Sex and Youth.* London: Tavistock/Routledge.

Royal College of Psychiatrists. 1986. *Alcohol: Our Favourite Drug.* London: Tavistock.

Spring, J. A., and D. H. Buss. 1979. Three cultures of alcohol in Britain. Pp. 22–30 in D. Robinson (Ed.). *Alcohol Problems: Reviews, Research and Commentaries.* London: Macmillan.

Stringer, P., and G. Robinson. 1991. *Social Attitudes in Northern Ireland.* Belfast: Blackstaff Press.

Trotter, T. 1804. *An Essay, Medical, Philosophical and Chemical, on Drunkenness.* London: T. N. Longman and O. Rees.

Tuck, M. 1989. *Drinking and Disorder: A Study of Non-metropolitan Violence.* Home Office Research Study 108. London: HMSO.

Warner, J. 1992. North, South, male, female: Levels of alcohol consumption in late medieval Europe. Personal communication.

Williams, G. P., and G. T. Brake. 1982. *The English Public House in Transition.* London: Edsall.

Wilson, P. 1980. Drinking habits in the United Kingdom. *Population Trends* 22:14–18.

# 27

# The United States of America

## David J. Hanson

About two-thirds of adults in the United States consume alcoholic beverages, and over 1.5 million people are directly, and nearly 5 million are indirectly, employed in the production and distribution of beer, wine, and spirits. Taxes on the industry in 1992 were almost $17.5 billion; the total economic activity generated by the alcoholic beverage industry (including cans, bottles, transport, etc.) in the same year was almost $3 trillion. Clearly the contribution of this eminently legal industry to the U.S. economy is enormous (Heien and Pittman 1993; Barnsky 1993).

Yet alcohol is not universally viewed as desirable. A substantial minority do not drink, and for some the issue is a religious or moral one. The abuse of alcohol is widely recognized as contributing to traffic accidents that result in injuries and deaths, to diseases such as cirrhosis of the liver, to disorderly and sometimes destructive behavior, and to interpersonal conflict. Alcohol education routinely catalogs and stresses the extent of such problems.

Although the moderate use of alcohol is generally recognized as beneficial in relieving stress, in facilitating social interaction, in enhancing camaraderie, and in contributing to a "good time," much less widely recognized is the well-documented fact that it contributes to a reduction of heart disease and an increase in longevity. Thus, some scientists emphasize that moderate consumption can contribute not only to making life more enjoyable but also to making it last longer (Ford 1988).

Differences in beliefs about alcoholic beverages and their proper role in society have existed to some degree throughout U.S. history.

## A LOOK BACK

The place of alcohol in U.S. society has long been ambivalent. Drinking "has been blessed and cursed, has been held the cause of economic catastrophe and the hope for prosperity, the major cause of crime, disease, military defeat, and depravity and a sign of high prestige, mature personality, and a refined civilization" (Straus and Bacon 1953, 8).

The perception of alcohol and attitudes toward it have changed back and forth over time. In the colonial period (1620–1775), alcohol was widely and heavily consumed. Toddlers drank alcohol with their parents, and regular use was seen as healthful for everyone. Taverns were considered an integral part of community life and often served as the church building, town hall, or courtroom. There was widespread agreement over proper drinking behavior; social control was strong; and drunkenness was not tolerated. Alcohol was considered a "good creature of God"; abstainers were often suspect, and drinking problems were infrequent.

The Revolutionary War (1776–83) was followed by social upheaval, a relaxation of anti-drunkenness laws, and an increase in drinking problems. The first use of federal troops was to suppress the Whiskey Rebellion when those who converted surplus grain on the frontier into whiskey, a commodity that had high value in small volume and was easy to ship, protested the first federal tax, imposed on their product. Drinking, which had been regulated by strong families and cohesive communities, increasingly became, by the early 1880s, an individualistic activity of men drinking in sex-segregated saloons that tolerated masculine aggression and antisocial behavior. The many social and economic problems associated with the developing industrialization, urbanization, social change, and social conflict were increasingly blamed on the abuse of alcohol and, as time passed, on any use of beverage alcohol.

With the settling of the West (which brought the moderating influence of women and children, improved social conditions, and the establishment of institutions such as churches), drunkenness became less acceptable. Ironically, as moderate drinking practices were reestablished, prohibitionism grew in power and influence.

What had begun as a religiously motivated movement favoring temperance (that is, moderation) in the early 1800s became a prohibition movement by 1835. What had begun as the "good creature of God" became "demon rum," a destroyer of all good things in society (Asbury 1950). By 1850, half of the states had enacted their own prohibition laws, but they did not last long.

An especially important conflict was that between the established, largely rural, and small-town majority population of northern European Protestant background and the newer Catholic arrivals from southern Europe, who were largely poor urban settlers. The growing popularity of the prohibitionist movement among the established population may have been motivated to a considerable degree by a desire to maintain control over the new arrivals and their culture.

Abstinence groups provided speakers, books, pamphlets, posters, sermons, and curriculum materials. Most temperance materials made no distinction between drinking and alcohol abuse, which were portrayed as one and the same. A typical poster presented the virtue and blessings of the abstainer on one side and the sin and misery of the drinker (synonymous with the drunk) on the other. Textbooks prepared by the Woman's Christian Temperance Union (WCTU) asserted that "any quantity of alcohol in any form was toxic and when consumed regularly produced inheritable disorders into the third generation" (Kobler 1973, 140). The WCTU taught fiction as scientifically proven facts: that the majority of beer drinkers die from dropsy; that alcohol burns the skin off the throat, leaving it bare and burning; and that alcohol turns the blood to water.

An avalanche of such materials for a period of decades contributed significantly to the passage of the Eighteenth Amendment to the U.S. Constitution, establishing national prohibition in 1920. Also important were the effective lobbying of numerous well-organized temperance organizations, the argument that the alcohol beverage industry diverted foodstuffs needed for the war effort, the association of alcohol with the "threatening" new urban immigrants, poor organization on the part of "wets," and political intimidation (Gusfield 1963).

In spite of the optimistic hopes of temperance workers, national prohibition proved to be a failure. It did not prevent consumption and led to the extensive production of unregulated and untaxed (bootleg) alcohol, the expansion of organized crime, increased violence, massive political corruption, and widespread contempt for the law. The counterproductive "great experiment" was repealed in 1933.

The repeal of prohibition returned control of alcohol to the individual states. Today, prohibition is limited to a small number of counties, some Indian reservations, and communities that by local option are "dry," and to all people under the age of twenty-one. Nevertheless, opposition to alcohol remains powerful. It is current federal policy to reduce average per capita consumption, and a former director of the National Institute on Alcohol Abuse and Alcoholism described alcohol as "the dirtiest drug of all" (Cahalan 1987, 5). Not surprisingly, debate continues as to the proper nature and degree of alcohol beverage regulation.

A second major movement has been the redefinition of alcoholism as a disease rather than a moral failure. An early proponent was the physician Benjamin Rush in 1795. The concept gained popularity through its promotion by Alcoholics Anonymous (A.A.), founded in 1935. It received additional popularity following a 1946 study by E. M. Jellinek. Although his research was very seriously flawed and inadequate, powerful lobbying organizations such as the National Council on Alcoholism, the American Medical Association, the National Institute on Alcohol Abuse and Alcoholism, and the World Health Organization actively promoted the disease concept.

An important motive in promoting the idea of alcoholism as a disease was to decriminalize alcoholic behavior and increase the probability that alcohol abusers would seek help. Alcoholics would be seen as victims of a disease rather than individuals with a bad habit, weak willpower, or a moral failing. Another motive was to make treatment eligible for financial support through medical insurance. Society is generally willing to help people with a disease (which is "not their fault"), whereas those with a bad habit, weak will, or a moral failing are expected to accept responsibility for their behavior and to fend for themselves.

Today, a treatment industry based on the disease theory generates more than $1 billion a year in revenues, and both supports and serves hundreds of thousands of individuals who have an emotional commitment (in the case of alcoholics) or an economic commitment (on the part of treatment providers) to the medical model of alcoholism. Although most alcoholism counselors argue that it is a disease, alcoholism is clearly unlike other known diseases. There is no alcoholism virus, fungus, or germ. It is not caused by parasites. It is not caused by any physical accident or injury. Even those who support the theory cannot explain what causes the alleged disease, how it operates, or where it is located in the body. Of course, excessive use of alcohol can cause a broad range of diseases, such as cirrhosis of the liver, pancreatitis, and peripheral neuropathy. But heavy drinking results from learning rather than from disease. People must voluntarily consume alcohol before they can abuse it and have drinking problems. These and other obvious inadequacies of the disease model have led increasingly in recent years to statements that the "disease" of alcoholism is a myth (e.g., Fingarette 1988; Peele 1989).

## CURRENT DRINKING BEHAVIORS

The apparent per capita consumption of absolute alcohol in the United States was 2.46 gallons in 1990, the lowest level since 1967. The current level continues a downward trend from 2.76 gallons in 1980–81, a decrease of nearly 11 percent.

Beer makes the largest contribution to per capita consumption (about 53%), followed by spirits (about 31%) and wine (about 16%). However, the proportions of beer drinkers, wine drinkers, and spirits drinkers in the total population have decreased significantly since 1984. In addition, the proportion of weekly and of heavy drinkers declined significantly over that period. This is reflected in alcohol sales figures, which indicate that since 1981, beer consumption is down about 4%, wine is down about 6%, and spirits about 24% (Midanik and Clark 1994).

Despite long-standing societal ambivalence, the use of alcoholic beverages is characteristic of most social categories and groups in the United States. Although about two-thirds of adults in the United States drink, the generalization ignores the many differences within the population. Important differences exist among genders, ages, income levels, religions, regions of residence, and ethnic groups.

Although the absolute rates vary by time, place, and sample, a larger proportion of men than of women drink. In 1990, about 71% of adult males and about 59% of adult females were drinkers. These proportions were both significantly lower than few years earlier. There is also evidence that the difference between men and women has been narrowing over the past several decades. Not only are men more likely to drink, but they are likely to drink larger quantities of alcohol. For example, men are more likely (9.7%) than women (1.7%) to report having had two or more drinks on any day within the past two weeks.

People are increasingly likely to drink as they move toward young adulthood; later, they are less likely to drink as they age. Among college students, the proportion of drinkers increases as they progress through their college careers but, contrary to popular belief, heavy drinking and problems related to drinking decrease through the college years.

The proportion of the population over age eighteen who drink ranges from a high of 70% in Wisconsin to a low of 30% in West Virginia. States with a low proportion of drinkers tend to be concentrated in the Southeast, with a notable exception being heavily Mormon Utah (31% drinkers). The percentage of drinkers is highest (76%) in the Northeast and lowest in the South (59%) and Mountain regions (54%). The percentage decreased in all regions and among both genders between 1983 and 1990.

The higher the educational level, the higher the proportion of drinkers. The percentage ranges from a low of 50% of those who did not graduate from high school to a high of 75% of those who graduated from college.

About 66% of whites, about 62% of Afro-Americans, and about 67% of Hispanics drink. In each case, a much higher proportion of men than of women consume alcohol (National Institute on Alcohol Abuse and Alcoholism 1993).

## CULTURAL GROUPS

### Blacks

Blacks (African-Americans) constitute about one-eighth of the U.S. population and are the nation's largest racial minority. The ambivalence regarding alcohol that is generally characteristic of U.S. attitudes is especially strong among them; patterns of both heavy drinking and abstention have been reported. Surveys of behavior suggest that although Black men are less likely than are White men to drink, those who do drink are more likely to suffer physiological complications related to chronic heavy consumption. And although Black women are much less likely than are White women to drink, those who do drink are much more likely to drink heavily (Spiegler et al. 1985). However, among college students, Blacks are much less likely to drink or to experience drinking problems than are others (Herd 1991). Most Blacks trace their ancestry to West Africa, where beer was socially and symbolically important on numerous important ceremonies, such as weddings, funerals, and work agreements. Drinking was socially regulated, with moderation being encouraged and abuse strongly discouraged; drinking problems were rare (Herd 1985).

This tradition was brought to the American colonies, where it was supported and reinforced by the dominant White culture. Subsequently, alcohol problems were rare among Blacks, just as they were among Whites. By the beginning of the nineteenth century, concern about alcohol abuse increased. Social and economic upheaval following the Revolutionary War and an increase in alcohol abuse led to the popularization of temperance. Blacks were especially attracted because the movements for temperance and for abolition of slavery were closely connected. Both were linked with reform Protestant churches that opposed slavery, were associated with political and economic interests of the North, and shared many leaders.

In the early 1800s, Black churches called for abstinence, and Black support for temperance increased dramatically in the 1830s as the temperance and abolitionist movements grew in strength. Black abolitionist leaders compared enslavement to alcohol with enslavement to slaveholding masters. Increasingly, alcohol was seen as a threat to emancipation, political equality, economic advancement, and social improvement (Herd 1985).

By about 1850, abstinence had assumed great importance in Black life and changed the role of alcohol. Any use of alcohol became widely unacceptable, a view that continued to permeate Black culture throughout the rest of the century. Following the Civil War (1861–65), abstinence was seen as a major vehicle for promoting the political, economic, and social advancement of Blacks. The success of abstinence is reflected in the fact that alcohol problems appear to have been so low that some observers believed Blacks were physiologically immune to alcoholism (Herd 1985).

By the final decades of the nineteenth century, economic problems and social unrest had led to increased racial conflict and Blacks had become convenient scapegoats. Especially among poor Whites, Blacks were seen as competitors; a campaign developed for "White supremacy," racial segregation, and Black disenfranchisement. In spite of their long support for temperance, Blacks became stereotyped as frequent alcohol abusers whose vote would be used to thwart the increasingly popular prohibition movement.

By 1900, the prohibition movement had became racist and hostile to the interests of Black people. Temperance lost its appeal; and the decision to drink, and how to drink, became a matter of individual preference as Black society provided conflicting norms. Alcohol was no longer seen as a symbol of slavery and social oppression. With the passing of time, it was seen as a symbol of sophistication and freedom from the racist prohibition movement.

Early in the twentieth century there began a major migration of Blacks from the South to northern cities. They moved from largely rural areas, heavily influenced by family and religious organizations, to large urban environments, with relative impersonality, freedom, and exciting night life. Alcohol consumption increased dramatically, and a tendency to romanticize it was noticeable among many Blacks. A lack of consensus regarding appropriate drinking behavior was soon accompanied by a dramatic increase in drinking problems.

Today, abstinence is encouraged by many churches and religious organizations, by many secular social improvement organizations, and often by the family. Simultaneously, however, drinking is encouraged through the importance of drinking establishments and the role of alcohol in contributing to one's prestige and image as being worldly and sophisticated. A result of this cultural ambiguity is a lack of consensus; thus social regulation of drinking is often ineffective (Herd 1985).

### Hispanics

Hispanics constitute about 9% of the U.S. population. The proportion of Hispanic males who drink is slightly lower than that of non-Hispanics as a whole. They tend to drink more often than non-Hispanics but to consume less on each occasion; thus, the total amount of alcohol consumed is similar. Hispanic women tend to drink much less often and to consume much less on each occasion. Therefore, their total consumption level is much lower than that of their non-Hispanic counterparts. It also appears that Hispanics (both male and female) tend to have their first drink, and to begin drinking on a regular basis, at least a year later than non-Hispanics. Beer is the beverage of preference for males, followed by spirits, with wine being a distant third; women strongly prefer mixed drinks and wine.

Although there is great diversity in drinking practices among Hispanics, there are also common characteristics. Hispanic men's drinking habits tend to be very different from Hispanic women's. Men are much more likely to drink and much more likely to consume more (Caetano 1991). Their attitudes toward alcohol are different, as are their typical drinking environments and companions.

Those Hispanic women who do drink tend to restrict their alcohol consumption to family parties and events (weddings and other ritual celebrations) at which there is strong social control of drinking and drinking behavior. Drinking in same-sex groups is rare, and when it does occur, such as at a dance, the major focus of the event is interaction with men. By contrast, drinking in same-sex groups is common among men, where it strengthens friendships, increases camaraderie, and enhances masculine self-concept.

Men tend to view drinking as an appropriate reward for hard work. Therefore, a man is old enough to drink when he is old enough to work. Drinking tends to be viewed as deviant only when it interferes with work, social relations, or the successful performance of other role-related obligations. Women are constrained by the rigid concepts of virtue and respect. Inappropriate use of alcohol can easily convince others that a woman has no virtue. And inappropriate use by either males or females can indicate a lack of respect for family, especially a lack of respect for parents.

Regional, class, and other differences exist among Hispanics. For example, among Mexican-Americans of south Texas, drinking in front of one's parents in public shows disrespect for both parents and family. However, this is generally not the case in California. Similarly, drinking preferences and behaviors often vary by social class. For example, high-status Hispanics drink in ways very similar to their Anglo counterparts and very different from lower-status Hispanics (Gilbert 1985; Trotter 1985).

Nor should the label "Hispanic" imply homogeneity. Striking differences have been documented in drinking behaviors among Hispanics in the United States who have immigrated from the Dominican Republic, Guatemala, Puerto Rico, and Cuba (Gordon 1985; Page et al. 1985).

Dominicans started to immigrate to the United States largely as a result of political turmoil following political upheavals in 1961. Dominicans in the United States are highly goal-oriented, seeking economic success and upward social mobility. This has led them to abandon attitudes and practices that would interfere with their goals but are common in the Dominican Republic. After coming to the United States they typically drink less and usually drink only on weekends rather than on weekdays, as is usual in their homeland. In the United States they typically drink with family and friends; there is less intoxication, fewer conflicts, and a general rejection of the *parrandero* (one who follows a life of rum, women, and song) image. Dominicans are entrepreneurial and dedicated to hard work. Because they want to maintain self-control and to avoid any misunderstandings, they generally drink in moderation. This norm of moderation is often strictly enforced in the Dominican social clubs, the rules of which specify in detail how moderation is to be maintained. Dominicans demonstrate their upward mobility and status by drinking the brands of alcoholic beverage with the very highest prestige. Their beverage of preference is scotch, although they enjoy beer in hot weather. Drinking behavior is important to Dominican group identity and helps them distinguish themselves from other Hispanics, especially Puerto Ricans, with whom they are often confused. Dominicans assert that their moderate use of prestige brands is unlike that of other Hispanics, who, they claim, abuse cheap beverages on a daily basis.

Like Dominicans, Guatemalans immigrated to the United States in search of economic advancement and a better life for their families. However, their experiences have been vastly different. Unlike Dominican men, Guatemalan men typically emigrate without their families. Their goal is to earn enough money to return to their homeland to start a business. But without the support of a family unit, they tend to become distracted and sidetracked. Many play the role of a traditional *pícaro* (wandering adventurer who flouts social convention), spending money on alcohol instead of saving it. Drinking, which typically occurs in bars with other males, almost always leads to intoxication. Reciprocity in buying drinks is expected, and the pace of drinking is fast. Nevertheless, the speed of purchases exceeds the speed of drinking, and a backlog of drinks quickly accumulates. There are few norms against heavy drinking; on the contrary, the drunk is glamorized and seen as a victim of sad circumstances.

Puerto Ricans long ago began immigrating to the mainland United States to improve their social and economic status. However, a tradition of dependency on welfare in Puerto Rico, racial discrimination, life in Puerto Rican ghettos, and poor education are all hindrances to progress. The limited ability of men to fulfill their traditionally expected roles as breadwinners and family leaders undermines their dignity. Both alcohol and drugs are widely used to help them cope with their frustrations. Daily drinking, combined with heavy drinking on weekends, occurs in the absence of norms of moderation. The rate of alcohol abuse among male Puerto Ricans is high.

Cubans began migrating to the United States in large numbers following the revolution in 1959. They have settled largely in south Florida in general and in Miami in particular. Although the first waves of immigrants were largely middle- and upper-class professionals, they were later followed by a broader cross section of Cuban society. Although they have enjoyed a reputation for hard work, ambition, and other values similar to the U.S. Puritan ethic, Cuban immigrants appear to be disproportionately poor. Many are elderly women with poor education and low occupational skills, and children who lost one or both parents as a result of immigration. In spite of the many difficulties faced in adapting to a new culture, Cuban immigrants do not rely heavily on alcohol for solace or other relief.

Cuban culture has long encouraged moderation in the enjoyment of alcohol. Consuming enough to stimulate pleasant social interaction and an atmosphere of happiness was acceptable, but not intoxication to the point of slurred speech or other loss of self-control. Although men could drink in taverns and occasionally come home intoxicated, the norms were much more strict for women. They were not permitted to drink publicly except at recreational gatherings, at which time they could drink small quantities. These traditional norms against visible intoxication remain largely intact among Cuban immigrants for both men and women.

### Jews

Jews, who constitute about 2% of the U.S. population, widely use alcohol but rarely experience any drinking-related problems. This is true whether they are Orthodox, Conservative, or Reform; male or female; young or old; rich or poor; rural or urban; highly educated or poorly educated. Their success in enjoying the use of alcohol with very few problems cannot be because they experience few anxieties or stresses (they experience many and show a high rate of neurosis). Drunkenness was common before about 600 B.C. and then became very uncommon. However, consumption and genetics were remarkably constant throughout the entire time and, therefore, cannot explain the dramatic increase in Jewish sobriety.

Alcohol use is important in Judaism. Beginning at an early age, children are taught benedictions for alcohol and proper rituals for drinking. Alcohol is drunk at circumcision, at rituals each Sabbath, and on holy days, weddings, and festivals. Although alcohol consumption is expected throughout life, sobriety is stressed as a religious obligation.

Jews learn at an early age how to drink properly and, at the same time, how *not* to drink. This is important because sobriety is considered a Jewish virtue, whereas drunkenness is seen as a Gentile vice. Because of this belief, sobriety is important in maintaining both self-worth and group identity.

Jews begin to drink alcohol at an early age; they drink beer, wine, and spirits; and they drink in a variety of religious and secular settings. There is consensus that moderate use is desirable and that drunkenness is unacceptable; violations of acceptable drinking behaviors are quickly and severely sanctioned. In this cultural environment, well over 90% of Jews drink, with a very low incidence of drinking problems.

Although high use and low problem rates are characteristic of Jews, the farther they are from the Orthodox tradition, the higher the chance of intemperate drinking. As religious affiliation moves from Orthodox to Conservative to Reform, there is a systematic (although still very low) increase in drinking problems. Those Jews for whom religion is less important are more likely to be problem drinkers (Snyder 1958; Glassner 1991).

## Italians

Italians, like Jews, are a group whose members tend to drink and to have low rates of alcohol problems. The attitudes and behaviors of Italians in the United States are a reflection of those in Italy, where children are introduced to alcohol as part of their regular family life and learn to drink moderate amounts while still young. In both countries, alcohol is commonly drunk with meals and is considered a natural and normal food. Most people agree that alcohol in moderation, for those who choose to drink, is necessary, and that abuse is unacceptable and results in immediate sanctions. People are not pressured to drink, and abstention does not offend others; drinking reflects sociability and social cohesion rather than a means to achieve them. Very few people drink for the physiological effect, and most people take alcohol for granted, with no mixed feelings or uncertainty about it.

As Italians in the United States lose the traditional attitudes and behaviors concerning alcohol, they begin to lose the protection of the Italian culture and to experience more drinking problems. But their rate of problems remains significantly below that of others in the United States in general (Lolli et al. 1958; Simboli 1985).

## Irish

Irish in the United States experience a high level of drinking problems, which distinguishes them from Jews and Italians. Current Irish attitudes and behaviors regarding alcohol can be traced back to the nineteenth century in rural Ireland. Life was very difficult on the numerous inefficient small farms that could not support the growing population. Men could not marry until they owned a farm, which was difficult to obtain. Unless he owned a farm, a man was called a boy and had the social status of one, regardless of his age.

Men were segregated from women in both work and leisure, even after marriage. Drinking and male companionship were encouraged; male identity was associated with heavy and boisterous drinking. Drunks were often envied and abstainers were suspect. Men were encouraged to sublimate their sexuality and to deal with any emotional problem by "drinking it off." Thus, men were expected not only to drink but also to drink heavily (Bales 1962).

The approval of drinking to "solve" (or ignore) problems and to drink heavily has been preserved among Irish in the United States. In addition, conforming to the traditional stereotype of the hard-drinking Irishman has become a way in which Irish in the United States assert their ethnic identity and pride (Stivers 1985). This stands in marked contrast to Jews, for whom sobriety is a way to assert their ethnic identity and pride. It also illustrates the importance of attitudes and beliefs in influencing behavior.

### Native Americans

Although they comprise less than 1% of the total population, Native Americans (or Indians) constitute over 300 different tribes. Social, economic, political, and other conditions and customs vary dramatically among tribes, even those living close to each other. Tribes differ greatly in drinking attitudes and beliefs, drinking customs and patterns, and the extent of drinking problems. Some are largely abstinent, whereas in others, most people drink, often abusively. In general, the Native American population consists of a large proportion of abstainers and a large proportion of drinkers, with a relatively small proportion of moderate drinkers (Heath 1985). Binge drinking is characteristic of many tribal groups, especially among males, and may contribute to a high rate of drinking problems in those tribes.

Except for several tribes in the Southwest, Native Americans did not have alcoholic beverages before their introduction by Europeans in the 1600s. The Apache and Zuñi drank alcoholic beverages that they produced for secular consumption, and the Pima and Papago produced alcohol for religious ceremonial consumption. Although Papago consumption was heavy, it was limited to a single peaceable annual ceremony; the drinking among other groups was infrequent and not associated with any drinking problems (MacAndrew and Edgerton 1969).

Some Native American tribes consumed newly introduced alcohol with few resulting problems, whereas for others the consequences were very negative. The frequently abusive drinking behavior of the European traders, trappers, soldiers, and settlers provided a negative role model to indigenous peoples for the use of the new beverages. Natives quickly learned that alcohol should be consumed rapidly, in large amounts, and that the resulting intoxication could be used as an excuse for engaging in otherwise unacceptable behaviors, often of an aggressive and/or sexual nature.

But why do some tribes now have very few drinking problems while others have many? It appears that groups with an individualistic hunting-gathering tradition have more drinking problems than do those with an agricultural tradition stressing communal values and ceremonies. Groups that have traditionally stressed communal values and have developed social controls to regulate alcohol-related behaviors appear generally less likely to experience alcohol problems (Stratton et al. 1978).

Although generalizations are easy to make, they are weakened by numerous exceptions and qualifications among the hundreds of tribes with different cultural traditions and historical experiences, different beliefs about alcohol and its meaning and role in life, different degrees of ambivalence toward alcohol, and different levels of unemployment and economic hardship.

### Chinese

Chinese, who represent less than 1% of the population, tend to use alcohol in moderation and experience few problems. This tradition extends back to China, where drinking was a part of everyday life. Children drank and watched others drink in a variety of settings, learning that although drinking in moderation was acceptable, intoxication was not. Both Confucian and Taoist philosophies stress the need for moderation; those who violated the norm were promptly sanctioned. Lack of moderation was seen as a defect not only of the individual but also of the family (Barnett 1955).

In the United States, most Chinese drink in moderation, many (especially women) choose not to drink, and very few experience any drinking problems. However, as traditional beliefs decrease, they tend to experience more drinking problems. Some have suggested that Chinese may limit their alcohol intake to avoid discomfort associated with the "Oriental flushing reflex," of which the primary manifestations are facial reddening, rapid breathing, itching, and other discomfort. A majority of Chinese (as many as 85%) experience the reflex, whereas as few as 3% of Caucasians do (National Institute on Alcohol Abuse and Alcoholism 1993). However, flushing is only slightly associated with reduced alcohol use. Furthermore, because it is physiological in origin, the reflex cannot explain differences in alcohol use over time or between generations.

### SUMMARY AND CONCLUSION

The cultures that are most successful in preventing alcohol abuse are those whose members tend to view alcohol as a natural, normal part of life about which they have no ambivalence; to teach their young by example how to drink in moderation; to encourage drinking among family and friends rather than in same-gender settings; to discourage heavy, episodic drinking; to sanction negatively and promptly any unacceptable drinking behaviors; to respect the decision of those who choose not to drink and not pressure them to drink; and to be free of the belief that alcohol can solve problems, signify adulthood, grant power, or confirm manhood.

Influences from numerous nations and cultures strongly affect alcohol beliefs, attitudes, and behaviors in the United States. The family plays a central role in teaching these alcohol norms and behaviors. Parents, through their power of example, may be the most important long-term influence on the behavior of their offspring. The strength of their power, often reinforced by religious teachings, is usually underestimated.

Young people, in particular, tend to be affected by their peers. Although people tend to conform to the expectations of others, the long-term effects of youthful peer pressure are not well documented. Similarly, the role of television and other mass media has been virtually impossible to document. Advertising, popularly thought to increase alcohol consumption, appears only to influence brand selection rather than overall consumption level (Fisher 1993).

Faith in the ability of education to solve social problems and improve life is strong in the United States. As a result of the rapid spread of illegal drug use in the 1960s, drug education programs proliferated in elementary and secondary schools throughout the country. The content of these programs has changed somewhat over time, but the thrust has largely been to stress problems associated with alcohol abuse and to portray alcohol as a dangerous substance to be avoided. In spite of the enormous human and monetary resources employed in this educational approach, it has not been effective (Hanson 1994). Not surprisingly, any alcohol education that is inconsistent with prevalent beliefs and behaviors in a group or society is likely to be ineffective.

## REFERENCES

Asbury, Herbert. 1950. *The Great Illusion: An Informal History of Prohibition.* New York: Doubleday.

Bales, Robert. 1962. Attitudes toward drinking in the Irish culture. Pp. 157–187 in David J. Pittman and Charles R. Snyder (Eds.). *Society, Culture, and Drinking Patterns.* New York: John Wiley & Sons.

Barnett, Milton L. 1955. Alcoholism in the Cantonese of New York City: An anthropological study. Pp. 179–227 in Oskar Diethelm (Ed.). *Etiology of Chronic Alcoholism.* Springfield, Ill.: Charles C. Thomas.

Barnsky, Steve L. 1993. Economic contribution of the distilled spirits and alcohol beverage industries to the United States economy, 1992. Molalla, Oreg. Unpublished paper.

Bennett, Linda A., and Genevieve M. Ames (Eds.). 1985. *The American Experience with Alcohol: Contrasting Cultural Perspectives.* New York: Plenum.

Caetano, Raul. 1991. Findings from the 1984 National Survey of Alcohol Use among

U.S. Hispanics. Pp. 293–307 in Walter B. Clark and Michael E. Hilton (Eds.). *Alcohol in America: Drinking Practices and Problems.* Albany: State University of New York Press.

Cahalan, Don. 1987. *Understanding America's Drinking Problem.* San Francisco: Jossey-Bass.

Clark, Walter B., and Michael E. Hilton (Eds.). 1991. *Alcohol in America: Drinking Practices and Problems.* Albany: State University of New York Press.

Ewing, John A., and Beatrice A. Rouse (Eds.). 1976. *Drinking: Alcohol in American Society: Issues and Current Research.* Chicago: Nelson-Hall.

Fingarette, Herbert. 1988. *Heavy Drinking: The Myth of Alcoholism as a Disease.* Berkeley: University of California Press.

Fisher, Joseph C. 1993. *Advertising, Alcohol Consumption, and Abuse: A Worldwide Survey.* Westport, Conn.: Greenwood Press.

Ford, Gene. 1988. *The Benefits of Moderate Drinking: Alcohol, Health and Society.* San Francisco: Wine Appreciation Guild.

Gilbert, M. Jean. 1985. Mexican-Americans in California: Intracultural variations in attitudes and behavior related to alcohol. Pp. 255–277 in Linda A. Bennett and Genevieve M. Ames (Eds.). *The American Experience with Alcohol: Contrasting Cultural Perspectives.* New York: Plenum.

Glassner, Barry. 1991. Jewish sobriety. Pp. 311–326 in David J. Pittman and Helene Raskin White (Eds.). *Society, Culture, and Drinking Patterns Reexamined.* New Brunswick, N.J.: Rutgers Center of Alcohol Studies.

Gomberg, Edith L., Helene R. White, and John A. Carpenter (Eds.). 1982. *Alcohol, Science and Society Revisited.* New Brunswick, N.J.: Rutgers Center of Alcohol Studies.

Gordon, Andrew J. 1985. Alcohol and Hispanics in the Northeast: A study of cultural variability and adaptation in alcohol use. Pp. 297–313 in Linda A. Bennett and Genevieve M. Ames (Eds.). *The American Experience with Alcohol: Contrasting Cultural Perspectives.* New York: Plenum.

Gusfield, Joseph R. 1963. *Symbolic Crusade: Status Politics and the American Temperance Movement.* Urbana: University of Illinois Press.

Hanson, David J. 1994. Alcohol, drug, and smoking education programs. Pp. 1610–1614 in Torsten Husen and T. Neville Postlethwaite (Eds.). *The International Encyclopedia of Education.* Vol. 3. 2nd ed. Oxford: Pergamon.

Heath, Dwight B. 1985. American Indians and alcohol: Epidemiological and sociocultural relevance. Pp. 207–222 in Danielle Spiegler, Diane Tate, Sherrie Aiken, and Charles Christian (Eds.). *Alcohol Use among U.S. Ethnic Minorities.* Research Monograph 18. Rockville, Md.: National Institute on Alcohol Abuse and Alcoholism.

Heien, Dale M., and David J. Pittman. 1993. The external costs of alcohol abuse. *Journal of Studies on Alcohol* 54:302–307.

Herd, Denise. 1985. Ambiguity in Black drinking norms: An ethnohistorical interpretation. Pp. 149–170 in Linda A. Bennett and Genevieve M. Ames (Eds.). *The American Experience with Alcohol: Contrasting Cultural Perspectives.* New York: Plenum.

———. 1991. Drinking patterns in the Black population. Pp. 308–328 in Walter B. Clark and Michael E. Hilton (Eds.). *Alcohol in America: Drinking Practices and Problems.* Albany: State University of New York Press.

Hilton, Michael E., and Walter B. Clark. 1991. Changes in American drinking patterns and problems: 1967–1984. Pp. 105–120 in Walter B. Clark and Michael E. Hilton (Eds.). *Alcohol in America: Drinking Practices and Problems.* Albany: State University of New York Press.

Kobler, John. 1973. *Ardent Spirits: The Rise and Fall of Prohibition.* New York: G. P. Putnam's Sons.

Lolli, Giorgio, Emidio Serianni, Grace M. Golder, and Pierpaolo Luzzatto-Fegiz. 1958. *Alcohol in Italian Culture: Food and Wine in Relation to Sobriety among Italians and Italian Americans.* Glencoe, Ill.: Free Press.

MacAndrew, Craig, and Robert B. Edgerton. 1969. *Drunken Comportment: A Social Explanation.* Chicago: Aldine.

Midanik, Lorraine, and Walter B. Clark. 1994. The demographic distribution of U.S. drinking patterns in 1990: Description and trends from 1984. *American Journal of Public Health* 84:1218–1222.

Milgram, Gail G. 1990. *The Facts about Drinking.* Mount Vernon, N.Y.: Consumers Union.

National Institute on Alcohol Abuse and Alcoholism. 1993. *Alcohol and Health.* 8th Ed. Rockville, Md.: National Institute on Alcohol Abuse and Alcoholism.

Odegard, Peter H. 1928. *Pressure Politics: The Story of the Anti-Saloon League.* New York: Columbia University Press.

Page, J. Bryan, Lucy Rio, Jacqueline Sweeney, and Carolyn McKay. 1985. Alcohol and adaptation to exile in Miami's Cuban population. Pp. 315–332 in Linda A. Bennett and Genevieve M. Ames (Eds.). *The American Experience with Alcohol: Contrasting Cultural Perspectives.* New York: Plenum.

Peele, Stanton. 1989. *Diseasing of America: Addiction Treatment out of Control.* Lexington, Mass.: Lexington Books.

Pittman, David J., and Helene R. White (Eds.). 1991. *Society, Culture, and Drinking Patterns Reexamined.* New Brunswick, N.J.: Rutgers Center of Alcohol Studies.

Simboli, Ben James. 1985. Acculturated Italian-American drinking behavior. Pp. 61–76 in Linda A. Bennett and Genevieve M. Ames (Eds.). *The American Experience with Alcohol: Contrasting Cultural Perspectives.* New York: Plenum.

Sinclair, Andrew. 1962. *Prohibition: The Era of Excess.* Boston: Little, Brown.

Snyder, Charles R. 1958. *Alcohol and the Jews: A Cultural Study of Drinking and Sobriety.* Glencoe, Ill.: Free Press.

Speigler, Danielle, Diane Tate, Sherrie Aitken, and Charles Christian (Eds.). 1985. *Alcohol Abuse among U.S. Ethnic Minorities.* Research Monograph 18. Rockville, Md.: National Institute on Alcohol Abuse and Alcoholism.

Stivers, Richard. 1985. Historical meanings of Irish-American drinking. Pp. 109–129 in Linda A. Bennett and Genevieve M. Ames (Eds.). *The American Experience with Alcohol: Contrasting Cultural Perspectives.* New York: Plenum.

Stratton, Ray, Arthur Zeiner, and Alfredo Paredes. 1978. Tribal affiliation and prevalence of alcohol problems. *Journal of Studies on Alcohol* 59:1166–1176.

Straus, Robert, and Selden D. Bacon. 1953. *Drinking in College.* New Haven: Yale University Press.

Trotter, Robert T. 1985. Mexican-American experiences with alcohol: South Texas examples. Pp. 279–296 in Linda A. Bennett and Genevieve M. Ames (Eds.). *The*

*American Experience with Alcohol: Contrasting Cultural Perspectives.* New York: Plenum.

Watts, Thomas D., and Roosevelt Wright, Jr. 1989. *Alcoholism in Minority Populations.* Springfield, Ill.: Charles C. Thomas.

# 28

# Zambia

## Alan Haworth

Shortly after Zambia gained its political independence, Zambians were prone to boast that their nation had the reputation of being one of the heaviest-drinking nations in Africa. They had no objective proof of this, but concerns with lack of access to alcohol had featured prominently in the political struggle for independence and political leaders, notable among them President Kenneth D. Kaunda, repeatedly complained of the effects of drinking upon the newborn nation. Some twenty-five years later, alcohol is hardly mentioned as a major problem by the politicians or in the media. If an individual were asked if the rate of drinking has gone down, he or she would probably assert that it has increased and that there has been a reversion to the consumption of illicit beverages, in view of the high cost of factory products. It still seems to be important for Zambians to believe that they are Africa's "best" drinkers. Yet, as with many neighboring countries, it is extremely difficult to determine the extent of drinking and one can only provide snapshots taken from particular perspectives, at definite times.

## CONTEMPORARY DRINKING PATTERNS

Data on drinking patterns in urban Lusaka were first obtained as part of an unpublished study of patients attending urban health centers that I carried out in 1969; it revealed very little youthful drinking, and about one-third of men and two-thirds of women were abstainers. It appeared that in the late 1960s, Zambians were mistaken in their assessment of the amount of heavy drinking: at least in Lusaka, fully half the adult population claimed not to drink at all. This picture was confirmed by a general population survey carried out in Lusaka and in a rural area some 80 kilometers to the northwest in 1978, as part of an international collaborative study sponsored by World Health Organization (Haworth et al. 1981). In this Community Response Study, 44% of males and 73% of females over the age of fifteen claimed to be abstainers. The report was received with disbelief and there was speculation that, in responding to questions in such a survey and probably in ordinary conversation, a person would not describe himself or herself as having been "drinking" unless this involved some degree of intoxication. It was also postulated that because it was impossible to carry out many of the interviews without another member of the household being present, younger respondents and many women (even up to the age of thirty) might have been unwilling to admit to even light or occasional drinking.

Further confirmation of the proportions of men and women drinking in Lusaka has come from another survey, conducted by the author in 1991 (and as yet unpublished), of a random sample of just under 2,000 respondents that was specifically looking at the relationship of drinking to sexual behavior and risk of acquiring HIV infection. In this survey, 43.7% of men and 73% of women stated that they had never taken alcohol. Thus it seems likely that there is a segment of the population who never drink or whose involvement in drinking is occasional and at most incidental, or perhaps opportunistic, rather than institutionalized as a meaningful part of their lives.

It would be a mistake, however, to assume that little change in patterns and styles of drinking has occurred; the process of change is ongoing. As Roizen (1989, 112) remarked, in reviewing a description of drinking in the Gwembe valley in Zambia given by Colson and Scudder (1988), "We see beer change from the glue of *gemeinschaft* [close community relations] to a cash commodity, move from sacred to secular, from highly structured ritual use to leisure-time and egoistic use; we see the beer supply, at first confined by the limits of the local harvest and competing demands on grain later made virtually unlimited by commercialization; we see the site of drinking moved from one's own homestead and fields to the public tavern." Numerous factors contribute to the process and rate of change in developing countries (where it can often be expected to be extremely rapid), and many of them affect patterns of alcohol consumption, sometimes in subtle fashion.

I will be describing some of these factors and changes, but we should also recognize that new factors must constantly be taken into account. For instance, the availability of home brew is beginning to be affected as AIDS reduces the capacity of peasants to produce grain, and both HIV infection and the combined economic recession and inflation reduce the urban dwellers' capacity to buy increasingly expensive factory brews. HIV (the AIDS virus), already probably infecting fully one-fifth of the adult population in major cities in Zambia, will continue to have a major impact for many years. And so drinking patterns may change while the underlying cultural underpinnings of particular beliefs and practices remain hardly affected.

Zambia has many cultures. There are about seventy ethnic groups; the exact number would depend upon the criteria used in determining "ethnicity." Although they have a common core of basic culture, there are many differences among the ethnic groups (or tribes, in lay usage) with regard to language, belief in specific aspects of sorcery or spirit possession, bringing up children, marriage customs, mutual obligations in marriage, inheritance, and so forth. For villagers, whether their principal economic activities are primarily pastoral or not remains extremely important. The constituent peoples of Zambia (such as the Lunda, Bemba, Ngoni, Chewa, Lozi, and Tonga) had established their territories long before the colonial scramble for Africa in the final two decades of the 1800s. Zambia (then Northern Rhodesia) became commercially important with the opening of copper mines on a large scale in the early 1930s. The area that came to be known as the "Copperbelt" had special significance in describing the history of drinking in Zambia. Zambia rapidly became more highly urbanized than its neighbors, and its cities experienced spectacular rates of growth. Lusaka, the capital, which had a population of only about 62,000 in 1954 (including 12,000 non-Zambians) is currently estimated to have a population of about a million.

## HISTORY OF DRINKING

In a sense, the history of drinking in Zambia since its colonization is also a history of conflict of cultures and a reflection of the struggle for political freedom as well as for power between various economic and other interests. The early missionaries were not fully in agreement in their attitude to beer-drinking but were at one in condemning drunkenness. Although there was an influx of European liquor meant for the settler population, various institutional arrangements were made to prevent Africans from having access to these beverages. The colonial administration began to show some interest in establishing its position on "the liquor question" when licensing regulations were drawn up in 1903. These and similar regulations were much influenced in their content by beliefs on the part of the ruling Whites concerning African susceptibility to alcohol, especially spirits, and with regard to their alleged proneness to drunkenness and its assumed effects, such as sexual aggressiveness and violence (Ambler 1990). Africans were not allowed to drink any beverage other than home-brewed beer.

Over the years, various regulations were made, and in 1930 they were consolidated into the Native Beer Ordinance (later called the Traditional Beer Act), which defined for Africans what and where they could drink. It also provided local authorities with a monopoly over the production and sale of African beer and established beer halls in the major urban centers. Although there was a fear of the consequences of drunkenness, it was also recognized by the management of the large mines that their employees (living in barracks without families) would need recreation. It was assumed that drinking the type of beer most familiar to them at home, in large beer halls, would be suitable, especially if such facilities were open only for very limited hours and were always under close supervision. The creation of a government monopoly had been justified on grounds that the profits would be used exclusively for "amenities." The nature of these amenities remained a bone of contention for many years, and as profits grew, there was increasing pressure to put them into the general revenue of municipalities, and in some cases to use them for infrastructure that the local Africans had been long demanding.

Although traditional beer could not be manufactured or sold in municipal areas except by the official monopoly, brewing for home consumption was allowed in rural areas and for sale, by special permit. In 1946, Zambians from all over the country were able to voice their views on beer-drinking restrictions in the African Representative Council, formed that year. At its first session, a motion that Africans be permitted to purchase European-style bottled beer and wine (but not spirits) was passed by a vote of 18 to 4. Within two years, the sale of wine and bottled beer was allowed in the beer halls. Besides a strong fear of the effects of drinking upon the African population, the Whites felt equally strongly about racial segregation and hence would not permit "mixed" drinking (by Blacks and Whites in the same place). The pressure continued for drinking rights of Africans to be on a par with those of Europeans and for the right of Africans to make and sell beer. The brewers were women who needed money to feed their families and to supplement their families' incomes. They protested strongly at the restrictions; in Lusaka, discontent erupted into one of the capital's largest pre-independence demonstrations, the 1954 beer riots. More than 2,000 women were involved, many with babies on their backs; they were tear-gassed and clubbed by the police for protesting the regulations that prohibited brewing and sale in towns.

But these were just the opening shots in what quickly proved to be a much more complicated political war. The beer halls became a very visible target for protest, whether on economic or social grounds. They were widely believed to promote criminal and immoral behavior, and the political party that eventually led Zambia to independence strongly promoted the notion that they were not fit places for women. The United National Independence Party leaders spoke of the need to strengthen the family and to promote the dignity of women, who, if they drank, should do so at home. But the movement to allow women to prepare and sell traditional brews in town, which had been so prominent in the 1950s, did not finally produce results. All restrictions on the African consumption of factory-made beverages in towns were swept away at independence in 1964 and many of the beer halls were closed, but the old regulations remained in force and homemade brew could not legally be sold. However, men with money to invest were able to take advantage of the new climate of opportunity and set up small taverns, so-called "tea rooms" (selling not tea but beer), bottle stores, and bars; even the beer halls were revived under the new name of "municipal taverns."

## TYPES OF BEVERAGES

A description of current modes of drinking that takes account of the cultural context can be anchored partially upon a review of the various types of beverages. In Zambia several symbolic meanings can be discerned as changes have occurred and are continuing. Beer was significant in the ritual, work, and leisure life of peoples in all parts of Zambia. In general it tended to be available only when there was sufficient grain for both food and beer. It is noteworthy that marijuana, which grows readily and was much used, never achieved any kind of ritual status—perhaps due to the much greater variation in its effects on the individual smoker. A whole group might have to agree that a particular brew of beer was bad, but such consensus would be much less frequent regarding marijuana.

The following classification of types of beer used traditionally in the eastern part of Zambia, taken from an account prepared as background material for the Community Response Study, can serve to set the basic picture, although it must be kept in mind that there are many local variations in practice, and limitations of space dictated that only a superficial account be given. "Work beer" was brewed for clearing trees, burning and preparing a garden for planting, weeding, and so forth, and for the many tasks involved in building a house, such as thatching. On the agreed day, those invited would gather for a preliminary taste before embarking on the work. Even if the beer was bad (and up to 20% of brews, at some times of the year, were of poor quality), they would do the work they had undertaken to do. "Ceremonial beer" was prepared for the important transitions of life, such as the death of a person. In this case, the "first beer" was brewed immediately after a person died; its purpose was to cleanse the relatives of the pollution of contact with death. The drinking of the first beer was also associated with the determination of the cause of death. The beer was not taken to the grave of the deceased.

The "second beer" was prepared some three months later, and its purposes were twofold: paying respect to the dead person and determining inheritance. In the presence of the whole village, the person appointed would take a sip from a calabash of beer, spit it on the grave and pray to the spirit of the deceased to keep the living safe from disease, and to provide a good harvest. Small shrines might be built at the graves of headmen for an annual offering. With all due ceremony, the occasion was looked upon as joyful, and dancing would go on for the whole day and night. Shrines were also erected within the villages for lineage spirits, and if beer was prepared for economic or social purposes, it was offered to the spirits before it was drunk. Beer was also prepared for other transitions, each with its particular style of usage. In addition to work, ceremonial, and social beer, there was "political" beer, which was sent by those seeking appointment to office, or wishing to keep public support, in amounts of a calabash or two, to the local village headman or chief.

Colson and Scudder (1988) give a detailed and rich account of some aspects of drinking among the Tonga people living in the valley of the Zambezi River. In eastern Zambia, ancestral and some other spirits were assumed to share the human fondness for beer, and although some might more appropriately receive offerings of chickens or goats, beer was the basic element in rituals in the region and was associated with household and lineage. A woman's marriage was fully established only when her own and her husband's kin gave her the right to make beer both for her own and for her husband's ancestors. Household (symbolized by hearth) and field (symbolized by grain) were brought together in the synthesis of beer, made by the wife and poured out over the doorway of the couple's house by representatives of the husband's and wife's lineages. In the olden days, beer could be and was taken socially, but the circumstances depended greatly upon the supply. Harvests not always being reliable, and with no factory beer, "hidden beer," prepared for an older man and his closest friends by a woman willing to brew it in secret, might be necessary. As the road network was extended and shops were built, the sale of beer became a means of generating cash income; sometimes advantage could also be taken of improved means of producing more beer, in the form of abandoned oil drums that were readily converted to the purpose of brewing on a much larger scale than had been possible with clay pots and calabashes. The White man's evening drink with his companions, the "sundowner," became the Black man's occasion as well, often with food and entertainment to go with the beer.

There were thus established patterns of drinking superseding the old customs when bottled beer and the commercial form of the traditional beer (*chibuku*) arrived. Social occasions were now more likely to bring together strangers, and although in a tavern men might sort themselves out by age, if a man—even a young man—had money, he would be welcome. In Gwembe, binge drinking was rare in the 1950s, but it became common in the 1970s and thereafter, and with it came drinking problems. Class differences emerged, with schoolteachers and other members of the rural elite drinking in their homes. Colson and Scudder (1988) remark that by the late 1970s, few adults other than young wives and a few fundamentalist Christians abstained completely. On the surface that contrasts sharply with the picture reported by the Community Response Project, but it still essentially conforms to the same pattern: a marked tendency to drink to get drunk, especially away from the homestead, and with very limited opportunities for women under the age of thirty-five to drink much. This kind of drinking was more likely to be associated with aggressive behavior and loose tongues, so that villagers returning home from the tavern at night might well voice what normally would never be said in public, including accusations of sorcery.

If one examines which beverages are consumed by which people, it is evident that there is a hierarchy, based largely upon socioeconomic status of the drinker, although there is a danger of oversimplification in arranging beverages in such an order. In the view of the town dweller, home brews fall one notch below *chibuku* (but above illicit beverages) because home brews still manifestly occupy a special place in social organization within the village. There is some recognition that homemade beer for traditional ceremonial use has its own aura, but this is less and less shared by urban youths. Occasionally one finds a drinker in a bar pouring a little of the beverage he has just purchased onto the floor, in imitation of the traditional gesture, but his action is often looked on as an embarrassing joke.

Even in a village, the beers made for work and for ritual purposes can sometimes be replaced by imported, factory-produced opaque beer. Or a home brew can be made from corn flour that has been purchased, rather than home-grown. There is a lack of clarity in people's thinking in distinguishing legal from illicit beverages, and the law itself can be confusing. Home brew, made in the traditional way over a period of about seven days, not sold without a permit, and used in the traditional manner, is not illegal. Many people assume that any beer of this type, bought and consumed convivially in a rural area, is provided legally. The style of life in town does not allow for such a long process of brewing; hence "home brews" made in town (the sale of which is illegal) are likely to fall into the illicit category in other ways. For example, they are more likely to have more than 6% alcohol, to be made from unacceptable ingredients (as defined in the law), to contain other forms of alcohol, or to have various contaminants. For these reasons, all home-distilled spirits are illegal.

There is an interesting ambiguity about illicit beverages in that although they are widely consumed, they are believed to be potentially very dangerous. However, the vendor is hardly likely to wish to poison her customers, and both analyses of specimens and follow-up of reports of alleged poisonings confirm that even illicit beverages are generally potable and not toxic; in fact, they are often of highly acceptable quality. The illicit beverages are also found in rural areas, where their quality will depend upon the skill of the maker and, to some extent, upon the frequency with which they are made. They have a higher alcohol content (usually two or three times that of ordinary seven-day beer), so that anyone wanting to get drunk quickly can do so, sometimes at the cost of becoming quite ill in the process.

Home brew (usually made of water, sugar, and yeast, and ready for consumption within twenty-four hours) is the basic ingredient of one form of a recent addition to the list of beverages, called *akiki* wine. It is made by substituting a brew of tea for the water; another form of *akiki* is fermented for about three weeks and, although it includes some fruit, hardly corresponds to the pressed-fruit wines known elsewhere. The illicit beverages are drunk by various strata of society, not just by the poorest. In fact, *akiki* is popular even among those who are usually lager drinkers, who do not think of *akiki* as being "dangerous" like other illicit beverages. The fact that it is called wine, which is looked upon as a drink of the rich, its darker color, and some doubt about whether it can even be classed as illegal have led to its use by urban youth.

The type of factory-produced beer designed to be similar to homemade beer is called *chibuku*. Like home brew, it is a thin, gruellike liquid in which fermentation is allowed to continue, thus giving it the potential to sour very quickly. This is one of the reasons why, on large-scale drinking occasions when beer is plentiful, there is much intoxication; beer should not be wasted by being allowed to go sour. Although drinking "too much" beer (more than one's share) is frowned upon when beer is in short supply, there is a ready excuse for drinking to the point of intoxication. *Chibuku* is the "beer of the common man" in urban areas and a replacement for home brew in rural areas, where it can be taken by tanker and arrive before it deteriorates. In a study of the drinking habits of students in 1980, it was noted that *chibuku* was the preferred drink of primary-school teacher trainees, corresponding to their relatively low status in the student hierarchy.

The next group of beers is the locally produced lagers, only one of which has survived. One proved to be too strong, preventing regular drinkers from estimating their expected rate of intoxication. Another was looked upon as a woman's drink but did not survive a drive against women's drinking in bars and taverns in the era of the miniskirt. *Mosi* (the surviving lager) is the preferred beverage of workingmen and of male university students. It is the beverage of those who have a secure socioeconomic status, whether in town or village; and, being bottled (and pasteurized), it can be bought anywhere in Zambia. The workingman will readily slip from *mosi* to *chibuku* and back, depending upon his financial status. This is reflected in the sales of *mosi* and *chibuku* during the course of a month, especially around paydays. It is not merely a preference for the taste of one beverage over the other—the actual composition of *chibuku* has changed greatly since it was first produced, and it now seems to be generally acceptable—but the sense of the status that goes with drinking it and, to some extent, the place of consumption.

Next in order of increasing status are imported beers, wines, and spirits, the higher-status ones being more expensive. In the student survey, wine, or its equivalents such as aperitifs, is the drink young women will expect to be offered by their escorts or boyfriends, and is not taken in large amounts. Beer, by contrast, is for getting drunk; male student drinkers report almost as high a rate of getting drunk as of drinking at all (Haworth 1983). For those who can afford them, wines and spirits are more likely to be taken for consumption at home and to show that one has "arrived" (from the socioeconomic point of view).

## RELIGION AND DRINKING

Zambia has relatively few members of the population, at least in most urban centers, who do not profess to be Christian; there are relatively few Muslims. It is possible to classify the types of churches along a continuum of strictness (or asceticism) in the following order: no affiliation; Roman Catholics; "liberal Protestants" (including Anglicans, Methodists, and various "reformed" churches); and "strict Protestants" (including Baptists, Salvation Army, Pentecostals, Seventh Day Adventists, and Jehovah's Witnesses). Although some members of certain denominations may object to being grouped with others, this classification has useful construct validity. In the Community Response Survey in 1978, religion was noted to have an impact upon a person's drinking. Those reporting that they were abstainers or very infrequent drinkers were, respectively, 48% no religion, 56% Catholic, 57% liberal Protestant, and 72% strict Protestant. Once the barrier "to drink or not to drink" had been overcome, the style of drinking, in terms of frequency and amount, was little affected by religious affiliation or frequency of participation in religious activities. In a survey carried out in Lusaka in 1991, the proportions of adherents of various churches reporting no drinking were almost the same. In addition, 65% of respondents who reported that religion played a major part in their lives had never taken alcohol, versus 44% of those for whom religion was not important. The constancy of these proportions, together with the constancy of proportions of Lusaka dwellers who apparently have never been drinkers, suggests that they are not just statistical artifacts.

There has been an important shift in religious practice in Zambia since the 1970s that may have influenced drinking. Traditionally, spirit possession was a common phenomenon, especially among women, and was seen as positive rather than imposing any severe disability. It was viewed in terms of the empowerment of these women because being possessed, far from disabling the "patient," may have often enabled her in terms of her having an increased measure of control over her own behavior, especially against her husband's wishes. The actual interpretation of the nature of the spirit(s) varies greatly from one ethnic group to another, but most allow that the possessing spirit would frequently impose taboos on the host's eating of certain foods, or on the consumption of alcohol. Studies of brain function during trance or possession states provide evidence for believing that alcohol is likely to disturb the process of possession. In fact, it is generally not drunk by anyone wishing to participate in a trance ceremony, except for the drummers, who work strenuously and consume large quantities of home brew, but who do not become possessed.

Alcohol is also declared taboo on many other occasions, and a proportion of women undoubtedly refrain from drinking on this account. This prohibition may lose its strength if the contract (for possession can fruitfully be looked upon as a form of contract between a spirit and the person it possesses) is not reaffirmed by repeated possession. A woman who has no need for the benefits thus conferred will often gradually slip into another pattern, if it suits her purpose. Roman Catholic and strict Protestant churches have united in designating traditional spirits of possession (such as *mashabe, masave, ngulu,* and *vimbuza*) as "evil" spirits. The attachment of the adjective is a relatively recent innovation and often leads to the need to exorcise these evil spirits. The possible influence of religion and church beliefs and practices on drinking is thus seen to be complex, potentially conflicting, and still evolving.

## PUBLIC AND PRIVATE CONTEXTS FOR DRINKING

The pattern of public drinking appears to have changed little since 1980, and is an extension of earlier styles. The majority of men who go out to drink do not do so with their spouses. The figures from the most recent survey (1991) confirm the earlier finding—only 15% of men reported usually drinking with their spouse. I have already mentioned the establishment and demise of the beer halls, with their limited hours of opening and overall drabness and lack of amenities. They were looked upon mostly as places where young men (and some of the older ones also) might meet with girlfriends; wives were not usually members of the drinking company. This attitude toward men's drinking with women was carried into other drinking places, but the municipal taverns that replaced the beer halls were little more than scaled-down versions, equally uninviting but probably seen much more as drinking places for men than as venues for meeting girlfriends. The private taverns at which *chibuku* is sold are much more comfortable and much more accessible to women. There are various other types of outlets, on a continuum between the bottle store and the most expensive hotel, each with its typical clientele. Bottle stores (which are officially not allowed to serve alcohol for consumption on or near the premises) often allow drinking of the bottled beer they sell in their vicinity. They may serve a regular group who may meet at a particular time, say for a drink after work or on a Saturday morning. The drinking style of many wealthier Zambians is now more likely to be modeled on their experiences when traveling abroad as well as on the preferences of foreign visitors.

The drinking places just described are all very visible because they are legal, but there is another group of less visible outlets, the *shebeens*. They initially evolved in towns, from the illicit sale of home brew. Women made and sold home brew in the yards of their homes. But *shebeens* have changed their character inasmuch as they now represent a measure of luxury, even a sort of private club for the blue-collar drinker. Contrary to stereotypes, whereas the municipal taverns and many other public drinking places can become noisy, drunkenness is fairly common, and there is a definite danger of assault or theft on the road home, the *shebeen* offers its clients the opportunity to drink in a small place where they are well known, with their usual friends, where there is usually little noise, and fights or quarrels are rare both within the *shebeen* or in the vicinity, and where comfort in drinking is assured. The regular customer will pay a little more for the bottled beer he is likely to drink there, and may be able to obtain it on credit. In contrast to their outdated image, most *shebeens* are not brothels. They are however, unlicensed and frequently condemned; they are, like youth, convenient scapegoats when need arises. Illicit beverages can be sold only from private homes. Depending upon the type of beverage and drinker, the image may be tarnished, but the drinking of a beverage defined as illegal does not necessarily predispose to unwanted behaviors.

## LEARNING TO DRINK

One of the most important recent changes in Zambian lifestyle concerns the position of children and youth. Whereas there was a relatively well-controlled transition from childhood to adulthood that often included a gradual introduction to alcohol and its use, modern youth must learn in a different way. The matter is simpler for girls, because they have always learned from their families and for the most part still do so. A girl in the village may be permitted to taste and sip beer, under the watchful eye of her mother or aunt. In town the introduction will often be at some special event, such as Christmas, a wedding, or a kitchen party. The institution of the kitchen party has come in for much criticism, especially because men are excluded. It occurs before marriage and is part of the process of informally coaching the young bride-to-be about her connubial duties; it serves as a replacement for, or sometimes as an addition to, the traditional ceremony of initiation for girls. The kitchen party is a time of great convivial drinking by the women attending, and some may even need to be carried away. This is not necessarily so much the result of having drunk too much as of having drunk far more than usual. Attendance at kitchen parties is now an important part of the social round for many middle-class housewives, who have found it a way—emulating their husbands' established habit—of drinking regularly, away from home. For the girl being initiated into drinking, it may remain little more than having the occasional sip until she is well established in marriage. Kitchen parties are for the mature and the successful.

Females are not expected to be regular drinkers. Even those who have escaped from direct parental control by attending training institutions or colleges tend to drink much less than their male friends. Survey data from Lusaka continue to support the general norm that few women are likely to be regular or heavy drinkers before the age of thirty-five. Women of childbearing age, who may be expected to bear seven or eight live children over a relatively short period, are already under considerable physical stress. The extra physiopathological burden of drinking is never mentioned as a reason why women should not be allowed to drink. The reasons are couched in moralistic terms, but the effect of the virtual ban is a healthful one.

The boy's progress to becoming a drinking man is very different. He may be given a sip of alcohol, like his sister; but it is no one's duty to do so. Nor will he necessarily have had the opportunity to observe his father drinking because, in town, this is mainly done away from home. Access to beer often comes first through a flagrant breaking of the law. When mother wants to have some *chibuku* at home, she often sends her son to get some from the nearest tavern. Taverns are not officially allowed to sell *chibuku* for consumption off the premises, but they often do so. Likewise, beer should not be served to anyone under the age of sixteen (in the case of *chibuku*), but the errand boys are often closer to twelve or thirteen. They soon learn that what they can buy for their parents, they can buy for themselves. In any case, a sip or two from a container of several liters will not be missed, especially if the container is topped up with water. Parents are not likely to notice the difference in view of the normal variation in quality, unless dilution has been too drastic.

The fact of having easily purchasable beer has made all the difference in the youthful drinking trajectory. And yet youth are in general blamed for much more drinking than they actually do. The many who are inexperienced drinkers readily show the effects of intoxication even from relatively small amounts of alcohol. Their drinking tends to be sporadic and infrequent. The traditional separation between the elders and the young men is maintained; for example, in Lusaka one particular tavern had become known as the "boys' tavern," where no older man would be seen drinking. A new phenomenon is the increasing population of street children (some of them orphans of parents who have died of AIDS), many of whom are drinking *chibuku* and experimenting with illicit beverages.

As the youths grow into adulthood and continue with their new styles of drinking, there will doubtless be further evolution of patterns of drinking and possibly some associated problems. On the whole, in spite of the reputation they claimed when Zambia gained its political independence, the people have been neither Africa's "best" nor "worst" drinkers—whatever those adjectives might mean.

## REFERENCES

Ambler, C. 1990. Alcohol, racial segregation and popular politics in Northern Rhodesia. *Journal of African History* 31:295–313.

Colson, Elizabeth, and Thayer Scudder. 1988. *For Prayer and Profit: The Ritual, Economic and Social Importance of Beer in Gwembe District, Zambia, 1950–1982.* Stanford: Stanford University Press.

Haworth, A. 1983. A preliminary report on self-reported drug-use among students in Zambia. *Bulletin on Narcotics* 35:1–9.

Haworth, A., M. Mwanalushi, and D. Todd. 1981. *Community Response to Alcohol-related Problems.* Institute for African Studies, Community Health Research Reports. Harare: University of Zambia.

Roizen, R. 1989. Book review of Colson and Scudder (1988). *Contemporary Drug Problems* 16:111–115.

# 29

# An Anthropological View of Alcohol and Culture in International Perspective

*Dwight B. Heath*

The preceding chapters afford a broad view of alcohol and culture in international perspective. In this chapter I will bring an anthropological viewpoint to bear on these data, underscoring some of the similarities that were found and calling attention to some of the more striking differences. In the next and final chapter, I will make some generalizations that combine those national-level data with what we know from anthropological research. A social science approach is one that deals with both uniformity and variation in human experiences, and the meanings of both alcohol and culture can better be appreciated by comparing these accounts, not only among themselves but also with accounts from other cultures throughout the world.

## COVERAGE OF THIS BOOK

This book is meant to fill an important gap in our understanding of alcohol use and its outcomes throughout the world. Many people know that ethanol is a substance that occurs in nature, without any intervention on the part of human beings. That does not mean it can be understood in the abstract, without a host of meanings, values, and attitudes that give it cultural context. Even though it is "natural" (rather than "artificial," a distinction nicely articulated in the chapter on China), this does not justify my having written (in Chapter 1 of this volume) that ethanol is "a relatively simple chemical compound." That is, in itself, an assertion that shows profound cultural bias, implying that there is some positivistic reality out there on which all agree, and that science is the best way of knowing about most of it. Whether one believes that or not, it must be obvious that there are others who do not, and that, at different stages of our own history, knowledgeable and respected people did not believe it. How much more does culture influence the ways in which we think about what, where, when, how, and how much to drink; in the company of whom; in what setting; with what utensils; for what purpose; and with what results! But this is not a book about the philosophy of science. It is a social scientist's attempt to derive meaning from contemporary world experience with alcohol and to make it accessible to others.

Even an international handbook cannot be encyclopedic in its coverage, but the chapters included here are a remarkably representative sample of nations around the world. Coverage is intentionally diverse. Every continent is represented, as is every latitude. The countries represent nearly 20% of the United Nations, and they included elected and hereditary monarchies, members of commonwealths, federated states, and independent republics, new and old, with a wide range of political and economic systems. Some of the world's largest countries are here, together with some of the smallest. Unlike other volumes that purport to deal with alcohol internationally, this includes developing countries as well as those that have long been at the forefront in terms of urbanization and industrialization. Several other countries would have been of special interest for one reason or another, but could not be included. It is rare to find an authority who is willing and able to write about alcohol, but it is next to impossible to find someone interested in doing it with a cultural emphasis. I was fortunate to be able to draw on colleagues (only one of whom was an anthropologist) for many of whom it was a wholly new way of considering the subject, and they were often a little surprised at what they learned.

The nations that are included range from culturally homogeneous (Denmark, Iceland) to extremely heterogeneous (Mexico, Zambia), from very restrictive about alcohol (Canada, Sweden) to unusually permissive (Italy, Spain), and from unusually high consumption (France) to extremely low (Egypt). To be sure, there are some countries that a reader might have wished to be covered in such a volume but that have been omitted for various reasons. For example, Norway's situation is so very close to that of Sweden and Finland that they often enact common laws and conduct joint research; the author for Portugal died before writing even an initial draft; Japanese colleagues were, for a variety of reasons, unable to contribute. Other cases from Central and South America, although unique in some details, would be largely repetitive in terms of general patterns, and the same could be said for much of Africa. Many of the Caribbean and Oceanic nations can be found in the ethnographic literature.

It would have been easier to write the book myself, organizing data in a uniform format and producing homogeneous essays that would have allowed quick and easy comparison. But that approach would have conveyed little sense of what knowledgeable people in each country consider important about the subject. I have been a light-handed editor, deliberately choosing to let each contributing author speak with his or her own voice. To be sure, I gave each chapter a number of close readings, changing many individual words, adding a colloquial translation here and there, reordering some sentences and even moving a paragraph from time to time in the interests in clearer or smoother communication; English is not the first language for many of these authors. But my editorial revisions were limited to expository style, and never affected content or intent. That is why each chapter tells about different national cultures of drinking, and does so in a distinct manner or voice. The authors come through both as spokespersons familiar with their subject matter and as individuals with their own special interests.

At the outset I did ask that each contributor pay some attention to history, to stereotypes and their fit (or lack of fit) with reality, to intranational variation among minority populations, and to recent changes. But I did not prescribe how much or how little should be said about each topic, nor what kind of "spin" to give to the thorny question of alcohol-related problems (if and when they occur) or other aspects of the presentations. That is why there is such variation. Far from being an impediment to the reader's understanding, such variation should help to convey the very real diversity that many people do not fully realize lies at the heart of the scientific enterprise of describing patterns of human belief and behavior transnationally or cross-culturally.

## Types of Nations

Our sample of twenty-seven nations ranges from the northernmost to southernmost, largest to smallest, densely to sparsely populated, historically dominant to newly emergent, highly developed to minimally, and along many other parameters. Major world areas (such as North Africa, sub-Saharan Africa, Latin America, Southeast Asia, Scandinavia, the Arctic, Oceania) are all represented, and so are a number of religions (Muslim, Jewish, Catholic, Orthodox, Protestant, traditional). Former colonies generally experienced major changes in alcohol use with independence, and most countries still recognize various and important impacts from other nations. Even though the units of analysis are nation-states, where political boundaries are of major importance, it is interesting to note that the contributing authors characterized their countries in different ways. Denmark is seen as intermediate between "the northern countries" and "the south" (of Europe), in cultural orientation as well as in geographic location. The Netherlands is characterized as a "low control" country, signaling a generally liberal view toward individual freedoms in more than the realm of access to alcohol.

## Types of Cultures

It is a crucial part of the anthropological perspective that boundaries be paid attention to where the local people say that they are important; often such boundaries are not geopolitical so much as ethnic, linguistic, or traditional. Over the years, anthropologists have tended to deal with relatively homogeneous societies, some of them rather small and isolated, and not with nation-states. Out of that anthropological tradition has grown a preoccupation with understanding holistically as much as possible of the entire culture (or way of life) of a people. I have no intention in this context of discussing in any great detail the more than 200 explicit definitions of "culture" that were cataloged by Kroeber and Kluckhohn (1952). In providing brief guidelines to the authors who contributed to this volume, I used my own: "*a system of patterns of beliefs and behavior that are familiar to, and, in significant degree, shared by a given population*" (Heath 1986, 234, italicized in the original). Such a way of life, or set of guidelines for understanding and dealing with the world, includes the most prosaic as well as the most exalted aspects of human thought and actions, and is clearly and firmly rooted in local history. As such, it is a useful tool for helping us to understand how and why different populations, often even in the same country, drink very differently and treat both drinking and its results in diverse ways.

   This approach, recognizing that there may be multiple cultures within a single nation, and that some cultures spill across national boundaries, fits with the general usage in sociology and anthropology, but it differs in some measure from usage that has become commonplace in alcohol studies (Heath 1984). Often a comparative account of drinking is called "cross-cultural" if it deals with two or more countries (where the data ostensibly refer to the country as a whole). Or the same label may be used if a study deals with as few as two different populations that may differ on such varied bases as religion, national ancestry, socioeconomic status (class), ethnicity (race), or other criteria.

   Many researchers in a broad range of disciplines share the anthropological interest in cultures as both reflecting and shaping behavior, and are even willing to concede that the "patterns of belief and behavior" that comprise a culture constitute a crucial part of the complex whole that determines drinking. In the formulation that calls alcohol use a complex "biopsychosocial" phenomenon (codified by Levin 1990), culture is largely subsumed as part of the social role, with some components being conceded to the psychological. In the formulation that identifies influential factors as the "drug," "set," and "setting" (following Zinberg 1984), culture is often presumed to be a major part of the setting. No one seriously denies the relevance of culture in this connection today, but most observers use the term in a very cavalier manner.

   The meaning is very close to the formulation of culture when the author describes many component "nations" in China, or different "tribes" in India or Zambia. Similarly, there is a brief mention of different "peoples" in Russia, and in Australia, the Aborigines are treated separately in some detail, as are the Maoris in New Zealand. The Mapuche Indians are culturally distinct in Chile, as are various Indian groups in Honduras and Mexico, and Canadian Natives (Indians) and Inuit (Eskimos) in Canada. These are all populations that have cultures in the anthropological sense, that is, systems of patterns of belief and behavior that are generally shared and agreed upon, or simply ways of life. Any reader who wants to learn in more detail about drinking and its sequelae in such minority populations will find a richly detailed (but very different) corpus of anthropological literature scattered through books and journals that do not necessarily have "alcohol" in their titles (guides are Heath 1975, 1987, 1991; Heath and Cooper 1981).

With specific reference to alcohol, it deserves mention that a few sociologists and epidemiologists have used the concept of culture in a very different way, to characterize overarching *types* of orientation that are international and macroscopic rather than intranational and more microscopic. For example, Poland is described as a "spirit-drinking culture" because distilled beverages are far more popular than fermented ones. By contrast, France, Chile, and Italy are prototypical illustrations of "wine culture," with wine not only the predominant beverage but also an integral part of sociability, hospitality, and so forth, and implying frequent use of wine with meals, by both sexes and all ages, with little drunkenness. Much of Germany is, and Australia was until recently, a "beer culture."

In some instances, the contributing authors use terms that may refer to geography or that reflect (for those who are familiar with drinking patterns) transnational similarities, such as "Latin" for France, "Mediterranean" for Italy, "Northern" and "Scandinavian" for Iceland. The authors of the Swedish chapter refer to their being in a "vodka belt" that stretches across northern Europe; presumably this is a convenient characterization of a band of countries where vodka is commonly drunk by groups of men in a context of binges. Similarly, Poland is described as having a "wet culture" (as France, Italy, Spain, and some others might be), with high consumption, liberal attitudes toward drinking, and a relatively low rate of abstention (all of which would be the opposite in a "dry" culture, such as that of Egypt). It is striking that so many of the countries described here have had strong temperance movements at various times, but few have been as long-lasting and pervasive as in Sweden, the United Kingdom, and the United States, all of which fit a criterion of "temperance cultures": having a long history of popular movements that label alcohol a major source of problems (Room 1992; Levine 1992).

## Types of Beverages

Most of the analytic studies of alcohol in its various aspects categorize all beverages into three basic types: beer, wine, and spirits. Beers are fermented, usually from a cereal base, and generally contain between 4% and 8% alcohol; also included in this category are mead, ale, stout, and other variants. Wines are also fermented, but usually from a fruit base, and generally contain between 8% and 20% alcohol. Spirits are distilled, and can contain up to 90% alcohol; this category refers to whiskey, rum, gin, brandy, cordials, and any other distillates.

Another kind of distinction has to do with manufacture: home brew is a fermented cottage-industry product (sometimes legal and sometimes not), and moonshine is similarly distilled in relatively small batches (usually illegal); there is no specific term for wine fermented on such a scale, perhaps because so much of the wine that was taxed and sold widely was, until recent years, handcrafted.

It is clear from the individual chapters that lay people do not ordinarily classify drinks this way, and the profusion of individual beverages in different countries is enormous. Grouping all beverages that contain alcohol into these three categories is a convenience for those who put real stock in statistics about average per capita annual consumption, which allows for easy comparison among populations (in countries, states, counties, or other jurisdictions that pay close attention to the sales of such beverages—and most do, because they are a ready source of tax revenue, and may even be a commercial monopoly of the government). There is little scientific justification for such categorization, as evidenced by the fact that the French decline to consider wine an alcoholic beverage.

Nevertheless, in this volume it is convenient to adhere to the tripartite classification, if only to be consistent with the enormous wealth of epidemiological and other literature that deals with alcohol internationally. These statistics have taken on a life of their own (see Appendix). It is also a convenience to be able to refer to such a broad class of beverages rather than always having to list the various forms of fermented beverages and the various forms of distilled beverages—for example, when referring to a historic change in popular taste (as from spirits to beer in Australia in the late 1800s, or from beer to spirits in Iceland and Denmark, and then back again in both countries). In Egypt, a rough rule of thumb identifies beer as an everyday food and beverage, wine as a celebratory drink, and spirits as taboo for religious reasons. The prototypical "wine culture" in Spain and Italy turns out to be little more than a century old, and may be superseded by beer if present trends continue. The Chinese experience is unusual, recognizing "natural alcohol" (made by nonhuman animals) and including mare's milk and a wide variety of flowers as a base for drinks. Cider is mentioned in a region of France, and it is known in some other countries that have apples. Palm wine, mentioned in Nigeria and Zambia, doubtless occurs elsewhere. Stout from an Irish manufacturer is popular in Malaysia, and the distinction between manufactured beers and home brews carries prestige in Zambia.

Some authors have tried to characterize their countries in broad terms, but the recognition of significant cultural differences among various regions makes them hesitant. Hence, whereas many writers in other books readily characterize Germany as a "beer culture," our author's focus on culture forces her to admit that one region is a "wine culture" and another favors spirits. Similarly, as important as wine unquestionably is in France, there is a region with a dominant "beer culture" and another where cider predominates.

In many of the countries, it is mentioned that different beverages are favored by different segments of the population. Indians and rural peasants in Guatemala, for example, prefer two illegal categories to the three legal categories that predominate in the cities; manufactured beers are more prestigious than home brews wherever they occur; women favor wine where men prefer spirits; Spanish youth prefer beer where their parents favor wine; and so forth.

In those few areas of the world where alcoholic beverages were not indigenous, they usually were adopted quickly when outsiders introduced them, and they often became tools of colonial and other economic exploitation. Spirits are often added to a beer or home-brew repertory, but drinks almost never disappear. (The peculiar history of absinthe in France, an interesting exception to that generalization, has yet to be fully documented.)

### Types of Drinking

One striking feature of drinking in virtually all of the countries in this volume is that it is essentially a social act. The solitary drinker, so dominant an image in relation to alcohol in the United States, is virtually unknown in other countries. The same is true among tribal and peasant societies everywhere.

In many instances, what we would call alcoholic beverages are thought of as food, an integral part of the diet rather than a special substance reserved for special purposes. Such has been the case with beer in Egypt for millennia, and such is the case with wine in France and Italy today. Many different kinds of drinking occur elsewhere: some excitedly celebratory, some solemnly ritualized, some integral to various kinds of work, and so forth. Whether it is by religious practitioners, by jurists or complainants, by suitors or coworkers, the context is always important, as is the participation by key individuals. In many societies, drinking is not even a frequent occurrence, but it can be important on those rare occasions when a binge is not only allowed but imperative.

In terms of classifying behavior, just as in terms of recognizing boundaries, an anthropological perspective looks not so much to impose any set of standards from the outside as to understand how things are viewed from the inside. Thus it is crucial that we recognize typologies of drinking that are pertinent in the ways of thinking of different peoples but that may never before have been mentioned in the analytic literature about alcohol. For example, we are told of different types of drinking (religious, medical, recreational, and other) in China; "wrong" and "normal" consumption in Denmark; "celebratory," "ritual," and "social" drinking in Honduras; "traditional" and "nontraditional" in India; and "proper ways," as well as very different (but locally appropriate) times, for drinking in Spain.

For any effort to understand not only the uses of alcohol but also the consequences of such use, it is crucial not only to understand how much a person drinks on one occasion but also how frequent such occasions may be. Chronic drinking without food can damage one's liver and other organs; if alcohol is taken with food, there is less likelihood of pathology. Episodic binge drinking carries virtually no such risk but may pose other risks (such as accidents). Because of these variant modes of quantity per occasion, similar per capita consumption figures can reflect very different customs and usages.

A few specific patterns that recur in different countries should perhaps be mentioned. The pattern of drinking in which a group of men take turns paying for drinks for everyone in the group—buying rounds in the UK, or "shouting" in Australia—not only has social and economic implications, but also implies that men more often stay longer in a bar and drink more than they would if they were paying just for their own drinks. The idea of offering drinks to friends and neighbors who join in a cooperative work effort (raising a building, taking in the harvest, or other reciprocal labor) assures the availability of labor at crucial times, and makes a pleasant social occasion of what otherwise might be drudgery. It is interesting that urban Zambian women are developing a gender-specific pattern of drinking in informal "kitchen parties" very similar to those in Sweden.

## THEORIES ABOUT DRINKING

The emphasis in this book is more descriptive than analytic, and most of the authors felt constrained by space limitations. There are a host of theories about alcohol and its use, emphasizing a host of different variables depending on the disciplinary orientation of the theorist. For a remarkably thorough and concise view—including genetic, neurobiological, neurobehavioral, psychoanalytic, personality, conditioning, learning, systems, availability, anthropology, and economic tendencies, see Chaudron and Wilkinson (1988).

Nevertheless, a few points deserve to be mentioned in setting these chapters into the context of the existing literature. For example, it is refreshing that so few of the authors made much of the ever-popular but simplistic notion that the primary reason people drink alcohol is to reduce tension or to relieve stress. Undoubtedly, it is one component among the motivations of many drinkers, but it is hardly informative when we try to understand similarities and differences at the cultural level among such diverse populations in such diverse situations.

The authors of these chapters are generally familiar with theories about drinking, and many have made substantive contributions. Without belaboring such points in detail, it is interesting to note some special features of theoretical importance in this book.

In its reference to dietary status, the typology of drinkers that is described in some detail in Chile differs from that used in other parts of the world. Inasmuch as Chile long served as the model for epidemiological studies of alcohol throughout Latin America, it will be interesting to see whether this typology gains broader acceptance.

In writing about Italian social thought, we are confronted with the absurdity (which often occurs elsewhere) that for political purposes, alcohol is often linked with crime and poverty in a causal manner—and vice versa. The five "sets of reasons for drinking" that are given for Russia may well be unique to the political and economic situation of that country. A personal sense of guilt is mentioned as a primary part of various alcohol-related problems only in Iceland, which has an exceptionally high rate of problem drinking with a low rate of consumption. This inverse relationship runs counter to the predictions of the World Health Organization and many authorities, although it is by no means unique. France, Italy, and Spain all have unusually high consumption and low problems; it is even suggested here that in France, problems appear to be *inversely* correlated with both the quantity and the frequency of drinking. For some years I have been making this same point with reference to many of the populations that have been studied by anthropologists, as will be discussed in the concluding chapter.

## ALCOHOL IN RELATION TO OTHER ASPECTS OF CULTURE

Duster (1983, 326) put it nicely: "Alcohol is to social science what dye is to microscopy. . . . What this dye does is to show up certain kinds of fundamental features of the structures of the cell, and I suppose that we can probably use alcohol the same way to penetrate the structure of social life." Using much the same logic, I have suggested that quite apart from the intrinsic interest the subject of alcohol may hold, it should be of interest to any social scientist inasmuch as it affords a sort of window into other aspects of culture. In a series of review articles that trace the evolution of anthropological writing about alcohol (Heath 1975, 1987, 1991), I have shown how various categories that are of theoretic and other interest are illuminated by studies of drinking in sociocultural context, whether the authors intended them to serve such purposes or not.

In this section, it seems appropriate to help the reader appreciate the degree to which alcohol affects other aspects of culture. In a broader sense, this discussion may dramatically illustrate the degree to which the various aspects of any culture are inextricably linked to each other, whether the integration is smooth and trouble-free or the opposite. There can be few more important points to be made in terms of understanding the concept of culture and its importance in human behavior.

### Social Organization

Fundamental to any society that has a culture is social organization. Without it, no one could know who's who, who should be doing what (and who should not), who should be where (and who not), and so forth. It includes not only the identification of individuals but also their grouping into categories (by age, sex, kinship, class, occupation, or any of a variety of other criteria that may be socially relevant in a given connection).

We have already mentioned the striking fact that drinking is primarily—and almost exclusively, in these countries—a social act, sometimes shared by a family with a meal, sometimes with coworkers, sometimes other men (or women), or otherwise used as a basis for inclusion or exclusion. To illustrate the specific ways in which alcohol provides insight into social organization, consider these examples from the preceding chapters.

Many authors said, in so many words, that "group drinking reinforces group cohesion" (Chile), "drinking together helps to integrate family and friends" (Poland), or "promotes social solidarity" (Spain). In both Australia and the UK, "mateship" (male bonding or friendship) is implied by drinking, much as female friends and neighbors bond during "kitchen parties" with drinking in Sweden and Zambia. "Social credit" is explicitly mentioned among Australian Aborigines, and it is implied in many other contexts, whereby even people who have little money can confirm ongoing networks of reciprocity by occasionally sharing a few drinks.

*Gender*

One measure of status that is recognized everywhere is gender (what many consider to be the sociocultural implications of the biological category of sex differentiation). Repeatedly our authors make the point that men drink more, and more often, than do women. (This is almost a cultural universal with only two peculiar instances—both small migrant groups in novel settings—known where the opposite holds [Heath 1993].)

In many groups, drinking together is an important way men act out their stereotypes of masculinity with boisterous behavior, frequent expressions of aggression, boasting about their capacities for drink and sex, and otherwise underscoring exaggerated caricatures, as in the "kiwi bloke" of New Zealand or the "macho" of Mexico or Chile. The settings in which such male demonstrative drinking takes place are often segregated to keep women away (Germany, Sweden), and youths are often eager to "prove their manhood" by drinking conspicuously (Italy, UK).

In the wine cultures around the Mediterranean, men often drink together without drunkenness, whereas in the beer- or spirits-drinking cultures to the north, they drink especially to get drunk. Associated with this difference is the cultural view in the south that men are responsible for social order, and hence they would be shamed by any breach of it; by contrast, in the north it is women who are expected to assure moderation and propriety. In Scandinavia, it is often expressly said that women oversee or control men's drinking (which is why binges usually occur away from women). Such imposed control is hardly necessary when a man's own honor is at stake, as is the case in the Mediterranean or Latin America.

A double standard often applies to the morality of drunkenness, with it expected of males but deplored among females. Associated with this is the frequent presumption that a woman who drinks in the company of men is sexually promiscuous and otherwise immoral. In France it is thought that men need wine, whereas women do not. A meal without wine may not be considered fit for a man, but it is commonplace for women to abstain or to drink different beverages (sometimes sweeter and usually with less alcohol). In Guatemala there are a few specific ritual occasions during which female drunkenness is not only accepted but actively sought as a form of spiritual transcendence. Sweden and Zambia recognize the "kitchen party" as an occasion on which drinking by women is a standard form of sociability, but it is clearly in a private setting with no men present.

Most countries report that women are drinking more than they used to, and more frequently, but not significantly so and not in ways that result in problems. Historically, it appears that drinking by women becomes a focus of public attention when they claim increased status, wealth, or other power. The epidemic of problem drinking that many predicted as women challenged traditional limitations (and supposedly suffered more stress through competing with men) in various countries did not materialize, dashing many superficial stereotypes about both feminist liberation and use of alcohol. An interesting countertrend is that most countries report men are drinking somewhat less, and less often, than in the 1980s. Such short-term changes, unless they are dramatic in scale or are linked with major increases or decreases in the rate of various important linked problems, are difficult to interpret, but collectively they make it obvious that gender significantly affects drinking.

Arguments can be made to the effect that women get the same impact from using less alcohol. This is true, partly because they tend to weigh less than men, partly because they have proportionally more fat and less muscle (so that alcohol is diffused through their bodies in less water), and partly because females have less of an enzyme that metabolizes alcohol, so it stays in their bodies longer. But none of these physiological data were known a generation ago, so we must again recognize how potent social organization is in shaping drinking customs. For interesting cultural studies that focus on female drinking, see Gefou-Madianou (1992) and McDonald (1994).

*Age*

Another criterion of social organization that is culturally significant is age. Although cultures may emphasize different ages in different ways and demand varying kinds of behavior, all recognize developmental stages and allot rights, privileges, obligations, and expectations on the basis of them. The ways in which age relates to drinking are many and diverse, although some patterns can be discerned.

One trend that appears to be widespread is that people are beginning to drink at an earlier age, and that young people are drinking more than they used to (e.g., Iceland, Mexico). Most of the contributors to this volume mention survey data that point in this direction, although the content, context, meanings, and outcomes of young people's drinking continue to be very different. Although I have no reason to question the data, they may be similar to those about women—an increase that is more apparent than real at a time when young people are testing the limits of their restricted status and power. In Spain, youth not only drink different beverages but also drink in different ways, and they drink for the effects (which few elders do). The idea of a minimum age before children should be "protected" from alcohol is alien in China and France; where it is a matter of law, the mid or late teens are favored.

Young students are said to have increasing alcohol problems in Nigeria and Iceland; adolescent drinking is interpreted as part of a youthful rebellion in Israel and Sri Lanka. Despite sensationalized accounts in the media, preadolescents in the UK are aware of alcohol but are not frequent or heavy drinkers. Children learn to drink early in Zambia by taking small quantities when they are sent to buy beer; children in France, Italy, and Spain are routinely given wine as part of a meal or celebration. Alcohol plays an important part in various rituals of the aged in China. Drinking is stratified by age in Zambia, with new taverns appearing now that young men have greater access to money, and thus to beer. All in all, the international data confirm the anthropological cross-cultural data in showing that the attitudinal context, rather than the beverage, shapes expectations and actions with respect to alcohol as it relates to age, just as it relates to other aspects of culture.

## Class, Caste, and Other Categories

A third aspect of social organization that tends to be important in most cultures is stratification, whether by class, caste, or other hierarchical ranking (such as schooling, income, occupation, religion, etc). Whereas Denmark prides itself on class equality, most of the countries admit to having very different drinking patterns in different socioeconomic classes. Fairly elaborate differences are spelled out in Malaysia and Spain, and the use of alcohol at all is an important status marker in religiously heterogeneous Sri Lanka. In India, where caste is important in many levels of human activity, alcohol is one of the few things to which the lower castes enjoy more access; the same is true in Sri Lanka. By contrast, in Guatemala, Indians may use home brew as ladinos use beer, with the emulation described as if it might facilitate social mobility. In Zambia, beer is the drink for most, but those who have achieved or aspire to upward mobility often shift to spirits as a sort of emblem.

In many countries, even religions are hierarchically ranked. Roman Catholicism incorporates wine into its sacraments and appears rarely to have been associated with major pronouncements against alcohol. By contrast, several Protestant sects hold to abstinence as an article of faith and denounce drinking as evil (Sweden, Iceland); Muslims do the same (Egypt, Malaysia). This, combined with vigorous missionary activity, has resulted in conversion by many who want to escape the social obligation to drink and to spend heavily in some countries that have traditionally been Catholic (e.g., Guatemala, Honduras). It is interesting to note that Buddhism, Hinduism, and Confucianism are not so ascetic as many believe (China, India), and that there is little difference in drinking between the few people who drink in Egypt, whether they are Christian or Muslim.

### Economics and Politics

Whatever else they may be, alcoholic beverages have become economic commodities that have played many different roles throughout history. In Russia and Poland, our authors emphasize their early and continuing manipulation to the economic and political advantage of a few; state monopoly of sale is still common (Canada, Egypt, Sweden), and heavy taxation prompts police to try to suppress home-brewing and moonshining (Guatemala, Nigeria). In France, Italy, Spain, and New Zealand, wine is an major export important to the national economy, as spirits are to Scotland (UK). In Malaysia, as in much of the developing world, breweries are viewed as an important symbol of economic development, just as the right to drink was involved with the movement toward political independence (in very different ways in India, Poland, and Zambia). Some minority populations still suffer restrictions similar to those that pertained during the colonial period: Aborigines in Australia, Mapuche Indians in Chile, Black natives in Zambia, and others. The economic value of alcohol as a tool in colonization is firmly imbedded in the "firewater" myth (Canada and the United States), and its use in maintaining debt peonage among peasants is similar in Denmark, Guatemala, Sweden, and elsewhere.

The political importance of alcohol in a few countries is implied by its being mentioned in the constitution (Honduras, India), or in major amendments to it (United States), although the Indian and U.S. experiments with total national prohibition both failed, as did most other such experiments in history. The pub as a center of political activity made it subject to regulation in both Germany and Italy, just as coffeehouses and chocolate shops were suspect at different times and places. The costs of drinking are one of the major sources of friction within some households, although the "social credit" that is built up thereby is not usually weighed in evaluating it. As beer and legally distilled spirits replace home brew and moonshine in Guatemalan ceremonial drinking, money that had been redistributed within the community is being siphoned off to outsiders. Furthermore, the role of alcohol in political rituals (China, Guatemala) is similar to what is found in many peasant and tribal societies. Here is another respect in which the international data conform—not in specific detail but in general pattern—with those described by anthropologists in small societies throughout the world.

### Interethnic Relations

To say that different ethnic populations have different patterns of belief and behavior with respect to alcohol is to imply that in many instances, drinking itself can be an important boundary marker between social groups. This is dramatically emphasized in countries as diverse as Australia, Canada, Guatemala, Malaysia, Mexico, New Zealand, and Sri Lanka. The various populations may be called "nationalities" (as in China), "ethnic minorities" (Malaysia), or "religions'' (Zambia, Sri Lanka), but it is clear that the way people drink (or don't drink) marks them as belonging in different social categories. Differential laws about the availability of alcoholic beverages have done much to aggravate ethnic tensions in Australia, Zambia, and elsewhere, including, at various times, attempts to impose prohibition on native people (Canada, New Zealand). The use of certain beverages (home-brewed palm wine, moonshine) may delineate one group from another (Honduras, Nigeria, India), in which case changing one's drinking pattern may be seen as a way of increasing one's social status. In Russia, it is suggested that acculturative stress is one of the factors that lead to heavy drinking among members of minorities; most other countries where there are significantly disadvantaged populations could probably say the same. As Third and Fourth World populations become increasingly involved with the capitalist economy and with manufactured beverages, this is a frequent (but not universal) trend.

## International Relations

Partly because of its economic value and partly because of evangelical views of morality, alcohol has long been subject to a variety of international policies and controls, and international differences are becoming increasingly important as trading blocs proliferate, threatening protective tariffs, introducing easier access to foreign goods, and so forth. Former colonies Australia, Canada, India, and New Zealand all show vestiges of domination by the UK. Denmark shows in microcosm how wars affect trade, diet, and manufacturing, and it is striking that the sale of the Virgin Islands saw a virtual end to the popularity of rum as a beverage. Tourists are credited—or blamed—for introducing new drinking patterns in such different countries as Iceland and Spain. Participation in both World Wars is cited as having introduced many volunteers from India to drinking on European models. Historically, the broad distribution of grape-growing in Europe is largely a heritage of the Roman Empire, just as wine production in Latin America was deliberately introduced by the Spaniards.

A few areas that had not had indigenous alcoholic beverages received them from European traders and often adopted them with alacrity (Canada, Malaysia, New Zealand). In regions where native drinks had long been used, the newly introduced beverages were generally added to the drinking repertory rather than displacing the old. The historical account of Nigeria includes the discussion of ambitious international efforts to restrict the alcohol trade—and, with it, slavery—throughout sub-Saharan Africa near the beginning of the twentieth century. Large-scale recent international efforts tend to follow the general guidelines that the World Health Organization has offered for national policies: restricting sales, indexing prices, increasing taxes, regulating advertising, and in various other ways limiting the availability of alcohol (Grant 1985). Such efforts at increasing controls are explicitly rationalized and recommended on the premise that alcohol-related problems occur in proportion to per capita consumption, a theory that we have disproved at least in France, Italy, Spain, Iceland, and Sweden, as well as in several ethnographic studies elsewhere.

### Diet and Nutrition

As our Russian contributor reminds us, ethanol is endogenous to the human body, not an alien substance. Nevertheless, the habitual use of any beverage affects diet, nutrition, and ultimately health of those who use it. Among "tribals" in India, Mexico, and Nigeria, for example, the various home brews are generally recognized—by scientists as well as by the drinkers—as foods that provide a wide range of vitamins, minerals, and other nutrients that are beneficial. In a similar manner, the populations of France, Italy, and Spain have long looked on wine as being healthful, and scientists in recent years have found increasing justification for that view (Ford 1993; Ellison 1993). Apart from vitamins and minerals, there are flavonoids that favorably affect cholesterol levels, thereby diminishing the likelihood of atherosclerosis and other coronary heart disease (the major cause of death in significant portions of the population). Anti-oxidants are other beneficial components of wine that justify its inclusion daily in the "Mediterranean diet" recommended by the Harvard School of Public Health, the WHO Regional Office for Europe, and the Oldways Preservation Trust (Oldways 1994). The French go so far as to consider wine a necessary component of "a good meal," and regard it as "the sanitary beverage," quite distinct from what they consider to be alcohol. Even commercially manufactured ferments are sometimes thought to be nutritious. The commercial slogan "Guinness [brand of stout] is good for you" has apparently been incorporated into the folk wisdom of much of Malaysia, and our author says it was not long ago that ale was "more healthful than milk or water" in the UK.

When too many food crops are distilled, as happened historically in Denmark, significant health problems can result. Land that is given over to growing crops for the production of alcoholic beverages is often taken out of service for producing local food crops, so that macroscopic economic factors can interfere with diet. The same can happen microscopically if too much of a household's income is diverted from food to drink. Another side to this coin is that for women (who usually are the producers of cottage-industry alcohol) it is a source of income that would not otherwise be available to them, and it is often spent on food or schooling for their children, benefiting not only them but also their communities. The way in which alcohol is drunk can also affect diet and nutrition; in both China and Denmark, distilled beverages are treated as an adjunct to food, so they have very different effects than when they are drunk without food.

### Language, Literature, and Folklore

Any cultural trait that has been the focus of as much attention as alcohol consumption will invariably be reflected in the language, literature, and folklore of a people. The Chinese credit monkeys with having discovered fermentation and tell stories about specific individuals (in different regions) who are culture heroes for having introduced people to alcohol. Egyptians tell of the god Osiris bringing beer to them, just as the Romans (of ancient Italy) credited the god Bacchus with having introduced wine, and the ancient Mexicans thought pulque was a gift from the gods. Drinking has played an important role in the arts, both visual (Egypt, Italy) and poetic (China, France, India). Drinking and drunkenness were important aspects of the legendary prowess of the ancient Vikings (Denmark). The vocabularies, proverbs, folktales, humor, and other realms of popular culture in China, Denmark, Poland, Italy, Spain, and Sweden are full of allusions to drinking, mostly favorable, and the concept of *ivresse* has special meaning in French thought, combining drunken intoxication with rapture and ecstasy. The symbolism of toasting is widespread as an important—and sometimes mandatory—component of sociability, often constituting a form of folk art in itself. Much of what is learned about drinking, whether favorable or unfavorable, is passed from one generation to another through stories, songs, poems, tales, and sayings that reflect long-term cultural experiences and attitudes.

### Conflict Management and Law

Few commodities are subject to as many laws and regulations, in as many countries, as are beverages containing alcohol. Most of the authors have taken pains to show how such controls have changed over time and how they currently affect alcohol use and outcomes. Laws about who may drink what and where ostensibly have to do with preserving public order, although it is not clear whether the resentment they engender may not often be more problematic than would be allowing, for example, members of different ethnic groups to drink together (India, Zambia). At any rate, it is evident that such official or formal controls are far less effective in shaping behavior than are the unofficial informal controls that people exert in their daily interactions, through gossip, exhortations, or other forms of social sanction. In one sense, this is the essence of culture as a system that makes it possible for us to live with others without frequent and insuperable conflicts.

When conflicts do arise, all societies have prescribed ways of dealing with them, even when there is no specific police force or written body of laws. One example is that of the Mapuche Indians in Chile, for whom an interesting sidelight is that the formerly competing parties at a hearing before the elders share a drink to symbolize their satisfaction at the end of deliberations. Such a pattern also exists among many tribal peoples in Africa. Similar drinking to "seal a bargain" is reported as an integral part of trading among some tribal societies in Africa.

### Religion and Ritual

The reality, magnitude, and emotional significance of differences among cultures is vividly displayed in contrasting views that people hold concerning alcohol and religion. Some consider it a gift of the gods, and others use it as a sacrament (China, India, Russia, Spain). Whereas some view alcohol as evil (Denmark, Iceland, many Protestant Christians throughout Latin America and Africa, Muslims anywhere), others consider it so holy that it is an ideal offering to deities or spirits of ancestors (China, India, Zambia). Drunkenness is often viewed as a religious experience, so that this shortcut to revelation is not only allowed but also approved on special occasions (even for women in Guatemala). It may surprise some readers that there is little difference between Muslim and Christian drinkers in modern Egypt. By contrast, Israel sees striking differences among different sects within Judaism. The long history of appreciation of alcohol among Muslims is noted in Spain; Muslims are now trying to enforce prohibition among others as well as themselves in Malaysia.

Religious differences can be discerned even in countries that superficially appear to be relatively homogeneous in terms of ethnicity, such as Germany and the Netherlands. Protestant abstinence appears to provide an alternative for some Latin Americans who want to opt out of the costly and time-consuming civil-religious hierarchy of community governance in which even secular rituals often involve heavy drinking and drunkenness. Some populations in China view drinking as necessary "to keep the world in balance," and some Zambians treat home brew as a sacred combination of key cultural factors—the household (hearth) and the field (grain)—brought together by women. Nevertheless, there are many others elsewhere who consider any alcohol an abomination. This is among the more dramatic and emotionally loaded respects in which alcohol and culture relate to each other, and it is by no means merely an archaic concern among people who know little about the rest of the world.

## Health and Curing

In most modern nations, the rationale that state authorities give for trying to restrict the availability of alcohol, even though it is a legal substance, is public health. It is ironic that at a time when the abundant evidence that the prophylactic effects of alcohol on blood vessels is rapidly mounting, there is strong institutional hesitancy to endorse regular consumption. By contrast, until the twentieth century, alcohol held a fundamental place in the pharmacopoeia of most cultures, and it is still credited with a variety of preventive and curative effects. In France and Italy, "wine builds the blood" and is thought to be positively healthful in many other respects. In Malaysia, "Guinness is good for you" because it supposedly maintains the balance of humors between "heaty" and "cooling." Tribal populations in China, India, and Nigeria specifically use alcohol as medicine and as an integral part of curing rites.

Conversely, heavy drinking (especially over a long time) is generally thought to be harmful. Nigerians recognize alcohol poisoning as a problem in children; the French and Italians are aware that a portion of their high rates of cirrhosis is probably due to alcohol; and many of the statistics that purport to relate to problem drinking are specific to health (admissions to hospitals, certain cancers, etc.). As is so often the case, the same substance is both embraced and reviled for its role in relation to physical well-being, underscoring how important cultural context is in the evaluation of an act that may look similar but that has very different meanings and impacts in different populations.

## Continuity and Change

Just as is the case with every other aspect of culture, beliefs and behaviors about alcohol are characterized sometimes by remarkable continuity and sometimes by rapid change. One of the most abrupt changes in many parts of the world was the introduction of new beverages (especially distilled spirits) to societies that had not known indigenous alcohol. Several of the authors writing about former colonies have described how alcohol was used in early trade or in markedly unequal kind of employment to take advantage of native populations (Australia, Canada, Guatemala, Nigeria, Zambia), or as a way of keeping lower-class workers in debt bondage (Denmark, Russia, Sweden). It is claimed that there has been little change in drinking in Egypt during 4,000 years except for the impact of Islamization. By contrast, the "gin epidemic" looms in English history as an important by-product of urbanization and industrialization, and many other countries point to these same processes as triggering major changes (Germany, Poland, Spain). Just as urbanization often crowds strangers together in a different and alien ambience, so industrialization separates the workplace from the home and creates a new distinction between work and leisure. In some countries, the history of the "wine culture" is more shallow than most readers would expect, with the prototypical French proletarian pattern only about 100 years old, prior to which wine was a luxury for the rich.

With few exceptions, populations appear to be drinking less now than they did in the 1970s, and the impact of such currents as tourism, the international youth culture, women's liberation, and growing common markets can be great on traditional drinking patterns. Shifts in popular preference for different beverages occur: from beer to spirits and back to beer in Denmark. Rapid changes in attitudes toward alcohol have occurred for largely political reasons in Germany, Poland, and Russia, and ideas about social mobility and the symbolism of drinking have affected practices in countries as different as Guatemala, India, Malaysia, and Zambia. Even the high occurrence of HIV/AIDS is reflected— for instance, in Zambia, where it interferes with peasants' production of home brew.

Movements ostensibly to inculcate temperance (but often aimed at achieving prohibition) have been remarkably widespread since the 1700s. Earlier prohibitions occurred in China, Russia, and elsewhere, but tended to be short-lived, disappearing with the monarch who decreed them. Movements with significant popular support are mentioned in most of the European countries, as well as in Australia, Canada, Iceland, and India; and sometimes they resulted in large-scale prohibition (Canada, Iceland, India, the United States) or in rationing (Sweden). It seems ironic that Iceland banned beer for several years while spirits were still legal, whereas most countries have generally been more restrictive of higher-proof drinks. The religious component of most temperance movements should not keep us from looking for other motives (Gusfield 1986), and the recurrent failure of most prohibitions should serve as a warning against relying on strict governmental controls to regulate drinking and other popular behavior.

## REFERENCES

Chaudron, C. Douglas, and Adrian Wilkinson (Eds.). 1988. *Theories on Alcoholism.* Toronto: Addiction Research Foundation.
Duster, Troy. 1983. Commentary. Pp. 326–330 in R. Room and G. Collins (Eds.). *Alcohol and Disinhibition: Nature and Meaning of the Link.* NIAAA Research Monograph 12. Rockville, Md.: National Institute on Alcohol Abuse and Alcoholism.
Ellison, R. Curtis. 1993. *Does Moderate Alcohol Consumption Prolong Life?* 2nd ed. New York: Americal Council on Science and Health.
Ford, Gene. 1993. *The French Paradox and Drinking for Health.* San Francisco: Wine Appreciation Guild.
Gefou-Madianou, Dimitra (Ed.). 1992. *Alcohol, Gender, and Culture.* London: Routledge.
Grant, Marcus (Ed.). 1985. *Alcohol Policies.* Copenhagen: World Health Organization, Regional Office for Europe.
Gusfield, Joseph. 1986. *Symbolic Crusade: Status Politics and the American Temperance Movement.* 2nd ed. Urbana: University of Illinois Press.
Heath, Dwight B. 1975. A critical review of anthropological studies of alcohol use. Pp. 1–92 in R. J. Gibbons, Y. Israel, H. Kalant, R. Popham, W. Schmidt, and R. Smart (Eds.). *Research in Alcohol and Drug Problems.* Vol. 2. New York: John Wiley and Sons.
———. 1984. Cross-cultural studies of alcohol use. Pp. 405–415 in Marc Galanter (Ed.). *Recent Developments in Alcoholism.* Vol. 2. New York: Plenum.
———. 1986. Concluding remarks. Pp. 234–237 in T. F. Babor (Ed.). *Alcohol and Culture: Comparative Perspectives from Europe and America. Annals of the New York Academy of Sciences 472.* New York: NYAS.
———. 1987. A decade of development in the anthropological study of alcohol use: 1970–1980. Pp. 16–69 in Mary Douglas (Ed.). *Constructive Drinking: Perspectives on Drink from Anthropology.* Cambridge: Cambridge University Press.
———. 1991. The mutual relevance of anthropological and sociological perspectives in alcohol studies. Pp. 125–143 in Paul M. Roman (Ed.). *Alcohol: The Development of Sociological Perspectives on Use and Abuse.* New Brunswick, N.J.: Rutgers Center of Alcohol Studies.
———. 1993. Cross-cultural perspectives on women and alcohol. Pp. 100–117 in E. S. L. Gomberg and T. D. Nirenberg (Eds.). *Women and Substance Abuse.* Norwood, N.J.: Ablex.
Heath, Dwight B., and A. M. Cooper. 1981. *Alcohol Use and World Cultures: A Comprehensive Bibliography of Anthropological Sources.* Bibliographic Series 15. Toronto: Addiction Research Foundation.

Kroeber, A. L., and Clyde K. M. Kluckhohn. 1952. *Culture: A Critical Review of Concepts and Definitions.* Papers of the Peabody Museum of American Archaeology and Ethnology 47 (1). Cambridge, Mass.: Peabody Museum of Harvard University.

Levin, Jerome D. 1990. *Alcoholism: A Biopsychosocial Approach.* New York: Hemisphere Publishing.

Levine, Harry G. 1992. Temperance cultures: Alcohol as problem in Nordic and English-speaking cultures. Pp. 16–36 in M. Lender and G. Edwards (Eds.). *The Nature of Alcohol and Drug-Related Problems.* Oxford: Oxford University Press.

McDonald, Maryon (Ed.). 1994. *Gender, Drink, and Drugs.* Oxford: Berg Publishers.

Oldways Preservation and Exchange Trust. 1994. *International Conference on the Diets of the Mediterranean.* Boston: Oldways.

Pernanen, Kai. 1991. *Alcohol in Human Violence.* New York: Guilford Press.

Room, Robin. 1992. The impossible dream? Routes to reducing alcohol problems in a temperate culture. *Journal of Substance Abuse* 4:91–106.

Zinberg, Norman E. 1984. *Drug, Set, and Setting: The Basis for Controlled Intoxicant Use.* New Haven: Yale University Press.

# 30

## Some Generalizations about Alcohol and Culture

### Dwight B. Heath

The varied sample of national experiences with alcohol that are described in this book prove again how diverse the cultural reactions to a substance can be, yet it also shows commonalities among the detailed differences. From an anthropological perspective, it was important to show the many and diverse ways in which drinking articulates with various other aspects of culture, such as social organization, economics and politics, interethnic and international relations, diet and nutrition, language and folklore, conflict management, religion and ritual, health and curing, and continuity and change. However, from the broader social science perspective, it is important also to highlight some generalizations that can be made about drinking and its outcomes, without repeating many of the close linkages between alcohol and culture that were emphasized earlier.

## ABSTINENCE, TEMPERANCE, AND AMBIVALENCE

Those who are new to the field of alcohol studies are often surprised to find out how many people do not drink at all. In the United States, this is more than one-third of the adult population, up from the 1980s. Abstainers (defined as those who drink no more than once a year) are thus a substantial segment of the population who should be taken into account when one tries to evaluate such figures as per capita consumption, the proportion of drinkers who have problems with drinking (about 10% in the United States), and so forth. For some, abstinence is a matter of religious faith; for others, a matter of personal taste, a resolution to maintain one's distance from alcohol in order to maintain one's sobriety, or some other reason. An unusually high percentage of Australian Aborigines abstain; the same is true of Egyptians, Indians, Irish, Lutheran Icelanders, and fundamentalist Protestants wherever they may be. Although drinking and drunkenness have long been popular in Germany, some famous men have spoken out forcefully in favor of greater moderation there.

"Moderation" and "temperance" are buzzwords in relation to alcohol that have very different meanings in different contexts. "Moderation" or "moderate drinking" differs in terms of quantity and frequency, depending on cultural context (e.g., Chile's idiosyncratic terminology allows for much more drinking than does that in Egypt or India, where drinking at all is out of the ordinary), but the latest scientific advice is that one to two drinks a day constitutes an appropriate part of a healthful diet for most persons (Ellison 1993). "Temperance" would appear to mean much the same as "moderation," but historically it has most often been used by those who deplore drinking and would curtail it if they could. Although their aim is usually prohibition, most temperance advocates have, during the twentieth century, generally recognized that the frequent rapid repeal of prohibition demonstrates popular opposition to such forceful involvement of the state with respect to a habit that many enjoy—and consider beneficial for a variety of reasons—so, tactfully, they are now speaking out for gradual rather than abrupt restriction of drinking.

This is not just the paranoiac projection of a libertarian moderate drinker who does not want to be told by others that he has to quit. Although few people who are not engaged in the study of alcohol are aware of it, both the World Health Organization (1981, 1992) and the U.S. Department of Health and Human Services (1991) have made official pronouncements calling for a 25% reduction in overall alcohol consumption.

This is only the most recent of many temperance movements. In the early 1800s, Canada, the UK, and the Netherlands joined the United States in strongly religious temperance movements. By the mid-1800s, Poland and Russia had their own such movements, and nearly half of the states in the United States had enacted local prohibition. By the late 1800s, those U.S. prohibitions had generally been repealed, but a strong wave of temperance sentiment swept over Australia, Sweden, and flourished again in Netherlands and the United States. In the early 1900s a temperance movement unexpectedly arose in Italy, and that in the United States gained momentum, culminating in nationwide prohibition (18th Amendment of the Constitution) in 1919, repealed by the 21st Amendment in 1933. Mexico, where one might not have foreseen a prohibition movement, had a brief one in the 1940s, and France had one in the 1960s. A "New Temperance Movement" has been influential not only in the United States but also throughout much of the world since the 1970s (Heath 1989; Pittman 1991). At first couched in religious or moralistic terms, the rhetoric has shifted toward science and pseudoscience, sometimes even distancing itself from religion and emphasizing public health, economics, or social welfare to appeal to new and broader constituencies. In India, Poland, and Sri Lanka—all in different ways—temperance was linked with anticolonialism and the push toward independence. Abstaining was never popular in Denmark, but the local category of "wrong consumption" shows that there is a fundamental ethic of moderation.

In the few countries where social historians have paid attention to temperance movements, there appear to be cycles of waxing and waning enthusiasm (Musto 1987; Blocker 1990) that are reflected in "long waves of consumption" (Skog 1986) and may be related to the ambivalence that many people hold with respect to alcohol, viewing it as both a boon and a bane, enjoyable but potentially dangerous. The frequently ambivalent reaction to alcohol accounts for much of the confusion that young people have about it and for many of the discontinuities that are reported in the histories of the nations described here. A sociologically sophisticated discussion of such ambivalence as an important portion of the human experience of alcohol is Room (1976).

## BENEFITS OF MODERATE DRINKING

In light of the negative evaluation of alcohol and drinking in many of the scientific and popular writings about them, stressing disease, death, and other costs to the individual and to society, it is remarkable that the attitudes, usages, proverbs, and experiences of the vast majority of the people and peoples dealt with in this book are positive. There are few cultures in which the dangers of excessive drinking are not deplored or even feared, but virtually all of our authors indicate that in most of the cultures with which they are dealing, the primary image is a positive one. Usually drinking is viewed as an important adjunct to sociability. Almost as often, it is seen as a relatively inexpensive and effective relaxant, or as an important accompaniment to food. The symbolic importance of drinking as a way of differentiating members of one population from another is closely linked with other emotionally laden symbolic meanings. Among these are a sense of identification with or participation in a more modern or cosmopolitan way of life, an indication of financial success and social status, or even of assertive masculinity. Its use in religions is ancient, and reflects social approval rather than scorn. Even some of the major religions that many outsiders believe to be abstemious do not enforce prohibition, and no secular state has succeeded in such experiments, although partial prohibition for various segments of the population based on age, sex, caste, or other criteria have sometimes been imposed.

One generalization that emerges from these chapters is the somewhat surprising virtual unanimity with which the authors have cited a broad range of benefits of moderate drinking. This is gratifying, not because I have any vested interest in promoting drinking but because it replicates at the level of the nation-state many of the findings that I have reported in my cross-cultural writing about tribal and peasant populations around the world. Some colleagues have questioned the reliability and validity of anthropological research methods, and others have wondered whether "modern" cultures may not be so wholly different from "primitive" ones that deep-seated customs and attitudes about drinking have become not only obsolete but also dangerous, and what is good for them may be bad for us. There are a few respects in which that may be true, but this does not appear to be one of them. It is in this connection that Room (1984) took ethnographers to task as "problem deflators"; however, few of those who commented on his article agreed with the charge.

But the contributors to this volume are not ethnographers, nor are they of the age, professional training, or cultural background that Room (1984) suggested prompted too many anthropologists to ignore the dangers of drinking while emphasizing its joys among other peoples. Almost every one of the contributing authors has described positive functions of drinking in his or her country— benefits that accrue to the social fabric as well as to individuals—even when they have viewed with alarm certain risks, dangers, and harm that sometimes result from excessive drinking. This is a little surprising in light of the fact that most of our authors are professionally engaged in public health and social wel- fare activities that are aimed at preventing, treating, or otherwise ameliorating such damage. Most of them are not simply teachers or researchers who might be thought to enjoy the luxury of academic detachment; they are psychiatrists, physicians, and others who work daily in clinical settings, faced with the need for realistic decisions that affect the lives of the people they serve. These authors are not "problem deflators" who seek to put a happy face on native people, or to find theoretically satisfying functional interpretations for disruptive customs. This explanatory aside may appear to verge on overkill, but emotions run high on this subject, so I feel it is necessary to reassure readers who may be concerned that contributors were chosen, or their works cunningly edited, to show drinking in an unrealistically good light. Such is simply not the case.

For that matter, such a finding about the good aspects of drinking should not be surprising. In the United States, which has been labeled a prototypically "temperance culture" (Room 1992; Levine 1992), national surveys—the same ones that tell us about drinking patterns and rates of problems—have repeatedly demonstrated that most of the serious drinking problems (of all kinds) occur in only about 10% of the drinkers (that is, less than 7% of the adult population), meaning that 90% of those who drink do so without such problems. Put another way, most people in the United States, Canada, and Sweden, when asked what emotions they associate with drinking, responded favorably, emphasizing per- sonal satisfactions of relaxation, social values of sociability, an antidote to fa- tigue, and other positive features, with little mention of violence, illness, or other harm (Pernanen 1991). Without for a moment wishing to diminish the human suffering that is unquestionably associated with certain kinds of drinking by a minority of those who drink, it is worthwhile in this context to summarize what an international sampling tells us about the benefits of moderate drinking, a theme that has been eclipsed in recent years by the mass and shrillness of writing about the harm that is done by excessive drinking. In fact, the same author who deplored "problem deflation" on the part of ethnographers (Room 1984) wrote a few years later: "We are definitely in a period of [problem] amplification when there are strong tendencies to overstate alcohol's role in health and social problems, to forget that its causation is usually conditional, and to overlook solutions to the problems that are not alcohol specific'' (Room 1990b, 1357).

### Sociability and Hospitality

Drinking is fundamentally a social activity, and sociability is unquestionably the reason for drinking that is most cited in all of the countries that are described here. The same is true in almost all of the populations that have been studied by anthropologists around the world (Heath 1975; Marshall 1979). Why this symbolism is so widespread is a complex question that involves an interplay of psychological and social variables, but the association is firmly established in most cultures (Douglas 1987). We are told that alcohol is "indispensable" for sociability (China, Denmark, Egypt). It is an integral part of "mateship" (male bonding) in Australia, Canada, and New Zealand; and "the regulars" are known and appreciated in pubs in Germany, Italy, and New Zealand. Drinking is "important to community solidarity" in Guatemala and among many of the tribal populations in India; it is said to be integral in relating to friends and general social participation in Spain and Mexico. Drinking games are a special expression of this in China, Germany, and Poland; drinking contests are common among men in France, Germany, and the UK. Almost every author speaks of an offer of alcohol as an important gesture of hospitality, even in countries that have relatively low overall consumption figures. Related to this is the recognition of drinking as a celebratory act, as is dramatically emphasized in the frequently elaborate secular ritual of toasting, which can go far to confirm one's acceptance within an alien group.

### Relaxation and Recreation

Alcohol seems often to be used, in small amounts, for just those purposes to which it is pharmacologically best suited, as a nontoxic relaxant that is readily metabolized. As such, it reduces fatigue. This is explicitly recognized by most of our authors, with special emphasis on the symbolic importance of drinking to mark the transition from workplace to leisure (in India, Malaysia, Zambia; see Gusfield 1987). It is a frequent adjunct to festivals (China, Guatemala, Mexico), and is sometimes mentioned as providing refreshing diversion when there are few other opportunities (Iceland, Nigeria). Specific recreational activities that focus on alcohol include drinking games (China, Germany) and drinking contests (France, China). Because socializing is often so integral a part of relaxation and recreation, it should also be considered in this connection.

### Food and Its Enhancement

We have already mentioned that some alcoholic beverages are thought of and treated as foods in themselves, and a few are judged by nutritionists as fully deserving that label. Others are viewed as having a gustatory or aesthetic quality that makes them valuable adjuncts to food because they stimulate the appetite, enhance flavor, aid digestion, and so forth. Wine is often an important part of a meal (France, Italy, Spain), and an elaborate sequence has evolved combining alcohol and food throughout the entire day (in Spain). This can involve elaborate ritualization, with a specialized vocabulary and matériel (as among wine connoisseurs), but it can also be simple and straightforward as an integral part of workaday eating. It is specifically noted that this is not a pattern in India, and it may also be absent in most of the settings where drinking takes place primarily in episodic binges, but it appears otherwise to be extremely widespread.

## Status and Health

To a remarkable degree, people seem to focus on what or how a person drinks—even more than on what or how one eats—as a marker of social status. This is reflected in the frequency with which our authors mention drinking as a symbol of manliness or valor (Chile, Denmark, France, Germany, Honduras, Mexico, Malaysia), and on people's changing their drinking habits as they achieve or aspire to upward social mobility (India, Sri Lanka, Zambia). In a more role-specific way, the effectiveness of a shaman in tribal India can be enhanced by the use of alcohol to alter consciousness. As a symbolic adjunct to ceremonies that confirm the assignment of specific titles in Nigeria, alcohol confers a special power on traditional ritual activities. Drinking patterns are often described as important boundary markers between ethnic groups, just as the choice to drink or to abstain is often a symbolic marker of importance to different religions, endowed with considerable affect and emotion.

Alcohol has long been viewed as a drug in the beneficial sense of helping to prevent or to cure a wide range of physical maladies, whether we speak of disease (in the sense in which scientists diagnose and treat symptoms) or of illness (the subjective dis-ease that a patient experiences). Chinese and Russian physicians still recognize a number of specific problems for which alcohol serves as a medicine, and there is the widespread belief in many wine cultures that "wine strengthens the blood," is beneficial to a nursing mother, or helps people to stave off the cold. Considerable scientific research has focused on "the French paradox" (Ford 1993; Perdue 1992), in which the French enjoy a relatively low rate of coronary heart disease (the leading cause of death for significant portions of the population in the United States and elsewhere) even though they eat far more saturated fats, exercise less, smoke more, and drink more. This is one of those instances where systematic research is confirming long-held popular beliefs, and wine turns out to be positively healthful in many respects. For that matter, it is not only red wine (as some originally thought) but any form of ethanol that has all of these benefits: "alcohol lowers harmful LDL-cholesterol levels; raises protective HDL-cholesterol levels; decreases formation of blood clots in the arteries; increases coronary blood flow; [and] increases estrogen levels'' (Ellison 1993, 3).

Fully cognizant that any discussion of the benefits of moderate drinking is likely to be highly controversial, I owe it to my readers to provide some caveats. The notion of ''moderate drinking'' is by no means a culture-free one, since any drinking at all may be seen as excessive by a devout Muslim or fundamentalist Protestant, or by a recovering alcoholic who fears that ''falling off the wagon'' could jeopardize his or her sobriety and do irreparable damage to physical health, mental stability, and social relations. Individuals vary enormously in their tolerance for alcohol (that is, how much reaction from a given dose)— just as they do in their tolerance for fava beans, sugar, salt, strawberries, lactase, or other substances. It is also clear that there are certain situations in which drinking can be inherently risky (such as prior to operating heavy equipment, or whenever immediate and substantial coordinated responses are requisite).

Otherwise, for most people, alcohol can serve all of the foregoing functions at levels that do no damage to the body, that are quickly metabolized, and that do not seriously impede the performance of normal daily activities. Following Ellison (1993), from whom these important data about recent scientific advances in medicine are summarized, I am using two drinks a day as a cautious and convenient measure for ''moderate drinking.'' Large-scale epidemiological research on various ethnic populations in many different parts of the world shows that people who have one or two drinks a day live longer than those who drink more—and also longer than those who drink less. The J-shaped curve is remarkably consistent, showing that healthy abstainers (not confusing them with sickly former drinkers who abstain after damage has already been done) have more deaths from virtually all other causes than do ''moderate drinkers,'' with rates rising rapidly as consumption increases beyond the ''moderate'' level.

In all fairness, mention should be made of what is perceived by many to be a benefit of immoderate (or heavy) drinking. A simple measure of ''heavy drinking'' that relates more to the potential for physical damage than to local culture or customs, would be about six drinks a day. Incidentally, the acute impact of alcohol on the system is such that even a moderate drinker's one or two drinks a day would not be innocuous if they were ''saved up'' to allow a seven to fourteen-drink binge on the weekend.

With reference to heavy drinking, it must be admitted that drunkenness is often considered to be a positive value in its own right, quite apart from the act of drinking and whatever benefits may accrue from it. Drinking that might result in drunkenness (for most people, at least five drinks within an hour) could usually be considered ''excessive''—except that the aesthetics of behavior differ markedly, as we have seen, and such heavier or faster drinking is not thought to be excessive by those who esteem and actively seek intoxication. In Chile, China, Denmark, Germany, and Mexico, it is mentioned specifically as an affirmation of masculinity; many tribal and peasant cultures make the same association. Guatemalan and Honduran Indians cherish it as a form of transcendence in connection with various rituals; this is also common in the ethnographic literature, and William James (1912) even spoke of it as important among the Western "varieties of religious experience." In Iceland, it is said to provide "release," and in France it is embraced as combining ecstasy with rapture. In Italy, where the traditional wine culture encourages considerable drinking, there are only a few festive occasions when "regulated abuse" is tolerated; drunkenness is considered foolish in other contexts. Some adolescents in India appear to have embraced drunkenness as a form of rebellion, just as impoverished Sri Lankans may have mistakenly adopted it as symbolizing fun and freedom that the wealthy enjoy.

Comparative studies clearly show that the effects of drunkenness are more cultural than they are pharmacological (MacAndrew and Edgerton 1969). This means that the drowsiness, clowning, violence, crime, sexual or verbal aggression, maudlin sentimentality, loquacity, spousal or child abuse, or other concomitants of drunkenness are shaped far more by expectations than by the interaction of alcohol with human physiology. Although drunkenness with such beneficial effects as those described above cannot properly be called the result of moderate drinking, it is not clear whether the heavy drinking that causes it should be called "excessive," inasmuch as the benefits appear to outweigh the costs in the judgment of those who matter most: the people whose lives are immediately affected by it.

## RISKS OF HEAVY DRINKING

It is clear that "heavy drinking" is no more a culture-free term than is "moderate drinking"; but in the interests of combining caution with convenience, I follow Ellison (1993) in using six drinks a day as an arbitrary measure (which is low in international perspective, as attested by the contributing authors). Although there are some contexts in which drunkenness is valued and actively sought (as described above), such drinking is not regularly accompanied by the positive benefits—for the individual as well as for society—that come with moderate drinking, and there are unquestionable risks.

Epidemiological researchers are not consistent in the quality of data they collect, nor do they always use the same numerical scales for counting quantity and frequency of alcohol consumption. However, there does appear always to be a rapid rise in the rate of damage (whether from coronary heart disease or other problems with health) as daily consumption exceeds six drinks. The authors in this book are not all specialists whose research focuses on the epidemiological coincidence of drinking and various problems, but they are all familiar with that literature, and most of them offer at least a few important generalizations with respect to the situation of their countries.

Liver cirrhosis, which used to be considered a good measure of alcoholism, proved to be caused by so many other factors that it lost its role as a direct index for all other drinking problems. Nevertheless, it is still important enough to have been mentioned in relation to Australia, France, and Italy. Traffic accidents, whether correctly linked with alcohol or not, are mentioned in Australia, Iceland, India, Israel, Mexico, and New Zealand. A few specific cancers tend to be associated with drinking (in Australia and Mexico), and alcohol poisoning sometimes occurs when too much alcohol is administered as a medicine to young children in Nigeria. Mental disorders and psychological problems are sometimes said to be caused by excessive drinking (Israel, Poland, Russia). Australian Aborigines, Mapuche Indians in Chile, and some Hondurans and Sri Lankans fear violence from heavy drinkers, but such behavior is invariably directed along lines that reflect stresses in the local culture rather than being random. In Guatemala, Mexico, New Zealand, and Russia, drunken violence is sometimes expressed within the family; in the UK, it tends to be public hooliganism associated with gangs of sports fans. The French fear losing self-control if one drinks too much, although they cherish the sensuality and esthetics of *ivresse* (being "high"), whereas Guatemalans and Malaysians are more concerned about the economic costs to the individual or to the household. In Italy, it is believed that drinking too much makes a woman sexually vulnerable, and in Iceland, divorce is cited (without further explanation) as a common outcome of drunkenness, which is frequent there despite overall low consumption of alcohol.

There is no doubt that most people are aware of certain risks associated with heavy drinking, but the specific nature of those risks differs considerably from one country to another, as it does in various cultures. There is remarkably little consensus about the nature of "alcohol-related problems" or, for that matter, whether the major problems are those suffered by the drinker, by others who are close to the drinker, or by the community at large. An abundant and insightful corpus of literature deals with the sociologically significant point that what constitutes a "problem" is socially defined (Gusfield 1981; Wiener 1981). An important warning to emerge from these data should be recognition that many of the associations that are so glibly presumed by the media are far from being commonplace, such as the supposed link between alcohol and violence, sexual forwardness, indecent language, sacrilege, and so on.

It may be that many of the authors would have listed more of the risks of heavy drinking and put more emphasis on them—as some of them have done in other contexts—if they had not been viewing alcohol at least partially through the lens of cultural analysis. A basic conceptual question must be faced: Why would a trait such as alcohol use have survived and flourished if it were so maladaptive as most critics make it out to be? Perhaps a major part of the answer lies in the fact that alcohol use for most people *means* moderate drinking, in ways that tend to be beneficial for both the individual and the social group. Frequent heavy or excessive drinking is an aberration in most societies, just as abstention is. Since both abstention and excessive drinking are extreme rather than normal behaviors in most cultures, there is a limited need for controls to lessen harm to individuals and to the group, which brings us squarely to the realm of policy.

## ALCOHOL POLICIES

Countries and social groups, like persons, seek to protect themselves from harm. That often requires that they encourage certain forms of behavior and discourage others. Alcohol was subject to strict control even in the earliest corpus of written law that we know; the Code of Hammurabi in Babylon, around 2000 B.C., contains more on alcohol, including a number of consumer-protection measures, than on any other subject. Since the 1890s, drinking has been subject to increasingly strict regulation, even in areas where it had been little controlled earlier. Furthermore, the growth of international bodies that conduct research, and of others that are concerned with public health and social welfare, has resulted in the promulgation of recommendations on a cross-cultural scale that had never been contemplated earlier.

Within the United Nations, the World Health Organization early paid attention to alcohol as a widely used psychoactive (or mood-altering) substance with the potential to impact health on a grand scale. From the beginnings, there were efforts to recognize national and cultural differences, without ignoring or homogenizing them, and interesting efforts have been made at doing collaborative research in different countries that would allow direct comparability (Rootman and Moser 1984). The results were not so promising as had been hoped, but authorities in many areas welcomed the interest, support, and expressions of concern from such a prestigious international agency.

Although there are many who still believe that drinking should be of interest to no one other than the drinker, social scientists discovered a conceptual ''handle'' for promoting international intervention in a finding that stemmed from a study in the Scandinavian countries: ''changes in the overall consumption of alcoholic beverages have a bearing on the health of the people in any society. Alcohol control measures can be used to limit consumption; thus, control of alcohol availability becomes a public health issue'' (Bruun et al. 1975, 90). From that innocuous statement, hedged about with scientific caution, there rapidly evolved a succession of pronouncements that became progressively more strident, converting what had been a mere inference into a virtual axiom.

The rapid progressive exploitation of this apparent scientific justification for political action was neatly documented in a paper by Room (1992) that traced a succession of quotations, each more assertive than the last. Perhaps the culmination was the assertion by the director general of WHO that ''any reduction in per capita consumption will be attended by a significant decrease in alcohol related problems'' (World Health Organization 1978, 4). Since then, although the exact nature of the ''bearing'' in the original cautious suggestion from Bruun et al. (1975) was never clear, it has been treated like an invariant scientific law linked with a moral imperative. It has become common for writers to assume (without any references or documentation) that it is common knowledge, or "everyone knows," that problems vary with consumption, and for that reason, consumption should be decreased. Such was the gist of World Health Assembly Resolution 32.40 (World Health Assembly 1979), which urged "all Member States to take all appropriate measures to reduce consumption among all sectors of the population."

A number of national policies concerning alcohol were analyzed (all in Europe and North America) and a bundle of restrictions on availability (Mäkelä et al. 1981; Single et al. 1981; Davies and Walsh 1985; Grant 1985) similar to those listed in the chapter on Nigeria were recommended. Significant increases in taxes on alcohol are supposed to discourage drinking, and to provide additional funds for prevention and treatment of problems. Stricter regulation of licensing, fewer hours of sale, and a higher minimum purchase age are supposed to make alcohol harder to get, especially for youth. The indexing of prices should assure that drinking does not become cheaper with monetary inflation. Restrictions (or, in some places a full ban) on advertising supposedly diminish popular interest, and warning labels on containers are meant to educate and discourage drinkers.

There is conflicting evidence about whether any of these measures would significantly curtail consumption, just as there is conflicting evidence about whether curtailing consumption would, in fact, diminish problems. But we must remember that these are political rather than scientific recommendations. Several of the chapters in this book show that problems do *not* occur in proportion to consumption; and, for that matter, so do many of the articles written by proponents of the additional controls on availability (e.g., in Single et al. 1981; Mäkelä et al., 1981; Grant 1985). Several critics have suggested that the control model is targeted at moderate drinkers who would be inconvenienced more than it is at heavy drinkers, who would continue drinking at whatever cost.

An alternative sociocultural model has been proposed (Heath 1992) that would not interfere with those moderate drinkers who wish to continue, for whatever social or personal benefit, but that would aim gradually to diminish problems by curtailing excessive drinking. It is striking that social attitudes have changed so rapidly with respect to alcohol in recent years. The infamous "three-martini business lunch" is history; newspapers and courts now take seriously DWI, which used to be treated as a joke unless someone was killed. Comedians find that most audiences do not appreciate jokes about drunks; and cocktail parties have become rare in many circles. Such sensitization or consciousness-raising is often not recognized as a product of education; the changing of cultural norms often takes place outside of the classroom. Much remains to be done in the way of broadening popular acceptance of the premises that heavy drinking is risky and that some forms of behavior are inexcusable, whether one is drunk or not. Addressing attitudes and values is probably the most effective way, in the long run, to change patterns of belief and behavior, because even the strictest nation-state is hard put to enforce its laws and regulations when they conflict with the culture of the people.

The human experience abounds with evidence, both cross-cultural and international, that people can use alcohol in a variety of responsible and fruitful ways. In recent years, a small minority of those who drink, many of whom also take a range of illegal drugs for various reasons, have acted in asocial and antisocial ways that harm themselves and others. Correcting and avoiding such misbehavior can probably be done more effectively by a combination of education (in the broad sense) and peer pressure than by the police, courts, or other remote authority. With such a sociocultural approach to alcohol, combined with letting people know honestly what it is and what it can do, many of the so-called alcohol-related problems would continue to lessen, probably at an accelerating rate. Those who want nothing to do with alcohol should be allowed to leave it alone. But those who want to drink moderately, for whatever among its benefits suits them at any time, should be confident that their behavior is neither deviant nor drug-addicted, but fits well in the vivid panorama of human history.

## REFERENCES

Blocker, Jack S., Jr. 1990. *American Temperance Movements: Cycles of Reform.* 2nd ed. Boston: Twayne.
Bruun, Kettil, Griffith Edwards, Martti Lumio, Klaus Mäkelä, Lynn Pan, Robert E. Popham, Robin Room, Wolfgang Schmidt, Ole-Jørgen Skog, Pekka Sulkunen, and Esa Österberg. 1975. *Alcohol Control Policies in Public Health Perspective.* Helsinki: Finnish Foundation for Alcohol Studies.
Davies, Phil, and Dermot Walsh. 1985. *Alcohol Problems and Alcohol Control in Europe.* London: Croom Helm.
Douglas, Mary (Ed.). 1987. *Constructive Drinking: Perspectives on Drink from Anthropology.* Cambridge: Cambridge University Press.
Ellison, R. Curtis. 1993. *Does Moderate Alcohol Consumption Prolong Life?* 2nd ed. New York: American Council on Science and Health.
Ford, Gene. 1993. *The French Paradox and Drinking for Health.* San Francisco: Wine Appreciation Guild.
Grant, Marcus (Ed.). 1985. *Alcohol Policies.* Copenhagen: World Health Organization, Regional Office for Europe.
Gusfield, Joseph R. 1981. *The Culture of Public Problems: Drinking-Driving and the Symbolic Order.* Chicago: University of Chicago Press.
———. 1987. Passage to play: Rituals of drinking time in American society. Pp. 73–90 in Mary Douglas (Ed.). *Constructive Drinking: Perspectives on Drink from Anthropology.* Cambridge: Cambridge University Press.
Heath, Dwight B. 1975. A critical review of ethnographic studies of alcohol use. Pp. 1–92 in R. Gibbins. Y. Israel, H. Kalant, R. Popham, W. Schmidt, and R. Smart (Eds.). *Research Advances in Alcohol and Drug Problems.* Vol. 2. New York: John Wiley and Sons.
———. 1989. The New Temperance Movement: Through the looking glass. *Drugs and Society* 3(3/4):143–168.

————. 1992. Prohibition or liberalization of alcohol and drugs? A sociocultural perspective. Pp. 129–145 in M. Galanter (Ed.). *Recent Developments in Alcoholism.* vol. 10. New York: Plenum Press.

James, William. 1912. *Varieties of Religious Experience: A Study of Human Nature.* Boston: Longmans, Green.

Levine, Harry G. 1992. Temperance cultures: Alcohol as a problem in Nordic and English-speaking cultures. Pp. 16–36 in M. Lender and G. Edwards (Eds.). *The Nature of Alcohol and Drug-Related Problems.* Oxford: Oxford University Press.

MacAndrew, Craig, and Robert Edgerton. 1969. *Drunken Comportment: A Social Explanation.* Chicago: Aldine.

Mäkelä, Klaus, Robin Room, Eric Single, Pekka Sulkunen, and Brendan Walsh. 1981. *Alcohol, Society, and the State.* Vol. 1: *A Comparative Study of Alcohol Control.* Toronto: Addiction Research Foundation.

Marshall, Mac (Ed.). 1979. *Beliefs, Behaviors, and Alcoholic Beverages: A Cross-Cultural Survey.* Ann Arbor: University of Michigan Press.

Musto, David F. 1987. *The American Disease: Origins of Narcotic Control.* 2nd ed. New York: Oxford University Press.

Perdue, Lewis. 1992. *The French Paradox and Beyond: Live Longer with Wine and the Mediterranean Lifestyle.* Sonoma, Calif.: Renaissance Publishing.

Pernanen, Kai. 1991. *Alcohol in Human Violence.* New York: Guilford Press.

Pittman, David J. 1991. The New Temperance Movement. Pp. 775–790 in D. J. Pittman and H. R. White (Eds.). *Society, Culture, and Drinking Patterns Reexamined.* New Brunswick, N.J.: Rutgers Center of Alcohol Studies.

Room, Robin. 1976. Ambivalence as a sociological explanation: The case of cultural explanations of alcohol problems. *American Sociological Review* 41:1047–1065.

————. 1984. Alcohol and ethnography: A case of problem deflation? *Current Anthropology* 25:169–191.

————. 1990a. Social science research and alcohol policy making. Pp. 315–339 in P. M. Roman (Ed.). *Alcohol: The Development of Sociological Perspectives on Use and Abuse.* New Brunswick, N.J.: Rutgers Center of Alcohol Studies.

————. 1990b. Review of D. Anderson, *Drinking to Your Health. British Journal of Addiction* 85:1355–1363.

————. 1992. The impossible dream? Routes to reducing alcohol problems in a temperance culture. *Journal of Substance Abuse* 4:91–106.

Rootman, Irving, and Joy Moser. 1984. *Community Response to Alcohol-Related Problems: A World Health Organization Project Monograph.* Washington, D.C.: National Institute on Alcohol Abuse and Alcoholism.

Single, Eric, Patricia Morgan, and Jan de Lint (Eds.). 1981. *Alcohol, Science, and the State.* Vol. 2: *The Social History of Control Policy in Seven Countries.* Toronto: Addiction Research Foundation.

Skog, Ole-Jørgen. 1986. The long waves of alcohol consumption: A social network perspective on cultural change. *Social Networks* 8:1–32.

U.S. Department of Health and Human Services. 1991. *Healthy People 2000: National Health Promotion and Disease Prevention Objectives.* Washington, D.C.: U.S. Government Printing Office.

Wiener, Carolyn. 1981. *The Politics of Alcoholism: Building an Arena Around a Social Problem.* New Brunswick, N.J.: Transaction Books.

World Health Assembly. 1979. *Resolutions of the 32nd World Health Assembly.* Geneva: World Health Organization.

World Health Organization. 1978. Report by the Director General, Executive Board, Sixty-third session. Provisional agenda item 23, Attachment E. In *Alcohol Related Problems: The Need to Develop Further the WHO Initiative.* Geneva: WHO.

———. 1981. *Global Strategy for Health for All by the Year 2000.* Geneva: WHO.

———. 1992. *Targets for Health for All: The Health Policy for Europe.* Copenhagen: WHO, Regional Office for Europe.

# Appendix: Annual Per Capita Consumption of Alcohol

By listing all alcoholic beverages that are sold, or reducing them to their absolute alcohol content, and dividing by the number of people, one can arrive at an average (that is, a mean) per capita consumption. Such a number would appear to be an objective, reliable, valid, and useful index for comparing how much people drink in different countries, and many of the authors who contributed to this book make it look as if it were easy to compare countries (in this instance—or, in other contexts, states, counties, or other jurisdictions) on a straightforward numerical scale. For example, France leads the world in wine consumption (91.5 liters), with second-place Italy fully 20% behind (see Table A.1). In overall alcohol consumption, France is one of the "wettest" countries; on the average, people drink twice as much as in Poland and three times as much as in relatively "dry" Iceland (Table A.2). In relative terms, that is close to being true, but there are several factors that should be taken into consideration before too much credence is given to such numbers.

In the first place, the term "per capita consumption" is often preceded by a qualifier, such as "apparent" or "estimated," to emphasize the lack of precision claimed by whoever put out the statistics. One reason for this imprecision is the fact that the total amount of alcohol supposedly drunk includes only that which has been "registered" (counted by some governmental agency, presumably in connection with taxation, or licensing, or reports from producers or wholesalers). Beverage alcohol that has not been "registered" is rarely estimated and never counted. In an area where home brew or moonshine may equal or even exceed the amount of "registered" beer and spirits—as in much of Africa, Asia, Latin America, and even some Scandinavian countries—relying only on "registered alcohol" for such a count leads to a major underestimation. Other sources of unregistered alcohol include duty-free imports (e.g., by returning tourists, sometimes after a brief ferry ride), goods bought in post exchanges, those brought in under diplomatic courtesy, and so forth.

Another factor that makes for imprecision in the numerator of the index is the lack of precision about the content (in terms of absolute alcohol) of the various beverages that

**Table A.1**
**Estimated Adult Per Capita Consumption of Beer, Wine, and Spirits in 1990**

| | Beer (liters) | | | Wine (liters) | | | Spirits (liters of ethanol) | |
|---|---|---|---|---|---|---|---|---|
| 1 | Czechoslovakia | 175.8 | 1 | France | 91.5 | 1 | Hungary(b) | 5.4 |
| 2 | Ireland | 171.4 | 2 | Italy | 73.7 | 2 | Poland | 5.1 |
| 3 | Germany(a) | 170.0 | 3 | Luxembourg | 70.4 | 3 | Czechoslovakia | 4.3 |
| 4 | Denmark | 153.3 | 4 | Portugal | 60.3 | 4 | Bulgaria | 4.0 |
| 5 | Belgium | 147.0 | 5 | Switzerland | 59.1 | 5 | Finland | 3.5 |
| 6 | Austria | 146.9 | 6 | Spain | 46.8 | 6 | Germany(a) | 3.4 |
| 7 | Luxembourg | 146.8 | 7 | Austria | 42.4 | 7 | Spain | 3.4 |
| 8 | New Zealand | 143.5 | 8 | Romania | 33.9 | 8 | France | 3.1 |
| 9 | Australia | 143.3 | 9 | Belgium | 30.3 | 9 | United States | 2.9 |
| 10 | United Kingdom | 135.7 | 10 | Hungary | 30.0 | 10 | Iceland | 2.8 |
| 11 | Hungary | 133.6 | 11 | Germany(a) | 29.5 | 11 | Canada | 2.7 |
| 12 | United States | 115.6 | 12 | Bulgaria | 29.3 | 12 | Japan | 2.7 |
| 13 | Netherlands | 110.1 | 13 | Denmark | 25.7 | 13 | U.S.S.R. | 2.7 |
| 14 | Finland | 103.3 | 14 | Yugoslavia | 24.0 | 14 | Romania(b) | 2.6 |
| 15 | Canada | 99.0 | 15 | Australia | 23.5 | 15 | Netherlands | 2.4 |
| 16 | South Africa | 94.8 | 16 | New Zealand | 19.0 | 16 | Ireland(b) | 2.4 |
| 17 | Spain | 89.9 | 17 | Czechoslovakia | 18.1 | 17 | Switzerland | 2.1 |
| 18 | Bulgaria | 83.5 | 18 | Netherlands | 17.8 | 18 | United Kingdom | 2.1 |
| 19 | Switzerland | 83.5 | 19 | Japan(c) | 16.1 | 19 | Sweden | 2.1 |
| 20 | Portugal | 82.6 | 20 | United Kingdom | 15.8 | 20 | New Zealand | 2.1 |
| 21 | Sweden | 72.3 | 21 | Sweden | 14.8 | 21 | Yugoslavia | 2.1 |
| 22 | Mexico | 68.7 | 22 | South Africa | 14.3 | 22 | Luxembourg | 1.9 |
| 23 | Romania | 66.5 | 23 | Finland | 12.6 | 23 | South Africa | 1.9 |
| 24 | Japan | 64.2 | 24 | Canada | 11.3 | 24 | Austria | 1.8 |
| 25 | Norway | 64.1 | 25 | Poland | 9.9 | 25 | Australia | 1.6 |
| 26 | Yugoslavia | 59.4 | 26 | United States | 9.9 | 26 | Denmark | 1.6 |
| 27 | France | 51.9 | 27 | U.S.S.R. | 9.2 | 27 | Belgium | 1.5 |
| 28 | Poland | 40.6 | 28 | Norway | 7.9 | 28 | Mexico | 1.3 |
| 29 | Iceland | 33.8 | 29 | Ireland | 6.1 | 29 | Norway | 1.2 |
| 30 | Italy | 27.6 | 30 | Iceland | 5.9 | 30 | Portugal(b) | 1.0 |
| 31 | U.S.S.R. | 24.3 | 31 | Mexico | 0.6 | 31 | Italy(b) | 1.0 |

(a) Includes the former German Democratic Republic (East Germany).

(b) Estimated.

(c) Includes sake.

*Source*: Adapted, with permission, from Ron Brazeau and Nancy Burr, *International Survey: Alcoholic Beverage Taxation and Control Policies*, 8th ed. (Ottawa: Brewers Association of Canada, 1992), Table 1, p. 480.

are reported in the aggregate. Beers tend to be anywhere in the range of 4–9% alcohol; wines, roughly between 5 and 20%; spirits, from 30 to 90%. Each country adopts a conventional percentage or tries to estimate for various brands within a type. Another distorting aspect is the assumption that all beverages sold during a year are drunk in that same year, with no provision for hoarding before a tax increase, replenishing stocks lost to disaster, stockpiling against the threat of inflation, and so forth.

**Table A.2**
**Estimated Adult Per Capita Consumption of Absolute Alcohol in 1990**

| Rank Order | Country | Liters |
|---|---|---|
| 1 | France | 16.5 |
| 2 | Luxembourg | 16.4 |
| 3 | Germany(a) | 15.0 |
| 4 | Austria | 14.0 |
| 5 | Hungary | 13.5 |
| 6 | Spain | 13.0 |
| 7 | Switzerland(b) | 12.9 |
| 8 | Portugal | 12.6 |
| 9 | Belgium | 12.0 |
| 10 | Denmark | 11.7 |
| 11 | Bulgaria | 11.6 |
| 12 | Czechoslovakia | 11.5 |
| 13 | Australia | 10.7 |
| 14 | Netherlands | 10.3 |
| 15 | Italy | 10.3 |
| 16 | New Zealand | 10.1 |
| 17 | Ireland | 10.0 |
| 18 | Romania | 9.9 |
| 19 | Finland | 9.6 |
| 20 | United Kingdom(b) | 9.4 |
| 21 | United States | 9.2 |
| 22 | Canada | 9.0 |
| 23 | South Africa | 8.5 |
| 24 | Japan | 8.0 |
| 25 | Poland | 7.9 |
| 26 | Yugoslavia | 7.9 |
| 27 | Sweden | 6.6 |
| 28 | Iceland | 5.2 |
| 29 | U.S.S.R. | 5.0 |
| 30 | Norway | 4.9 |
| 31 | Mexico | 4.8 |

(a) Includes the former German Democratic Republic (East Germany).
(b) Includes fermented cider.

*Source*: Adapted with permission, from Ron Brazeau and Nancy Burr, *International Survey: Alcoholic Beverages Taxation and Control Policies*, 8th ed. (Ottawa: Brewers Association of Canada, 1992), Table 2, p. 481.

Not only is the numerator (amount of alcohol consumed) imprecise, but so is the denominator (population). It is well known among demographers that the apparent precision of censuses is a comfortable artifact rather than a reflection of reality. No jurisdiction can confidently offer a precise count of its population throughout a year, and those that come close to doing so for a specific date are very few. A compounding factor in this connection is the fact that the figure in this index is not supposed to represent all persons, but only "potential drinkers" (sometimes those over fourteen years of age, sometimes over sixteen or eighteen, etc.). In some areas, the number of drinkers may be drastically distorted (for example, in southern Spain, where notoriously heavy-drinking tourists—who are not recorded in the census—outnumber "natives" for much of the year, leading to a major overestimation). Similarly, a jurisdiction that has unusually low taxes or prices on alcoholic beverages may attract buyers from nearby areas, again resulting in overestimation.

With all of these caveats, one must still admit that per capita consumption figures are interesting and provide a crude way of comparing at least something about the prevalence of alcohol in various areas. As with most statistics that are based on numbers collected for other purposes, it would be folly to take them at face value. Nevertheless, it seems in order, in an international handbook on alcohol and culture, to provide readers with an overview of such an index for the thirty-one countries that were included in what is probably the most reliable and authoritative source available (Brazeau and Burr 1992). Table A.1 shows estimated per capita consumption of each of the three major categories of beverages containing alcohol, and Table A.2 shows it for absolute alcohol, aggregating beer, wine, and spirits.

In areas where more detailed surveys of drinking have taken place, it is often possible to compare provinces, populations with various religions, occupations, age groups, and so forth. When such figures are then correlated with figures from other sources—such as rates of certain causes of death, arrests for certain crimes, highway fatalities, and so forth—associations between drinking and various problems can be inferred. As crude as such figures must necessarily be, they are widely used as a basis for many kinds of comparisons about drinking, and about its relation to many other factors. Such comparisons take on special importance when linked with the pseudoscientific assertion that a wide range of "alcohol-related problems" occurs in direct proportion to average per capita consumption. Evidence given in many of the chapters in this book contradict that assumption (notably France, with exceptionally high consumption and low problems, and Iceland, with low consumption but high problems). Nevertheless, with official backing by the World Health Organization and the U.S. National Institute on Alcohol Abuse and Alcoholism, this model still dominates most discussions about policies for the promotion of health and human services.

An inference or correlation is not a proof of causality, and it is unfortunate that too many who view such associations with alarm tend to ignore others. Ironically, it was the same sociologist who had earlier denied "problem deflation" on the part of anthropologists (Room 1984) who lamented the misuse of his discipline to inflate problems: "In the U.S. at least, alcohol epidemiologists often feel that the only political interest in their work is as a source of figures on alcohol's role in health and social problems, pushed as high as would seem credible ('up to 70% of X is due to drinking') to put at the front of official or quasi-official reports" (Room 1990, 1357). As the great mathematician and philosopher, Alfred North Whitehead cautioned long ago, in dealing with numbers it is important not to fall into the fallacy of misplaced concreteness.

## REFERENCES

Brazeau, Ron, and Nancy Burr. 1992. *International Survey: Alcoholic Beverage Taxation and Control Policies.* 8th ed. Ottawa: Brewers Association of Canada.

Room, Robin. 1984. Alcohol and ethnography: A case of problem deflation? *Current Anthropology* 25:169–191.

———. 1990. Review of D. Anderson, *Drinking to Your Health. British Journal of Addiction* 85:1355–1363.

# Glossary

Each of these chapters has been written and edited to be clear and comprehensible to the intelligent lay reader who may come to this reference source with no prior knowledge about a particular country, and with no special familiarity with alcohol studies. Nevertheless, a few words are used with meanings that would not be readily apparent in a dictionary of English. The following is a list, with brief definitions, of terms that are used in this book in special ways with reference to alcohol and culture.

ABSOLUTE ALCOHOL. Literally, 100% ethyl alcohol, but usually a mathematical convention indicating the alcohol content regardless of the overall volume of a drink or drinks. This allows easy comparison of various beverages that contain differing amounts of alcohol. For example, a typical "drink" (in the United States in 1995) contains about 12.5 g. of absolute alcohol, regardless of whether it is a 1 oz. shot of 84-proof liquor; a 12 oz. can, bottle, or glass of beer (at 4%); a glass of wine (at 12%); or a 2.5 oz. glass of cordial (at 20%)

ABSTAINER. A person who takes no more than one drink a year

ABUSE. Excessive or inappropriate use (of alcohol), resulting in problems

*AGUARDIENTE.* Spanish-language term for various kinds of distilled spirits (especially high-proof rum in Guatemala)

ALCOHOL. Unless otherwise specified, alcohol means ethyl alcohol, which is also called ethanol, ETOH, or $C_2H_5OH$

ALCOHOLIC. A person who "has alcoholism" (see ALCOHOLISM)

ALCOHOLISM. In simplest terms, drinking that results in chronic serious problems, especially for the drinker but frequently for others as well. Ironically, the term has been dropped for some years from the American Psychiatric Association's *Diagnostic and Statistical Manual,* but it remains very prevalent in professional as well as lay usage. Despite a vast and rapidly growing literature, there is no specific quantity or frequency of drinking that qualifies for this label, nor is there agreement on diagnostic criteria, symptoms, causes, or outcomes, nor even on whether it is a "disease"

*BOJ*. A home brew based on sugarcane juice (Guatemala)

BOOTLEG. To produce or distribute alcoholic beverages illegally

*BOUZAH*. A home-brewed beer (Egypt)

*CHIBUKU*. Although it began as a trade name, *chibuku* has come to be a virtual generic term for factory-made dark beer (Zambia)

*CHICHA*. Home brew, variously based on fruits, vegetables, or cereals (throughout Latin America)

CONSUMPTION. See PER CAPITA CONSUMPTION

DRINK (noun). See ABSOLUTE ALCOHOL

GROGGING. Secretive (and illegal) drinking (Australia)

*GUARO*. In some Spanish-speaking areas, any distilled spirit; in Guatemala, lightly distilled rum

HEAVY DRINKING. Highest consumption, usually among three categories (with "light" and "moderate"), defined in various ways by different authors. Heath's (conservative) measure is six or more drinks daily

HOME BREW. A fermented beverage produced by cottage industry for consumption in the home or for small-scale local sale; usually 5–10% alcohol

*IVRESSE*. French for "intoxication," with the special sense that combines rapture and exhilaration with other aspects of drunkenness

KUMISS. A fermented beverage based on mares' milk (China, Russia)

*KUXA*. Lightly distilled rum (Guatemala)

LIGHT DRINKING. Lowest consumption apart from abstaining, defined in various ways by different authors

LIQUEUR. A distilled spirit heavily flavored with additives (such as flowers, herbs, etc.), usually about 20–40% ethanol

MEAD. A fermented beverage based on honey (Scandinavia)

MODERATE DRINKING. Middle-range consumption (among three categories, with "light" and "heavy"), defined in various ways by different authors. Heath's (conservative) measure is up to two drinks daily

MOONSHINE. Illegally produced distilled spirits

*MOSI*. Although it began as a trade name, *mosi* has come to be a virtual generic in Zambia for factory-made lager (light) beer

PER CAPITA CONSUMPTION. Average (mean) intake of alcohol per adult per year within a population. For a discussion of the strengths and limitations of this as a quantitative basis for comparisons, see Appendix

PROBLEM DRINK(ER/ING). A drinker who has, or the drinking that results in, occasional problems, whether for self or for others. There is no general agreement about the number, severity, or nature of such problems, but they tend to be less— and less chronic—than in ALCOHOLISM (q.v.)

*SAMSU*. Moonshine (Malaysia)

SHOUTING. Buying and drinking of rounds, with each member of a group paying for drinks for all, by turns (Australia)

SPIRIT(S). A distilled beverage based on fruit, vegetable, or grain

# Bibliographical Essay

Alcohol is a subject about which there is an enormous wealth of written material at the highly specialized level. Some of it is about controversial theories, or about abstruse new technical data in every field from genetics to neurology, from anthropology to epidemiology, and dealing with baboons or rats as well as with human beings. It is also a subject about which much is written at the popular level. Some of that deals with the subjective experiences of recovering alcoholics, some with how to achieve sobriety and serenity, or how to help a friend who has drinking problems. Some of it is informative, but often at only a superficial or simplistic level. Some of it is, unfortunately, downright misleading. For example, too many of the popular books on alcohol claim that no one is responsible for his or her behavior, or state that alcohol is supposed to be as dangerous as tobacco or illegal drugs.

## GENERAL SOURCES

Between those extremes is an unfortunate gulf, in which far too few books provide a sound general introduction to alcohol, combining relevant aspects of chemistry, biology, neurology, physiology, psychology, the social sciences, history, and other fields. I hope to rectify that with my *Drinking: A Global Perspective on Alcohol* (New York: McGraw Hill, expected 1996). Although it is outdated in some details, Berton Roueché's *Alcohol: The Neutral Spirit* (Boston: Little, Brown, 1960) is still excellent; it was reprinted in 1971 and, with another title, *Alcohol: Its History, Folklore, and Its Effect on the Human Body*, in 1962. More up to date is Richard S. Shore and John M. Luce, *To Your Health: The Pleasures, Problems, and Politics of Alcohol* (New York: Seabury Press, 1976). A good college textbook that provides a fairly broad introduction to alcohol in general, with enough about alcoholism to make that subject comprehensible, is James E. Royce's *Alcohol Problems and Alcoholism: A Comprehensive Survey*, rev. ed. (New York: Free Press, 1989). The same holds for a collection of essays by various authors, used as a core text in the Rutgers Summer School of Alcohol Studies: Edith L. S. Gomberg, Helene

R. White, and John A. Carpenter (eds.), *Alcohol, Science, and Society Revisited* (Ann Arbor: University of Michigan Press; and New Brunswick, N.J.: Rutgers Center of Alcohol Studies, 1982).

The primary international and multidisciplinary journal on the subject is *Journal of Studies on Alcohol* (published by Rutgers Center of Alcohol Studies). The annual series *Recent Developments in Alcoholism*, edited by Marc Galanter, contains groups of articles on selected themes, in which specialists review important recent work. *ETOH* is the name of a computerized "alcohol science data-base analysis and dissemination project" that can be accessed broadly for titles and abstracts in the current literature. Specific questions can be directed to the National Clearinghouse on Alcohol and Drug Information, Box 2345, Rockville, Md. 20852 (telephone 1-800-729-6686); it prepares topical bibliographies on request, at no charge.

To keep abreast of what the U.S. government considers important on the subject (especially U.S. drinking patterns), see the series *Alcohol and Health*, published approximately every three years since 1971 by the National Institute on Alcohol Abuse and Alcoholism (one of the National Institutes of Health, within the Department of Health and Human Services). A number of books on alcoholism are both detailed and readable, but devote nearly half of their attention to major problems that are associated with long-term heavy drinking. Most of them relate to a single country (usually the United States).

Until recent years, it was customary to research and write about alcohol as quite distinct from drugs, partly on the basis of legality and partly because the users who had problems with them were very different populations. For the past decade or two, problem drinkers have increasingly become problem drug users as well, and both public and private funding agencies have encouraged scholars to write about "alcohol and other drugs." Researchers continue to focus on topics that interest them, however narrow they may be, but the literature is often aimed at a broader audience, with more titles that refer to "Drugs" or "Addictions" than to "Alcohol." *Addiction*, formerly *British Journal of Addiction*, published monthly, includes many more kinds of information than the usual journal, which has only research reports and book reviews. *Research Advances in Alcohol and Drug Problems*, edited by various scientists at Toronto's Addiction Research Foundation, is an excellent series; each annual volume contains several articles, each by a specialist reviewing the state of the art on some subject.

An excellent bibliography is available, but only up to 1960: various compilers produced *International Bibliography of Studies on Alcohol*, 3 vols. (New Brunswick, N.J.: Rutgers Center of Alcohol Studies, 1966–1980). Some of the same people, led by Mark Keller, put together *A Dictionary of Words about Alcohol*, 2nd ed. (New Brunswick, N.J.: Rutgers Center of Alcohol Studies, 1982).

## INTERNATIONAL DATA AND COMPARISONS

Other books that describe alcohol use and its outcomes in various countries are many and varied. Among the best for statistical data, including estimated per capita consumption, are two frequently revised compendiums: *International Survey: Alcoholic Beverage Taxation and Control Policies*, 8th ed. (Ottawa: Brewers Association of Canada, 1992); and *Hoeveel alcoholhoudende dranken worden er in de wereld gedronken?*, compiled and published by the Dutch Produktschap voor Gedistilleerde Dranken: in recent years, an English translation, *World Drinking Trends*, has been published yearly (Henley-on-Thames, UK: NTC Publications).

Descriptions of other countries tend to focus on the harmful aspects of excessive drinking. They are mostly European—see, e.g., Eric Single, Patricia Morgan, and Jan de Lint (eds.), *Alcohol, Society, and the State*, vol. 2: *The Social History of Control Policy in Seven Countries* (Toronto: Addiction Research Foundation, 1981); and Phil Davies and Dermot Walsh, *Alcohol Problems and Alcohol Control in Europe* (London: Croom Helm, 1983). On Latin America, see Institute of Medicine, *Legislative Approaches to Prevention of Alcohol-related Problems* (Washington, D.C.: National Academy Press, 1982). For Africa, see Lynn Pan, *Alcohol in Colonial Africa* (Helsinki: Finnish Foundation for Alcohol Studies, 1975); and Juha Partanen, *Sociability and Intoxication: Alcohol and Drinking in Kenya, Africa, and the Modern World* (Helsinki: Finnish Foundation for Alcohol Studies, 1991). Book-length studies on alcohol in individual countries are rare, and few of them deal with sociocultural aspects in any detail. Brief articles on several countries, including a few in the developing world, can be found in Gunno Armyr, Åke Elmér, and Ulrich Herz, *Alcohol in the World of the 80s: Habits, Attitudes, Preventive Policies and Voluntary Efforts* (Stockholm: Sober Förlags, 1982); and Timo Kortteinen (ed.), *State Monopolies and Alcohol Prevention*, Report 181 (Helsinki: Social Research Institute of Alcohol Studies, 1989); or Peter M. Miller and Ted D. Nirenberg (eds.), *Prevention of Alcohol Abuse* (New York: Plenum, 1984).

Alcohol use and its outcomes may seem important at specific times to specific audiences, but there have been long periods when they were simply taken for granted and, hence, ignored by scientific investigators or other writers. Research is sometimes regarded as a luxury, and few people have devoted much attention to systematically looking at alcohol until very recently. For all of these reasons, it has not been possible to compile equally detailed or useful lists of references on each of the countries covered in this book. Contributing authors have done their best to draw readers' attention to key sources, but even those may not be available except at major libraries.

## SOCIAL AND CULTURAL PERSPECTIVES

When we consider how widespread alcohol use is and how long the custom has survived in many cultures, it is compelling to note the benefits as well as the costs. It is striking that some of the populations who drink the most suffer the least, and even find it difficult to imagine that alcohol could be viewed in a negative light. The emphasis on pathology, whether phrased as alcohol *abuse*, or alcoho*lism*, alcohol-related *problems*, *problem* drinking, or alcohol *dependence*, predominates in the field, and few other than social scientists, some nutritionists, and recently heart specialists have dared to write about alcohol in a positive or value-neutral way, reflecting the experience and attitudes of most who drink.

For a focus on social and cultural aspects of alcohol, an excellent anthology is David J. Pittman and Helene R. White (eds.), *Society, Culture and Drinking Patterns Reexamined* (New Brunswick, N.J.: Rutgers Center of Alcohol Studies, 1991). A delightful little book that combines historical and ethnographic cases to illustrate the importance of such factors is Craig MacAndrew and Robert B. Edgerton's *Drunken Comportment: A Social Explanation* (Chicago: Aldine, 1969).

Anthropological reports focusing on tribal and peasant populations are listed in Dwight B. Heath and A. M. Cooper, *Alcohol Use and World Cultures: A Comprehensive Bibliography of Anthropological Sources* (Toronto: Addiction Research Foundation, 1981);

some are reprinted in Mac Marshall (ed.), *Beliefs, Behaviors, and Alcoholic Beverages: A Cross-Cultural Survey* (Ann Arbor: University of Michigan Press, 1979).

A group of vivid essays on the anthropological significance of drinking (of alcoholic and other beverages) is Mary Douglas (ed.), *Constructive Drinking: Perspectives on Drink from Anthropology* (Cambridge: Cambridge University Press, 1987); an early collection is Michael W. Everett, Jack O. Waddell, and Dwight B. Heath (eds.), *Cross-Cultural Approaches to the Study of Alcohol: An Interdisciplinary Perspective* (The Hague: Mouton, 1976). An attempt to relate the theoretical concerns of social scientists with the practical concerns of treatment-oriented personnel is Dwight B. Heath, Jack O. Waddell, and Martin D. Topper (eds.), *Cultural Factors in Alcohol Research and Treatment of Drinking Problems, Journal of Studies on Alcohol,* supp. 9 (Washington, D.C.: Smithsonian Institution, and New Brunswick, N.J.: Rutgers Center of Alcohol Studies, 1981). The Alcohol and Drug Study Group, affiliated with the American Anthropological Association, publishes an occasional newsletter that helps one to keep abreast of recent developments. The nearest we have to an international group sharing these interests is the Kettil Bruun Society for Social and Epidemiological Studies of Alcohol, affiliated with the International Council on Alcohol and Addictions; it publishes an occasional newsletter. *The Drinking and Drug Practices Surveyor,* published by the Alcohol Research Group of the University of California-Berkeley, occasionally focused on sociocultural aspects.

Some earlier attempts at sampling the international variation in how cultures treat alcohol are, as is this one, colored by the intellectual climate of their times: from Samuel Morehead's *A Philosophical and Statistical History of the Inventions and Customs of Ancient and Modern Nations in the Manufacturing and Use of Inebriating Liquors . . .* (Dublin: William Curry, Jun. and Company, 1838) to Daniel Dorchester's *The Liquor Problem in All Ages* (New York: Phillips and Hunt, 1884), to Ernest Crawley's *Dress, Drink, and Drums: Further Studies of Savages and Sex* (London: Methuen and Co., 1931), to Chandler Washburne's *Primitive Drinking: A Study of the Uses and Functions of Alcohol in Preliterate Societies* (New York: College and University Press, 1961).

For specifically historical discussions of drinking, see Susanna Barrows, Robin Room, and Jeffrey Verhey (eds.), *The Social History of Alcohol: Drinking and Culture in Modern Society* (Berkeley, Calif.: Alcohol Research Group, 1987); and Susanna Barrows and Robin Room (eds.), *Drinking: Behavior and Belief in Modern History* (Berkeley: University of California Press, 1991). There are many excellent monographs dealing with specific themes in the history of individual countries, especially on temperance and prohibition. In order to stay abreast of such studies, *The Social History of Alcohol Review,* published by the Alcohol and Temperance History Group, combines original articles with book reviews, bibliographical essays, and notes on work under way.

Links between literature and mood-altering experiences are the theme of *Dionysos: The Literature and Intoxication Triquarterly* (published at University of Wisconsin-Superior).

A predominantly cultural approach to alcohol use among many different populations in the United States is Linda A. Bennett and Genevieve M. Ames (eds.), *The American Experience with Alcohol: Contrasting Cultural Perspectives* (New York: Plenum, 1985); of related interest, although with a more epidemiological emphasis, is Danielle L. Spiegler, Diana A. Tate, Sherrie S. Aitken, and Charles M. Christian (eds.), *Alcohol Use among U.S. Ethnic Minorities,* Research Monograph 18 (Rockville, Md.: National Institute on Alcohol Abuse and Alcoholism, 1985). For other countries, see the references cited in chapters of this book.

The approaches that some other authors call "cultural" do not always coincide closely with that taken in this book. Thomas F. Babor edited *Alcohol and Culture: Comparative Perspectives from Europe and America, Annals of the New York Academy of Sciences* 472 (1986); it is an excellent collection, but the many highly specialized papers there have more to do with statistics (that nations deal in) than with attitudes, values, and behavior (which are more the stuff of cultures). Pertti Alasuutari's interesting *Desire and Craving: A Cultural Theory of Alcoholism* (Albany: State University of New York Press, 1992) combines an ethnographic account of pubs and clubs of recovering alcoholics in Finland, with a philosophically abstruse theory, more about personhood than social relations. John E. Tropman brings a cultural viewpoint to the limited question of social control in his *Conflict in Culture: Permissions versus Controls and Alcohol Use in American Society* (Lanham, Md.: University Press of America, 1986).

To cast your net further, check the list of references or the bibliography of any book or article that you find interesting or relevant, and never hesitate to consult a reference librarian. Happy hunting!

# Index

Identity, and drinking, 78

Immigrants, drinking habits of, 143, 285–286, 301. *See also* Introduction of alcohol by outsiders

Income and alcohol consumption. *See* Consumption patterns

Independence (political), and drinking: in India, 128–133; in Sri Lanka, 271

India, 128–141; change in drinking patterns, 130–135

Indians, American, 26, 34–37, 100–107, 111–114, 179–184, 310–311

Indians, East, in Malaysia, 168–175

Indigenous drinking patterns: in Chile, 32; in Honduras, 111; in India, 134–135; in Malaysia, 174; in Mexico, 179–180

Individualism, 85

Induction: in the military, 92, 157, 275; in the workplace, 275, 282

Industrialization, 53, 82, 160, 229, 290–291, 345

Inebriation. *See* Drunkenness

Inhibitions. *See* Disinhibition; Excuse, for inappropriate behavior; Time out

Insurance, 303

Interethnic relations and alcohol, 340–341. *See also* Ethnic groups; Stereotypes, of ethnic groups

Intoxication. *See* Drunkenness

Introduction of alcohol by outsiders, 334, 341; in Australia, 13; in Canada, 20; in Chile, 32; in Mexico, 180; in New Zealand, 203; in Nigeria, 216; in Russia, 238; in the U.S., 310

Irish, in the U.S., 309–310

Islam, 63, 132, 168–171, 195, 217, 254–257, 271–278. *See also* Muslims

Israel, 142–155; change in drinking patterns, 143–150; prevention program, 150–152, youth, drinking by, 147–148

Italy, 156–167; consumption patterns, 162–165; wine culture, 157–162

*Ivresse*, 79–84

Jellinek, E. M., 113, 302

Jews, 142–148, 273; as tavernkeepers,

225; in the U.S., 308–309. *See also* Anti-Semitism

Koran. *See* Islam

Kumiss, 45, 242

Labor unions, 54, 161, 225, 259

Ladino, *See* Mestizo

Language, and alcohol, 2, 37

Latin America. *See* Chile; Guatemala; Honduras; Mexico

Latin cultural zone, 79

League of Nations, 216

Learning, social. *See* Socialization, to drinking

Legends, alcohol in, 49, 131. *See also* China; Mexico

Leisure, drinking and, 138, 192, 229, 266

Lesbian, 210–211

Light drinking, 11, 63, 118, 183, 287, 370

Liquor. *See* Spirits (distilled liquors)

Liver. *See* Cirrhosis

Local option. *See* Prohibition, by local jurisdiction

Long waves (of historical change), 8, 33, 227–228, 350

Machismo. *See* Masculinity, drinking as

Malaysia, 168–178; ethnic groups, 169–175

Maori, 201–209

Mapuche, 34–37

Marital status, and drinking. *See* Consumption patterns

Marriage: alcohol in negotiating, 43–46, 134, 215; threatened by alcohol, 243, 284

Masculinity, drinking as, 337, 350; in Australia, 7–9; in Chile, 36; in Germany, 92; in Honduras, 115; in Israel, 149–150; in Malaysia, 173; in Mexico, 181–186; in the Netherlands, 197; in New Zealand, 202; in Nigeria, 215; in Poland, 224; in Sweden, 283–284; in the U.S., 306. *See also* Consumption patterns; Gender, differences in drinking

# About the Editor and Contributors

In accordance with various national traditions, paternal surnames are placed differently. The following list is alphabetized according to the English spelling, the surnames designated by all capital letters.

Walter Randolph ADAMS, Ph.D., is a Guatemala-born postdoctoral fellow at the Center for Alcohol and Addiction Studies at Brown University, Providence, Rhode Island. At the time he wrote this chapter, he was an assistant professor of anthropology and American ethnic studies at Kansas State University, Manhattan, Kansas.

Peter ALLEBECK, Ph.D., M.D., is a professor of social medicine at the University of Göteborg, and a researcher at the Karolinska Institute, in Stockholm, Sweden.

Charles Victor AROKIASAMY, Ph.D., is studying for the priesthood in his native Malaysia. When he wrote this chapter, he was an assistant professor of rehabilitation counseling at the Louisiana State Medical Center in New Orleans.

Abdel Monheim ASHOUR, M.D., is a professor of neurology and psychiatry, and director of the Geriatrics Unit, at Ain Shawms University in Cairo, Egypt.

Gylfi ÁSMUNDSSON, M.D., is an associate professor of medicine at the University of Iceland, and director of psychological services at the National University Hospital, Reykjavík.

Yuet W. CHEUNG, Ph.D., is a lecturer in sociology at the Chinese University of Hong Kong, in Shatin, N.T., Hong Kong. At the time he wrote this chapter with Dr. Erickson, he was a research scientist at the Addiction Research Foundation in Toronto, Canada.

Amedeo COTTINO, Ph.D., is professor of psychology, and of political and social sciences, at the University of Turin, Italy.

Patricia G. ERICKSON, Ph.D., is a senior scientist at the Addiction Research Foundation, adjunct professor of sociology at the University of Toronto, and director of the Collaborative Program on Alcohol, Tobacco and Other Psychoactive Substances, in Toronto, Canada.

Juan F. GAMELLA, Ph.D., is a professor of political science and sociology at the University of Granada, Spain.

Henk F. L. GARRETSEN, Ph.D., is director of the Alcohol Research Institute and professor at the University of Rotterdam, as well as head of the Department of Epidemiology and Health Policy of the Greater Rotterdam Municipal Health Service in the Netherlands.

Wayne HALL, Ph.D., is deputy director of the National Drug and Alcohol Research Centre, and a member of the faculty at the University of New South Wales, in Kensington, Australia.

David J. HANSON, Ph.D., is a professor of sociology at the State University of New York, in Potsdam.

Alan HAWORTH, M.D., is professor and head of psychiatry at the University of Zambia School of Medicine in Lusaka.

Dwight B. HEATH, Ph.D., is a professor of anthropology at Brown University in Providence, Rhode Island. While editing this book, he was also chair of the Task Force on Alcohol and Drugs of the American Anthropological Association.

Ernest HUNTER, M.D., M.P.H., is regional psychiatrist for Community Mental Health Services in Queensland, Australia.

Eduardo MEDINA Cárdenas, M.D., is a specialist in psychiatry and public health with the Chilean Ministry of Health, and an adjunct professor of anthropology, psychiatry, and public health at the University of Chile in Santiago.

Davinder MOHAN, M.D., is professor of psychiatry, and head of the Drug Dependence Treatment Centre, at the All India Institute of Medical Sciences in New Delhi.

Jacek MOSKALEWICZ, M.A., is acting head of studies on alcoholism and drug dependence at the Institute of Psychiatry and Neurology in Warsaw, Poland.

Véronique NAHOUM-GRAPPE, D.Phil., is a research historian and anthropologist at the Center for Transdisciplinary Studies in Sociology, Anthropology, and History at the School of Advanced Studies in the Social Sciences, in Paris.

Guillermina NATERA Rey, M.Ed., M.Sc., is head of the Department of Psychosocial Research at the Mexican Institute of Psychiatry in Mexico City.

Karin NYBERG, R.M.N., is on the faculty of Göteborg College of Health and Caring Sciences, and is a researcher at the Karolinska Institute in Stockholm, Sweden. At the time she wrote this chapter, she was a postdoctoral research fellow in psychology at Brown University in Providence, Rhode Island.

O. G. OSHODIN, D.Ed., is a professor of education, and dean of students, at the University of Benin in Benin City, Nigeria.

Julie PARK, Ph.D., is a professor of anthropology, and coordinator of several research programs in the Alcohol Research Unit, of the University of Auckland in New Zealand.

Martin A. PLANT, Ph.D., is a professor of psychiatry and sociology, and director of the Alcohol Research Group, at the University of Edinburgh, Scotland.

Diyanath SAMARASINGHE, M.D., is a professor of psychiatry in the School of Medicine of the University of Colombo, in Sri Lanka.

Peter SCHIØLER, Ph.D., M.D., is a specialist in sociocultural studies of alcohol in Virum, Denmark, and a founding member of The Amsterdam Group.

H. K. SHARMA, Ph.D., is a sociologist who has worked in the field of alcohol and drug dependence for several years, combining ethnographic and epidemiological approaches in India.

Pavel I. SIDOROV, D.Sc., is a professor of psychology and rector of the Archangel Medical Institute in Archangelsk, Russia. He is also a member of the Russian Academy of Natural Sciences and vice president of the International League of Temperance and Health.

Ien VAN DE GOOR, Ph.D., is affiliated with the Royal Netherlands Academy of Arts and Sciences. When she wrote this chapter, she was coordinator of alcohol research at the Addiction Research Institute of the University of Rotterdam.

Kenneth W. VITTETOE Bustillo, M.D., is deputy director of the Honduran Institute for the Prevention of Alcoholism, Drug Addiction, and Pharmacodependency, a professor of psychiatry at the Autonomous National University of Honduras, and a practicing psychiatrist in Tegucigalpa.

Irmgard VOGT, Ph.D., is a social psychologist and professor of social work at the University for Higher Education in Frankfurt am Main, Germany.

Shoshana WEISS, D.Sc., is a social researcher with the Israel Society for the Prevention of Alcoholism, in Karmiel.

XIAO Jiacheng, Ph.D., is a professor of ethnology at the Institute of Nationality Studies of the Chinese Academy of Sciences in Beijing, People's Republic of China.

Antoni ZIELIŃSKI, LL.D., is a professor of studies on alcoholism and drug dependence at the Institute of Psychiatry and Neurology in Warsaw, Poland.

ISBN 0-313-25234-3

90000>

EAN

9 780313 252341

HARDCOVER BAR CODE